UNJUST ENRICHMENT AND PUBLIC LAW

This book examines claims involving unjust enrichment and public bodies in England, France and the EU. Part 1 explores the law as it now stands in England and Wales as a result of cases such as *Woolwich EBS v IRC*, those resulting from the decision of the European Court of Justice (ECJ) in *Metallgesellschaft and Hoechst v IRC* and those involving Local Authority swaps transactions. So far these cases have been viewed from either a public or a private law perspective, whereas in fact both branches of the law are relevant, and the author argues that the courts ought not to lose sight of the public law issues when a claim is brought in the private law of unjust enrichment, or vice versa. In order to achieve this a hybrid approach is outlined which would allow the law access to both the public and private law aspects of such cases.

Since there has been much discussion, particularly in the context of public body cases, of the relationship between the common law and civilian approaches to unjust enrichment, or enrichment without cause, Part 2 considers the French approach in order to ascertain what lessons it holds for England and Wales. And finally, as the *Metallgesellschaft* case itself makes clear, no understanding of such cases can be complete without an examination of the relevant EU law. Thus Part 3 investigates the principle of unjust enrichment in the European Union and the division of labour between the European and the domestic courts in the ECJ's so-called 'remedies jurisprudence'. In particular it examines the extent to which the two relevant issues, public law and unjust enrichment, are defined in EU law, and to what extent this remains a task for the domestic courts.

Unjust Enrichment and Public Law

A Comparative Study of England, France and the EU

Rebecca Williams

·HART·
PUBLISHING

OXFORD AND PORTLAND, OREGON
2010

Published in the United Kingdom by Hart Publishing Ltd
16C Worcester Place, Oxford, OX1 2JW
Telephone: +44 (0)1865 517530
Fax: +44 (0)1865 510710
E-mail: mail@hartpub.co.uk
Website: http://www.hartpub.co.uk

Published in North America (US and Canada) by
Hart Publishing
c/o International Specialized Book Services
920 NE 58th Avenue, Suite 300
Portland, OR 97213-3786
USA
Tel: +1 503 287 3093 or toll-free: (1) 800 944 6190
Fax: +1 503 280 8832
E-mail: orders@isbs.com
Website: http://www.isbs.com

British Library Cataloguing in Publication Data
Data Available

ISBN: 978-1-84113-414-7

Typeset by Hope Services, Abingdon
Printed and bound in Great Britain by
CPI Antony Rowe Ltd, Chippenham, Wiltshire

For my parents; Roger and Rae Williams

PREFACE

Given how rapidly the law is evolving along the intersection between public law and restitution for unjust enrichment, it was perhaps inevitable that changes would take place in the period between going to press and final publication. In the event there have been several such developments.

THE TREATY OF LISBON

The first, and most significant event was the coming into force on the 1st December 2009 of the Lisbon Treaty. The European law discussed in this book is primarily the jurisprudence of the European courts, so the substance of the law discussed here remains unchanged, but of course there have been some important changes of terminology. The EC Treaty is now known as the Treaty on the Functioning of the European Union (TFEU) and the articles of what was formerly the EC Treaty have again been renumbered. And, of course, the so-called 'depillarisation' brought about by the TFEU means that rather than distinguishing between the 'first pillar' EC and the 'three pillar' EU structure,[1] we should now refer only to the EU as a collective whole.[2] As a result, throughout this book I have used the new TFEU numbering for Treaty articles, giving the pre-Lisbon, Treaty of Amsterdam numbering in brackets afterwards. I have also included a table of equivalences for the Treaty Articles referred to in the book, which gives their numbers under Lisbon, under the Treaty of Amsterdam, and their original pre-Amsterdam numbering. Similarly, wherever I have referred to the European Union or to European Law in a general manner or in the present tense, I have referred to the 'Union' or to 'EU' law. However, where I have quoted from cases decided under the old, three pillar structure, or referred to European law in the past tense, I have left in the old terminology of 'European Community' or 'EC' law, since that was what it was at the time.

[1] See further ch 7 p 233.

[2] There will still be exceptions to this rule regarding the Common Foreign and Security Policy, but these are beyond the scope of the current investigation.

THREE COURT DECISIONS

The other developments are court decisions; the decision of the Court of Appeal in the *FII Group Litigation* case;[3] the decision of Henderson J in the *Thin Cap* case,[4] and the decision of the Court of Appeal in *Chalke and A C Barnes (Wokingham) Ltd v The Commissioners for Her Majesty's Revenue and Customs*[5]. These decisions add in various ways to the discussion in the book, but what follows should be read alongside the relevant passages in the book itself, rather than as freestanding commentary.

1. The principle of 'effectiveness': is FII a 'milestone' case?

(a) The relationship between so-called 'San Giorgio' claims and state liability in damages and the involvement of the ECJ in the choice of cause of action

It will be argued in chapters four and eight[7] that the decision of the ECJ in *FII*,[8] largely reiterated in *Thin Cap*,[9] was significant in that for the first time both the Advocate General and the ECJ became involved in the definition of the cause of action at national level, undercutting in substance their formal adherence to the *Metallgesellschaft and Hoechst*[10] principle that the classification of claims at national level is for the courts of the Member States, not for the ECJ. The key paragraph of Advocate General Geelhoed's opinion in *FII* is as follows:

> [134] In principle, it is for the national court to decide how the various claims brought should be characterised under national law. However, as I observed above, this is subject to the condition that the characterisation should allow the test claimants an effective

[3] [2010] EWCA Civ 103 (Ch). Throughout the text of the book reference is made to the decision of the ECJ in Case C-446/04 *Test Claimants in the FII Group Litigation v Commissioners of the Inland Revenue* [2006] ECR I-11753, and to the decision of Henderson J in *Test Claimants in the FII Group Litigation v The Commissioners for Her Majesty's Revenue & Customs* [2008] EWHC 2893, [2008] STI 2726. 'FII' stands for 'Franked Investment Income'. I am very grateful to Rupert Shiers for his views on these cases from the tax perspective, though of course any remaining errors are mine alone.

[4] *Test Claimants in the Thin Cap Group Litigation v Commissioners for Her Majesty's Revenue and Customs* [2009] EWHC 2908 (Ch). 'Thin Cap' stands for 'thin capitalisation'; the practice by parent companies of funding their subsidiaries by loans, rather than by equity, in order to reduce their liability to tax.

[5] [2010] EWCA Civ 313. References throughout the book are to the first instance decision; *F J Chalke Ltd and AC Barnes (Wokingham) Ltd v The Commissioners for Her Majesty's Revenue and Customs* [2009] EWHC 952 (Ch).

[6] Case 199/82 *Amministrazione delle Finanze dello Stato v San Giorgio* [1983] ECR 3595. See further p 254.

[7] At pp 85–6, 104–5 and 261–4.

[8] Above n 3.

[9] Case C-254/04 *Test Claimants in the Thin Cap Group Litigation v IRC* [2007] ECR I-2107.

[10] Cases C-397/98 and C-410/98 *Metallgesellschaft and Hoechst v IRC* [2001] ECR I-1727.

> remedy in order to obtain reimbursement or reparation of the financial loss which they had sustained and from which the authorities of the member state concerned had benefited as a result of the advance payment of tax. This obligation requires the national court, in characterising claims under national law, to take into account the fact that the conditions for damages as set out in *Brasserie du Pêcheur*[11] may not be made out in a given case and, in such a situation, ensure than an effective remedy is nonetheless provided.

In *FII*, counsel for the applicants essentially argued that this paragraph should be interpreted as follows: (1) a cause of action for state liability in damages requires the presence of a sufficiently serious breach, which may be difficult to fulfil in a given case. (2) European law requires the claimant to be given an effective remedy. And crucially, (3) thus the *San Giorgio* unjust enrichment action should be broadly defined so that the claimants receive just and effective satisfaction when the state liability in damages action is unavailable. The Court of Appeal agreed that 'the Advocate General would seem to have supported this submission in paragraph [134] of his opinion' but refused to accept it themselves and held that the ECJ had rejected this approach. Similarly, in his decision in *FII*, Henderson J had assumed that the ECJ endorsed this approach,[12] but in *Thin Cap* he stated that he had been wrong to do so.[13]

Certainly, as the Court of Appeal in *FII* points out,

> The ECJ established the requirement of a sufficiently serious breach because it considered it just to do so. The difficulty that this creates for the Claimants is not an acceptable basis for striving to circumvent the requirement by enlarging the scope of a remedy that is not subject to this requirement. A claimant who cannot establish a sufficiently serious breach is not for this reason deprived of an effective remedy: he is not entitled to an effective remedy.[14]

However, it is not clear that even the Advocate General's opinion should be interpreted as suggesting such a thing. His paragraph [134] quoted above, followed on from his finding in paragraphs [132] and [133] that 'with one exception' (relating to the *FID* enhancements)[15] 'the claims . . . should be considered equivalent to claims for recovery of sums unduly paid, that is to say, claims for recovery of charges unlawfully levied'. On that basis his opinion could alternatively be read as being simply that where a claim *can in any event* be interpreted as a so-called *San Giorgio* unjust enrichment claim at European level, which would automatically give a right to reimbursement, it is not then open to a national court to make use of the *Metallgesellschaft* principle in order to choose instead a cause of action at national level which would subject the claim to the *extra* requirement of proving a

[11] Cases C-46/93 and C-48/93 *Brasserie du Pêcheur SA v Germany and R v Secretary of State for Transport, ex p Factortame Ltd* [1996] ECR I-1029. The condition in question is that the breach of European law be 'sufficiently serious', see further ch 8 p 239 and n 122.

[12] Above n 3 at [231].

[13] Above n 4 at [213].

[14] Arden LJ, giving the judgment of the Court, above n 3 at [137].

[15] See further below pp 103–5.

sufficiently serious breach. Rather than the Advocate General suggesting that the cause of action in state liability in damages should be examined first and the *San Giorgio* unjust enrichment action then altered to catch anything left over, the order of consideration would on this interpretation be the other way round; actions *already* available under *San Giorgio* on its own terms must not be limited by use of the rules on state liability in damages. There would then not be such a discrepancy between the opinion of Advocate General Geelhoed in *FII* and the decision of the ECJ, since neither would be suggesting the alteration of one cause of action to escape the requirements of another. The point would simply be that while in principle the choice of cause of action is open to a national court when there is nothing to choose between the options available, (*Metallgesellschaft*), when the *San Giorgio* action is, on its own terms, straightforwardly available, but the state liability in damages action seems likely to fail as a result of the 'sufficiently serious breach' requirement, the principle of effectiveness requires that a 'remedy' be given at national level for that *independently* available *San Giorgio* action (*FII*).

In any event, as argued in the book, the case remains important evidence of the involvement of the ECJ and its Advocates General in the choice of cause of action at national level,[16] and on this front it is submitted that it certainly can be regarded as a milestone. In addition the case is further evidence of the fact that a breach of European law will give rise more easily to a *San Giorgio* unjust enrichment action than to an action for state liability in damages, contrary to the views of Lord Scott in *Deutsche Morgan Grenfell.*[17]

(b) Whether the ECJ now regards interest as a central, rather than an 'ancillary' matter

In addition to seeing the ECJ's decision and Advocate General's opinion *FII* as a milestone in terms of the choice of 'remedy' available, Henderson J also regarded them as marking 'a significant advance' in the jurisprudence of the ECJ on the issue of interest.[18] 'His view was that until *FII* there was a consistent line of ECJ authority that *San Giorgio* claims are for the repayment of the unlawful charges and that it is for the national law to settle all ancillary questions such as the payment of interest and the date from which it must be calculated'[19] but that this was changed by the decision in *FII* so that

> *FII* . . . does . . . represent a significant advance on *Hoechst* in the jurisprudence of the Court. The identification of an underlying general principle, the linking of it to the principle of effectiveness, and the subsuming within the general principle of the loss of use claim in *Hoechst*, are important new milestones (or perhaps I should say kilometre posts) on a journey that is still far from completed. They are sufficient, however, to make it clear, to my mind, that the *San Giorgio* principle must now be regarded as entitling a

[16] See further p 262.
[17] *Deutsche Morgan Grenfell v IRC* [2006] UKHL 49, [2007] 1 AC 558 (HL). See further pp 77–86.
[18] *FJ Chalke (Chancery)*, above n 5 at [107].
[19] *F J Chalke* (CA), above n 5 at [35].

> claimant who has paid tax levied in breach of Community law not only to repayment of the tax itself, but also to reimbursement of all directly related benefits retained by the member state as a consequence of the unlawful charge. It is only in this way that the claimant can obtain an effective remedy for its loss, and effect can be given to the underlying principle that the member state should not profit from the imposition of the unlawful charge.[20]

On appeal, however, the Revenue argued that the Judge had been wrong to interpret *FII* in this way, and the Court of Appeal's response was that the issue was 'unclear':

> There is considerable cogency in the argument of the Commissioners and the analysis of the judge that, at least until *FII*, the settled jurisprudence of the ECJ in relation to *San Giorgio* claims was that, save in the *Metallgesellschaft* case of premature levying of tax, interest was an ancillary matter to be dealt with in accordance with national law, including whether there was a right to any interest at all and, if so, the rate and the time for which it was to be paid. It is also striking, as the Commissioners have forcefully submitted, that there is no clear statement by the ECJ, whether in *FII* or any subsequent case, that the former settled jurisprudence has been changed by the formulation of the *San Giorgio* principle in paragraph 205 of the ECJ's judgment in FII, and that, in cases of overpayment as much as cases of premature payment, the *San Giorgio* principle requires the recipient to pay compensation for the time value of the wrongful retention of tax when it was not lawfully due. On the other hand, it is clear, as the Judge found and as the claimants contend, that the formulation of the *San Giorgio* principle in paragraph 205 of *FII* is, on one interpretation, broad enough to encompass the claimants' claims to payment for the time value of the overpayments of VAT while retained by the Commissioners. It is also difficult to see any logical basis for distinguishing in this respect between the premature levying and payment of tax and the overpayment of tax. In both cases, only compound interest will normally give a full and effective remedy.[21]

In view of these 'doubts and difficulties and the importance and financial implications of the issue'[22] the Court concluded that 'it seems plainly desirable that there should be a reference to the ECJ for a preliminary ruling on the issue',[23] but since the Court also concluded that Henderson J had been right to hold that the claims for compound interest were in any event time barred, it would not be possible to make a reference from these proceedings since an answer to the question was not necessary to enable judgment to be given in the case.[24]

In the book I argue that compound interest is necessary if transactions are to be fully unravelled,[25] though not in the particular case of *Chalke* for the reasons given by Henderson J and upheld by the Court of Appeal.[26] However, it is harder to

[20] *FJ Chalke (Chancery)*, above n 5 at [107]. See further pp 44–9.
[21] *FJ Chalke* (CA), above n 5 at [40].
[22] Ibid at [41].
[23] Ibid.
[24] Ibid.
[25] See further pp 44–9.
[26] The Court of Appeal also held that the claimants in *FJ Chalke* had a year after the *Marks and Spencer* decision to institute proceedings before their claim became time-barred (above n 5 at [66]) and that in any case if they had brought their claims before the decision in *Sempra* it is not clear that those

know whether this conclusion ought to follow from the European principle of effectiveness or be left for domestic law to determine. In chapter eight I outline the problems associated with what is known as the ECJ's 'remedies jurisprudence' (a term which by its own vagueness indicates the lack of clarity surrounding the area) and I highlight the need for a more satisfactory determination of the division of labour between national and European courts.[27] And unless and until this occurs, and a clearer view is taken of what constitutes a 'remedy' which can be dictated by European law, it is inevitable that we will not know which issues fall into this category and which, by contrast, are 'ancillary' and thus to be left to the courts of the Member States. The question of compound interest in *Chalke*, therefore, is simply another illustration of this point, and no doubt it will not be the last.

2. The principle of equivalence

Of course it is the European requirement to provide an 'effective' 'remedy'[28] which is at issue in the questions above, but in addition to this there is, of course, the requirement of equivalence.[29] Throughout the book it is argued that while European law requires the provision of an effective 'remedy' for breach of that law, domestic 'remedies' for breach of European law are subject also to the principle of equivalence. Thus it would be perfectly acceptable to adopt the public law reason for restitution as an exclusive route to restitution in public body cases as proposed here, since that would provide an effective 'remedy' equivalent to anything provided for cases involving public bodies in a wholly domestic context, and a distinction between public and private law is perfectly acceptable as a matter of European law.[30] It is this argument which answers Henderson J's decision in *Thin Cap* that it would not avail the Revenue to establish that the *Woolwich* cause of action would, by itself, or with appropriate extensions, be sufficient to satisfy the claimants' *San Giorgio* claims when they also have the alternative open to them of making a mistake-based restitution claim.[31]

claims would have been dismissed, as indeed the claims in *Sempra* itself were not (at [71]). It may well be that the Court of Appeal was thus right to reject the claimants' assumption that any proceedings commenced by them would, as a matter of fact, undoubtedly have been dismissed, but what would in practice have happened is, of course, different from what the claimants could have been expected to predict. It would be undesirable to penalise claimants who assume that the law as it stands will continue to apply and who, as a result, do not go to the expense and trouble of bringing an action to challenge it, when in prospect they have no means of knowing the likelihood of success of such an action.

[27] See in particular pp 252–7 and 271–4.

[28] On which see further pp 237–41.

[29] On which see further pp 237 and 241.

[30] See further pp 100–1and 237–41.

[31] 'it is no part of the principle of effectiveness to say that [if English law provides two alternative causes of action] only the more restrictive of those causes of action is needed'. Above n 4 at [223]. The point is that English law need not provide the alternative cause of action based on mistake; the public law reason for restitution is in itself sufficient to fulfil the EU requirements of equivalence and effectiveness.

The approach taken in this book now receives support from the decision of the Court of Appeal in *FII*. This held that sections 320 of the Finance Act 2004 and 107 of the Finance Act 2007 were not precluded by the European principles of equivalence, effectiveness, legal certainty and legitimate expectations[32] because those provisions only limited mistake claims and mistake claims were not required by Community law. Similarly the Court held that the claimants' claim for overpaid corporation tax in *FII* bore greater similarities to other claims for excess tax paid by reason of a mistake in a return than to claims for repayment of tax paid under wholly ultra vires assessments, so that it would not be a violation of the principle of equivalence for s 33 of the Taxes Management Act 1970 to apply to them. Of course, whether or not the Court is correct on this point as a matter of fact depends in turn on the extent of invalidity of the UK rules (on which see further issue 5 below), but the point remains that, as I have argued in this book, it is not necessary for domestic law to provide the most extensive remedy imaginable, only the most extensive remedy applicable to equivalent, public, domestic claims, provided that this is in itself an effective remedy. It is submitted that the public law reason for restitution I outline fulfils both these requirements.

3. The relationship between *San Giorgio* and *Woolwich*[33]

This is, of course, closely connected to the fact that at first instance in *FII* Henderson J had argued that a mistake claim was necessary to give effect to the so-called '*San Giorgio*' principle at national level, whereas it is argued in the book that this is not the case and that, conversely, *San Giorgio* is a subset of *Woolwich* in the sense that all claims which are beyond the powers of the public body in question fall within the public law reason for restitution first created by *Woolwich*, but only some of these claims will be beyond the public body's powers as a matter of European law, as in *San Giorgio*. This view receives support from the decision of the Court of Appeal in *FII*, which held that Henderson J should have accepted the Revenue's submission that *Woolwich* alone provides a sufficient UK cause of action for *San Giorgio* claims.[34]

4. The need for a demand

Closely connected to the *San Giorgio-Woolwich* relationship is the question whether a '*Woolwich* claim' can only be made where the money was paid in response to a demand. In chapter three it will be argued that the public law reason for restitution (as *Woolwich* should properly be understood) does not have any such requirement;[35] the simple ultra vires nature of the payment is sufficient. However, at first

[32] On which see further ch 8 pp 237–41 and 265.
[33] *Woolwich Equitable Building Society v IRC* [1993] AC 70 (HL).
[34] Above n 3 at 157.
[35] pp 40–1.

instance in *FII* Henderson J had suggested that a demand would be necessary, hence his finding that *Woolwich* was not sufficient to absorb at national level all *San Giorgio* European claims. The Court of Appeal in *FII* has now added weight to the view taken here, holding that there is no authority to suggest that a demand is required, but that if there had been such a requirement it would be displaced in the context of European law.[36] Such a distinction would obviously be undesirable and this provides a further reason for preferring the interpretation of the *Woolwich* cause of action suggested in the book, according to which *San Giorgio* claims are merely a subset of cases in which the reason for restitution is public law.[37]

This approach would also provide an answer to a further question. At paragraph [227] of the *Thin Cap* decision, Henderson J asks whether the claimants in that case have any other claims which are not *San Giorgio* claims and as a matter of European law would give rise only to an action for state liability in damages but which nevertheless are good restitutionary claims as a matter of English domestic law. On the interpretation given here the answer to this question must inevitably be in the negative. If *Woolwich* is understood as establishing a right to restitution for unjust enrichment wherever there has been an ultra vires action by a public body which invalidates the payment in question, and if *San Giorgio* is understood as representing the subset of such claims in which the invalidity is a matter of European rather than domestic law, then any breach of Community law capable of generating what Henderson J calls 'a *Factortame* claim for damages'[38] which could also found a domestic '*Woolwich*' public law unjust enrichment claim, ought also, by definition, to be a *San Giorgio* claim. Indeed it would be more straightforward to make out such a claim than to make out a claim for state liability in damages, since as noted above, the latter would be subject to the additional requirement of sufficiently serious breach.[39] The fact that this is not yet clear as a matter of European law is almost certainly a further result of the fact that, as noted in chapter seven, unjust enrichment is regarded largely as a general principle of European law, rather than as a freestanding cause of action in its own right, a position which is inherently in tension with the ECJ's increasing involvement in the definition of aspects of the claim in cases originating in Member State courts.[40]

5. The claims in *FII* and *Thin Cap* which fall within the '*San Giorgio*' principle

This question of causation brings us to a further issue. Of the claims in *FII* three in particular were thought to fall outside the so-called '*San Giorgio* principle'.

[36] Above n 3 at [169]–[174].
[37] See further p 107.
[38] Above n 4 at [227].
[39] Above n 14 and surrounding text.
[40] See further pp 229–31, 259–64 and 271–4. See also R Williams, 'Case C-47/07, *Masdar (UK) Ltd v. Commission*; Case C-446/04, *Test Claimants in the FII Group Litigation v. Commissioners of Inland Revenue*' (2010) 47 *CMLR* 555.

Advocate General Geelhoed, the ECJ and Henderson J were all in agreement that the 'FID enhancements' could not fall within that principle; the ECJ and Henderson J added to this the waiver of tax credits in order to increase the liability to MCT against which ACT could then be offset, and Henderson J included a third category of claims excluded from *San Giorgio* concerning the 'consequential steps that were taken within the group to utilise surplus ACT, for example by setting it off against unlawful Case V corporation tax', both on the basis that this was not a 'direct and inevitable consequence' of the UK's breach of European law, and on the basis that the Revenue had not been enriched.[41] The exclusion of all three categories of claim will be discussed in more detail in chapters four and eight,[42] but it will be argued in particular that it is not clear that Henderson J was right to add this third category of cases to those already excluded by the Advocate General and ECJ. The decision of the Court of Appeal now supports this view, holding that the claim in respect of ACT set against the unlawful Case V charge is also a *San Giorgio* claim.[43] Of course, in reaching this conclusion the Court continued to rely on the 'inevitable consequence' reasoning of the ECJ,[44] and as long as that test remains at European level, this inefficient bar to mitigation will remain.[45]

In addition to the setting off of ACT against unlawful Case V corporation tax, the claimants in *FII* sought to argue that the setting off of group relief and management expenses against that Case V charge could also be included in a *San Giorgio* claim for recovery.[46] The Court of Appeal disagreed, though it is not wholly clear that they should have done so. Their principal reason for rejecting these claims was a lack of enrichment on the part of the Revenue.[47] However, there is no reason to suppose that this means the claims must be barred in principle. If the argument is that reliefs were used in the first year against an unlawful tax so that that those reliefs were not then available in the second and subsequent years then it is difficult to see why in principle the Revenue should not be regarded as unjustly enriched. Surely 'spending' reliefs against an unlawful tax is (subject to questions of valuation) not so different from spending money on that tax? Of course it must be borne in mind that valuing the enrichment would be problematic in circumstances where it is not clear what would have happened to the reliefs had the unlawful tax not existed.[48] And if those reliefs would not have been available for anything else in the first year and would not have been available at all in the second year[49] then that would obviously also defeat the enrichment argument. But these are questions of fact and do not mean that management expenses and

[41] See further p 118 onwards.
[42] See further pp. 111–118 and 259–264.
[43] Above n 3 at [151].
[44] Ibid at [149].
[45] See further pp 113–6 and 263–4.
[46] Above n 3, 'Issue 13' at [175]–[9].
[47] 'Utilisation of the other reliefs may have been a detriment to the Claimants, but did not represent a gain to the Revenue for the purpose of a restitutionary cause of action'. Above n 3 at [179].
[48] Ibid at [180].
[49] Ibid at [183].

group relief can be distinguished from the payment of ACT against unlawful MCT as a matter of principle.

Similarly in the *Thin Cap* decision Henderson J was asked to consider whether various claims should be regarded as *San Giorgio* claims or not.[50] 'Thin cap' stands for 'thin capitalisation', the practice by which parent companies finance their group members by loans rather than equity. This is done in order to reduce their liability to tax, since in many Member States companies are permitted to deduct interest payments on loans for the purposes of calculating their taxable profits, whereas in the case of equity finance, distributions paid to shareholders are not similarly deductable. However, since the practice of thin capitalisation essentially involves presenting what is in substance an equity investment as a loan, and manipulating the manner in which capital is provided so as to choose where profits will be taxed, many Member States regard the practice as abusive and have taken measures to counter it.[51] On a reference to the ECJ, the UK's rules were found to have involved a difference in treatment between resident and non-resident borrowing companies which constituted a restriction on freedom of establishment which could not be justified by the need to ensure cohesion of the UK's tax system,[52] and while it could be justified on the ground of prevention of abusive practices, Henderson J found that in fact the UK thin cap provisions were not proportionate to achieve this purpose because they did not allow for a separate defence of commercial justification.[53] The UK provisions were thus in breach of the rules on freedom of establishment and liability was in principle made out.

As for recovery, however, three claims in particular were in dispute: (c) a claim for repayment of corporation tax paid by the borrowing company where a lesser amount of interest on the loan was paid to the lending company because the lending company funded the borrower with equity capital or converted existing debt to equity due to the thin cap provisions;[54] (d) a claim for repayment of corporation tax paid by the borrowing company where a lesser amount of interest on the loan was paid to the lending company because the rate of interest was reduced or the loan was made interest free due to the thin cap provisions[55] and (e) a claim for restitution or compensation in respect of losses or other tax reliefs or credits of the borrowing company or other companies used by the borrowing company to offset the additional corporation tax liabilities said to have arisen in the above claims.[56]

In chapter four I state that in relation to the *FII* decision 'it is at least arguable that since the[actions taken were] the result of the companies' attempts to mitigate the loss to them caused by the IRC's unlawful discrimination against them it was

[50] Above n 4 at [199].
[51] See further above n 4 at [1]–[2].
[52] Ibid at [9].
[53] Ibid at [75].
[54] Issue (c), ibid at [199] .
[55] Issue (d), ibid.
[56] Issue (e), ibid.

equally unlawful for the Revenue to receive the benefit of those constrained choices'.[57] And for these three issues (c), (d) and (e) in *Thin Cap* the same argument applies; on Henderson J's assumption that a causal link can be established between the actions of the Revenue and the actions of the claimants,[58] if as a result of the unlawful thin cap rules the companies (c) replaced debt with equity, (d) reduced their rate of interest or (e) used reliefs to offset tax, meaning that in each case they paid tax which they would not have done if the unlawful thin cap rules had not been in place, then it must be at least arguable that receipt of this extra tax was in each case beyond the powers of the Revenue. Of course the case is stronger in relation to (e) where the companies' actions are simply responding to the tax already imposed, whereas in (c) and (d) their actions are anticipatory, changing their behaviour in order to alter the tax rules applicable in the first place, which may be thought to introduce more problematic questions of remoteness. However, while simple responses may be more predictable and straightforward than anticipatory actions, surely the whole point of tax legislation is that companies will alter their commercial arrangements accordingly. So if a company acts in advance to rearrange its dealings in order to produce certain tokens, rather than just spending those tokens once received, surely that is still something the Revenue can be held to have caused. The *Thin Cap* decision thus provides further evidence for two points made in the book: first, that it is vital that we adopt the correct test for causation, and that it is by no means obvious that the 'direct consequences' test chosen by the ECJ is the best one for this purpose, especially since it discourages efficient mitigation.[59] And second, that it is imperative that we adopt the hybrid public and private approach suggested here so that we can address questions of remoteness directly from both points of view. We should be asking not only what the tests of causation and remoteness are in unjust enrichment but also how far the invalidity of the UK rules should extend as a matter of public law.[60] If the thin cap rules themselves were beyond the powers of the UK as a matter of European law, we need also to examine the extent to which this unlawfulness invalidated subsequent and consequential receipts of tax or reliefs from it.

6 The definition of mistake

As noted at several points in the book, this approach would also avoid the difficulties associated with trying to interpret such cases as turning on the existence of a mistake.[61] A further example of such difficulties is provided by paragraphs [231] and [232] of Henderson J's decision in *Thin Cap*. Here, as he himself notes, 'much may depend on the level at which the relevant mistake of law is identified'. This in

[57] See further p 112.
[58] See n 4 at [203]–[5].
[59] See further pp 113–6 and 263–4.
[60] See further pp 110–13.
[61] See further eg 64–7, 86–8, 94–7, 109–10 and 121–2.

turn opens up the possibility of disagreement over the precise kind of mistake necessary to found a claim[62] and of discrepancy between the treatment of mistakes and other causative factors.[63] If, rather than becoming sidetracked by or entangled in the correct definition of mistake we were instead to deal with the problem head on, examining the extent of the invalidity as a matter of public law and using this as the reason for restitution instead, these difficulties could be avoided.

7. Miscellaneous other points

For the sake of completeness it is worth recording that in addition to the points discussed above, in *FII* the Court of Appeal confirmed that it did not think the defence of change of position would be compatible with the requirement to provide an effective remedy in *San Giorgio* cases,[64] and that it did not regard the breach of European law in that case to have been sufficiently serious to found an action for state liability in damages.[65] And in *FII*, confirmed in *Chalke*, the Court held that a mistake would only be relevant for the purposes of section 32(1)(c) of the Limitation Act 1980 if it is an essential element of the cause of action.[66]

[62] As in those paragraphs themselves, and see further ibid
[63] See further p 116.
[64] Above n 3 at [191]. See further pp 136–49.
[65] Ibid at [201]. See further ch 4 n 198. For general details of the sufficiently serious breach requirement see ch 8 n 122.
[66] Ibid at [230]–[245] and above n 5 at [44]. See further ch 4 pp 74–5, n 16 and J Edelman, 'Limitation Periods and the Theory of Unjust Enrichment' (2005) 68 *MLR* 848.

ACKNOWLEDGEMENTS

This book began as my PhD thesis, and so my first thanks are due to the Law School of the University of Birmingham, whose excellent Postgraduate Teaching Assistantship scheme allowed me to complete my PhD and take my first steps as an academic lawyer. I cannot rate this scheme too highly and have since recommended it to countless students on the basis of my experience there. Similarly, I owe a huge debt of gratitude to two people in particular; Anthony Arnull, my PhD supervisor and mentor, and Graham Virgo, who helped me a great deal with the process of readying my PhD for publication after I moved to Cambridge. While of course any remaining errors are mine alone, there is no question that the book would not have existed in its current form without Tony and Graham's help, which in both cases went far beyond anything I had any right to expect. I am enormously grateful to both of them. Since I am also one of the many people who first encountered unjust enrichment and restitution in seminars led by Peter Birks on the Oxford BCL, I am therefore one of the many people who owes him particular thanks and, again like many others, I am only sorry that I cannot deliver those thanks in person.

However, I am also grateful to a large number of other people whose help and support has been invaluable during the process of writing this book, in particular John Bell, Monica Bhandari, Sophie Boyron, Andrew Burrows, Anne Clayton, Matthew Conaglen, Cathryn Costello, Eric Descheemaeker, James Edelman, Ariel Ezrachi, Christopher Forsyth, Judith Freedman, Joseph Howard, Angus Johnston, Gareth Jones, Charles Mitchell, Rupert Shiers, Andrew Simester, Robert Stevens, William Swadling, Magali Veneau, and Simon Whittaker.

I would of course also like to thank all those from whom I've received research assistance, namely Jason Goodman, Benoit Kohl, Robyn Llewellyn, Shane Sibbel and, in particular, Francesca Galli and Catherine Lee, as well as all those at Hart Publishing, especially Richard Hart, who have been so patient with me in the process of producing the book.

Finally, my thanks would not be complete without reference to the unfailing support and often very practical help I have received from my family; my husband John, my sister Jen, and my parents Roger and Rae, who will never look at a Marks & Spencer's teacake the same way again.

TABLE OF CONTENTS

ABBREVIATIONS AND GLOSSARY FOR FRENCH SOURCES

Courts

CE	Conseil d'Etat
Civ (1)	First Civil Chamber of the Cour de Cassation (responsible predominantly for matters relating to contract). (Older reports do not necessarily list the number of the chamber hearing the case.)
Civ (2)	Second Civil Chamber of the Cour de Cassation (responsible predominantly for matters relating to delict).
Ch mixte	Chambre mixte of the Cour de Cassation. Because there are six chambers of the Cour de Cassation, each with specific responsibilities, there is the potential for conflict over interpretation of legislation. To resolve this, a chambre mixte comprising the Premier President of the Cour together with the president and three senior members of each chamber concerned (between 13 and 25 people in total) can be convened.[1]
Com	The fourth, Commercial Chamber of the Cour de Cassation
Soc	The fifth, Social Chamber of the Cour de Cassation
Trib d'inst	Tribunal d'instance. Judges of the Tribunal d'instance are members of the ordinary judiciary and since 1958 they have been grouped into 475 courts located in the main towns of départements, arrondissements and cantons. Their jurisdiction is limited to €10,000.[2]

Reports and Journals

AJDA	Actualité juridique, droit administratif
Bull civ	Bulletin Civil; Bulletin des arrêts des Chambres civiles de la Cour de Cassation (decisions of various civil chambers of the Cour de Cassation which are reported in five different sections, hence the five different Roman numerals used to label them).
Bull civ, AP	Decisions of the Assemblée Plénière reported in the Bulletin. The Cour de Cassation sits in Plenary Session where a case is appealed from a Cour d'Appel to which it has been remitted after cassation. It may also be involved in other important cases. It is composed of

[1] See further J Bell, S Boyron and S Whittaker (eds) *Principles of French Law*, 2nd edn (Oxford, Oxford University Press, 2008) 46.

[2] See also: ibid, 45.

	the First President, the president, oldest conseiller and two others from each of the six chambers, giving 25 judges in total.[3]
CJEG	Cahiers juridiques de l'électricité et du gaz
D	Recueil Dalloz
D chr	Dalloz Chronique (the Dalloz series includes jurisprudence, législation and 'chroniques', ie academic articles).
DH	Recueil Dalloz hebdomadaire
DP	Recueil Dalloz périodique
Gaz Pal	Gazette du Palais
JCP	Juris Classeur Périodique (also known as La Semaine Juridique) (édition générale)
Lebon	Recueil Lebon or Recueil des décisions de la Conseil d'Etat
Rec CE	Recueil des décisions du Conseil d'Etat
RDP	Revue de droit public et de science politique
RFD adm	Revue Française de droit administratif
RJF	Revue de jurisprudence fiscale
RTD civ	Revue trimestrielle de droit civil
RTD eur	Revue trimestrielle de droit Européenne
S	Sirey

Other abbreviations

Obs	Observations
c	Contre, ie v

[3] See also: ibid, 47.

TABLE OF EQUIVALENCES

European Treaty Article Numbering: Table of Equivalences

Original, pre-Amsterdam numbering (used until 2/10/1997)	**Numbering introduced by the Treaty of Amsterdam (used from 2/10/1997 to 1/12/2009)**	**Current Numbering (Introduced by the TFEU, Lisbon, 1/12/2009)**	**Subject Matter**
Article 5	Article 10	Repealed and replaced in substance by Article 4	Cooperation between the Union and the Member States
Article 52	Article 43	Article 49	Right of establishment
Article 85	Article 81	Article 101	Competition (concerted practices)
Article 73b	Article 56	Article 63	Free movement of capital
Article 86	Article 82	Article 102	Competition (abuse of a dominant position)
Article 92	Article 87	Article 107	State aids
Article 93	Article 88	Article 108	State aids
Article 173	Article 230	Article 263	Judicial review of Union acts
Article 176	Article 233	Article 266	Voidness of Union acts
Article 177	Article 234	Article 267	Preliminary rulings
Article 178	Article 235	Article 268	ECJ jurisdiction over compensation for damage (see Article 340 below)
Article 215	Article 288	Article 340	Contractual and 'non-contractual' liability of the Union in damages

TABLE OF CASES

Australia

Canada

European Commission

European Commission and Court of Human Rights

European Court of Justice

Alphabetical

Chronological

France

India

Ireland

South Africa

United Kingdom

TABLE OF LEGISLATION

Australia

European Union

Directives

Regulations

France

Germany

Ireland

United Kingdom

Statutory Instruments

TABLE OF CONVENTIONS

INTRODUCTION

If a public body such as the Inland Revenue charges too much tax, should it have an obligation to repay the excess? If a local authority pays out money when it does not have the capacity to do so should it be able to reclaim the money paid? The answer 'yes' to these questions seems to flow from simple common sense because it seems unfair or unjust to let the recipient keep the money and it would therefore surprise a non-lawyer to learn that the law of England and Wales did not reflect this until recently.

Perhaps more difficult is the question whether it makes any difference that in these two examples one of the parties is public. Should the resulting claims be treated as if they had occurred between two private parties, or should the law recognise that public bodies require different rules? If changes are to be made, then what should they be and does it matter whether the public body is the claimant or the defendant? And where is the line to be drawn between what is public and what is private?

To a 'restitution' lawyer it will be immediately obvious that these are the kind of questions raised by cases such as those following the 'swaps transactions' and by *Woolwich EBS v IRC* [1993] AC 70. To a 'public' lawyer it will be the questions concerning the division between public and private law in these examples that appear more familiar. It is thus one of the purposes of this book to try to bring together these two spheres of study and to articulate fully the relationship between ultra vires action by public bodies and the reason for restitution in these cases.

Broadly speaking there are two different approaches to the area of law known controversially as 'Restitution'. While the English common law system, at least in the past, has relied on specific 'reasons for restitution' known as 'unjust factors', the civilian approach is the reverse, being reliant on a general principle of *unjustified* enrichment, or enrichment *without cause*. Recently it has become increasingly apparent that the relationship and indeed the choice between these two approaches is very important to the future development of the law in England. It is therefore of particular interest that much of the discussion on their various merits has centred on the cases involving public bodies considered here.

It is thus apparent that in order to understand this area of English law it is necessary also to have an understanding of the civilian approach. This comparative technique is not new to English 'Restitution' lawyers. Much of the work done so far in this field in England has used German law as a comparator system, but this is not the only relevant civilian system and part two of the book will examine the situation in France. In addition to this, in France the division between public and private law is, at least institutionally, more complete than it is in England. From the initial consideration of the English claims the first branch of the investigation will thus be into the French system, which will shed light on both the important public and private law issues.

Finally, it is now often the case either that the public body involved in such a claim is not domestic at all but one of the institutions of the EU, or that the law permitting or forbidding certain actions on the part of a public body will come, not from its own domestic law, but from the law of the EU. It thus becomes clear that in order to complete this study it is necessary also to understand the EU law that applies to this issue and in particular the division of labour between the European courts and the national courts in formulating the relevant claims and responses. To what extent are the structure and operation of such claims still the responsibility of national law and to what extent are they in fact claims in EU law? How must each of the two systems, domestic and European, respond to the challenges of their public nature? An investigation of the European dimension of the domestic claims will thus form the second branch from the central English cases, but of course, while any relevant European law will obviously have its own content and identity, it may often contain ingredients drawn from the constituent national systems and this provides a further reason for understanding as fully as possible the operation of both the civilian and common law systems. And in addition to this, in its own terms we need to understand more clearly what is meant by the ECJ's 'remedies jurisprudence' and the relationship between Member State courts and the ECJ. The 'remedies jurisprudence' concerning unjust enrichment provides an important insight into precisely this issue and thus gives us another reason why it is crucial that we examine it.

Part 1

Unjust Enrichment and Public Law in England and Wales

1

Definitions and Controversies

TO BEGIN TO investigate 'restitution' and 'public bodies' the starting point must be a definition of those terms. It is necessary, therefore, briefly to outline the relevant matters from each sphere in order to provide a secure foundation for the specific investigation which will combine the two.

'Restitution' or 'Unjust Enrichment'

The first important thing to note is that, like the law of obligations more generally, this area has Roman origins. The *Digest* contains two versions of a fragment excerpted from Pomponius. One reads 'this is indeed by nature fair, that nobody should be made richer through loss to another'.[1] The other reads '[i]t is fair by the law of nature that nobody should be made richer through loss and wrong to another.[2] In Gaius' *Institutes*, the law of obligations was divided by the events that brought the obligations into being. Gaius, unable to fit the case of a reclaimed mistaken payment into his statement that all obligations arose from contract and tort,[3] listed another category: other miscellaneous events. Either he, or 'someone later interfering with his text',[4] then broke this third category into two, creating the categories of obligations arising *quasi ex contractu* and *quasi ex maleficio*,[5] which were subsequently adopted by Justinian.[6] In this context, the Latin term was less inappropriate than the common law term quasi-contract: the Roman category included all obligations which were not contracts, but whose consequences were similar to the results of a contract. It could thus genuinely be said that they arose 'as if upon a contract', a term that made it perfectly clear that there was no actual contract. It is important for our purposes to realise that these Roman origins are the starting point both for the development of English law[7] and of our comparator system,

[1] *Cum alterius detrimento, Digest*, 12.6.14.

[2] *Cum alterius detrimento et iniuria, Digest*, 50.17.206.

[3] Gaius, *Institutes*, 3.88.

[4] P Birks, *An Introduction to the Law of Restitution* (Oxford, Clarendon Press, 1985) 30.

[5] *Digest*, 44.7.1, (Gaius, 2 *Aurea) Obligationes aut ex contractu nascuntur aut ex maleficio aut proprio quodam iure ex variis causarum figuris.*

[6] Justinian, *Institutes*, 3.13.1.2.

[7] All references to 'England' and 'English Law' throughout this book should of course be taken to refer to the law of England and Wales. The phrase is shortened only for convenience.

French law. However, whereas in France this area of law remained separate from other branches of the law of obligations, in English common law the terminological connection with the law of contract for many years deprived the subject of an independent existence and of a reasoned basis.

The historical confusion surrounding the subject has been well documented.[8] Its result was that in England the subject did not begin to develop as a discrete area of the law until the demise of the 'implied contract' theory in the twentieth century. This process has often entailed reinterpretation of rules and decisions previously thought to belong to a variety of disparate areas of the law. Consequently, there is still great controversy over the extent to which this process of gathering and reinterpretation should continue and thus over the content and reach of the area itself.[9]

One example of this controversy concerns the very name given to the area. The first major gathering exercise was undertaken by Goff and Jones in 1966, but one of the most important steps in the reinterpretation exercise in English law came from Birks' *An Introduction to the Law of Restitution* in 1985. He began by pointing out that from a theoretical perspective 'restitution' cannot be aligned with 'contract' and 'tort' because it does not denote an 'event', but rather the response to an event.[10] We do not refer to tort as 'compensation' or to contract as 'expectation damages', so although thus far the terms 'unjust enrichment' and 'restitution' have been used without specific import, from now on the relevant area will be referred to as 'unjust enrichment' rather than 'restitution'. Whatever the other problems concerning the relationship between the two terms, it is this initial event with which we will be concerned.

A second instance of controversy concerns the technique used, particularly by Birks, to explain and analyse unjust enrichment. This is the technique of 'mapping' or 'topography'. He argues that 'case-law grows without much regard for principle or for the coherence of one piece of law with another'[11] and, in particular, he sees it as the role of academic investigations to find a 'line of best fit' through the existing law. However, as he himself notes, such an exercise is not purely descriptive, but also contains normative elements: '[a] skeleton of principle is not just the common sense behind a legal topic, but rather a particular organisation of its common sense, a version chosen from a number of possibilities'.[12] Thus, when

[8] See especially: D Ibbetson, *A Historical Introduction to the Law of Obligations* (Oxford, Oxford University Press, 1999); H Baker, 'The History of Quasi-Contract in English Law' in W Cornish and others (eds), *Restitution, Past, Present and Future: Essays in Honour of Gareth Jones* (Oxford, Hart Publishing, 1998) and Birks, *Introduction* (n 4), especially 29–39.

[9] Notable examples of the debate can be found in the contrast between Birks' technique in his *Introduction* (n 4) and subsequent work as compared to that of S Hedley, 'Unjust Enrichment as the Basis of Restitution—an Overworked Concept' (1985) 5 *Legal Studies* 56; S Hedley, *A Critical Introduction to Restitution* (London, Butterworths, 2001) especially ch 1; S Hedley, *Restitution: Its Division and Ordering* (London, Sweet and Maxwell, 2001) especially ch 8; and I Jackman, *The Varieties of Restitution* (Sydney, The Federation Press, 1998).

[10] Birks, *Introduction* (n 4) 9 ff.

[11] ibid 1–2. He argues that it is the 'generations of textbooks' which have given tort and contract the structure lacking in the law of unjust enrichment until recently.

[12] ibid 1.

the cases do 'reflect back the framework selected as best-fitted to the subject', it is a framework which contains conclusions about how best the law *should* be seen.[13] For this reason, however, others see the map as 'an attempt to squeeze the law into a mould it patently does not fit'.[14] It is, therefore, to a certain extent, impossible to separate the analytical technique used in such an investigation from the controversy underlying the area as a whole. This investigation will use the existing topography as a starting point, because it will be seen that the choices made by the process so far present a helpful way of highlighting the relationship between the two areas of law, public law and unjust enrichment, brought together in this study. However, this does not mean that the mapping process can by itself provide enough normative justifications for the courts to answer the questions before them in public body cases. Nor does it mean that those cases will automatically be fitted into the existing map without independent justification. Like any map, this one will provide a basic structure to prevent the investigation from becoming lost, but it will not by itself dictate the route to be followed in future.

Using the Map

The first thing to note is that if the law is to be divided up, or classified into various 'territories', then there is a variety of possible means of categorisation. Moriarty lists several: Birks' system is known as 'event-response' classification, but it would also be possible to divide the law up by the *subject-matter* of the obligation (money, goods, work) or by social context (family law, company law, labour law) as happens in universities. The point is, Moriarty argues, that since tort and contract already follow the event-response classification it is this one we should use to discuss unjust enrichment.[15]

This is particularly important in the present context, since the current investigation seems to span two such types of classification: private law questions relating to causes of action in unjust enrichment which belong to the event-response Birksian classification, and the relationship between public and private law, which seems initially more like the 'social context' classificatory system.

Remaining for the moment with the event-response classification, Birks has developed this as follows: 'All rights are either (by jurisdictional origin) legal or equitable and (by the nature of their exigibility) proprietary or personal; and all

[13] Burrows in particular divides this normative aspect into three categories of consequences; the tailoring and development of defences; the rejection of irrelevant rules which are mere historical accidents and which restrict the application of the relevant underlying principles; and the ability to treat like cases alike by gathering them together and recognising their similarity. See: A Burrows, *The Law of Restitution*, 2nd edn (London, Butterworths, 2002) 8.

[14] S Hedley, '"Unjust enrichment" today: the theory' ch 1 pt D in S Hedley and M Halliwell (eds), *The Law of Restitution* (London, Butterworths, 2002) 8.

[15] S Moriarty, 'Review of *An Introduction to the Law of Restitution* (1st edn) by Peter Birks' (1986) 45 *Cambridge Law Journal* 128.

such rights arise from wrongs, from consent, from unjust enrichment or from other causative events'.[16]

It is true that often the law does not use the language of 'events' and 'responses', preferring the terms 'right' and 'remedy'. However, in his lecture entitled 'Rights, Wrongs and Remedies' (delivered as the 23rd Blackstone Lecture in May 1999),[17] Birks defends the event-response classification from the threat posed by the word 'remedy' by abandoning this word and concentrating instead on the word 'right' since this will allow us to see that the courts 'realise rights not only from wrongs, but also from not-wrongs, and, more exactly, from three categories of not-wrongs'.[18] This will mean in turn that we can focus properly on the causative event relied on by the claimant, and ensure that the law responds correctly.

If the law is to be divided by causative events into consent, wrongs, unjust enrichment and 'others', it becomes necessary at the next level of detail to examine the boundaries within each of those categories. In the category entitled 'unjust enrichment' we are again immediately confronted by further controversy. In his *Introduction*, Birks argued that the law of unjust enrichment was divided into two. Sometimes the enrichment was at the claimant's expense because there had been a direct transfer of value from C to D, for example where C pays D £100 by mistake. This became known as 'autonomous unjust enrichment' because it was totally independent of all other events. On the other occasions D wronged C and in doing so made a profit, for example where X pays D £100 to hit C, and Birks called these cases 'enrichment by doing wrong'.[19] However, in his more recent work Birks concluded that in the wrongdoing cases the operative event is the wrong itself.[20] Thus for Birks, the boundary is no longer one within unjust enrichment, but one which defines the edges of the subject. This also provides one reason why, even after the event-response distinction is made, for Birks the response of restitution no longer quadrates with the event of unjust enrichment.[21] It should not be thought that this is only of semantic interest. If the event in question is a wrong, then policy arguments from the law of wrongs will be allowed to limit recovery. If, on the other hand, the relevant event is

[16] P Birks, 'Equity in the Modern Law: An Exercise in Taxonomy' (1996) 26 *University of Western Australia Law Review* 1, 9. It should be noted that to avoid the last category, 'others', 'swallowing' the first three categories, an event should only be placed in this fourth category if it cannot be placed in any of the other three. This follows simply from the position taken above that it is desirable to remove categories of like cases from the 'residual miscellany' so that they can be seen as alike and treated as such.

[17] Later published as: P Birks, 'Rights, Wrongs and Remedies' (2000) 20 *Oxford Journal of Legal Studies* 1.

[18] ibid 36.

[19] Birks, *Introduction* (n 4) 22–25.

[20] P Birks, 'Misnomer' in W Cornish and others (eds), *Restitution, Past, Present and Future: Essays in Honour of Gareth Jones* (Oxford, Hart Publishing, 1998); and Birks, 'Equity in the Modern Law: An Exercise in Taxonomy' (n 16) 32.

[21] A separate debate over 'quadration' has arisen concerning the relationship between the law of property and the law of unjust enrichment. See especially: *Foskett v McKeown* [2001] 1 AC 102 (HL); P Birks, *Unjust Enrichment*, 2nd edn (Oxford, Oxford University Press, 2005) at 28–38; Burrows, *Law of Restitution* (n 13) 60–77; A Burrows, 'Unmasking Unjust Enrichment' (2001) 117 *Law Quarterly Review* 412; and G Virgo, *The Principles of the Law of Restitution*, 2nd edn (Oxford, Oxford University Press, 2006) 9–11 and 425–31.

an unjust enrichment, then it is policy arguments from that sphere which must operate. The controversy arises because Birks' new viewpoint has not been universally accepted. On the contrary, it has been challenged descriptively by Friedmann,[22] normatively by Tettenborn[23] and Kull,[24] and at least temporarily by Burrows.[25] This debate has the potential to affect the current investigation in various ways. The standard examples of overpaid tax and money transferred under contracts that public bodies had no power to form seem initially to fall into the 'autonomous unjust enrichment' category. On the other hand, since these charges or payments are unlawful as a matter of public law, if they are not to be placed alongside cases where money is gained through a wrong, this decision will require justification.[26] Even if we conclude that they do not, it will of course remain possible that there are other situations in which a public body may gain money through wrongdoing.[27]

The Criteria for a Claim in 'Autonomous' Unjust Enrichment

It is generally accepted[28] by supporters of the unjust enrichment principle that four elements must be fulfilled in order for a claim in unjust enrichment to succeed:

1. The defendant must have been enriched.
2. This enrichment must have been received at the expense of the claimant.
3. The enrichment must be unjust.
4. There must be no defences.

Two of these criteria are particularly relevant to this investigation.

The Enrichment Must Be Unjust

It is on this question that much of the investigation will be based since it is arguable that this element is the most important factor in explaining the law's intervention. For example, this is the element which has, at least in the past, contained the greatest difference between common law and civil law systems such as in France and it is this element on which some of the most recent controversy has focused. In *Orakpo v Manson Investments Ltd* Lord Diplock said that:

> [T]here is no general doctrine of unjust enrichment recognised in English law. What it does is to provide specific remedies in . . . cases of what might be classified as unjust enrichment in a legal system that is based upon the civil law.[29]

[22] D Friedmann, 'Restitution for Wrongs: The Basis of Liability' in W Cornish and others (eds), *Restitution, Past, Present and Future: Essays in Honour of Gareth Jones* (Oxford, Hart Publishing, 1998).
[23] A Tettenborn, 'Misnomer: A Response to Professor Birks' in W Cornish and others (eds), *Restitution, Past, Present and Future: Essays in Honour of Gareth Jones* (Oxford, Hart Publishing, 1998).
[24] A Kull, 'Rationalizing Restitution' (1995) 83 *California Law Review* 1191.
[25] Burrows, *Law of Restitution* (n 13) 5–6.
[26] See below pp 12–13 and 148.
[27] Such cases are, however, beyond the scope of this investigation, see: (n 100).
[28] See, eg: *Banque Financière de la Cité v Parc (Battersea) Ltd* [1999] 1 AC 221 (HL) 227 (Lord Steyn); Burrows, *Law of Restitution* (n 13) 15; and P Birks and R Chambers (eds), *Restitution Research Resource* (Oxford, Mansfield Press, 1997) 2.
[29] *Orakpo v Manson Investments Ltd* [1978] AC 95 (HL) 104.

In his *Introduction to the Law of Restitution*, Birks made it clear that 'nothing' in that book 'is meant to contradict' Lord Diplock's position, but he also argued that such a general doctrine would be 'unusably vague'[30] and he was therefore concerned to find a better order for the specific instances Lord Diplock did recognise. Thus the burden was to rest with the claimant of proving a reason for restitution, an 'unjust factor'[31] to show why the defendant should have to give up the enrichment. It would not be open to the claimant, as it is in civilian systems, to claim that the enrichment was without cause and thus to place the burden of proving a legal cause on the defendant. Clearly, when he was writing his *Introduction*, Birks' view was that it was desirable that the burden should remain on the claimant, so that 'unjust' can be made to 'look downwards to the cases'.[32] For this reason, Birks argued, fears that the concept of 'unjust enrichment' will lead to abstract and uncontrollable 'palm-tree' justice[33] are unfounded. The phrase is only used to identify the situations in which the law will respond to an enrichment of one person at another's expense. If it is undesirable for the law to respond to this in an abstract way, it is perfectly possible to construct rules to ensure that it does not do so.

However others, and more recently Birks himself,[34] have argued on the contrary that a generalised right to unjust enrichment is either preferable or necessary.[35] It is therefore important to examine whether there is any practical difference between a generalised right concretised by specific rules and a right based only on specific causes of action, but justified by an underlying general principle. In

[30] Birks, *Introduction* (n 4) 27.

[31] The terms 'unjust factor' and 'reason for restitution' will be used interchangeably.

[32] Birks, *Introduction* (n 4) 23. See also Krebs, who has argued against the introduction of the civilian approach in England, on the basis that 'while the German approach is undoubtedly elegant and works well in German law, there is no evidence to suggest that it would work equally well in English law. Moreover there is no reason to change the traditional English approach, given that it cannot be shown to lead to unjust or unsatisfactory results': T Krebs, *Restitution at the Crossroads: a comparative study* (London, Cavendish, 2001) 254.

[33] A Burrows, 'Contract, Tort and Restitution—A Satisfactory Division or Not?' (1983) 99 *Law Quarterly Review* 217, 234 at fn 65, identifies such sentiments in *Baylis v Bishop of London* [1913] 1 Ch 127 (CA) 140 (Hamilton LJ); W Holdsworth, 'Unjustifiable Enrichment' (1939) 55 *Law Quarterly Review* 37, 51–53; P Winfield, *The Province of the Law of Tort* (Cambridge, Cambridge University Press, 1931) 131 ff.

[34] See especially: Birks, *Unjust Enrichment,* (n 21) particularly part 3

[35] See especially: Krebs (n 32) 2 and 244–50, citing S Meier, *Irrtum und Zweckverfehlung (Mistake and Failure of Purpose)* (Tübingen, Mohr Siebeck, 1999) and R Zimmermann, 'Unjustified enrichment: the modern civilian approach' (1995) 15 *Oxford Journal of Legal Studies* 404. Some of the debate has focused on the precise effect of the decision of the HL in *Criterion Properties plc v Stratford UK Properties LLC* [2004] UKHL 28, [2004] 1 WLR 1846 in which Lord Nicholls in particular worked on the basis that a valid agreement between the parties would justify benefits transferred between them. However, it was Lord Scott's opinion which received majority support and he held that the question was simply whether the contract between the parties was enforceable or not. He thus did not reject the traditional analyses of 'knowing receipt' and 'knowing assistance', but rather held them to be inapplicable to the facts in front of him. It was therefore not clear even before the decision of the HL in *Deutsche Morgan Grenfell plc v IRC* [2006] UKHL 49, [2007] 1 AC 558 that *Criterion Properties* could be taken as authority that Birks' *Unjust Enrichment* view has prevailed; it could simply have been a case about the general subsidiarity of unjust enrichment claims in relation to valid contracts. However, since then the decision of the HL in *Deutsche Morgan Grenfell* makes it clear that 'unlike civilian systems, English law has no general principle that to retain money paid without any legal basis (such as debt, gift, compromise, etc) is unjust enrichment': at [21] (Lord Hoffman).

Deutsche Morgan Grenfell v IRC,[36] Lord Walker regarded English law as being 'at something of a crossroads'[37] between the two approaches, and indicated that his own 'tentative inclination' was to align English law with Scottish law and other civilian systems,[38] but ultimately concluded that 'the choice is one which will rarely make much if any practical difference to the outcome of any particular case before the court'.[39] Burrows' view is similar, especially since the English approach is not static and is capable of recognising new unjust factors,[40] and even Birks himself accepts that even if 'absence of basis' is to be the final reason for recovery, beneath this apex of the pyramid 'at the base, the particular unjust factors such as mistake, pressure, and undue influence become the reasons why, higher up, there is no basis for the defendant's acquisition'.[41]

Indeed, as Lord Walker pointed out, 'the recognition of "no basis" as a single unifying principle would preserve . . . the purity of the principle on which unjust enrichment is founded, without in any way removing . . . the need for careful analysis of the content of particular "unjust factors" such as mistake'.[42]

This issue is particularly important in relation to claims against and by public bodies in relation to ultra vires payments, as *Deutsche Morgan Grenfell* itself shows, since it will be seen that here the 'unjust factor' itself can appear to be simply an absence of cause, in the sense that there was no legal basis for the claim made by the public body and the claim was therefore beyond the body's powers.[43] The proper interpretation of this apparently civilian approach will be discussed further in the detailed examination of the English system, and will be seen to be an important stage in the argument made there.[44] It also follows that this area in particular will benefit from a comparison with the French system, which does adopt

[36] *Deutsche Morgan Grenfell* (n 35).

[37] ibid [154].

[38] ibid [158].

[39] ibid [155].

[40] A Burrows, 'Understanding the Law of Restitution: a Map Through the Thicket' (1995) 18 *University of Queensland Law Journal* 149, 160. One possible distinction between the schemes relates to the burden of proof, but even here, Burrows argues that the burden of proof could be put on the claimant to establish the absence of basis and that in any event it could only be in a very few cases that a difference in the burden of proof on the unjust question would lead to a difference in result: A Burrows, 'Absence of Basis. The New Birksian Scheme' in A Burrows and A Rodger (eds), *Mapping the Law: Essays in Memory of Peter Birks* (Oxford, Oxford University Press, 2006) 45. Ultimately, he concludes that the new Birksian absence of basis scheme is no simpler or more elegant than the system of unjust factors: 46–47. On the relationship between the two approaches, see also: J Edelman, 'The Meaning of "Unjust" in the English Law of Unjust Enrichment' (2006) 3 *European Review of Private Law* 309: and R Stevens, 'Is there a law of Unjust Enrichment?' in S Degeling and J Edelman (eds), *Unjust Enrichment in Commercial Law* (Sydney, Law Book Co, 2008). There is, of course, a separate and more practical debate over whether English law as it currently stands could cope with such a change without the need for many consequential amendments to be made, see generally: Krebs (n 32).

[41] Birks, *Unjust Enrichment* (n 21) 116, 'The Pyramid: A Limited Reconciliation'.

[42] *Deutsche Morgan Grenfell* (n 35) [158].

[43] Indeed, it is these cases that have led Birks to conclude that the 'change of direction' to the civilian approach is necessary: Birks, *Unjust Enrichment* (n 21) 112–28. See also: Krebs (n 32) 1–3, who argues that the move towards the civilian approach in England comes not only from such cases, but also from *Kleinwort Benson Ltd v Lincoln CC* [1999] 2 AC 349 (HL) on mistake of law.

[44] See, eg ch 2 below pp 29–30 and 36.

the civilian approach, so that the focus there is on finding a cause to *justify* the enrichment, rather than finding a means of '*unjustifying*' it.[45]

But in the meantime, since the common law approach has not yet adopted this generalised right to restitution and instead requires proof of specific unjust factors or reasons for restitution,[46] it will be necessary to identify what that reason is in the case of ultra vires payments to and from public bodies.

There Must Be No Defences

This element is also important and it is often the availability of a particular defence that is the primary reason for classifying a particular claim as belonging to the law of unjust enrichment or not, since some defences may be confined to cases of unjust enrichment while others may apply more broadly. Many defences and other related arguments are (at least theoretically) possible to a claim in unjust enrichment: time limits, change of position, estoppel, bona fide purchase, impossibility of counter-restitution, submission to an honest claim, ultra vires, passing on, fiscal disruption, exhaustion of statutory mechanisms for recovery and prospective overruling. The role of each defence in relation to the cases under investigation here will be discussed when more is known about the operation of those claims and will be seen to be closely connected to identification of the correct unjust factor.

Controversies surrounding the meaning of the word 'enriched' will only occasionally be relevant to this investigation, which is primarily concerned with the payment of money to and by public bodies. The requirement that the enrichment must have been received at the expense of the claimant will be relevant only in relation to cases where the defendant argues that the claimant passed the expense on to third parties.[47]

'Public Bodies' and 'Public Law'

Having thus laid the basic ground from the point of view of unjust enrichment, it is necessary next to give a similar outline of 'public law'.

At the outset it should be noted that there are those who argue that such a discrete area either does not or should not exist. The starting point for claims involving

[45] See further ch 6.

[46] Lord Hoffman states that 'In England, the claimant has to prove that the circumstances in which the payment was made come within one of the categories which the law recognizes as sufficient to make retention by the recipient unjust': *Deutsche Morgan Grenfell* (n 35) [21]. However, ultimately Lord Hoffmann concluded that it was not necessary to decide on the fundamental basis of enrichment liability because the case simply concerned the question whether DMG's action could be regarded as being 'for relief from the consequences of a mistake' within the meaning of s 32(1)(c) of the Limitation Act 1980: ibid [22]. See further: Edelman (n 40). As noted above, the terms 'unjust factor' and 'reason for restitution' will be used interchangeably throughout the rest of this book.

[47] See below, 'Passing On', ch 5.

public bodies in England is the Diceyan orthodoxy that even public officials should be liable in the ordinary way before the 'ordinary' courts of the land, and there are those who argue that this either is or should be the case.[48] Certainly at a very abstract level, the law applicable to public bodies and to private parties may well share similar values[49] and even in more specific areas the rules applicable to both types of entity may be the same.[50] Nevertheless, whatever one's view of the desirability or precise location of the public/private divide, for the following two reasons it seems impossible to deny that to some extent it exists.[51] The first and most concrete reason is that public law contains 'remedies' that are not available in private litigation. These 'prerogative remedies'[52] must be sought through a separate public law procedure, an application for judicial review.[53] Whatever one's normative view of the distinction, then, it is apparent that in this very concrete sense the law currently does regard public bodies as being subject to different rules from those applicable to private parties. But in addition to this immediate distinction it appears that public bodies also have both more and less power than private parties. Public bodies may be empowered to act in a way which in many cases is only permissible because the actor is a public body, the Revenue's[54] ability to levy tax being a prime example of this. Conversely, it may be desirable to restrain public bodies from acting in certain ways without this behaviour giving rise to any private law causes of action.[55] This means that public law must contain events *in addition to those on the private law map* to which the law must respond but which do not fit easily into the private law categories.

Administrative law does not generally regard itself as charting a 'taxonomy' of these 'events' in the manner discussed above in relation to private law. Indeed, the

[48] See, eg: C Harlow, '"Public" and "Private" Law: Definition without Distinction' (1980) 43 *Modern Law Review* 241.

[49] See, eg: D Oliver, 'Common Values of Public and Private Law and the Public/Private Divide' [1997] *Public Law* 630.

[50] See, eg: the similarities between '*Wednesbury* unreasonableness' (made famous by *Associated Provincial Picture Houses Ltd v Wednesbury Corp* [1948] 1 KB 223 (CA)) and the principles used in the context of trusts in the cases of *Sieff v Fox* [2005] EWHC 1312 (Ch), [2005] 1 WLR 3811 and *Hastings-Bass (Deceased), Re* [1975] Ch 25 (CA). See further: S Taube, 'The Principle in *Hastings-Bass* and *Sieff v Fox*: Analogies with Administrative Law' (2006) 3 *Private Client Business* 155.

[51] This is inevitably a somewhat pragmatic approach. For a more developed theoretical investigation of the relationship between public and private law in this context see C Mitchell and P Oliver, 'Unjust Enrichment and the Idea of Public Law' in R Chambers, C Mitchell and J Penner (eds), *Philosophical Foundations of the Law of Unjust Enrichment* (Oxford, Oxford University Press, 2009).

[52] Namely quashing orders (formerly certiorari); prohibiting orders (formerly prohibitions) and mandatory orders (formerly mandamus).

[53] Supreme Court Act 1981 s 31 and RSC 1965 Ord 53, now contained in the CPR Pt 54 (SI 2000/2092 (Schedule 1)).

[54] Up until 18 April 2005 direct taxes were levied by the Commissioners for Inland Revenue (IRC), while indirect taxes were collected by Her Majesty's Commissioners of Customs and Excise (CC&E). However, on 18 April 2005 these entities were merged to form Her Majesty's Revenue and Customs (HMRC). Where appropriate, these abbreviations will be used throughout the book, while 'the Revenue' will be used generically to refer to both the IRC and HMRC.

[55] See, to this effect: *R v Somerset County Council, ex p Fewings* [1995] 1 All ER 513 (QB) 524 (Laws J). For a similar definition based on extraordinary power and extraordinary limitations see the definitions of public law discussed in the French system, below at p 170.

concrete manifestation of the public/private divide has, at least in the past,[56] centred around the existence of a separate procedure for judicial review, and even now accounts of public law generally see the 'nucleus' of the subject as being based around the public law 'remedies' now known as 'quashing orders', 'prohibiting orders', 'mandatory orders', together with at least declarations, injunctions and damages.[57] This contrasts with the private law focus on events and responses discussed above. On the other hand, although it is clear that such a taxonomy of public law would look very different from anything found in the private law sphere, administrative law does essentially perform the same function. It certainly seems possible to define a biased decision as an 'event' to which the law responds, for example, with a quashing order. We are now not very far removed from public law's second controversial debate over the role of the 'ultra vires' doctrine,[58] with those of the 'common law school' arguing that the development of grounds of judicial review should operate in a similar way to the development of private law causes of action.[59] From this viewpoint, the term 'ultra vires' is a universally applicable 'umbrella term' that adds nothing to the existence of the 'event' as elaborated by the common law.[60] While my own preference is for this latter approach, it is in fact possible to separate the current investigation from the ultra vires controversy, because it is precisely the universality of the term 'ultra vires' which will make it useful here as a general expression for 'public law event'. Thus, whatever the constitutional source of the courts' authority to declare a particular rule or action 'ultra vires', that term will be used here simply to indicate that there has been an event which could give rise to a successful action for judicial review, an instance of public law illegality of some kind. We can thus leave aside the further analysis and justification of judicial review but retain an awareness that public law may well have its own internal system of events and responses, however the creation of those events and responses may be constitutionally justified.

It could, perhaps, be argued that all such public law events are in fact wrongs and thus do fit into that private law category. For example, in *Test Claimants in the*

[56] The decision in *Clark v University of Lincolnshire and Humberside* [2000] 1 WLR 1988 (CA) is discussed further below, at pp 14–15.

[57] See, eg: H Wade and C Forsyth, *Administrative Law*, 9th edn (Oxford, Oxford University Press, 2004) 32 and 591. Habeas corpus has been omitted from this list because it is possible that it more closely resembles the old forms of action in which the event and response are combined into what Birks has called an 'actionable story': Birks, 'Rights, Wrongs and Remedies' (n 17) 10–12.

[58] See, eg: C Forsyth, 'Of Fig Leaves and Fairy Tales: The Ultra Vires Doctrine, the Sovereignty of Parliament and Judicial Review' (1996) 55 *Cambridge Law Journal* 122. See also: M Elliott, 'The Ultra Vires Doctrine in a Constitutional Setting: Still the Central Principle of Administrative Law' (1999) 58 *Cambridge Law Journal* 129; M Elliott, *The Constitutional Foundations of Judicial Review* (Oxford, Hart Publishing, 2001) chs 2–4; and M Elliott, 'The Demise of Parliamentary Sovereignty?: The implications for justifying Judicial Review' (1999) 115 *Law Quarterly Review* 119. Compare: P Craig, 'Ultra Vires and the Foundations of Judicial Review' (1998) 57 *Cambridge Law Journal* 63; P Craig, 'Competing Models of Judicial Review' [1999] *Public Law* 428; and P Craig, 'Constitutional Analysis, Constitutional Principle and Judicial Review' [2001] *Public Law* 763.

[59] Craig, 'Competing Models of Judicial Review' ibid 432–35.

[60] While those in favour of its retention, such as Elliott and Forsyth, argue that retaining a reference to Parliament's intention is the only way of preserving constitutional orthodoxy: (n 58). Those in favour of the common law approach argue that this is unnecessary.

FII Group Litigation v The Commissioners for Her Majesty's Revenue and Customs,[61] Henderson J held that the change of position defence should not be available where the claim was 'founded on the unlawful levying of tax and therefore on the commission of a legal wrong,'[62] but it is clear that this is not correct for two reasons. First, it is already plain that these extra 'wrongs' concerning public bodies are different from the wrongs concerning private parties that can be found in the private law category. It would therefore be odd to group both kinds of wrongs together when there is such a clear division between them and it is difficult to see what this would achieve when they do not overlap. Even if this first objection is not fundamental, it appears that to place all such extra events into the 'wrongs' category is to deny that public law is a separate area at all. On the one hand, it is true that decisions may be quashed because of the bias of the decision-maker, because the wrong considerations were taken into account, or because the resulting decision was unreasonable, all of which could be described in a general sense as 'wrongs'. But this does not add anything to our understanding of public law and indeed it obscures the fact that public law has its own internal taxonomy, and to some extent procedure, which is separate from that of private law.

Of course, once it is established that public law is thus separate from private law, in events, responses and to some extent procedure, the next task is to locate the division between the two. What will trigger the application of public law to an entity as opposed to purely private law? Again, it is the differences in procedure between the two systems that have in the past largely provided the answer to this question. On the one hand, it is advantageous for litigants to have these extra 'remedies' (events and responses) available, but the public law procedure can also have disadvantages for litigants, including a short time limit, and reduced chances for cross-examination and disclosure.[63] For unjust enrichment claimants in the past, these disadvantages also included the unavailability of restitution as a response under the public law procedure.[64] Unsurprisingly, therefore, over the years there was much litigation over which procedure was applicable to a particular case, with some litigants trying to argue their way into the public law procedure and others trying to argue their way out of it.[65]

Those who wanted to use the private law procedure in preference to an application for judicial review had for a long time to contend with the decision of Lord Diplock in *O'Reilly v Mackman.*[66] Prior to the institution of the application for judicial review there had been a long line of authority to the effect that a plaintiff

[61] *Test Claimants in the FII Group Litigation v The Commissioners for Her Majesty's Revenue and Customs* [2008] EWHC 2893 (Ch), [2008] STI 2726.

[62] ibid [339]. For further discussion see below, ch 5, pp 148–9.

[63] See: PP Craig, *Administrative Law,* 6th edn (London, Sweet and Maxwell, 2008) 26-006; and Wade and Forsyth (n 57) 650–60.

[64] *Wandsworth LBC v Winder* [1985] AC 461 (HL) 480 (Robert Goff LJ). The position has now been changed by the Civil Procedure (Modification of Supreme Court Act 1981) Order 2004 SI 2004/1033. See: Wade and Forsyth (n 57) 798 and app 2 (pt 5).

[65] See: Wade and Forsyth ibid ch 18.

[66] *O'Reilly v Mackman* [1983] 2 AC 237 (HL).

could choose whether to apply for a prerogative writ (a specifically public law remedy) or to sue for a declaration (an equitable remedy). However, in 1977 the Rules of the Supreme Court Order 53 were substantially amended to make two important changes. One was the provision of a unified procedure[67] for an application for judicial review and the other was that in addition to the prerogative remedies, private law remedies of declarations, injunctions and damages would from then on be available on an application for judicial review. In *O'Reilly*, Lord Diplock inferred from these changes that since the position of applicants for judicial review had been made so much easier by the new rules it would henceforth,

> as a general rule be contrary to public policy, and as such an abuse of the process of the court, to permit a person seeking to establish that a decision of a public authority infringed rights to which he was entitled to protection under public law to proceed by way of an ordinary action and by this means to evade the provisions of Order 53 for the protection of such authorities.[68]

Thus, following *O'Reilly*, there was a presumption of 'procedural exclusivity' in favour of judicial review unless the applicant could show that his or her case fell within one of four recognised exceptions to the *O'Reilly* rule, namely: waiver by the public body of the protections available to it under the judicial review procedure;[69] 'collateral challenge' in which the invalidity of the public body's actions are raised as a defence in another case;[70] cases in which the fact finding capabilities of the judicial review procedure are deemed to be insufficient for dealing with matters in which the specific facts are key[71]; and, most importantly, cases in which the claimant has sufficient private law rights to bring the action through the normal private law procedure.[72] Originally this last exception was relatively narrow. Essentially the applicant would have to be able to show that he or she had a complete cause of action in private law to which the public law issue was only incidental,[73] but over the years the category has broadened.[74] The most significant development in this context, however, occurred in *Clark v University of Lincolnshire and Humberside*,[75] and was again motivated by legislative alterations to the judicial review procedure. On 2 January 2000, Part 54 of the Civil Procedure Rules was enacted and again these made various changes to the procedure for judicial review applications, one of which was Part 24. As Lord Woolf MR pointed out in *Clark*, Part 24 is important because it enables the court, either on its own motion or on the application of a party, if it considers that a claimant has no real

[67] Until that point the rules for standing, time limits etc had differed for each of the prerogative remedies.

[68] *O'Reilly* (n 66) 285.

[69] See: ibid 285 and *Gillick v West Norfolk and Wisbech AHA* [1986] AC 112 (HL).

[70] See: *Boddington v British Transport Police* [1999] 2 AC 143 (HL), though see also *Wandsworth* (n 64).

[71] See, eg: *Dennis Rye Pension Fund Trustees v Sheffield CC* [1998] 1 WLR 840 (CA).

[72] See: *O'Reilly* (n 66) for the origin of this exception.

[73] See, eg: *Roy v Kensington and Chelsea and Westminster Family Practitioners Committee* [1992] 1 AC 624 (HL).

[74] See, eg: *Mercury Communications v Director General of Telecommunications* [1996] 1 WLR 48 (HL).

[75] *Clark* (n 56).

prospect of succeeding on a claim or an issue, to give summary judgment on that claim or issue.[76] On the facts, *Clark* was not particularly significant, since it already fell within the private law exceptions created by *O'Reilly* itself, *Roy* and *Mercury*.[77] The importance of the decision instead lies in the fact that Lord Woolf clearly regarded the procedure chosen as essentially irrelevant in deciding what rules should apply to the claim.[78] If the claim is brought as an application for judicial review then of course the time limits and other procedural safeguards in Part 54 will apply. However, Part 24 and *Clark* now mean that the court can still give summary judgment when it thinks there has been undue delay, insufficient interest in the case and so on, even if the case is brought through the ordinary private law procedure. In other words, the choice of procedure will no longer be a watershed between the two sets of rules. Those who bring their cases through the private law procedure will no longer be safe simply because they have brought their claim within the relevant limitation period. Thus in *Carter Commercial Developments v Bedford BC*[79] when the claimant initiated ordinary proceedings in respect of a public law issue this was not in itself held to be determinative of the case. The court went on to hold that use of this procedure had been a deliberate attempt to circumvent the time limits which would have applied had Part 54 been used and thus on that basis the use of ordinary proceedings was held to be an abuse of process. The result is not that the public/private divide has vanished; it has just shifted to a different level. Rather than litigating over the correct *procedural channel* to be used, on the assumption that the applicable rules follow automatically from that choice of channel, the applicants will instead have to litigate over the correct *rules* to be applied to their claim.[80] A wholly procedural public/private divide has thus been replaced with a more substantive divide, though the rules at issue are still relatively procedural, such as time limits. This is not to make any comment at all on the desirability of such a divide, nor on the desirability of its current location, merely to show its current existence and functioning.

Conversely, for those trying to argue their way *into* the public law system in order to access its unique 'remedies' (events and responses), perhaps the most important indicator that public law should apply is the nature of the power being exercised by the body against which the challenge is being brought. In *R v Panel on Takeovers and Mergers, ex p Datafin plc*[81] the question arose whether the panel's decision to dismiss the applicants' complaint was susceptible to judicial review. In

[76] ibid [27].

[77] *Roy* (n 73) and *Mercury* (n 74).

[78] See also: M Elliott, *Beatson, Matthews and Elliott's Administrative Law: Text and Materials*, 3rd edn (Oxford, Oxford University Press, 2005) 468–69; and T Hickman, '*Clark*: The Demise of *O'Reilly* Completed?' (2000) 5 *Judicial Review* 178.

[79] *Carter Commercial Developments v Bedford BC* [2001] EWHC 669 (QB) (Admin), (2001) 34 EG 99.

[80] As Elliott puts it, 'The relevance of the public/private distinction therefore survives *Clark*: the public authorities' safeguards still apply in relation to public law matters, albeit that those safeguards are now upheld by effectively invoking them irrespective of the type of proceedings used, rather than by rigidly enforcing the procedural dichotomy of *O'Reilly v Mackman*' (n 78) 469.

[81] *R v Panel on Takeovers and Mergers, ex p Datafin plc* [1987] QB 815 (QB).

holding that it was, Lloyd LJ held that a claim would fall into Order 53 if the *source* of the challenged body's power was statutory. If the source of the power were contractual, on the other hand, it would not. Between these two extremes, however, the '*nature* of the power' (emphasis added) became relevant to the determination.[82] In *ex p Datafin*, the nature of the body was held to be public for a number of reasons. First, although self-regulating, the Panel on Takeovers and Mergers did not operate consensually, but imposed a collective code on those within its ambit, and it was not possible to trade without being subject to this code.[83] Second, it was held that the government had impliedly devolved its power to the Panel, because the government had limited legislation in this area, and certain legislation presupposed the existence of the Panel.[84] Third, the Panel's powers were reinforced by statutory powers exercisable by the government and the Bank of England.[85] Finally, the applicants did not have any cause of action in contract or tort against the Panel.[86]

Two aspects of this decision are important for our purposes. First, the monopolistic and reinforced nature of the Panel's power was important to its determination as a body amenable to public law and it is this amenability that is the key to what is meant by 'public body' for the purposes of this investigation. And second, cases based on the private law event of contract are excluded from the sphere of public law.[87]

This means that although, particularly over the last 40 years,[88] the concept of judicial review has developed exponentially in cases which *do not* have a parallel in private law. For those cases which *do* fall under a private law heading, such as contract, tort or unjust enrichment, the Diceyan orthodoxy remains; the presence of a public body essentially makes no difference and the claim is treated as if it were between two private parties. Thus even when the Crown Proceedings Act 1947 removed Crown immunity, it did so by making the Crown vicariously liable for its servants as if it 'were a private person of full age and capacity'.[89] However, this does not mean that in those instances the simultaneously greater and more limited nature of public power vanishes and thus it is often the case that traditionally-private law is used by public bodies for purposes that are significantly different

[82] ibid 847. It should be noted that Ord 53 has now been replaced by CPR pt 54.

[83] ibid 852.

[84] ibid 849.

[85] ibid 838.

[86] ibid 839.

[87] The idea that claims based on private law events should belong outside public law is reinforced by cases from the opposite direction, where the litigants are trying to get out of the public law procedural rules. Such cases include: *Lonrho plc v Tebbit* [1991] 4 All ER 973 (Ch); [1992] 4 All ER 280 (CA); *Davy v Spelthorne BC* [1984] AC 262 (HL); *Wandsworth* (n 64) and arguably *Roy* (n 73). See also: Forsyth (n 58).

[88] Lord Mustill stated in *R v Secretary of State for the Home Dept, ex p Fire Brigades Union* [1995] 2 AC 513 (HL) 567: 'To avoid a vacuum in which the citizen would be left without protection against a misuse of executive powers the courts have had no option but to occupy the dead ground [left by the reduction of Parliamentary control of the executive] in a manner, and in areas of public life, which could not have been foreseen 30 years ago'.

[89] Crown Proceedings Act 1947 s 2(1).

from those pursued by private individuals or undertakings. One example of this is 'regulation by contract,' whereby 'the economic or bargaining power of government in procurement is used to regulate matters which are collateral to the main object of the contract'.[90]

Similarly, although the whole of public law cannot simply be subsumed into the category of private law 'wrongs' for the reasons given above, public bodies can commit 'wrongs' which are properly so-called even in comparison to the other public law events. At present, ultra vires acts per se will not give rise to damages liability in purely domestic law. Indeed, if they did, it would be easier to argue that in fact all public law events should be regarded as belonging in the category of 'wrongs'. Instead, to succeed the claim must be brought within one of the recognised *private law* causes of action. In the case that established this principle, *X (Minors) v Bedfordshire CC*,[91] Lord Browne-Wilkinson identified several possible causes of action which could be used against public bodies: first, actions for breach of statutory duty; second, actions for breach of a common law duty of care arising from the imposition of a statutory duty or from its performance; and third, misfeasance in a public office.[92] In addition to these, a fourth source of liability comes from sections eight and nine of the Human Rights Act 1998, a fifth is nuisance, as established by *Rylands v Fletcher*[93] and a sixth comes from the EU context,[94] where in *Francovich*[95] the ECJ held that breach of Community law could give rise to state liability in damages before the national courts. In the subsequent joined cases of *Brasserie du Pecheur* and *Factortame III*[96] the Court held that liability would only arise where the breach by the state was 'sufficiently serious', which would be the case where the Member State had 'manifestly and gravely disregarded the limits on its discretion'.[97] In some cases *Francovich/Brasserie/ Factortame III* damages actions have been brought within the framework of breach of statutory duty,[98] while in others they have been regarded as free-standing public law torts.[99] It is clear, therefore, that to a large extent the same is true of tort as it was of contract. The special position of public bodies means that the kind of wrongs they can

[90] C Harlow and R Rawlings, *Law and Administration* 2nd edn (London, Butterworths, 1997, reprinted 2006) ch 8, 'A Revolution in the Making' at 208.

[91] *X (Minors) v Bedfordshire CC* [1995] 2 AC 633 (HL). Indeed, since *Barrett v Enfield LBC* [2001] 2 AC 550 (HL) and *Phelps v Hillingdon LBC* [2001] 2 AC 619 (HL) the relationship between ultra vires activity and liability in tort has been even more complicated, since those cases established that a finding of ultra vires is neither a sufficient nor, in some cases, a necessary condition of liability in tort.

[92] *X (Minors)* ibid 730–40.

[93] *Rylands v Fletcher* (1868) LR 3 (HL) 330.

[94] For further detail, see discussion of the EU system below ch 8 at pp 238–39.

[95] Cases C-6 and 9/90 *Francovich and Bonifaci v Italian Republic* [1991] ECR I-5357.

[96] Cases C-46 and 48/93 *Brasserie du Pecheur SA v Germany; R v Secretary of State for Transport, ex p Factortame Ltd* [1996] ECR I-1029. Confusingly, from the UK perspective the case was the fifth in the *Factortame* series and is therefore known as '*Factortame V*', whereas for the ECJ it was the third in the series and is thus known to EU lawyers as '*Factortame III*'.

[97] ibid [55]–[56].

[98] *Garden Cottage Foods Ltd v Milk Marketing Board* [1984] AC 130 (HL).

[99] *Application des Gaz SA v Falks Veritas Ltd* [1974] Ch 381 (CA) 395–96. Craig prefers the latter approach: Craig, *Administrative Law* (n 63) 29-059.

commit is different from those of private parties, but the extent to which the law has recognised this is very limited. On the other hand, not all public law events will give rise to liability in damages, even under the EU system, nor is it possible to argue either that all public law events belong in the private 'wrongs' category or that these cases are simply further examples of purely public events. Instead it is clear that in both instances there are events which contain elements of reasoning from both public and private law.[100] Nevertheless, the tendency is still to regard them as belonging solely to one sphere or the other. Thus, on the one hand we have the Diceyan orthodoxy of the Crown Proceedings Act and the need for a private law cause of action in *X*, while on the other hand commentators, such as Harlow, Rawlings, Hogg and Monahan[101] argue against the introduction of a special public law of contract to cover such cases, and do so largely on the basis of the coincidental usefulness of private law as a means of public regulation, rather than the belief that it makes no difference whether the parties to the private claim are both private or not.[102] The tendency therefore is to regard the current situation either from the purely private perspective, or from the purely public law perspective.

Conclusion

It was noted above[103] that there are various potential means of classification. The one adopted by those mapping the area so far is the event-response system, but it was also noted that the relationship between public and private law seems initially more like the 'social context' classificatory system. Given the existence of these extra 'public law events', however, it now becomes apparent that the public law/private law divide does in fact have a place on the *existing* map and does not require a change to the method of classification. Thus although so far the event-response division has been thought to be the largest-scale map, in fact there is a level above this; the division between public and private law. It should be noted that Birks himself separates 'private law' from 'public law' before he begins the event-response system of classification and he expressly only connects this to the

[100] Here the investigation is into public body claims in unjust enrichment by subtraction. It is of course possible that a public body could also profit from committing one of the specific wrongs recognised as giving rise to financial liability listed above. In such cases it would also no doubt be necessary for both the public and private aspects of the claim to be recognised, in addition to discussion over the nature of such claims of the kind described above, but such cases are beyond the scope of the current investigation.

[101] P Hogg and P Monahan, *Liability of the Crown*, 3rd edn (Toronto, Carswell, 2000).

[102] For example, Hogg and Monahan write 'for the most part, the "ordinary" law does work a satisfactory resolution of the conflicts between government and citizen. Indeed the parts of the law that seem . . . to be most unsatisfactory are those where the courts have refused to apply the ordinary law to the Crown . . . conclude that Dicey's idea of equality provides the basis for a rational, workable and acceptable theory of governmental liability': ibid 3.

[103] Above, 'Using the Map' at p 5.

former. He states that it follows from his event-response 'map' that he will not discuss, 'unless tangentially', public law.[104] The event-response division can then be seen to be a subdivision of each of these two initial spheres. Using this analysis, it is clear that it is the two 'ends' of the existing map and the relationship between them that will be important to this investigation: at the one end, the largest-scale map of the division between public and private law, and at the other the most detailed, smallest-scale map of the specific reasons for restitution.

[104] Birks, 'Rights, Wrongs and Remedies' (n 17) 10. At 3, Birks also writes that he is '[a]ccepting without comment the difficult division between public and private law, and staying within the latter'. See further Mitchell and Oliver, n 51.

2

Woolwich and the Creation of the Public Law Reason for Restitution

THE FIRST CASE to raise sharply the relationship between public law and the law of unjust enrichment was *Woolwich Equitable Building Society v IRC*,[1] which entailed a claim for the return of money from a public body.

The Facts

Until 1985, the tax position of building societies, so far as concerned accounting for tax deducted by a society on interest paid or credited to its members, was regulated by extra-statutory arrangements between individual building societies and the Commissioners of Inland Revenue (IRC) which were formalised by statute in section 23 of the Finance Act 1951 and section 343 of the Income and Corporation Taxes Act 1970. These arrangements meant that building societies had to account to the IRC for lump sums representing the interest paid to members. For the financial year 1985–86, the lump sum paid by Woolwich only took into account the period up to 30 September 1985. No interest was therefore paid for the period from 1 October 1985 to 5 April 1986, the 'omitted period'. The Finance Act 1985 empowered the IRC to introduce subordinate legislation by way of regulations to alter the mechanics of collecting income tax on building society deposits.[2] It was explicitly not to raise extra tax, but 'transitional provisions' in the introduced regulations meant that tax was charged for the omitted period in order to prevent the building societies from receiving a windfall. The building societies, however, argued that this was a new tax and was thus beyond the powers granted to the IRC under the Finance Act 1985. Nevertheless, Woolwich paid, under protest, most of the disputed tax (£56,998,220), fearing that if it did not do so it would give the impression to its customers that it could not pay, and this would lead them to withdraw their money.

[1] *Woolwich Equitable Building Society v IRC* [1993] AC 70 (HL).

[2] For a detailed account of the facts, see: N Jordan, 'Retrospection and Restitution: The Woolwich Building Society Rulings' (1991) *Butterworths Journal of International Banking and Financial Law* 481.

Woolwich therefore had two complaints. First, that the tax was invalid, and second, that the money should be repaid with interest. These two arguments are interesting for our purposes because they belong to either side of the public/private divide: the invalidity of the tax involved a claim in public law, while the claim for return of the money belonged in private law, under the Diceyan orthodoxy.

As soon as the regulations were made, Woolwich had brought proceedings by way of judicial review, seeking a declaration that the transitional provisions were ultra vires. The Treasury Minister promptly responded by introducing a late amendment into the Finance Bill 1986 retrospectively widening the IRC's regulation-making power to cover the situation, and this became section 47 of the Finance Act 1986. However, deficiencies in the drafting of section 47 encouraged Woolwich to pursue its case[3] and the House of Lords unanimously found in its favour on 25 October 1990.[4]

Once Woolwich had been successful in this first complaint, the IRC agreed to return the principal amount, but they denied any obligation to pay interest unless they had previously agreed to do so. It was this matter which formed the basis of the claim in *Woolwich*, under section 35A of the Supreme Court Act 1981. Woolwich would only be entitled to interest[5] at the court's discretion if the plaintiff could establish a legal entitlement to the principal sum, so that it constituted a debt. Thus, only if the IRC had had an obligation to repay the principal sum under the law of unjust enrichment could Woolwich get interest on the repayment.

The Background to the Claim

Before *Woolwich*, success for individuals in such claims was mixed. Some cases, such as *Newdigate v Davy*,[6] *Campbell v Hall*,[7] *Steele v Williams*,[8] *Hooper v Exeter Corp*,[9]

[3] ibid.

[4] *R v IRC, ex p Woolwich Equitable Building Society* [1990] 1 WLR 1400 (HL).

[5] Interest awarded under the Act is simple interest. The possibility of awarding compound interest was considered by the HL in *Westdeutsche Landesbank Girozentrale v Islington LBC* [1996] AC 669 (HL), but the majority decided against awarding it because Islington had not been able to address the issue. Lord Goff and Lord Woolf, however, were of the opinion that all restitutionary claimants, whether pursuing a personal or proprietary claim, should be entitled, where appropriate, to compound interest. For further detail see: A Jones, *Restitution and European Community Law* (London, Mansfield Press, 2000) 31–35. However, in *Sempra Metals Ltd v IRC* [2007] UKHL 34, [2008] 1 AC 561, the HL held, distinguishing *Westdeutsche*, that courts had jurisdiction at common law to award compound interest where the claimant sought a restitutionary remedy for the time value of money paid under a mistake. *Sempra Metals* is one of the domestic cases that has followed the ECJ's decision in Cases C-397/98 and C-410/98 *Metallgesellschaft and Hoechst v IRC* [2001] ECR I-1727, discussed below in ch 8. For further discussion of the implications of this case see below at n 115.

[6] *Newdigate v Davy* (1701) 1 Ld Raym 742, 91 ER 1397 (KB).

[7] *Campbell v Hall* (1774) 1 Cowp 204, 98 ER 1045 (KB).

[8] *Steele v Williams* (1853) 8 Ex 625, 155 ER 1502 (Excheq).

[9] *Hooper v Exeter Corp* (1887) 56 LJQB 457. (QB).

Queens of the River Steamship Co v Conservators of the River Thames,[10] *AG v Wilts United Dairies*[11] and *South of Scotland Electricity Board v British Oxygen Co Ltd (No 2)*[12] suggested that such money could be recovered as of right, and indeed, this had been argued by Birks[13], G Jones[14] and Cornish.[15] However, other cases suggested that a private law unjust factor such as duress would be necessary.[16] For example, in *Meadows v Grand Junction Waterworks Co*[17] the claimants recovered for mistake of fact, while in *Sebel Products Ltd v Customs and Excise Commissioners,*[18] although the claimants succeeded through implied contract rather than through unjust enrichment, the method used was still purely private. In *Slater v Burnley Corp,*[19] *Twyford v Manchester Corp*[20] and *Eric Gnapp Ltd v Petroleum Board,*[21] the unjust factor required was duress, but here there were also the beginnings of a public law element, since it was held that the payments could be recovered if they were paid *colore officii.*[22] This provides an interesting parallel with the relationship between the private law category of wrongs and public law. The starting point in wrongs, as with unjust enrichment, is the Diceyan orthodoxy that the liability of a public body arises on exactly the same basis as the liability of an individual. But, just like the *colore officii* claim in unjust enrichment, an exception has been made and a specifically public law tort has been created where an official misuses his or her powers (misfeasance in public office).[23] Nevertheless, although the *colore officii* claim did have these public law features, it was still a close relative of the private law ground of duress and some threat, express or implied, to withhold a service or benefit to which the plaintiff was entitled was necessary. A simple threat to sue was not enough to found such a claim,[24] and it would certainly not succeed solely on the basis that the demand was ultra vires. The cause of action was thus still very much a private one, even if some account was taken of the greater potential for duress where one of the parties is private and the other public.

[10] *Queens of the River Steamship Co v Conservators of the River Thames* (1899) 15 TLR 474 (QB).

[11] *AG v Wilts United Dairies* (1921) 37 TLR 884 (CA), (1922) 127 LT 822 (HL).

[12] *South of Scotland Electricity Board v British Oxygen Co Ltd (No 2)* [1959] 1 WLR 587 (HL).

[13] P Birks, 'Restitution from the Executive, a Tercentenary Footnote to the Bill of Rights' in P Finn (ed), *Essays on the Law of Restitution* (Sydney, Law Book Co, 1990).

[14] G Jones, 'Restitutionary Claims against Public Authorities: A Comparative Study' in *Restitution in Public and Private Law* (London, Sweet and Maxwell, 1991).

[15] WR Cornish, '"Colour of Office": Restitutionary Redress Against Public Authority' (1987) *Journal of Malaysian and Comparative Law* 41.

[16] See generally: G Jones (n 14) 14–19.

[17] *Meadows v Grand Junction Waterworks Co* (1905) 3 LGR 910 (KB).

[18] *Sebel Products Ltd v Customs and Excise Commissioners* [1949] Ch 409 (Ch).

[19] *Slater v Burnley Corp* 59 LT 636 (QB).

[20] *Twyford v Manchester Corp* [1946] Ch 236 (Ch).

[21] *Eric Gnapp Ltd v Petroleum Board* [1949] 1 All ER 980 (CA).

[22] Birks has defined this as a case in which 'the demand is made in respect of something which the applicant wants and which it is the duty of the authority to provide, where the potentiality for duress consists in the withholding of the applicant's entitlement': P Birks, 'Restitution from Public Authorities' (1980) 33 *Current Legal Problems* 191, 199.

[23] See: P Craig, *Administrative Law,* 6th edn (London, Sweet and Maxwell, 2008) 29-031—29-036 and H Wade and C Forsyth, *Administrative Law,* 9th edn (Oxford, Oxford University Press, 2004) 416–19 and 773–88.

[24] *William Whiteley Ltd v R* (1909) 101 LT 741 (KB).

A Wholly Private Approach? Potential Unjust Factors Available to the Woolwich

The question for the Woolwich, then, was whether its case could be brought within these existing precedents, or any of the other existing unjust factors.

Duress or *Colore Officii*

It is certainly true that the Woolwich had felt compelled to pay the IRC, and indeed Lord Browne-Wilkinson held that:

> [A]s a matter of principle the *colore officii* cases [listed above] are merely examples of a wider principle, viz that where the parties are on an unequal footing so that money is paid by way of tax or other impost in pursuance of a demand by some public officer, these moneys are recoverable since the citizen is, in practice, unable to resist the payment save at the risk of breaking the law or exposing himself to penalties or other disadvantages.[25]

Thus the concept of 'payment under implied compulsion' was 'in play'.[26] Similarly Lord Slynn held that:

> Although . . . the facts do not fit easily into the existing category of duress or of claims *colore officii*, they shade into them. There is a common element of pressure which by analogy can be said to justify a claim for repayment.[27]

However, Lord Keith held that:

> [N]o pressure to pay was put upon Woolwich by the revenue. Woolwich paid because it calculated that it was in its commercial interest to do so. It could have resisted payment, and the revenue had no means other than the taking of legal proceedings which it might have used to enforce payment. The threat of legal proceedings is not improper pressure. There was no improper pressure by the revenue, and in particular there was no duress.[28]

Lord Goff agreed that:

> [S]ince the possibility of distraint by the revenue was very remote, the concept of compulsion would have to be stretched to the utmost to embrace the circumstances of such a case as this. It is for this reason that Woolwich's alternative claim founded upon compulsion did not loom large in the argument and is difficult to sustain.[29]

And Lord Jauncey argued that:

> Duress to be relevant must be found within the four walls of the transaction. In this case Woolwich would, in relation to the revenue, have been no worse off if they had refused

[25] *Woolwich* (n 1) 198.
[26] ibid.
[27] ibid 204.
[28] ibid 161.
[29] ibid 173.

payment of the tax claimed and raised the defence which subsequently proved successful . . .Woolwich are not entitled to recover on the ground of duress.[30]

This majority viewpoint is also supported in the academic literature.[31] None of this is intended to deny that public bodies have even greater power to compel individuals than large companies, or indeed even when the private party *is* a large undertaking such as Woolwich. The argument is that the elements of the private law *colore officii* ground must be satisfied and it is difficult to do this when there is no 'entitlement threat' or private law compulsion.

Inequality

Birks in particular[32] has suggested this factor as a possible explanation for the result in *Woolwich* and, as McKendrick notes,[33] the view received some support from Lord Slynn when he stated that the *colore officii* cases were based on the fact that the payer and payee were not on an equal footing. Certainly this is an important aspect of the current cases, but the majority decision was not based on the idea of transactional inequality alone. It is clear, particularly from Lord Jauncey's judgment,[34] that in cases such as *Morgan v Palmer*,[35] used as authority for the significance of the 'unequal footing,' the inequality was significant to their Lordships only because it allowed the payee to demand payment; it was not itself the reason for restitution.

No Consideration

This 'unjust factor' has been the subject of much academic criticism. Although in fact the most significant judicial support for it came from the judgment of Hobhouse J (as he then was) at first instance in *Westdeutsche*,[36] several of their Lordships[37] in *Woolwich* referred to *Queens of the River Steamship Co* as being authority for recovery where there was 'no consideration' and Lord Goff pointed out that in *Campbell v Hall*[38] 'recovery was stated to be founded upon absence of consideration for the payment'.[39] Furthermore there are other cases in the late

[30] ibid 194.

[31] See, eg: G Virgo, 'Restitution of Overpaid Tax—Justice at the Expense of Certainty' (1993) 52 *Cambridge Law Journal* 31; A Burrows, 'Restitution from Public Authorities' (1993) 4 *The King's College Law Journal* 97, especially at 98; and Birks, 'Objections to the Duress Requirement' in 'Restitution from Public Authorities' (n 22) 196.

[32] Birks, 'Restitution from the Executive' (n 13).

[33] E McKendrick, 'Restitution of Unlawfully Demanded Tax' [1993] *Lloyd's Maritime and Commercial Law Quarterly* 88, 94.

[34] *Woolwich* (n 1) 181.

[35] *Morgan v Palmer* (1824) 2 B & C 729, 107 ER 554 (KB).

[36] *Westdeutsche Landesbank Girozentrale v Islington London Borough Council* (QB) [1994] All ER 890.

[37] See, eg: *Woolwich* (n 1) 183 (Lord Jauncey) and 197 (Lord Browne-Wilkinson).

[38] *Campbell v Hall* (n 7).

[39] *Woolwich* (n 1) 198 and 166 respectively.

eighteenth and early nineteenth centuries, of which *Dew v Parsons*[40] is a significant example, which support this approach. Nevertheless, Lord Keith pointed out that the report in *Queens of the River Steamship Co* contained no citation of authority nor any account of the argument, so that the decision could not be regarded as significant,[41] and although Lord Browne-Wilkinson believed that 'no consideration' was 'in play' in the *Woolwich* case *alongside* 'implied compulsion', crucially he did not believe that either of those factors was sufficient on its own to found the claim.

There are two reasons why this conclusion is welcome. First, and perhaps most importantly, 'absence of consideration' may perhaps not be an unjust factor at all, and its adoption could lead to an abandonment of the whole scheme of unjust factors, or specific reasons for restitution. This is because, were we to adopt 'absence of consideration', all the existing unjust factors could be swallowed up into this one 'reason for restitution'. Such a move would thus in fact be a change to the civilian approach of enrichment *without cause* outlined in chapter one and discussed in more detail below, in part two. It was noted in chapter one that there is nothing inherently 'wrong' with such an approach, nor would it be impossible for English law to adopt it. It was even suggested that there may not be any great difference between the two approaches,[42] and that at least Birks and Meier advocate such a change.[43] Indeed, Birks in particular thinks that it is public body cases (albeit of a potentially different kind) which necessitate the change.[44] Nevertheless, for this area of law to adopt the civilian structure would be a significant intellectual change if not a practical one, and since the advantages and disadvantages of doing so were not considered by Hobhouse J or their Lordships it is unlikely that this is what they intended. This is particularly so given that Lord Goff expressly pointed out that English law has not developed so as to recognise a general *condictio indebiti*.[45]

Second, in the first edition of his book, Virgo pointed out that even apart from these structural objections there is another reason for rejecting 'no consideration' as the unjust factor on which to found recovery in *Woolwich*. Rather than focusing on the fact that the contract is void, he believes we should instead be focusing on the reasons why it is void.[46] Thus in the cases of payment out by a local authority

40 *Dew v Parsons* (1819) 2 B & Ald 562, 106 ER 471 (KB).

41 *Woolwich* (n 1) 156.

42 See ch 1 at 7–10. Even Birks' book contains 'a limited reconciliation' between the two approaches which supports this conclusion: P Birks, *Unjust Enrichment*, 2nd edn (Oxford, Oxford University Press, 2005) 116–17.

43 See ch 1 at 7–10. It was noted in ch 1 (n 35) that the decision of the House of Lords in *Criterion Properties plc v Stratford UK Properties LLC* [2004] UKHL 28, [2004] 1 WLR 1846 could be seen as support for this approach in English law, though that is by no means the only possible interpretation of the case.

44 Birks, *Unjust Enrichment* (n 42) 108–28.

45 Lord Goff stated that 'To the simple call of justice, there are a number of possible objections. The first is to be found in the structure of our law of restitution, as it developed during the 19th and early 20th centuries. That law might have developed so as to recognise a *condictio indebiti*—an action for the recovery of money on the ground that it was not due. But it did not do so': *Woolwich* (n 1) 172.

46 His chief criticism is that it confuses the contractual notion of consideration with the restitutionary notion of consideration. If a contract is void, then there is indeed no contractual consideration, but restitution requires a reason, typically based on vitiation of consent, and the voidness itself is not

(as in the swaps cases)[47] the reason for restitution he suggests is incapacity, and in the cases such as *Woolwich*, the reason for restitution he suggests is 'unauthorised receipt by a public authority'. Both of these are policy-orientated unjust factors that belong alongside other miscellaneous public policy cases of restitution.[48]

Failure of Consideration[49]

Similarly, Lord Browne-Wilkinson certainly thought that there was a 'close analogy' between failure of consideration and the basis for the claim in *Woolwich*,[50] but this makes it clear that failure of consideration did not apply directly as the unjust factor either. On the contrary, he made it clear that *both* want of consideration and payment under implied compulsion were 'in play'.[51] Thus, even if failure of consideration reasoning was relevant in *Woolwich*,[52] it could not capture all the relevant aspects of that case.

Mistake of Law

The first point to be made here is that at the time of the decision in *Woolwich* it was not possible to recover after a mistake of law, only after a mistake of fact. However, even if the House of Lords had wanted to remove this rule in the *Woolwich* case, rather than waiting for *Kleinwort Benson Ltd v Lincoln CC*,[53] the

sufficient: G Virgo, *The Principles of the Law of Restitution*, 2nd edn (Oxford, Oxford University Press, 2006) 383. The relationship between the various forms of consideration—the promise, the performance of the promise and the validity of the performance of the promise—will be discussed in further detail in ch 3, p 63, See further: R Stevens and B McFarlane, 'In Defence of *Sumpter v Hedges*' (2002) 118 *Law Quarterly Review* 569, 576–77; J Edelman, 'The Meaning of "Unjust" in the English Law of Unjust Enrichment' (2006) 3 *European Private Law* 309, 316; and R Stevens, 'Is there a Law of Unjust Enrichment?' in S Degeling and J Edelman, *Unjust Enrichment in Commercial Law* (Sydney, Lawbook Co, 2008).

[47] Discussed in their own terms below ch 3 at pp 57–69.

[48] Virgo, *Principles* (n 46) 384–86.

[49] On the other hand, in *Westdeutsche* (n 36) 924, Hobhouse J (as he then was) reinterpreted this potential unjust factor to be, not a *failure* of consideration, but an *absence* of consideration: '[I]n the case of ultra vires transactions such as those with which I am concerned where there is not and never has been any contract, I prefer to use the phrase 'absence of consideration'. I note that this was the phrase used by the House of Lords in the *Woolwich* case'. The relationship between 'absence' and 'failure' of consideration will be considered in more detail below, pp 58–63, when *Westdeutsche* is investigated on its own terms.

[50] *Woolwich* (n 1) 197.

[51] ibid 198.

[52] Virgo has suggested that failure of consideration could in any case never provide a ground for recovery because no consideration can ever come from the Revenue in tax cases. Even if the tax had been valid the discharge of the liability would have 'arisen by virtue of the taxpayer's act of payment': G Virgo, 'The Law of Taxation is Not an Island—Overpaid Taxes and the Law of Restitution' [1993] *British Tax Review* 442. However, in ch 3 it will be noted that others argue that the validity of a transaction can itself constitute consideration, See also: p 63.

[53] *Kleinwort Benson Ltd v Lincoln CC* [1999] 2 AC 349 (HL).

question did not arise on the facts. It will be remembered that the Woolwich were at no point mistaken as to their legal rights. From the time of introduction of the ultra vires regulations they challenged the tax, and when they did pay they did so under protest. The only mistake, therefore, was on the part of the IRC, not on the part of the Woolwich. Indeed, while there are various dicta in *Woolwich* casting doubt on the mistake of law rule and hinting at the change that was to come in *Kleinwort Benson*,[54] Lord Goff pointed out that:

> [I]f there is to be a right to recovery in respect of taxes exacted unlawfully by the revenue, it is irrelevant to consider whether the old rule barring recovery of money paid under mistake of law should be abolished, for that rule can have no application where the remedy arises *not from error on the part of the taxpayer*, but from the unlawful nature of the demand by the revenue.[55] (emphasis added)

Thus regardless of the independent desirability of mistake of law as a ground for recovery in such cases[56] it did not arise on the facts of *Woolwich.*

Two New Options for Recovery

It can therefore be seen that on its particular facts, none of the existing private law-based unjust factors were available to the Woolwich. If the Woolwich were to win, the House of Lords had two options. It could extend the private law grounds of recovery to cover the case,[57] or it could develop a new, public law unjust factor. The majority of their Lordships (Lord Goff, Lord Browne-Wilkinson and Lord Slynn) chose the second 'public law unjust factor' option, and at its very narrowest the ratio of *Woolwich* is that:

> a citizen who makes a payment in response to an unlawful demand for tax that was unlawful because of the invalidity of the relevant subordinate legislation has a prima facie right in restitution to the repayment of the money, irrespective of whether the payment is mistaken or made under duress.[58]

[54] See, eg: *Woolwich* (n 1) 164 (Lord Goff) and 199 (Lord Slynn).

[55] ibid 176.

[56] This matter will be discussed in more detail pp 64–67, 94–97, 109–10 and 121–22.

[57] In the past Burrows had suggested this option, A Burrows, 'Public Authorities, Ultra Vires and Restitution' in A Burrows (ed) *Essays on the Law of Restitution* (Oxford, Clarendon Press, 1991). A similar argument was made by R Collins, 'Restitution from Government Officials' (1984) 29 *McGill Law Journal* 407. But Burrows has since expressed himself to be in line with Birks who, like Beatson argued that the public law aspects of the case should be fully recognised: A Burrows, *The Law of Restitution*, 2nd edn (London, Butterworths, 2002) 442; P Birks, 'Public and Private' in *Restitution: the Future* (Sydney, Federation Press, 1992) 82; and J Beatson, 'Restitution of Taxes, Levies and Other Imposts: Defining the Extent of the *Woolwich* Principle' (1993) 109 *Law Quarterly Review* 401, 412.

[58] Law Commission, '*Restitution: Mistakes of Law and Ultra Vires Public Authority Receipts and Payments*' (Law Com No 227 Cm 2731, 1994) [6.33].

Even the minority's rejection of this unjust factor was not based on any objection to its operation in principle, but on the fact that:

> To give effect to Woolwich's proposition would . . . amount to a very far reaching exercise of judicial legislation. That would be particularly inappropriate having regard to the considerable number of instances which exist of Parliament having legislated in various fields to define the circumstances under which payments of tax not lawfully due may be recovered, and also in what situations and upon what terms interest on overpayments of tax may be paid . . . [F]ormulation of the precise grounds upon which overpayments of tax ought to be recoverable and of any exceptions to the right of recovery, may involve nice considerations of policy which are properly the province of Parliament and are not suitable for consideration by the courts.[59]

What is the *Woolwich* Unjust Factor?

Clearly then, *Woolwich* created a new 'reason for restitution'. But what exactly is it?

Illegality

One option might be to regard the *Woolwich* unjust factor as a form of illegality. However, there are several reasons why we cannot simply assume that illegality will, on its own, found a claim following *Woolwich.* First, of course, it is not clear that illegality can provide a ground for recovery at all; it may only operate as a defence. Both Birks and Burrows, on the other hand, argue that withdrawal within the *locus poenitentiae* can furnish an unjust factor based on the policy of discouraging unlawful conduct,[60] and Burrows would add to this another ground of restitution which exists where the illegality is designed to protect the vulnerable class to which the claimant belongs.[61] Put this way, an analogy with this policy-motivated unjust factor seems at first attractive, but even if illegality is potentially an unjust factor, its application to this type of case was rejected by Estey J of the Supreme Court of Canada in *Hydro Electric Commission of Township of Nepean v Ontario Hydro.*[62] Although he was dealing in that case with a situation of mutual

[59] *Woolwich* (n 1) 161 (Lord Keith) and 196 (Lord Jauncey).

[60] Burrows *Law of Restitution* (n 57) 425, citing P Birks, *An Introduction to the Law of Restitution* (Oxford, Oxford University Press, 1985) 229–303 and 424–32. On the other hand, Virgo argues that this ground of restitution is effectively failure of consideration. He points to the fact that this would give rise to an anomaly, since sometimes illegality can operate as a defence to claims based on total failure of consideration and yet there are other examples in which total failure of consideration does seem to ground recovery in spite of, or (if Burrows and Birks are correct) because of, the illegality: Virgo, *Principles* (n 46) 728–29.

[61] Burrows *Law of Restitution* (n 57) 269–71.

[62] *Hydro Electric Commission of Township of Nepean v Ontario Hydro* [1982] 132 DLR (3d) 193.

mistake as to the law, he held that this 'cannot be classified as an illegal transaction as neither party has offended any prohibition in law, but rather each party has respectively asked for and paid a charge not included in the statutory term 'cost'.[63]

It is arguable that this reasoning does not depend on the presence of a mistake and so applies equally to the *Woolwich* case. On that basis it could not be said that the *Woolwich* unjust factor is based purely on private illegality of the kind envisaged by Birks and Burrows, though on the other hand that does not mean that the concept of illegality has nothing at all to contribute to the *Woolwich* reason for restitution.

Incapacity

Remaining with the idea of 'policy-motivated unjust factors', Virgo, in rejecting absence of consideration as an unjust factor, prefers to focus on the underlying policy which removes the consideration.[64] In some cases, he argues, this is the policy of continuing to protect those in whose favour the capacity rules were created.[65] This would mean that the *Woolwich* unjust factor belonged either in the category of policy-motivated restitution or in the category of unjust factors vitiating intent. It is arguable, though, that cases of incapacity seem more closely linked to the *Woolwich* unjust factor than they actually are. First, it should be noted that this type of unjust factor is far more relevant to situations where the public body is the *claimant* (discussed in chapter three) than it is to the unjust factor in *Woolwich*, since wherever the incapacity unjust factor belongs, its purpose is to justify restitution to the incapax. In *Woolwich* on the other hand, the incapacity was the defendant IRC's. Further, as Birks points out, claims against companies or minors are not based on incapacity but on total failure of consideration,[66] the question of capacity only being relevant as a defence. It thus appears that even for public-body-as-claimant cases the category of incapacity is not secure. Nevertheless, as with illegality, although we cannot fit the result of *Woolwich* neatly into the private law concept of incapacity, this does not mean that the concept has no role at all to play in explaining what the reason for restitution in *Woolwich* really was.

Absence or failure of basis

Similarly, as noted above,[67] there are several reasons why absence of basis should not, by itself, be regarded as explaining the reason for restitution in *Woolwich*. As

[63] ibid 239.
[64] See text at (n 46).
[65] eg: in relation to *Westdeutsche* (n 36), Virgo writes: 'At the very least, by basing the restitutionary claim on the plaintiff's incapacity, it is easier to justify the award of restitutionary relief simply because of the policy of ensuring that the interests of those who provided the funds in the first place should be protected against the misuse of the funds': Virgo, *Principles* (n 46) 399.
[66] Birks, 'Restitution from Public Authorities' (n 22) 207.
[67] See above, pp 24–26.

far as failure, rather than absence of basis is concerned, we have already seen that the court in *Woolwich* did not feel confident basing its decision on total failure of consideration alone,[68] and from a more general point of view, when cases of unjust enrichment in which the public body may be the *claimant* are discussed in chapter three it will be noted that in any case the 'failure of consideration' approach ignores the important question of *why* the consideration has failed.[69] Nevertheless, it is no coincidence that the principal cases cited in support of 'absence of consideration' all come from the public law context.[70]

Inequality

Finally, Birks has, on more than one occasion,[71] suggested that the true basis for recovery in *Woolwich* was some kind of transactional inequality. Burrows too thought that there may be advantages in using this reasoning, but pointed out that transactional inequality cases usually require some form of *substantive* unfairness, or actual exploitation rather than depending on the prima facie disparity between the parties.[72] The problem with extending this kind of reasoning to the *Woolwich* case is, however, that it is in the very nature of a public–private relationship such as that between the Woolwich and the IRC that there will be 'transactional inequality'. In normal circumstances, we *want* this to be the case, and we *want* the inequality to be used to the disadvantage of the weaker party. That is exactly what tax collection is.[73] The issue, therefore, is not whether cases can be found in which transactional inequality was thought to be relevant despite the absence of substantive unfairness or illegitimate threats. Instead the real question is what is different about cases such as *Woolwich*, so that instead of seeing transactional inequality used to the disadvantage of the weaker party as desirable and necessary, we see it as wrong, and something which unjust enrichment should help to correct. The answer to this new question must obviously be the ultra vires nature of the demand made by the public body in cases such as *Woolwich*.

[68] See above, p 26.

[69] See pp 61–64.

[70] eg: *Westdeutsche* (n 5); *Rochester CC v Kent CC* (The Times, 5 March 1998), in which Sullivan J specifically referred to the fact that there was 'no consideration' for the money received, and of course *Woolwich* (n 1).

[71] Birks, *Restitution: the Future* (n 57) 83; and P Birks, 'The English Recognition of Unjust Enrichment' [1991] *Lloyd's Maritime and Commercial Law Quarterly* 473, 506.

[72] Burrows, 'Public Authorities, Ultra Vires and Restitution' (n 57) 64. This takes the ground into ideas of unconscionable behaviour on the part of the defendant.

[73] It is this point which answers the argument in Birks, 'The English Recognition of Unjust Enrichment' (n 71) 506: 'the species of restitutionary right based on transactional inequality has nothing peculiarly public about it, though it does happen to cross this public terrain. It cannot be said to be a creature of public law'.

A Wholly Public Approach: Could Restitution Simply be a Response to a Public Law Event?

In other words, conversely, perhaps it is therefore insufficient simply to recognise the relevance of public law in cases such as *Woolwich* and instead it should be given centre stage. Why should we not simply regard the ultra vires demand in *Woolwich* as an entirely public event to which the law can now respond, either with a mandatory order for restitution or (since 2004) with restitution as a response in itself?[74] This suggestion receives support from several quarters. As Jordan notes, the Woolwich's second lawsuit was originally seen as merely 'a technical postscript to the main case'.[75] Pannam refers to 'questions that follow in the wake of a declaration of unconstitutionality' as 'in one sense . . . rather like litter that remains to be cleared up after a football game', especially by 'comparison with the rather glamorous debate over the extent of governmental power'.[76] Also, Alder has argued that the principle in *Woolwich* should not be regarded as part of the private law of restitution creating a private law right but as a free standing public law principle enforceable in the Administrative Court, broadly analogous to a legitimate expectation.[77] By far the most significant support for this view, however, comes from the decision of the Supreme Court of Canada in *Kingstreet Investments Ltd v New Brunswick (Finance)*.[78] This case concerned the constitutional validity of a user charge paid on alcoholic beverages by nightclub owners in New Brunswick. The trial judge held the charge to be unconstitutional and this was upheld by the Supreme Court, so that that Court was essentially concerned only with the claim for relief. The case had been argued on the basis of unjust enrichment, but Bastarache J, giving the judgment of the court, held that an unjust enrichment analysis was 'ill-suited to deal with the issues raised by *ultra vires* taxes'.[79] Instead, he held, the taxpayers had 'recourse to a remedy as a matter of constitutional right'.[80] Significantly for our purposes, this was because '[r]estitution for *ultra vires* taxes does not fit squarely within either of the established categories of restitution. The better view is that it comprises a third category distinct from unjust enrichment'.[81]

[74] The Civil Procedure (Modification of Supreme Court Act 1981) Order 2004 SI 2004/1033) added restitution as a response available on an application for judicial review. See Wade and Forsyth (n 23) 798 and app 2 (pt 5) for more detail.

[75] Jordan (n 2).

[76] C Pannam, 'The Recovery of Unconstitutional Taxes in Australia and the UnitedStates' (1964) 42 *Texas Law Review* 777, 778.

[77] J Alder, 'Restitution in Public Law: Bearing the Cost of Unlawful State Action' (2002) 22 *Legal Studies* 165. For another alternative view, see L Sossin, 'Public Fiduciary Obligations, Political Trusts, and the Equitable Duty of Reasonableness in Administrative Law' (2003) 66 *Saskatchewan Law Review* 129.

[78] *Kingstreet Investments Ltd v New Brunswick (Finance)* [2007] SCC 1, [2007] 1 SCR 3.

[79] ibid [12]. It should be noted that the decision has since also been applied by the Supreme Court of British Columbia to car parking charges exacted by the University of British Columbia on the basis that the latter was also a public authority: *Barbour v the University of British Columbia* [2009] BCSC 425.

[80] ibid [34].

[81] ibid [40].

This was held to be so for several reasons. One was the separate origins of the two kinds of 'remedies'. Although actions for recovery of taxes and actions of unjust enrichment 'both address concerns of restitutionary justice', the action for recovery of taxes was held to be:

> firmly grounded, as a public law remedy in a constitutional principle stemming from democracy's earliest attempts to circumscribe government's power within the rule of law. Unjust enrichment, on the other hand, originally evolved from the common law action of *indebitatus assumpsit* as a means of granting plaintiffs relief for quasi-contractual damages.[82]

Interestingly, earlier in his judgment Bastarache J had also pointed out that Lord Goff had not referred to the principle of unjust enrichment when he held that restitution was available as a matter of 'common justice'.[83]

A second reason for rejecting the 'unjust enrichment framework' in such cases was that Bastarache J regarded it as adding 'an unnecessary layer of complexity to the real legal issues'.[84] In his view, restitution 'as a matter of constitutional right' was the only 'appropriate remedy because it raises important constitutional principles which would be ignored by treating the claim under another category of restitution'. It is not precisely clear which are the 'constitutional principles' that he fears will be ignored, nor which are the 'policy considerations' from unjust enrichment law that he fears will conflict with them, but his reasoning for this proposition seems to be as follows. In the first place he is concerned that technical interpretations of 'benefit' and 'loss' are hard to apply in tax recovery cases[85] and in addition to this he regards the framework of restitutionary rules established in *Garland v Consumers' Gas Co*[86] as 'very complex'.[87] *Garland* had established a two-part analysis for unjust enrichment in Canada. First the plaintiff would be required to show that no established category of juristic reason for the enrichment existed. If he or she could do this, the burden would then shift to the defendant to show that there was some other reason why recovery should be denied. At this stage, the Court had explicitly recognised that the juristic reasons for the enrichment had to be considered in the light of the reasonable expectations of the parties and also certain policy considerations.[88] In the past, this second stage had been used to deal with what Bastarache J calls the 'difficulties' of applying 'private law principles in the realm of public and constitutional law'.[89] In his view, however, matters such as those concerning preservation of the public purse do not belong to this second stage of the *Garland* test, which should instead be confined to '*proper* policy considerations'; those that are 'rooted in the policy considerations that are

[82] ibid.
[83] ibid [17], citing *Woolwich* (n 1) 172 (Lord Goff).
[84] ibid [35].
[85] ibid.
[86] *Garland v Consumers' Gas Co* [2004] SCC 25, [2004] 1 SCR 629.
[87] *Kingstreet Investments* (n 78) [38].
[88] ibid [36].
[89] ibid.

traditionally found in unjust enrichment cases'[90] and that avoid the potential for 'palm tree justice'.[91] This conclusion is not surprising given that he had earlier held that such matters are in any case not for the courts at all, but for Parliament.[92] What is not so clear is why he still regards the unjust enrichment claim as inappropriate for tax recovery cases even when such matters are removed from it and the 'policy considerations' considered in the *Garland* test *are* confined to 'proper policy considerations'. It would, perhaps, have been helpful to have some indication of which remaining 'policy considerations' might in his view still cause problems for such 'important constitutional principles' and which difficulties of applying private law principles in the realm of public law are raised by the relationship between the unconstitutionality of taxes and the cause of action in unjust enrichment. Nevertheless, his overall argument seems to remain that, 'the ordinary principles of unjust enrichment should not be applied to claims for the recovery of monies paid pursuant to a statute held to be unconstitutional'[93] on the basis that 'components of the modern doctrine are of little use to a principled disposition of the matter, but are rather liable to confuse the proper application of the key principles of constitutional law at issue'.

Certainly it is true that private law cannot, as shown above, single-handedly provide the reason for restitution in cases such as *Kingstreet Investments* and *Woolwich*. However, it seems likely that it would be equally misguided to allow the pendulum to swing too far in the opposite direction chosen by the Supreme Court of Canada.

The first reason for this concerns the availability of restitution in a purely public law action. Under the current law it is possible to obtain restitution as part of the public law procedure in two ways. The first, a mandatory order to repay the money, was available even when the House of Lords decided *Woolwich*.[94] However, like all public law 'remedies', that order is discretionary. Various factors operate to determine whether such orders will be granted, including waiver, bad faith, the premature nature of the application, the absence of any injustice and the impact on third parties and on the administration.[95] For example, in *R v Secretary of State for Social Services, ex p AMA*,[96] relief was withheld because to grant it would cause serious public inconvenience. It is clear that one of the reasons why the Supreme Court of Canada favoured the purely public approach to restitution of unconstitutional taxes was that 'the Court's central concern must be to guarantee respect for constitutional principles'[97] and that as a result, the taxpayers had 'recourse to a remedy as a matter of constitutional right'.[98] It thus seems as if

[90] ibid [38].
[91] ibid.
[92] ibid [25].
[93] ibid [39].
[94] Alder (n 77) 179.
[95] See, eg: Craig, *Administrative Law* (n 23) ch 25 and 26-055.
[96] *R v Secretary of State for Social Services, ex p AMA* [1993] COD 54.
[97] *Kingstreet Investments* (n 78) [14].
[98] ibid [34].

Bastarache J, giving the judgment of the Court, favoured the purely public approach on the basis that this would make the taxpayer's right to restitution stronger.[99] However, when the discretionary approach to public law 'remedies' is considered it appears that, at least in English law, use of a purely public approach might have the opposite effect. After all, it would not be impossible in some cases to argue that the return of large sums of money would have such a detrimental impact on the administration or third party recipients that the court's discretion should not be exercised to grant a mandatory order for repayment. Thus whereas restitution *would* have been given as a matter of right following a successful private law unjust enrichment claim, it need not be so given in public law.

Of course, such problems would not necessarily arise in relation to the second possibility; obtaining restitution as of right as a response to a public law event. Nevertheless, that option would not be without difficulties either. For example, it is clear that Bastarache J comforts himself with the thought that if recovery as of right were to lead to fiscal chaos in a given case, this should be left to Parliament and the legislatures to address, should they choose to do so. For instance, he suggests, it would be open to the Canadian Parliament and the legislatures to enact valid taxes and apply them retroactively so as to limit or deny recovery of ultra vires taxes.[100] The problem, however, is that, as he concludes, 'obviously, such legislation must also be constitutionally sound'. In the English system this requirement presents particular problems as a result of membership of the EU.[101] It is possible to introduce time limits which reduce the period within which repayment of sums collected illegally may be sought, as long as this period is reasonable, includes transitional provisions and is not completely retroactive.[102] Crucially for the decision in *Kingstreet Investments*, however, retroactivity targeted specifically at the effects of a particular decision of the ECJ is especially prohibited.[103]

The result is that there are then only two remaining options for limiting recovery as of right. One is to deny it on the basis that discretion should not be exercised to grant a mandatory order when to do so would cause serious inconvenience to the public, and the other, applicable equally to mandatory orders and restitution as a response in itself, would be to leave it to Parliament to enact whatever legislation it could, within its obligations under EC law, to ameliorate the fiscal chaos

[99] Similar concerns seem to have motivated Kirby J of the High Court of Australia in *British American Tobacco Australia Ltd v Western Australia* [2003] HCA 47, (2003) 217 CLR 30 to hold that a cause of action derived from the Constitution itself permits recovery of an invalid tax levied in breach of that Constitution on the basis that such a right would not be vulnerable to abolition in the same way as 'common law rights'.

[100] *Kingstreet Investments* (n 78) 25.

[101] For further detail of the requirements and limitations imposed by the EU's 'remedies' jurisprudence, see ch 8.

[102] See Case C-62/00 *Marks and Spencer v Commissioners of Customs and Excise* [2002] ECR I-6325 and M Chowdry, 'How long can section 80 last?' [2004] *British Tax Review* 106. Case C-255/00 *Grundig Italiana SpA v Ministero delle Finanze* [2002] ECR I-8003 held that retroactive time limits are possible as long as there is an adequate transition period.

[103] Case 309/85 *Barra v Belgium* [1988] ECR 355 and Case C-343/96 *Dilexport srl v Amministrazione delle Finanze dello Stato* [1999] ECR I-579.

resulting from such a decision. In each case the choice would seem to be between absolute recovery and denial of restitution altogether. Of course, such an approach could be adopted, but it is difficult to see why we should do that if a better alternative could be found.

Two other matters also suggest that it would make little sense to regard restitution as purely a public law response, available as of right following a finding of ultra vires without the need also to make out an unjust enrichment claim. First, in his article advocating the purely public approach, Alder suggests that 'the value of certainty, and therefore of a formalistic solution is perhaps more important in private law'[104] whereas 'a claim based only on the voluntary payment of an unlawful demand', as in *Woolwich*, 'might be subject to the more flexible and context sensitive regime of public law'. However, this is to miss the point that in some cases public bodies may unlawfully receive payments in an otherwise relatively private context, for example as a result of the private finance initiative.[105] In such cases certainty is imperative for the financial institutions with which they deal, but the public law need for 'context sensitivity' is no less than it is in a tax receipt case; the money at stake is still public money, which may well have been spent on providing public services and which will still have to be replaced through other public means.

Second, if the law fails to recognise the unjust enrichment event and concentrates solely on the public law finding of ultra vires, it becomes very difficult to explain why the appropriate response should be *restitution.* As Alder points out, public law concerns 'relate primarily to the concerns of limiting government power. They point to a prima facie obligation to disgorge the gain, but do not require the gain to be paid to any particular person as of right'.[106] Of course, if the rule of law is to be upheld, the law must provide *a* response when a public body has acted ultra vires, but there has never been any general requirement that this should take the form of transferring money to the citizens or private entities who have suffered as a result. In the context of compensation for wrongdoing the tendency is in fact often in the other direction.[107] Thus were we to ignore the private law aspects of these claims, namely the enrichment of the public body at the expense of those making the payment, there would be nothing to justify the second stage of the Woolwich's challenge. The judicial review action would be sufficient and there would be no reason for the law to ensure restitution of the money received.

[104] Alder (n 77) 172.

[105] The so-called 'swaps' transactions provide a perfect example of this. See also: ch 3, p 57 onwards.

[106] Alder (n 77) 176.

[107] See, eg: *X (Minors) v Bedfordshire CC* [1995] 2 AC 633 (HL).

The Solution: A Hybrid Approach

The answer must therefore be that neither a wholly private nor a wholly public approach can possibly be used to explain cases such as *Kingstreet Investments* and *Woolwich*, precisely because recovery in such cases is based on *both* unjust enrichment and the public law ultra vires event.

From the private law point of view, the reason we cannot explain the *Woolwich* decision neatly using *only* illegality, incapacity, transactional inequality or absence of basis is that in fact the reason for restitution in *Woolwich* is based on all four of those elements. While we look at the case only from the purely private point of view this presents huge problems of analysis and classification, but once we move beyond that to adopt the public law point of view, nothing could be simpler or more obvious.

Beginning with the 'inequality' and 'duress' aspects of the decision, chapter one discussed the *ex p Datafin* test (used to establish whether a sufficient private law element is present in the nature of the power exercised by the challenged body) which contains extremely similar concerns.[108] For example, in that case the fact that the Panel did not operate consensually but imposed a code on its members, and the fact that the Panel's power was reinforced by statute both played a part in determining that it should be subject to judicial review. It follows from this that the role of inequality is to be found at an earlier stage in the determination of the unjust factor than that suggested by the purely private law analysis. In the specific case of *Woolwich*, the inequality between the parties *as a result of their public–private relationship* had already been relevant to the choice of the public law procedure for the judicial review hearing and it was the finding of invalidity as a matter of public law that then formed the basis later on for the ground of recovery in *Woolwich*.

The existence of this public law finding also reveals why it is that the concept of 'absence of consideration' keeps emerging in cases involving public law. A declaration that an act was ultra vires as a matter of public law is a declaration that it never existed in the first place, because it could not; it was void *ab initio*. In referring to 'absence of consideration' it thus becomes clear that the courts have not, within private law, deliberately been toying with the idea of moving towards the civilian system (though that is the practical danger inherent in their use of the expression). Rather they have been attempting to handle a public law concept using only private law tools, leading to a private law mistranslation with potentially far-reaching consequences. This in turn suggests that Birks is wrong to argue that this different approach of enrichment 'without cause' is necessary for the accommodation of public body cases.[109]

[108] *R v Panel on Takeovers and Mergers, ex p Datafin plc* [1987] QB 815 (CA). See also: ch 1 above, text at n 81.

[109] Birks, *Unjust Enrichment* (n 42) 108–28.

Similarly, it is no wonder that although incapacity and illegality cannot by themselves found the decision in *Woolwich* they have been suggested as explanations for or relative to it. The very essence of public law, as discussed in chapter one, is that public bodies, as a result of their greater powers, have a correspondingly narrower capacity than private entities. It is precisely this idea of limited 'capacity', and the 'illegality' of actions taken beyond it, that provide the substance of administrative law.[110] The reason for restitution in *Woolwich* was therefore that an ultra vires event had occurred as a matter of public law in the sense that a public body had taken action to which the law could respond in an action for judicial review. None of this is particularly remarkable to a public lawyer, but because we have tended to see claims such as *Woolwich* through entirely 'private law spectacles'[111] we have mistranslated the public law event variously as 'transactional inequality', 'incapacity', 'absence of basis' for the transfer or 'illegality' as single concepts in private law. In doing so we have thus missed the point that all four of those concepts go together in public law to produce the *ab initio* voidness of actions taken beyond the body's capacity or powers, the limits on that capacity having themselves been imposed as a result of the inequality between citizens and the bodies who have power over them. It is for this reason that Lord Browne-Wilkinson could not choose between the different factors he regarded as being 'in play'; none of them could found the decision alone because they were each only part of the real issue. It was argued in chapter one that we cannot regard all ultra vires actions as 'wrongs' in the private sense, and the point now is that it would be similarly inaccurate to regard them all as examples of 'transactional inequality', 'illegality', 'absence of basis' or 'incapacity' in that private law sense. Once it is understood that attempts to do so are essentially attempts to force public law concepts into a private law framework, it is perhaps less surprising that such an attempt should have potentially serious consequences for the framework itself.[112]

Conversely, as seen above, from the public law point of view there are equal dangers inherent in failing to recognise that in cases such as *Woolwich* and *Kingstreet Investments* the defendant public body has been unjustly enriched and, for example, such an approach cannot satisfactorily explain why the remedy for the ultra vires taxation must take the form of return of the money to the claimant. The conclusion must therefore be that such transactions cannot be classified as wholly public or private; instead the law must recognise their inherently hybrid nature and address the concerns of both areas of law. Neither the certainty of private law nor the flexible discretionary nature of public law can prevail absolutely; a balance must be struck between them.

110 See ch 1 pp 10–18, especially n 55.

111 The phrase is Burrows', 'Public Authorities, Ultra Vires and Restitution' (n 57) 40.

112 The reference here is of course to the danger that 'absence of consideration' would lead to an adoption of the civilian system. The extent to which attempts to use private law to deal with public issues can have detrimental impacts on the structure of private law will be seen again in relation to the French system in ch 6 and in ch 3.

On reflection, then, it is hardly surprising that when two systems are asked to choose between such approaches one should opt for the purely private approach[113] and the other the purely public approach. It simply provides further evidence that in fact there are two relevant legal events to which the law is responding.[114] If we really did have to choose one option over the other we could do so, if necessary by tossing a coin, but there seems little point in making such an unnecessary and fortuitous choice when conceptual accuracy can be better served by recognising that the law should be allowed to respond to both the public and the private law aspects of the claim, and that neither kind of legal event should preclude consideration of the other. The correct approach is thus to regard *Woolwich* claims as hybrid claims, in which the reason for restitution, the 'unjust factor', is provided by the existence of a public law ultra vires event, leaving the definition of enrichment, the claimant's expense and relevant defences to be worked out by the law of unjust enrichment in the usual manner.[115] Private law defences to a claim in unjust enrichment can then be tailored to take account of Alder's competing public and private interests[116] without giving rise to the 'palm tree justice' that Bastarache J feared would arise from trying to accommodate public law concerns in a *purely* private framework.

Not only does this provide a more accurate description of the claim in *Woolwich* itself, it also receives support from another Commonwealth jurisdiction, this time Australia, in the case of *British American Tobacco*.[117] Here, in their joint judgment, McHugh, Gummow and Hayne JJ (with whom Callinan J agreed) held that the common law action for money had and received attracted federal jurisdiction because it was the operation of section 90 of the Constitution which 'render[ed] the retention of the money against conscience'.[118] However, this did not mean that liability to repay on the part of the State 'springs without more from s 90 of the Constitution';[119] rather their Honours cited the decision of Fullagar J in *Antill Ranger and Co v Commissioner for Motor Transport*[120] that 'the right asserted is a common law right, but an essential element in the cause of action is that the

[113] For further support for the purely private approach see *Deutsche Morgan Grenfell v IRC* [2006] UKHL 49, [2007] 1 AC 558 and ch 4.

[114] The same argument can be made in relation to the decision of Plender J in *Jones v Powys Local Health Board* [2008] EWHC (Admin) 2562, see also: ch 3 pp 50–52.

[115] This also includes the relevant rules on payment of interest. In *Sempra Metals* (n 5), (a further case in the *Metallgesellschaft and Hoechst* line (n 5), the Revenue had argued that claims based on private law unjust factors such as mistake should be treated differently from claims based on the unlawful nature of the demand, ie on the public law unjust factor. (See, eg: [123]–[124] (Lord Nicholls). Since the issue of interest goes to the extent to which repayment of the enrichment received at the claimant's expense must be repaid, rather than to the reason why the enrichment was unjust, this is one of the issues in the case which should be governed by private law and not by public law. *Metallgesellschaft* will itself be discussed in more detail in chs 4 and 8 below.)

[116] Alder (n 77), especially at 166.

[117] *British American Tobacco Australia* (n 99).

[118] ibid [41].

[119] ibid [40].

[120] *Antill Ranger and Co v Commissioner for Motor Transport* (1955) 93 CLR 83 (HCA); affd *Commissioner for Motor Transport v Antill Rangers and Co Pty Ltd* (1956) 94 CLR 177, [1956] AC 527 (PC).

moneys in question were unlawfully exacted from it'.[121] This is precisely the kind of hybrid approach advocated here.[122]

Understanding the precise nature and content of the reasons for restitution in *Woolwich* in this way not only enables a better understanding of that decision, it also allows us to ascertain the scope of the judgment and how it should be applied in future cases and it is this issue which will occupy the following three chapters.

[121] *Antill Ranger* ibid 102–3. See also: *British American Tobacco Australia* (n 99) [168] (Callinan J).

[122] Significantly, their Honours McHugh, Gummow and Hayne JJ also went on to hold that British American Tobacco's claim could be placed on the 'further' ground of mistaken payment: *British American Tobacco Australia* ibid [43]. It will be argued in ch 4 below that while mistake does indeed provide a 'further' ground for recovery, there are reasons why the public law unjust factor approach is preferable and where applicable it should therefore always be used as the principal ground of recovery and it should certainly not be replaced by other grounds, even if these grounds are pleaded in addition to it lest the public law reason for restitution should not be held to apply (which would then only occur where the claim was not found to involve public law).

3

The Scope of the Public Law Reason for Restitution

The Scope of the Public Law Reason for Restitution: Eight Key Questions

HAVING ESTABLISHED THAT THE reason for restitution in *Woolwich* is simply the existence of a public law ultra vires event,[1] it becomes possible to answer some questions about its scope and application in future cases. In particular, there are eight questions left open after the *Woolwich* decision, all of which can now be answered.

The first five of these questions are relatively procedural:

Need There Have Been a Demand for the Public Law Reason for Restitution to Operate?

As the Law Commission points out, Lord Goff's reasons for the new restitutionary right first established in *Woolwich* do not focus on the particular requirements of a demand or a tax 'but on the manifest injustice of allowing moneys unlawfully extracted from the subject by a public authority to be retained by it'.[2] Academic discussion of this question unanimously supports this answer[3] as does the understanding of the public law reason for restitution outlined here. There would be no reason to limit recovery in such an arbitrary manner and no justification for doing so: recovery will be available under the principle first established in *Woolwich* whenever there has been an ultra vires event to which public law will respond. It is true that in *Boake Allen Ltd v Revenue and Customs Commissioners*[4] the Court of

[1] *Woolwich Equitable Building Society v IRC* [1993] AC 70 (HL). The term '*Woolwich* principle' obviously signifies the reason for restitution or 'unjust factor' first established in *Woolwich*. In ch 2 it was established that this reason for restitution is simply that as a matter of public law there has been an ultra vires event. This will be referred to as the 'public law unjust factor' or 'public law reason for restitution'.

[2] Law Commission, 'Restitution: Mistakes of Law and Ultra Vires Public Authority Receipts and Payments' (Law Com No 227 Cm 2731, 1994) [6.41].

[3] See, eg: A Burrows, *The Law of Restitution*, 2nd edn (London, Butterworths, 2002) 448; F Toube, 'Restitution for Public Lawyers' (1996) 1 *Judicial Review* 92, 96.

[4] *Boake Allen Ltd v Revenue and Customs Commissioners* [2006] EWCA Civ 25, [2006] STC 606. The HL did not discuss the issues of restitution for unjust enrichment on the basis that the CA had been

Appeal, as Henderson J put it in *Test Claimants in the FII Group Litigation v The Commissioners for Her Majesty's Revenue and Customs*,[5] did 'adopt a narrow approach' to the '*Woolwich* principle' and gave no encouragement to attempts to broaden the concept of a 'demand',[6] but neither did it contradict the position proposed here. The issue of 'demands' received the greatest attention from Lord Justice Mummery in *Boake Allen* and even he did not deny that the '*Woolwich* principle' could apply where a taxpayer had paid in accordance with the terms of a statute rather than a specific 'demand'. He merely held that on the facts of the case, even if there had been a 'demand', it had been lawful.[7] Similarly, although Henderson J stated that 'a *Woolwich* claim must involve, *at least in some sense*, the making of a demand by the Revenue'[8] (emphasis added) of a kind which would not be required in a claim based on mistake, it is again difficult to read much into this, given first that his only authority for so holding was *Boake Allen*, second, the weakness of the terms in which this view was expressed ('at least in *some* sense') and third, the lack of reasoning to support a stronger view.

Need There Have Been a Protest for the Public Law Reason for Restitution to Operate?

Again, the answer is 'no'. Academic discussion of this question unanimously concludes that a protest should not be necessary for the unjust factor to operate[9] and on the basis of the argument outlined here this is correct. Not only does it not fit with the reasoning in *Woolwich* itself, the requirement of a protest would again be an arbitrary and normatively irrelevant hurdle for claimants to cross, since the claimants need not necessarily have recognised the public law event before paying the money. Although he was discussing the requirement in a different context,[10] support for these arguments comes from Bastarache J, giving the judgment of

correct to hold the tax in question to be lawful on the specific facts of the case: [2007] UKHL 25, [2007] 1 WLR 1386.

[5] *Test Claimants in the FII Group Litigation v The Commissioners for Her Majesty's Revenue and Customs* [2008] EWHC 2893, [2008] STI 2726.

[6] ibid [258] and [260].

[7] A view upheld by the HL. *Boake Allen* (HL) (n 4). Indeed, if the decision in *Boake Allen* runs counter to the argument here at all, it is on this issue of whether or not the receipt was unlawful and the question of the type of ultra vires action necessary to found a claim. See also: below, '*What Sort of Invalidity Triggers this Unjust Factor?*' and in particular n 99 and surrounding text where it will in fact be argued that the case is still perfectly compatible with the view outlined here.

[8] ibid [245].

[9] G Virgo, *The Principles of the Law of Restitution*, 2nd edn (Oxford, Oxford University Press, 2006) 416; Toube (n 3). This view is also implicit in Burrows' view that there need not have been a demand on the part of the public authority either: Burrows, *Law of Restitution* (n 3) 448.

[10] Referring to P Maddaugh and J McCamus' argument, *The Law of Restitution* (Aurora: Ont, Canada Law Book 2004, updated 2005) (at 11–44 and 11–45: 'the defence of passing on [discussed further in its own right below in ch 5] would no longer be available once the taxpayer signaled, through protest, that the unlawfulness of the taxation measure was being challenged'). Nevertheless, Bastarache J stated that since he had already rejected this defence on its own terms his ensuing statements were made as 'useful general comments', which suggests they may thus be more applicable even outside the context of the passing on defence.

the Supreme Court of Canada, in *Kingstreet Investments Ltd v New Brunswick (Finance)*.[11] He held that there should be no burden on the taxpayer to prove that they were paying under protest, because 'the right of the party to obtain restitution for taxes paid under *ultra vires* legislation does not depend on the behaviour of each party but on the objective consideration of whether the tax was exacted without proper legal authority'.[12] Further, he was concerned about 'horizontal equity' between claimants if only those who had protested were able to recover the unlawful tax.[13] He did hold that courts should insist on compulsion in fact, which protest would be neither necessary nor sufficient to establish, but it is clear from the rest of his judgment,[14] that this can only have meant that the taxpayer must not have waived its right to restitution, rather than that Bastarache J was insisting on a cause of action based on duress.

To What Extent is the Public Law Reason for Restitution Overridden by Statute?

Although there are several statutory provisions for the recovery of overpayments of tax, none applied to the *Woolwich* case. The most likely seemed to be section 33 of the Taxes Management Act 1970 (TMA), which provides for the recovery of such sums of overpaid income tax, corporation tax, capital gains tax, or petroleum revenue tax as is 'reasonable and just'. However, it did not apply to *Woolwich*, first because it was doubted whether the section applied to the composite rate tax at issue in *Woolwich* and second, and more importantly, because no valid 'assessment' had been, or could have been made, as required by section 33, since there was no lawful basis whatever for the demand of ultra vires tax. Finally, even if there could have been a valid assessment, section 33 would not have applied in this case because it would not have been excessive 'by reason of some error or mistake in a return,' as required by section 33. Naturally any common law cause of action such as that first recognised in *Woolwich* can in principle be overridden where a statute expressly excludes it, and it appears from the *Woolwich* case itself that the common law right will be narrow and limited to situations where the statute does not cover the case expressly or by necessary implication.[15]

It is, however, worth noting that the application of statutory principles rather than the common law, or vice versa, is left largely to chance, as is clear from the facts of *Woolwich* itself. Similarly left to chance is the question of *which* statutory provisions apply in any particular context. It cannot even be said that the applica-

[11] *Kingstreet Investments Ltd v New Brunswick (Finance)* (2007) SCC 1, [2007] 1 SCR 3.

[12] ibid [53].

[13] ibid [56].

[14] Discussed in more detail above at pp 31–35.

[15] See: *Monro v Commissioners for Her Majesty's Revenue and Customs* [2007] EWHC 114 (Ch), [2008] EWCA Civ 306, [2008] STC 1815. See generally: Burrows, *Law of Restitution* (n 3) 447–48 and J Beatson, 'Restitution of Taxes, Levies and Other Imposts: Defining the Extent of the *Woolwich* Principle' (1993) 109 *Law Quarterly Review* 401, 418.

tion of the statutes, however haphazard, is at least the application of consistent principles. On the contrary, there is a great deal of inconsistency between the statutory provisions and between the approaches of the common law and Parliament.[16]

The relationship between the common law right in *Woolwich* on the one hand and the statutory rights to recovery on the other was considered by the Law Commission. It recommended that in respect of ultra vires receipts and payments by public authorities there should be a 'series of specific amendments to the recovery provisions for overpaid tax in the taxation legislation to reflect the emergence of the *Woolwich* principle'.[17] In particular, they recommended:

> [A] repeal of TMA 1970 s 33, and replacement by a right on the part of all taxpayers charged to tax, whether under an assessment or otherwise, to recover tax paid but not due irrespective of the presence or absence of any mistake on the part of the taxpayer.[18]

Obviously, such a reform would remove the application of the common law right to the *Woolwich* situation itself, as explained above.[19] Apart from these specific alterations to the statutory provisions, the Commission had a choice between three possible responses to *Woolwich*. The first possibility was to recommend a general statutory right to recovery of ultra vires or mistaken[20] payments to public bodies. This was rejected, in particular, because of the uncertainties surrounding the term 'public body'.[21] The second option was to devise a list of public bodies to whom such a statutory provision would apply. This too was rejected as being too arbitrary, and capable of producing injustice.[22] The Commission thus chose the third option, and recommended that 'development of the right to restitution of ultra vires receipts by public authorities should, save for the specific recommendations . . . made in [the] Report, [concerning the specific statutory provisions, as listed above] be left to the common law'.[23] This was desirable, they argued, because 'the potential variety of claims which may arise make this an ideal area for the common law to operate in as it can, in this field, provide the flexibility which would be lacking in a statutory provision'.[24] They also agreed with Beatson that 'it

[16] See: Virgo, *Principles* (n 9) 420 and S Arrowsmith, 'Recovery of Unlawful Taxes—Part 2' (1992) 142 *New Law Journal* 1761, 1762.

[17] Law Commission (1994) (No 227, above n 2) [1.18].

[18] ibid [9.24].

[19] Further, the Law Commission recommended that this new statutory provision replacing s 33 TMA should also apply to the PAYE system, self-assessment, inheritance tax and stamp duty (ibid [12.7], [12.17], [13.11] and [13.23] respectively). No recommendations were made for changes to the statutory schemes for VAT or insurance premium tax (ibid [14.19] and [14.24] respectively) and overpaid excise duty was to be recoverable in the same circumstances as overpaid VAT, with legislation to be modelled on the unchanged VAT Act 1994 (ibid [14.23]). For National Insurance and Council Tax, the Commission recommended that no changes should be made, except that contributions under ultra vires secondary regulations should be included in the range of recoverable payments (ibid [15.12] and [15.26]).

[20] Throughout its report no 227 the Law Commission lists ultra vires and mistake cases as alternatives. Law Commission (1994) (n 2). Their true relationship will be discussed fully below, pp 64–69.

[21] ibid [16.1]–[16.5].

[22] ibid [16.6]–[16.8].

[23] ibid [16.10].

[24] ibid [16.10].

is likely that there will be very few cases which fall within the residual right, and that those will turn on their particular facts'.[25] However, as will be discussed further in this chapter and the next, there has, since *Woolwich*, been a series of cases dealing particularly with the incompatibility of national tax rules with EC law which has given rise to a variety of different common law claims. As a response to this, Section 100 and Schedule 52 of the Finance Act 2009 contain provisions for amending S 33 TMA 1970 so that all claims for overpaid corporation, capital gains and income tax will, from 1 April 2010, be available only via a new Schedule 1AB to the TMA, to the complete exclusion of the common law. Nevertheless, it is worth noting first that the courts will be likely to have to deal with a surge of claims brought before the new rules take effect, and second that the application of any given statute is subject always to its compatibility with EU law.[26]

What Exactly Does the Claimant Recover?

This question does not wholly belong with the other seven questions considered here, because the answer to it comes not just from an inherent understanding of the public law reason for restitution, but also from the decisions in two key cases. Nevertheless, it is convenient to deal with it here as part of the process of defining the operation of the public law reason for restitution. In *Sempra Metals v HMRC*[27] the claimants argued that they should be entitled to compound, as opposed to simple, interest on their claim. A majority of the House of Lords agreed, Lord Hope, Lord Nicholls and Lord Scott holding that compound interest would be available at common law,[28] thereby departing from the decision of the House of Lords in *Westdeutsche.*[29] Lord Hope justified this change on the basis that *Westdeutsche* was not relevant, because it had dealt with the question of whether compound interest could be awarded in equity, and furthermore because *Westdeutsche* did not deal with situations where interest was itself the principal sum, as was the case in *Sempra.*[30] Similarly, Lord Nicholls pointed out that the unavailability of compound interest at common law had been conceded rather than argued in

[25] ibid [16.10].

[26] See also: *F J Chalke Ltd and AC Barnes (Wokingham) Ltd v The Commissioners for Her Majesty's Revenue and Customs* [2009] EWHC 952 (Ch) [107]–[8] in which Henderson J held that the statutory scheme in ss 78–80 VAT Act 1994 was in principle exhaustive as far as repayment of overpaid VAT and interest were concerned, but that these national rules could be trumped by the entitlement to compound interest as a result of a combination of the decisions in Case 199/82 *Amministrazione delle Finanze dello Stato v San Giorgio* [1983] ECR 3595, Case C-446/04 *Test Claimants in the FII Group Litigation v Commissioners of Inland Revenue* [2006] ECR I-11753 and *Sempra Metals Ltd (formerly Metallgesellschaft Ltd) v Her Majesty's Commissioners of Inland Revenue and another* [2007] UKHL 34, [2008] 1 AC 561. See also: ch 8.

[27] *Sempra Metals* (n 26).

[28] Lord Hope, ibid [22], Lord Nicholls, ibid [112] and Lord Scott, ibid [153].

[29] *Westdeutsche Landesbank Girozentrale v Islington LBC* [1996] AC 669 (HL).

[30] *Sempra*, n 26, Lord Hope [34]–[5]. *Sempra* is one case among many following the decision of the ECJ in Cases C-397/98 and C-410/98 *Metallgesellschaft and Hoechst v IRC* [2001] ECR I-1727. For a detailed discussion of the facts of this case and other subsequent decisions, see ch 4 p 75 onwards.

Westdeutsche, so that it was open to the House of Lords in *Sempra* to re-examine that basic point of law.[31] The minority Lord Walker and Lord Mance preferred to regard compound interest as being available, if at all, through equity, on the basis that this would allow for the exercise of discretion in awarding it.[32] However, their Lordships gave no indication of the circumstances in which this equitable discretion should or should not be exercised, and indeed Lord Walker did not envisage it differing at all from the common law approach in terms of practical outcome.[33] If it is accepted that compound interest should be available because, as Lord Nicholls and Lord Walker put it, otherwise 'the unravelling would be partial only',[34] it is difficult to see why compound interest, and thus full unravelling, should not be available as a matter of common law right, and so the conclusion of the majority is thus preferable to that of the minority.

However, having established the availability of compound interest in principle, it then became necessary to work out how this would be calculated in practice, and again this matter produced a 3:2 split.[35] A majority of their Lordships assumed that use of money for a period of time would constitute an enrichment which must be returned via compound interest, rather than requiring the claimant to prove this enrichment specifically. Lord Hope's judgment is the strongest in this direction, holding that:

> Once the claimant has shown that prima facie he is entitled to a restitutionary remedy, direct knowledge of the extent of the benefit, if any, that has been received can be assumed to lie with the recipient. It is open to the recipient to demonstrate that there was no actual enrichment when the money fell into his hands notwithstanding the opportunity to turn it to account . . . It seems to me that . . . the assumption that the revenue derived some benefit from the receipt of the money prematurely has not been displaced, and that this justifies resort to a conventional rate of interest as the measure of that benefit.[36]

However, Lord Nicholls and Lord Walker also held that the Revenue could prima facie be supposed (as the agreed 'conventional basis' recognised) to have taken full advantage of receipt of the money. It could thus be regarded as having been enriched by the amount that it would have cost to borrow the amount in question for the relevant period,[37] subject to the defendant proving otherwise.[38] In other

[31] *Sempra*, n 26, Lord Nicholls [111].

[32] *Sempra*, n 26, Lord Walker [184] and Lord Mance [236].

[33] *Sempra*, n 26, Lord Walker [188].

[34] *Sempra*, n 26, Lord Walker [178], citing Lord Nicholls in *Nykredit Mortgage Bank plc v Edward Erdman Group Ltd (formerly Edward Erdman (an unlimited company)) (No 2)* [1997] 1WLR 1627, 1637.

[35] The split on this second occasion was between Lord Hope, Lord Nicholls and Lord Walker in the majority, with Lord Scott and Lord Mance in the minority, whereas on the question of common law versus equitable jurisdiction to award compound interest in the first place the split had been between Lord Hope, Lord Nicholls and Lord Scott in the majority, with Lord Mance and Lord Walker in the minority.

[36] *Sempra*, n 26, Lord Hope [48].

[37] *Sempra*, n 26, Lord Nicholls [103], [116] and [118]; Lord Walker [186] and [188].

[38] According to Lord Nicholls this would take the form of an argument based on 'subjective devaluation' or 'change of position', *Sempra*, n 26, Lord Nicholls [119], whereas Lord Walker felt more

words, according to the majority, the presumption would be that the defendant had been enriched by the use of money over time, and it would then be up to the defendant to disprove this, for example by demonstrating that it had, as Lord Mance put it (in dissent), put the money in a non-interest bearing current account or even under the bed.[39]

In the minority, on the other hand, Lord Scott was not prepared to accept the premise:

> that the possession of mistakenly paid money—and accordingly the ability to use it if minded to do so—is sufficient to justify not simply a restitutionary remedy for recovery of the money, but a remedy also for recovery of the wholly conceptual benefit of an ability to use the money. Why should a restitutionary remedy be concerned with a benefit that is no more than conceptual?[40]

Lord Mance's dissent from the majority turned on a difference in perception concerning the roles of subjective devaluation and/or change of position. For him, 'the basic test of recovery looks to actual benefit' with the change of position defence being 'a separate matter, arising after any actual benefit has been ascertained'[41]. And 'far from operating as a control on or qualification of some objective or hypothetical measure of recovery', for Lord Mance 'the principle of "subjective devaluation" makes actual or "incontrovertible" benefit the very test of and precondition to recovery'.[42] Ultimately, however, as he himself noted, 'in a fully investigated context' the approaches of the majority and minority should in any event 'assimilate . . . in the end result',[43] and given the inherently enriching nature of money and the ease with which defendants can prove that they were not enriched as compared with the ability of claimants to prove enrichment, it is submitted that again the approach of the majority is to be preferred.

The question of compound interest was subsequently revisited by Henderson J in *F J Chalke*[44]. The facts of this case differed from those in *Sempra* because in *Chalke* the tax itself had been invalid, so the claim had originally been for a principal sum plus interest, whereas in *Sempra* the interest was itself the principal sum. However, even in *Chalke* the Revenue had already repaid the unlawful tax with interest, so that the only remaining claim was for this to be 'upgraded' to compound interest.[45] Henderson J held that this distinction between the cases made no difference:

> no sensible distinction can be drawn in relation to interest between cases where tax is levied prematurely (as in *Hoechst* [and thus *Sempra*]) and cases where the tax itself has

uncomfortable with use of this terminology from the context of benefits in kind ([187]) and thus preferred the discretionary, equitable approach.

[39] *Sempra*, n 26, Lord Mance [233].
[40] *Sempra*, n 26, Lord Scott [145]. See also Lord Mance at [233].
[41] *Sempra*, n 26, Lord Mance [233].
[42] *Sempra*, n 26, Lord Mance [232].
[43] *Sempra*, n 26, Lord Mance [233].
[44] *F J Chalke*, n 26.
[45] *F J Chalke*, n 26 [36].

> to be repaid. In each case, the claimant should receive by way of 'interest' a sum which represents the loss of use of the money, or (perhaps more accurately) the benefit of the use of the money to the member state, over the relevant period. If anything, common sense suggests that this right should be stronger in cases where the tax itself has to be repaid than in cases where the tax was merely levied prematurely . . . the measure of such loss of use or benefit, in the context of a restitutionary claim brought in an English court, should normally be compound, not simple, interest.[46]

Certainly this seems consistent with the reasoning of the House of Lords in *Sempra* that compound interest should be awarded because only this would truly represent 'the time value' of the money,[47] although it does mean that one of Lord Hope's grounds for distinguishing *Sempra* from *Westdeutsche* can no longer be used.[48]

In addition, although the House of Lords in *Sempra* had been unanimous that an English court has jurisdiction under domestic law to award compound interest,[49] Henderson J held (obiter) that

> if the guiding principle of Community law is that the member state should not profit from the imposition of the unlawful charge, compound interest would seem to be required as a matter of Community law, because it is only in that way that full effect can be given to the guiding principle.

This also meant that the entitlement to compound interest would 'trump' any national rules concerning interest.[50] However, it did not mean that the claimants in *Chalke* could recover compound interest. The problem was that the mistakes which had caused Chalke to make the overpayment of tax in the first place had been discovered at the end of June 1997 at the latest, and thus the extended limitation period under s 32(1)(c) Limitation Act 1980 had expired by no later than the end of June 2003, so that Chalke's claims for compound interest were time-barred.[51] It is true that the claimants did not discover that they could also have claimed compound interest until the decision of the House of Lords in *Sempra* in July 2007, but this mistake that they were entitled to simple interest only was not an operative mistake for the purposes of the present claims. The only operative mistakes were their 'liability mistakes'; that is, their mistake that they had been

[46] *F J Chalke*, n 26 [108].

[47] See, eg: *Sempra*, n 26, Lord Nicholls [103].

[48] (n 30).

[49] *F J Chalke*, n 26 [116]. As was noted above, the House of Lords split 3:2 on the question of whether this jurisdiction came from the common law or from equity, but whatever its origin, their Lordships were unanimous in holding that it existed.

[50] *F J Chalke*, n 26 [57]–[125]. The national rules at issue in *Chalke* were ss 78–80 of the Value Added Tax Act 1994, but the same point could be made in relation to Virgo's concern that the decision in *Sempra* 'does not sit easily with the statutory regime for simple interest under the Supreme Court Act [1981]' (G Virgo, 'Compound Interest Made Simple' [2007] *Cambridge Law Journal* 510, 512).

[51] *F J Chalke*, n 26 [143]. Nor could the claimants derive any help from s 29(5) Limitation Act 1980 because the payment by the Commissioners of the principal sum with simple interest had been a payment under s 80 VATA, not a payment which acknowledged the non-statutory common law restitutionary right to compound interest [149].

liable to pay the tax in the first place.[52] Their claim to 'upgrade' from simple to compound interest could not be regarded as free-standing. On the contrary, the claim was simply 'for the one element which remains unsatisfied of [their] restitutionary claim arising from the overpayments'.[53] Nothing about this rule would infringe the EU requirements to provide an equivalent and effective remedy for breach of EU law,[54] and nor was there any hope for the claimants that they could recover via an action for state liability in damages, since Henderson J held that the breaches in question were not sufficiently serious and were in any event also time-barred.[55]

In policy terms, if the purpose of the Limitation Acts is to encourage litigants to bring claims as promptly as possible then it is worth noting that the claimants in *Chalke* could not have brought their claims for compound interest any sooner than the decision of the House of Lords in *Sempra.* It is also worth observing, in answer to Henderson J's statement that 'it is no part of the function of the law of limitation to provide that time should start to run afresh whenever a development in the law brings the possibility of making a new type of claim into the foreground', that this was precisely the function of the law of limitation in the decision of the House of Lords in *Kleinwort Benson v Lincoln*[56]. Finally, it is also the case that as a result of Henderson J's decision in *Chalke* the claimants *were* to some extent worse off than if they had been claiming interest as the principal sum, despite Henderson J's concerns that such a disparity should not be created.[57]

However, notwithstanding these arguments, ultimately it is difficult to see how Henderson J could have concluded otherwise. As he points out, there is a need for certainty in public expenditure,[58] and this would be severely undermined by allowing claimants effectively to reopen actions previously thought to have been closed. If the claimants here had been entitled to receive compound interest, it would be difficult to argue that a tort claimant should not equally be entitled to reopen a claim should a subsequent House of Lords decision open a new head of damages. If claimants who recover simple interest as a principal sum are also denied the ability to 'upgrade' this to compound interest more than six years later, the potential disparity between such claims and those in which the interest is only ancillary to a principal sum disappears. The conclusion must therefore be that while compound interest is available as a matter of both domestic and perhaps EU law, this only applies when the claim for the principal sum is not time-barred.

Finally, to return to the point from which we started, it was noted above that this question does not fit perfectly with the other seven questions considered in this section, because the answer to it comes to a large extent from the decisions in

[52] *F J Chalke*, n 26 [163].
[53] Ibid [143].
[54] *F J Chalke*, n 26 [169]. On which see also: ch 8.
[55] *F J Chalke*, n 26 [188]–[9] and [191]. Again, for further detail of this cause of action see ch 8 pp 238–39.
[56] *Kleinwort Benson Ltd v Lincoln CC* [1999] 2 AC 349 (HL).
[57] *F J Chalke*, n 26 [108] and text to n 46.
[58] *F J Chalke*, n 26 [164].

Sempra and *F J Chalke* rather than being derived from a proper understanding of the nature of the public law reason for restitution itself. Nevertheless, that understanding does now allow us to move beyond the decisions in *Sempra* and *Chalke* to argue that while in both those cases the court was concerned with claims based on the unjust factor of mistake, the reasoning employed there ought to apply equally to claims based on the public law reason for restitution. Nothing in this suggestion contradicts the decided cases because it is clear that nothing turned on the particular reason for restitution in either *Sempra* or *Chalke*.[59] Indeed, as Lord Scott pointed out, the mistake that had been made 'and on which the restitutionary claim is based was the mistake of the payer, Sempra in the instant case',[60] and Lord Nicholls regarded mutual mistake as being more likely to give rise to a situation in which the recipient might make no actual use of the money, not less.[61] As a matter of principle it is surely even more important that full 'unravelling' should take place when the reason for restitution is the existence of an ultra vires act, particularly if Henderson J is right that, in some instances, this is required as a matter of EU law. There is therefore no reason to suppose that compound interest should not be available for claims based on the public law reason for restitution, and every reason to suppose that it should.

Is it Always Necessary to Bring Two Separate Cases, One Action for Judicial Review and One Private Law Claim?

The inefficiency, cost and clumsiness of the 'bifurcation' of the claims in *Woolwich* was much criticised,[62] and in *British Steel plc v Customs and Excise Commissioners*[63] it was finally established that both issues could be decided in the same case. Although this decision was welcome it did of course mean that a choice had to be made between the two procedures. In the event, the private procedure was chosen for two reasons. First, at the time of the claim in *British Steel* it was not possible to obtain the response of restitution through the public law procedure,[64] and second,

[59] On other fronts, the precise relationship between the cause of action based on mistake and the cause of action based on the public law reason for restitution will be discussed in more detail in ch 4.

[60] *Sempra*, n 26 [145].

[61] *Sempra*, n 26 [118].

[62] See P Birks, '"When Money is Paid in Pursuance of a Void Authority . . ."—a Duty to Repay?' [1992] *Public Law* 580, 589 and J Beatson, 'Public Law, Restitution and the Role of the House of Lords' (1993) 109 *Law Quarterly Review* 1, 5.

[63] *British Steel plc v Customs and Excise Commissioners* [1997] 2 All ER 366 (CA).

[64] See ch 1 text at n 57, although Birks had also suggested that the prerogative writ of mandamus could be used to grant restitution, see: P Birks, 'Restitution from the Executive: A Tercentenary Footnote to the Bill of Rights' in P Finn (ed), *Essays on Restitution* (London, Sweet and Maxwell, 1990) 200. In *R v Barnet Magistrates Court, ex p Cantor* [1999] 1 WLR 334 the Divisional Court refused to issue such a mandatory order, but this was on the ground that it would not be clear whether in a civil action a payment would have to be made. Alder has criticised this decision on the basis that mandatory payments should not be dependent on the existence of private law rights: J Alder, 'Restitution in Public Law: Bearing the Cost of Unlawful State Action' (2002) 22 *Legal Studies* 165, 180.

the decision in *O'Reilly v Mackman*[65] meant that although in principle procedural exclusivity would operate in favour of the public law procedure, an exception to this would exist where 'private rights' were at stake.[66] It therefore made sense to use the cause of action in unjust enrichment to bring the case outside the public law procedure so that restitution could be granted.

However, since the reforms to the procedural rules and the decision in *Clark*,[67] one case suggests that the authority of *British Steel* might no longer be so straightforwardly applied. In *Jones v Powys Local Health Board*[68] an elderly man had paid for his care and accommodation in a nursing home for the six years prior to his death. Following his death, his son requested a retrospective review of his father's care and nursing needs and it was found that in the eight weeks prior to his death his father would have been entitled to the care without paying for it. However, the son argued that the defendant's review panel should in fact have conducted a multi-disciplinary assessment of his father's needs at the time of his admission to the nursing home, and that had the defendant done so it would have discovered that his father was entitled to free care throughout the whole six year period. The son thus sought restitution of the whole amount. However, Plender J held that it was an abuse of process to try to bring this claim outside the procedure for judicial review.[69] His reasoning was that it was necessary to ascertain whether the son was in substance asserting an entitlement to a subsisting right in private law, which incidentally involved the examination of a public law issue, or whether the primary focus or dominant issue was to challenge a public law act or decision. Since on the facts of the case it was clear that the claimant could not succeed without establishing that the review panel had erred in assessing his father's needs, the complaints made of the review panel were central, explicit and suitable for determination by judicial review. By proceeding through the private law procedure the claimant had therefore deprived the defendant of both the stringent time limit and the requirement of permission applicable to applications for judicial review.[70]

As was noted in chapter one, even before the decision in *Clark*[71] brought the *substantive* public/private divide to the fore, litigation over the *procedural* public/private divide has always served as a proxy for it. It is not therefore difficult to see how use of the private procedure for claims based on the '*Woolwich* unjust factor' has led to a substantive assumption that this reason for restitution is no different from any other private law ground such as mistake or failure of consideration. Similarly, it is not difficult to see why, when trying to establish the procedure applicable to such hybrid claims, the court in *British Steel*[72] felt able to classify it

[65] *O'Reilly v Mackman* [1983] 2 AC 237 (HL).

[66] See also: ch 1 n 72.

[67] *Clark v University of Lincolnshire and Humberside* [2000] 1 WLR 1988 (CA). See also: ch 1 pp 14–15.

[68] *Jones v Powys Local Health Board* [2008] EWHC 2562 (Admin). I am very grateful to James Edelman for bringing this case to my attention.

[69] See also: ch 1, pp 14–15.

[70] ibid.

[71] *Clark* (n 67).

[72] *British Steel* (n 63).

(for pragmatic reasons) as a claim in private law, while Plender J in *Jones v Powys*[73] felt the necessity to classify it as suitable for determination by judicial review, just as on the more substantive level the Supreme Court of Canada in *Kingstreet Investments*[74] wished to classify the cause of action as arising wholly in public law while, as will be seen further in chapter four, the House of Lords has tended to take a wholly private view of such claims.[75] However, it should now be clear that, far from having vanished, the existence of a public law ultra vires event remains absolutely at the heart of claims such as those in *Woolwich* because it provides the very reason for restitution even when such claims are brought through the private procedure. This is especially so given that choice of the private procedure in *British Steel* was in any case largely a matter of chance based on essentially pragmatic reasoning. Conversely, it should be apparent that while the validity of the review panel's decision in *Jones v Powys* was indeed central and suitable for determination by judicial review, this did not alter the fact that if the claimant son was to receive any money overpaid by his father, this would constitute an action for restitution to reverse an unjust enrichment.[76]

Inevitably, in order to avoid the 'bifurcation' of claims so criticised following the *Woolwich* decision[77] one procedure must be chosen over the other. In order to avoid unnecessary litigation, and for the sake of uniformity and certainty, it seems desirable that the same procedure should be used in all cases. It is therefore unfortunate that to some extent the decision in *Jones v Powys* may now have reduced this certainty and uniformity by reopening the choice made in *British Steel*. The really key point, however, is that whichever procedure is chosen, that procedure should no longer be allowed to hide the substance of the claim, so that in future *both* the relevant unjust enrichment *and* public law ultra vires events should be recognised as being central to the claim. Giving sufficient attention to each of these two aspects of the claim regardless of the particular procedure chosen is therefore ultimately more important than the choice of procedure itself. Inevitably, since the choice between the two procedures is, at least in the abstract, 50:50, good arguments can obviously be made for adopting each of them. Whichever procedure is chosen, from it will tend to flow the expertise necessary for addressing one of the two relevant events, and it will always remain important to ensure that the expertise from the procedure not chosen is not lost as a result. Thus, were *Jones v Powys* to be followed across the board it would be crucial that the administrative courts should not lose sight of the existence of an unjust enrichment event and the wealth of authority so far established on the different elements of such a claim. Conversely, were *British Steel* to be followed, it would be crucial for the civil courts to remember that there is a wealth of authority on the nature and operation of

[73] *Jones v Powys* (n 68).

[74] *Kingstreet* (n 11) See also: ch 2 pp 31–35.

[75] See the discussion of *Deutsche Morgan Grenfell v IRC* [2006] UKHL 49, [2006] 3 WLR 781, ch 4 p 94 onwards.

[76] See also: ch 2 p 35, where it was argued that the return of the money *to the claimant* cannot be explained purely as a response to the public law ultra vires event.

[77] Birks (n 62).

judicial review which should be borne in mind when considering the reason for restitution.

In practice, however, there are three reasons why the private law procedure should probably be chosen. First, we do not have complete carte blanche to make the decision anew. *Jones v Powys* is a relatively isolated decision, whereas it has been assumed since *British Steel* that all such claims can be brought via the private law procedure. Second, it should be noted that claims against public bodies in tort (even torts specific to public bodies, such as state liability in damages or misfeasance in public office) are also brought through the private law procedure rather than as applications for judicial review.[78] Third, there may well be instances in which only one entity needs to challenge the validity of the initial payment, but many entities subsequently wish to recover the money they have paid on that basis. Since none of these subsequent claims would need to revisit the question of validity, it would seem more natural for such subsequent claims to be heard through the private law procedure, even though the existence of the ultra vires event would of course remain relevant as one of the two relevant events at the heart of the claim and as the reason for restitution, as proposed here. If this were to happen, then private law would already have to make the necessary adjustments to accommodate the public law aspects of the claim, as it has been argued here that it should. It therefore seems more consistent and indeed more efficient to allow all the claimants to use the same, private, procedure, adjusted to take into account the relevant public law concerns, rather than making the first claimant use the public procedure while all subsequent claimants can use the (adjusted) private one. For the considerations of uniformity and certainty noted above, and for simplicity, therefore, it seems sensible to remain with the private law procedure for all such claims, and it will be argued in chapter five that they should, in any event, have their own time limit.[79]

In addition to these five questions concerning the practical operation of the *Woolwich* unjust factor, knowledge of its true nature also gives the answer to three other questions concerning its substantive scope.

Over What Subject Matter does the Public Law Reason for Restitution Extend?

It is clear that uncertainty surrounding the precise limits of the '*Woolwich* principle' presents a significant source of concern to judges who have considered applying it in other cases. In *Deutsche Morgan Grenfell v IRC*,[80] for example, Lord Hope and Lord Walker both referred to the lack of precision in the expression 'taxes and other similar charges' from the *Woolwich* ratio.[81] This uncertainty arises

[78] See, eg: *Watkins v SSHD* [2006] 2 AC 395 (HL) on misfeasance in public office and *R v Secretary of State for Transport, ex p Factortame (no 5)* [2000] 1 AC 524 (HL) on state liability in damages.

[79] See also: ch 5 p 128 onwards.

[80] *Deutsche Morgan Grenfell* (n 75).

[81] ibid [46] and [140].

because, as the Law Commission notes,[82] the majority of the Court of Appeal in *Woolwich* held that the key was in the 'public law' nature of the demand. Glidewell LJ included licence fees and similar imposts as well as tax and customs duties,[83] while Butler-Sloss LJ, agreeing with Glidewell LJ, referred to 'tax, duty, licence fee, or other payment on behalf of central and local government'.[84] The House of Lords, however, appeared to suggest a narrower application for the principle. Lord Goff's formulation appears to exclude licence and other fees,[85] Lord Slynn only referred to tax, and Lord Browne-Wilkinson talked of 'money paid by way of tax or other impost'[86]. But the Law Commission's conclusion is that there is no positive indication that they intended a narrower scope for the principle and nothing turned on this in the case itself.[87] Furthermore, having considered Lord Goff's reasoning, the Law Commission concluded:

> We do not think that the *Woolwich* right is limited to payments of tax or to Governmental or quasi-Governmental exactions, or to payments made in accordance with a demand. We believe that the crucial element is that the payment is collected by any person or body which is operating outside its statutory authority, that is, it is acting ultra vires. The requirement of ultra vires is not in our view confined to the excess of statutory power but also extends to procedural abuses, abuse of power and error of law on the part of the charging authority.[88]

Now that we know that the unjust factor or reason for restitution is in fact provided by an event in public law it is clear that the Law Commission is right. Whenever money has been obtained in an ultra vires manner, as defined by public law, it should in principle be recoverable using the public law reason for restitution and there is no further need to be concerned with the specific definition of any such payment as a tax or licence fee etc.[89] A proper understanding of the reason for restitution, then, provides a much clearer and simpler definition of the scope of the principle than any that was available when the case was viewed in a wholly private law light.

[82] Law Commission (1994) (n 2) [6.38].

[83] (n 1) 79. Crucially, Glidewell LJ drew a distinction between 'private law' cases and cases 'in which the defendant is an instrument or officer of central or local government, exercising a power to require payment of a tax, customs duty, licence fee or other similar impost' which he regarded as 'public law' cases.

[84] (n 1) 138.

[85] (n 1) 177.

[86] (n 1) 198.

[87] Law Commission (1994) (n 2) [6.38].

[88] ibid [6.42].

[89] Interestingly, although the approach they take to the substance of such claims was rejected in ch 2, the Canadian courts have followed a similar approach to that suggested here on the question of the relevant subject matter, holding that the decision of the Supreme Court of Canada in *Kingstreet Investments* (n 11) also applies to charges for car parking applied by the University of British Columbia, on the basis that it was a public body: *Barbour v the University of British Columbia* [2009] BCSC 425.

What Sort of Invalidity Triggers this Reason for Restitution?

Similarly the Law Commission Report states that:

> There is doubt as to whether that ultra vires quality must stem from the invalidity of subordinate legislation, or may also be due to error of law, abuse of discretion, or possibly procedural unfairness. This doubt arises because Lord Goff and Lord Slynn expressly reserved judgment on this question. However, the misconstruction of a relevant statute or regulation is an error of law and any administrative decision based on such a misconstruction is likely to be ultra vires and may, therefore, fit into the basic formulation.[90]

Some further guidance came from the case of *British Steel*,[91] which established that misinterpretation of a valid statute was included in the *Woolwich* unjust factor and in *Kingstreet Investments*;[92] Bastarache J, giving the judgment of the Supreme Court of Canada held that 'there is no need to distinguish between cases involving unconstitutional legislation and cases where delegated legislation is merely *ultra vires* in the administrative law sense'.[93] However, once the reason for recovery in *Woolwich* is understood as simply being the existence of a public law ultra vires event, it no longer becomes necessary to wait for further elaboration of the rule on this case by case basis. Again, whenever money has been obtained in an ultra vires manner, as defined by public law, it should in principle be recoverable using the *Woolwich* unjust factor. As was noted in chapter one,[94] the expression 'ultra vires' is thus used in its 'umbrella sense' to indicate that money could be recovered under *Woolwich* where it has been levied in disproportionate breach of the applicant's legitimate expectations,[95] following a biased hearing,[96] following a mistake of law or of fact,[97] following a misuse of powers,[98] or following any other action to

[90] Law Commission (1994) (n 2) [6.39].

[91] *British Steel* (n 63). See also: *Hillsdown Holdings plc v IRC* [1999] STC 561 (Ch); *Mallusk Cold Storage Ltd v Dept of Finance and Personnel* [2003] NIQB 58 (QB); *Carvill v IRC (No 2)* [2002] EWHC 1488 (Ch), [2002] STC 1167; *British Sky Broadcasting Group plc v Customs and Excise Commissioners* [2001] EWHC 127 (QB), [2001] STC 437; and *Waikato Regional Airport Ltd v Attorney-General* [2003] UKPC 50.

[92] *Kingstreet Investments* (n 11).

[93] ibid [57]. Obviously it is more controversial in English law to regard legislation as 'unconstitutional' in quite the same sense as applies in a system with a comprehensive written constitution such as Canada. Nevertheless, the basic point remains. Distinctions should not be drawn between, for example, wholly ultra vires statutes and those which are intra vires in themselves but have been applied in a manner which is ultra vires.

[94] At p 12.

[95] Established as a ground of review: *R v North and East Devon Health Authority, ex p Coughlan* [2001] QB 213 (CA).

[96] For the most recent definition of this ground of review, see: *Porter v Magill* [2001] UKHL 67, [2002] AC 357.

[97] For examples of these grounds of review in operation, see, eg: *R v Lord President of the Privy Council, ex p Page* [1993] AC 682 (HL); and *E v Secretary of State for the Home Dept* [2004] EWCA Civ 49, [2004] QB 1044.

[98] For an example of this ground of review in operation, see: *Wheeler v Leicester CC* [1985] AC 1054 (HL) as well as Browne-Wilkinson LJ (CA).

which the law could respond on an application for judicial review.[99] Of course, in addition to these questions concerning the kind of invalidity which will give rise to the public law reason for restitution, there will also be important questions relating to the scope and extent of its operation. However, it will be much easier to discuss these questions with reference to the facts of the cases in which they have been in issue, and thus it will be convenient to reserve that discussion until those cases have themselves been examined in more detail.[100]

Which Kinds of Body Will Give Rise to this Reason for Restitution?

Finally, as the Scottish Law Commission notes:

> [M]any of the justifications could be invoked as a reason for introducing a rule of automatic recovery applying to *private* sector debts as well as to public sector debts. Second, there are other justifications which apply well enough to powerful governmental bodies such as the defendant in *Woolwich* . . . but which seem inapt or unconvincing when applied to less powerful public or semi-public bodies . . . and appear especially inapt and even absurd when applied to a small private trader . . . Third, the only remaining justification is the public law principle of legality. But this is a formal justification which, unlike the *Woolwich* case, has nothing to do with the relative strength of the parties, and seems to create an arbitrary and uncertain boundary. The distinction between private and public law, and . . . between private and public bodies, is very ill-defined.[101]

So again, no particular answer is given by the *Woolwich* case itself and, as a result, judges in subsequent cases have been reluctant to apply the reason for restitution derived in that case to the issues in front of them. Thus in *Deutsche Morgan Grenfell*,[102] Lord Hope was also concerned that the *Woolwich* principle might involve 'treating the Revenue differently from all other public authorities which receive payments'.[103] However, just as before, once the true significance of *Woolwich* is understood, this objection vanishes. It is not the *Revenue* specifically that will be treated differently as a result of *Woolwich*, rather it is all public bodies which are *already* treated differently by being subject to judicial review and thus liable for events in public law.[104] As was seen in chapter one,[105] although in some

[99] Again, the decision of the CA in *Boake Allen* (n 4) might be thought to run counter to this argument, but once more it does not in fact do so. In that case the CA held and the HL confirmed that the tax in question was not unlawful because the relevant double taxation conventions had not been brought into force in the UK and a reference would be needed to the ECJ under Art 267 TFEU (ex 234 EC) to establish whether the tax was contrary to Art 63 TFEU (ex 56 EC) EC law on free movement of capital. The claimants did plead a cause of action in mistake in the alternative, but this mistake was that the law was valid, and on the facts of the case that was held to be true, as just noted. There was therefore no question of the Revenue in this case receiving money to which it was not entitled.

[100] See also: below: ch 4, '*How Wide are the Effects of the Public Law Reason for Restitution?*'

[101] Scottish Law Commission, 'Unjustified Enrichment, Error of Law and Public Authority Receipts and Disbursements' (Scot Law Com No 159, 1999) [2.61]–[2.63].

[102] *Deutsche Morgan Grenfell* (n 80).

[103] ibid [44].

[104] Again, note the similar decision reached by the Canadian courts (n 89).

[105] At pp 13–16.

cases it may not be clear whether a particular body is subject to judicial review or not, this is an issue with which the law already has to grapple and to which it has already, in most cases, provided an answer.

Indeed, we can go even further than this: if the public law reason for restitution simply means that the enrichment was the result of an ultra vires event in public law, we are thus able to move beyond the eight questions identified above and onto the first of the more significant conclusions to be drawn from the true nature of the reason for restitution in *Woolwich.*

The Scope of the Public Law Unjust Factor: Restitution *for* Public Bodies

Once we understand that the real reason for restitution in *Woolwich* was the existence of a public law ultra vires event, there is no reason why this should not also provide the reason for restitution in cases where the public body has *paid money out* in excess of its powers. In this sense the corollary of *Woolwich* is the case of *Auckland Harbour Board v The King,*[106] in which Viscount Haldane held that 'any payment out of the consolidated fund made without Parliamentary authority is simply illegal and ultra vires, and may be recovered by the Government'.[107] In fact, two limitations on the right were suggested by Viscount Haldane's reasoning: that the claim is proprietary and therefore dependent on tracing; and that the money must have been paid out of the consolidated fund. *Commonwealth of Australia v Burns,*[108] however, held that the reference to tracing was not to tracing in the equitable or proprietary sense, but to tracing the identity of the recipient of the money, and Burrows removes both restrictions to regard *Auckland Harbour Board* as the true 'mirror' of *Woolwich.*[109] It is also clear that Lord Goff regarded *Auckland Harbour Board* as being relevant to the decision in *Woolwich* in terms of reciprocity:

> [I]t is well established that, if the Crown pays money out of the consolidated fund without authority, such money is *ipso facto* recoverable . . . see *Auckland Harbour Board v The King* . . . The comparison with the position of the citizen, on the law as it stands [before *Woolwich*] is most unattractive.[110]

But the argument here goes further than this. The cause of action in *Woolwich* is not just the mirror or fair corollary of *Auckland Harbour Board*; they are one and the same thing. In both cases there has been a private law unjust enrichment at the expense of the claimant and the injustice or reason for restitution arises from the

[106] *Auckland Harbour Board v The King* [1924] AC 318 (PC).
[107] ibid 326.
[108] *Commonwealth of Australia v Burns* [1971] VR 825 (SC Victoria).
[109] Burrows, *Law of Restitution* (n 3) 420–23.
[110] *Woolwich* (n 1) 177 (Lord Goff).

existence of a public law ultra vires event. The law does not, however, recognise that this is the case, and as a result it has again, in a series of well-known cases, struggled to find an appropriate reason for restitution.

The 'Swaps' Cases[111]

These cases concerned hundreds of transactions entered into by local authorities throughout England with various banks. Under the swap agreements, the parties exchanged interest rates, so that one party paid to the other sums calculated by reference to a fixed rate of interest in return for the other party paying sums calculated by reference to the market rate of interest upon a notional principal sum. At the time these cases came to court some of the transactions were still 'open', meaning that they were still running and payments were still being made. Others were 'closed swaps', meaning that they had run for the whole of the specified period and all the necessary payments had been made.

Hazell v Hammersmith and Fulham LBC[112]

Just as in the *Woolwich* case, these swaps transactions gave rise to two legal issues, one from either side of the public/private divide. First it was necessary to decide whether the transactions were within the powers of the local authority, a public law question. *Hazell v Hammersmith and Fulham LBC* answered this question in the negative: the transactions were ultra vires the local authorities. The second issue again concerned the reclaiming of money transferred under these contracts,[113] just as in *Woolwich*, the difference this time being that the public body could in principle have been either the defendant or the claimant.[114]

Before claims for recovery could be brought at all, the claimants had to overcome the hurdle posed by the House of Lords decision in *Sinclair v Brougham*,[115] which held that an action for money had and received could not succeed if the award of restitution would involve the indirect enforcement of an invalid transaction. Thus in that case, restitutionary relief would be unavailable at common law because repayment of the loan was exactly what was required under the invalid loan contract.

[111] For the most recent significant work on the swaps cases, see: P Birks and F Rose (eds), *Lessons of the Swaps Litigation* (London, Mansfield Press, 2000).
[112] *Hazell v Hammersmith and Fulham LBC* [1992] 2 AC 1 (HL).
[113] Again the action for money had and received operated as a vehicle for unjust enrichment reasoning.
[114] Although in the cases discussed below the public body was in fact the defendant.
[115] *Sinclair v Brougham* [1914] AC 398 (HL).

Westdeutsche Landesbank Girozentrale v Islington LBC[116] *and* Guinness Mahon and Co Ltd v Kensington and Chelsea RLBC[117]

In *Westdeutsche*, both Hobhouse J (at first instance)[118] and the Court of Appeal[119] held that this principle was inapplicable to the facts of the case simply because the swaps transactions were not borrowing transactions: by definition they did not include the lending of money, and because the banks were not seeking directly or indirectly to enforce the ultra vires contracts (quite the reverse).[120] However, Lord Goff's solution appears to be wider than this. He suggests that even where the transaction does involve a loan there can still be restitution simply because it is now recognised that the obligation to make restitution is imposed by law and is independent of the contractual obligation to repay the loan:

> I myself incline to the opinion that a personal claim in restitution would not directly enforce the ultra vires contract, for such an action would be unaffected by any of the contractual terms governing the borrowing and moreover would be subject (where appropriate) to any available restitutionary defences.[121]

Once this issue had been dealt with, the way was clear for the courts to try to find an appropriate reason for restitution, a matter complicated by the fact that some of the swaps were 'open', while others were 'closed'. Various such reasons were used in the ensuing litigation.

Perhaps the best-known swaps case, *Westdeutsche* was brought when the transaction was in its third year of ten, and the bank had paid approximately £1m more to Islington LBC than it had received.

Absence of consideration

At first instance, Hobhouse J allowed recovery on the basis of 'absence of consideration' and in doing so he relied on the judgments in *Woolwich*.[122] Similarly, in the Court of Appeal Dillon LJ held that:

> The *Woolwich* case . . . [was a case] in which it would be more accurate to say that there had been no consideration for the payment than to say that the consideration had wholly failed; the transactions in issue did not obviously involve any consideration or performance,

116 *Westdeutsche* (HL) (n 29).
117 *Guinness Mahon and Co Ltd v Kensington and Chelsea RLBC* [1999] QB 215 (CA).
118 *Westdeutsche* (first instance) [1994] All ER 890 (QB).
119 *Westdeutsche* (CA) [1994] 1 WLR 938.
120 *Westdeutsche* (first instance) (n 118) 917–19 and *Westdeutsche* (CA) (n 119) 952.
121 *Westdeutsche* (HL) (n 29) 688 (Lord Goff).
122 *Westdeutsche* (first instance) (n 118) 924 (Hobhouse J). He also held that the money had, from the time it had been received by the local authority, been held on resulting trust for the bank, which was entitled in equity to the return of the lump sum. The bank was also entitled to compound interest from the date of receipt by the local authority. These matters are beyond the scope of the current investigation, which is concerned with the operation of the unjust factor, but see further: P Birks and F Rose (eds), *Lessons of the Swaps Litigation* (n 111) and for further discussion of the question of compound interest see above, 'What Exactly does the Claimant Recover?'.

> moving from the payee to the plaintiff, in the sense of the phrase 'the consideration had wholly failed'.[123]

It is less easy to establish the reason for restitution to which Leggatt LJ refers in his judgment, but it appears to be the same:

> There can have been no consideration under a contract void *ab initio*. So it is fallacious to speak of the failure of consideration having been partial. What is meant is that the parties did, in the belief that the contract was enforceable, part of what they would have been required to do if it had been. As it was they were not performing the contract even in part: they were making payments that had no legal justification instead of affording each other mutual consideration for an enforceable contract . . . The payments made are in those circumstances recoverable by Westdeutsche in so far as they exceed the payments made by Islington, as money had and received to the use of Westdeutsche by which Islington have been unjustly enriched.[124]

As has already been seen in discussion of the *Woolwich* decision,[125] there are two structural objections to the use of 'absence of consideration' as a reason for restitution. First, as Swadling[126] and Virgo[127] point out, Leggatt LJ is confusing the unjust enrichment sense of the word 'consideration' with the contractual sense of the word, a distinction first made in *Fibrosa Spolka Akcyjna v Fairbairn Lawson Combe Barbour Ltd*, where Viscount Simon LC held that:

> In English law an enforceable contract may be formed by an exchange of a promise for a promise, or by the exchange of a promise for an act . . . and thus, in the law relating to the formation of a contract, the promise to do a thing may often be the consideration, but when one is considering the law of failure of consideration and of the quasi-contractual right to recover money on that ground, it is, generally speaking, not the promise which is referred to as the consideration, but the performance of the promise. The money was paid to secure performance, and if performance fails the inducement which brought about the payment is not fulfilled'[128]

If the consideration is seen as a valid promise, then it is true that this cannot arise under a contract void *ab initio*, but that would be the contractual sense of the word 'consideration'. Performance of the promise, on the other hand, can happen whether or not the initial promise is void.[129]

Second, 'absence of consideration' is not in fact an unjust factor at all, but rather an abandonment of the whole scheme of unjust factors, or specific reasons for restitution, and it would be a significant intellectual change for this area of law to

[123] ibid 960.

[124] ibid 969.

[125] Above ch 2 at pp 24–26 and 29–30.

[126] W Swadling, 'Restitution for no Consideration' [1994] *Restitution Law Review* 73, 78–79.

[127] G Virgo, 'Failure of Consideration: Myth and Meaning in the English Law of Restitution' in D Johnston and R Zimmermann (eds), *Unjustified Enrichment: Key Issues in Comparative Perspective* (Cambridge, Cambridge University Press, 2002) 120.

[128] *Fibrosa Spolka Akcyjna v Fairbairn Lawson Combe Barbour Ltd* [1943] AC 32 (HL) 47 (Viscount Simon LC).

[129] See also: below p 63.

adopt the civilian structure.[130] Since again the advantages and disadvantages of such a change were not considered by the courts it is similarly unlikely that this is what they intended here, any more than in relation to the *Woolwich* case. Thus, as before, we should reject 'absence of consideration' as a potential 'unjust factor'. Nevertheless, the fact that the courts were tempted to use the concept of absence of consideration in both *Woolwich* and *Westdeutsche* remains significant.

Of course, among the other reasons for restitution 'failure of consideration' is unusual in that it is a negatively-defined unjust factor. Whatever one's views on their individual validity, it is clear that unjust factors such as 'mistake', 'ignorance', 'duress' and 'undue influence' etc all suggest positive reasons for recovery; only 'failure of consideration' refers to the absence of something instead although it is true that mistake could also be characterised in this way: the facts were not as C thought they were. In any case, for failure of consideration, unlike mistake, it is necessary for both parties to be aware of the condition for the payment.[131] The focus of the ground of recovery is therefore the *failure* of this state of affairs to emerge *when it ought to have done* rather than the fact that C was positively mistaken about something that was never supposed to be the case. It is therefore possible that it was simply this negativity that brought the English system so perilously close to the reverse civilian approach and made it possible for the courts to slide from 'failure' to 'absence' as the particular variety of negativity.[132]

Nevertheless, although use of the concept of 'absence of consideration' can to some extent be explained in these linguistic terms, its use in the swaps cases is significant in two important and interrelated ways. First, as was seen in relation to the *Woolwich* decision,[133] from the private law perspective 'no consideration' is not enough, we need a specific reason for restitution. From the public law perspective, on the other hand, the concept of 'no consideration' begins to make more sense. In relation to the *Woolwich* case, it was argued that a declaration that a public law act was ultra vires is a declaration that it never existed in the first place, because it could not, it was void *ab initio*, and that it was a recognition of this public law finding that became mistranslated into the private law concept of 'absence of consideration'. Further support for this proposition can now be found in the swaps cases. For example, in explaining the use of 'absence of consideration' in *Guinness Mahon*,[134] Robert Walker LJ suggested that:

> Where a contract is void *ab initio* there is in the eyes of the law no contract at all, and so speaking of failure of consideration, in the sense of failure of contractually promised performance, may be confusing. That is why Hobhouse J preferred, as he explained, to speak

[130] See, eg: T Krebs, *Restitution at the Crossroads: A Comparative Study* (London, Cavendish, 2001) pt V. See also ch 1 nn 32, 35.

[131] *Craven-Ellis v Canons Ltd* [1936] 2 KB 403 (CA). See Virgo, *Principles* (n 9) 306.

[132] Incidentally, a tangential result of this slide is that whereas failure of consideration entails a time lag between the receipt of the enrichment and the generation of the reason for restitution when the condition fails, once the ground is allowed to slide into absence of consideration this time-lag is lost.

[133] See above ch 2 at pp 24–26 and 29–30.

[134] *Guinness Mahon* (n 117).

of 'absence of consideration' in the case of a purported contract which was void because ultra vires.[135]

The swaps cases thus provide further evidence for the argument that 'absence of consideration' is merely a private law mistranslation of *ab initio* voidness in public law.[136] Second, the fact that this inherently public concept arose in both the *Woolwich* and the swaps cases underscores the argument that the reason for restitution in both instances should actually be the same. In both *Woolwich* and the swaps cases there were two relevant events, one dealt with by judicial review and the other dealt with by unjust enrichment. The event at issue in the first case thus provides the reason for restitution in the second, producing an overall hybrid claim, regardless of whether the money was unlawfully paid out or received by the public body.

As with claims from public body defendants, this hybrid approach would also avoid many of the disadvantages associated with recognising only one of the two relevant events. For example, it was noted in relation to claims from public bodies that a move to a wholly public approach, especially one involving the prerogative mandatory order for repayment, could mean that the law's response would become discretionary.[137] If this had been the approach adopted for the swaps transactions, it is by no means impossible that, as a result, restitution would have been denied. The general consensus among public lawyers[138] was that *Hazell v Hammersmith* had stifled the private finance initiative and made banks extremely unwilling to deal with local authorities in the future, which seems like precisely the kind of 'serious public inconvenience in upsetting the impugned order' that led to the withholding of relief in *ex p AMA*.[139] Even were this danger to be avoided, the other dangers canvassed in relation to claims from public bodies would also remain.[140] Conversely, from the private law perspective, not only would the hybrid public law unjust factor approach avoid the complications associated with 'absence of consideration', it would also remove some of the problems associated with other reasons for restitution used in the swaps cases.

Failure of Consideration

One other such reason is of course failure of consideration. Even if this ground were to be adopted in preference to absence of consideration, it runs immediately into a problem. Despite frequent criticisms of the rule, in claims for money had

135 ibid 236. A similar point is made by P Birks, 'Private Law' in *Lessons of the Swaps Litigation* (n 111) 19–21.

136 See also: *Boake Allen* (CA) (n 4) [161] (Mummery LJ).

137 See ch 2 at pp 33–34.

138 See, eg: M Loughlin, 'Innovative Financing in Local Government: The Limits of Legal Instrumentalism—Part II' [1990] *Public Law* 568, 572; R Clutterbuck, editorial, (1991) *Journal of Business Law* 105; and J Convery, 'Lord Goff's Swansong: Restitution, Mistake of Law and the Retrospective Effect of Judicial Decisions' (1999) 3 *Edinburgh Law Review* 202 and 'Coda' at 216.

139 *R v Secretary of State for Social Services, ex p AMA* [1993] COD 54. For further discussion see: ch 2 at p 33.

140 See: ch 2 at pp 33–35.

and received it has repeatedly been made clear by the courts that the failure of consideration must be total.[141] The problem here is that, if we correctly analyse the consideration for the purposes of unjust enrichment as being performance of the swaps contracts, then the consideration has not totally failed as sums have been paid between the parties. In order to investigate this further it is necessary to look at another of the swaps cases.

Guinness Mahon[142] was essentially an appeal from the Sandwell closed swap in *Westdeutsche*. Birks had argued that it should not be possible to recover in such a case[143] but the Court of Appeal held that it should. The key thing is to notice how Morritt LJ defines the failure of consideration in *Guinness Mahon*:

> [I]t is the very fact that the contract is ultra vires which constitutes the total failure of consideration justifying the remedy of money had and received or restitution for unjust enrichment. If partial performance of that assumed obligation in the case of an open swap does not preclude a total failure of that consideration then there is no basis on which complete performance of a closed swap could do so . . . If the relevant consideration for each swap was the *performance* of the obligation each party thought it was under in respect of that swap then each swap would be fully performed and neither party could recover from the other, either during the term of the swap agreement or thereafter, the amount by which what he had paid exceeded what he received. If on the other hand the consideration for each swap was the *benefit* of the contractual obligation then there was a total failure of consideration in the case of each swap either before or after the term of the agreement had elapsed, thereby entitling the loser to recover the balance under a closed swap as well as an open one.[144]

And later:

> The bank did not get in exchange for [its] performance all it expected, for it did not get the benefit of the contractual obligation of the local authority. Likewise, in reference to paragraph 47 of the *American Restatement*, the bank did not get the benefit it expected in the form of a contractual obligation.[145]

Similarly Robert Walker LJ held that:

> The recipient's title is . . . overshadowed by the payer's personal restitutionary claim, and if that shadow is there throughout the period of the transaction, it would be paradoxical if it vanished at the moment when, and simply because, the contract, had it been a valid contract, would then have been fully performed. With a valid contract total failure of consideration and full performance are at the opposite ends of the spectrum. The same is not true of a void contract. That is . . . the real force of the argument based on absurdity. The injustice of the . . . enrichment does not vanish because the term of the void contract ran its course.[146]

[141] eg: *Stocznia Gdanksa SA v Latvian Shipping Co* [1998] 1 WLR 574 (HL). For criticism of the requirement, see, eg: Burrows, *Law of Restitution* (n 3) 327–31 and Virgo, *Principles* (n 9) 323–26.

[142] *Guinness Mahon* (n 117).

[143] P Birks, 'No Consideration: Restitution after Void Contracts' (1993) 23 *University of Western Australia Law Review* 195.

[144] *Guinness Mahon* (n 117) 227–28.

[145] ibid 230.

[146] ibid 240.

The *Guinness Mahon* decision was cited with approval by the House of Lords in *Kleinwort Benson Ltd v Lincoln CC.*[147]

It is therefore possible that the Court of Appeal, in *Guinness Mahon*, has found a way to rescue the dictum of Legatt LJ, cited above.[148] Perhaps the problem is not a confusion over the meaning of 'consideration' but rather that there are three potential and competing definitions in these cases. First there is the contractual conception of consideration, rejected in *Fibrosa*, namely the promise itself. Then, there is the standard unjust enrichment conception of consideration accepted in *Fibrosa*; the performance of the promise. Here we are presented with a third conception, specific to contracts which are void *ab initio*; *the benefit*, or, as McKendrick would put it,[149] the *enforceability* of the performance of the promise. There has indeed been a total failure of this third kind of consideration in the swaps cases, as Stevens, McFarlane and Edelman point out.[150] If the enforceability of the performance of the promise is thus a third meaning of 'consideration' then crucially 'failure of consideration' is preserved as a single unjust factor (however negative) and the intellectual shift into the civilian system is avoided. Conversely the fine nature of the line between these alternative explanations supports the conclusion that the distinction between the civilian and traditional common law approaches is similarly thin.

Nevertheless, even failure of consideration is not without its problems in this context. For example, Virgo criticises this qualification of the claimant's consent as being artificial,[151] arguing that the consideration can only be said to have failed as a matter of law, rather than fact. McKendrick, on the other hand, has a different objection.[152] He argues that the failure of consideration is unique among the unjust factors because there is a time-lag between the transfer of the enrichment and the emergence of the reason for restitution. For him, this is not merely a descriptive observation about the usual operation of failure of consideration; it is necessary for the claim to succeed. He concludes that if the failure is present when the benefit is conferred, the true basis for the claim should be mistake, not failure of consideration.[153] In any case, whatever the merits of these various other criticisms, surely the overriding objection must be that even if we accept that 'failure of enforceability' provides us with the requisite failure of consideration in these

[147] *Kleinwort Benson Ltd v Lincoln CC* [1999] 2 AC 349 (HL) 387 (Lord Goff): '[I]t is incompatible with the ultra vires rule that an ultra vires transaction should become binding on a local authority simply on the ground that it has been completed'. For further discussion of this statement, see below ch 4, text following n 278. See also: ibid 415–16 (Lord Hope).

[148] See text to n 124.

[149] E McKendrick, 'The Reason for Restitution' in P Birks and F Rose (eds), *Lessons of the Swaps Litigation* (London, Mansfield Press, 2000) especially at 102.

[150] R Stevens and B McFarlane, 'In Defence of *Sumpter v Hedges*' (2002) 118 *Law Quarterly Review* 569, 576–77 and J Edelman, 'The Meaning of "Unjust" in the English Law of Unjust Enrichment' (2006) 3 *European Private Law* 309, 316.

[151] Virgo, 'Failure of Consideration' (n 127) 121.

[152] McKendrick (n 149) 105.

[153] Thus in relation to 'open' swaps, monies already paid are recoverable *either* for mistake, or because the consideration is that the swap would run its course and that has failed: ibid 106.

instances,[154] this is still a private law mistranslation of the public law concept of ultra vires. The promise is unenforceable because the public body did not have the power to make it in the first place. Thus whatever private law terminology we try to use, we ultimately cannot escape the fact that the real reason for restitution is simply the existence of an ultra vires event in public law. As Meier puts it, the different reasons for restitution listed in the swaps cases 'do nothing else than to mirror the reasons why the contract is invalid'.[155]

Kleinwort Benson Ltd v Lincoln CC[156]—*mistake of law*

As a final example of this, even McKendrick's preferred ground of mistake[157] is not wholly without difficulty.

In four separate cases, the appellant bank in *Kleinwort Benson v Lincoln* sought the recovery of monies which had again been paid to the respondent local authorities under swaps transactions. In each case, the transactions had been fully performed, and the monies paid to the banks more than six years previously. They were therefore outside the normal six year limitation period for the recovery of money paid under a mistake, and as a result, the bank sought to rely on section 32(1)(c) of the Limitation Act 1980 which provided that where an action was for relief from the consequences of a mistake 'the period of limitation shall not begin to run until the plaintiff has discovered the . . . mistake . . . or could with reasonable diligence have discovered it'.

The High Court had to follow precedent and hold that there could be no recovery for mistake of law, but the matter was then allowed to leap-frog to the House of Lords, which was asked to consider four issues:

i) Whether the mistake of law rule generally precluding a restitutionary remedy for money paid under a mistake of law should be maintained;
ii) If the rule were to be abrogated, whether recovery should still be precluded if either:
    a) the money was paid under a settled understanding of the law which was subsequently changed by judicial authority; or
    b) the money had been the subject of honest receipt by the defendant;
iii) Whether recovery was precluded by the fact that the transactions had been fully performed; and
iv) Whether section 32(1)(c) applied to mistakes of law.

154 Above n 150.

155 S Meier, 'Restitution after Executed Void Contracts' in P Birks and F Rose (eds), *Lessons of the Swaps Litigation* (London, Mansfield Press, 2000) 211. Crucially, she does not distinguish between invalidity in public as opposed to private law, as the argument here does.

156 *Kleinwort Benson* (n 147).

157 McKendrick (n 149).

On the first issue[158] Lord Goff held that:

> [T]he mistake of law rule should be abrogated, or at least reformulated, so that there should be a general right of recovery of money paid under a mistake, whether of fact or law, subject to appropriate defences. This is because a blanket rule of non-recovery, irrespective of the justice of the case, cannot sensibly survive in a rubric of the law based on the principle of unjust enrichment; and because recognition of a defence of change of position demonstrates that this must be proved in fact if it is to justify retention, in whole or in part, of money which would otherwise be repayable on the ground that the payee was unjustly enriched by its receipt.[159]

This view was also held by Lord Hoffmann and Lord Hope.[160]

Should mistake of law be the reason for restitution? McKendrick argues that it should have been the ground of restitution across the swaps cases, but for its belated recognition.[161] Similarly, Bamforth regards it as 'the most straightforward route to restitution' in future cases[162] and as the law stands this must be so. On the other hand, for Krebs it poses as great a threat to the common law approach as does absence of consideration. His view is that:

> *Kleinwort Benson* purports to remain within the established typology. In reality it undermines it in a similar fashion . . . Their Lordships' view of what constitutes a mistake . . . was so wide that it effectively based restitution on the nullity of the obligation which the transfer in question was supposed to discharge. The challenge in *Kleinwort Benson v Lincoln* is therefore surprisingly similar to the challenge in *Westdeutsche*: restitution is based not on a concrete reason for restitution such as mistake or failure of consideration, but on the absence or nullity of a supposed underlying obligation'[163]

Indeed it is not completely clear that mistake *can* provide the ground of recovery in such cases. Much time was spent in *Kleinwort Benson v Lincoln*, and in the Law Commission's preparations for its Report, discussing whether the claimant in such cases had in fact been mistaken.[164] Is it possible to be *mistaken* when the situation is, as far as is ascertainable at the time, exactly as the claimant believes it to be? Lord Browne-Wilkinson thought not. While agreeing with the abolition of the rule precluding recovery for mistake of law, he nevertheless rejected the interpretation of the present case as one of mistake, holding that:

> The main effect of [the majority's] decision in the present case is to abolish the rule that money paid under a mistake of law cannot be recovered, which rule was based on the artificial assumption that a man is presumed to know the law. It would be unfortunate to

[158] Issue (ii)(a) will be dealt with below, as one of two matters which related to the choice of unjust factor in *Kleinwort Benson* (n 147). Issue (ii)(b) will be dealt with in ch 5 pp 151–52. Issue (iii) will also be dealt with below as the second unjust-factor related issue. Issue (iv) will be dealt with below, pp 74–75.

[159] *Kleinwort Benson* (n 147) 373. See also: 375 and 389.

[160] ibid 398 (Lord Hoffmann) and 405 and 418 (Lord Hope).

[161] McKendrick (n 149) 111.

[162] N Bamforth, 'Public Law' in P Birks and F Rose (eds), *Lessons of the Swaps Litigation* (London, Mansfield Press, 2000) 56.

[163] : Krebs (n 130) 2.

[164] Law Commission (1994) (n 2) [5.2] onwards.

> introduce into the amended law a new artificiality, viz, that a man is making a mistake at the date of payment when he acts on the basis of the law as it is then established. He was not mistaken at the date of payment. He paid on the basis that the then binding Court of Appeal decision stated the law, which it did: the fact that the law was later retrospectively changed cannot alter retrospectively the state of the payer's mind at the time of payment . . . In my judgment, therefore, if a man has made a payment on an understanding of the law which was correct as the law stood at the date of such payment he has not made that payment under a mistake of law if the law is subsequently changed.[165]

Similarly, while Lord Lloyd held that:

> The critics of the mistake of law rule have waited long enough. The plaintiffs in these proceedings should have the benefit of a change which is long overdue . . . the mistake of law rule should not stand in their way as it would if we were to wait for Parliament to take a hand.[166]

There was no mistake in the present case '[f]or when the parties entered into the contract the law was as they believed it to be. How then could they claim to have been mistaken?'[167] Even where the truth is ascertainable at the time of entry into the contract, controversy surrounds the level of doubt that is compatible with a mistaken belief. Obviously this is closely linked to the question of the causative operation of the mistake. In *Barclays Bank Ltd v WJ Simms Son and Cooke (Southern) Ltd*,[168] Robert Goff J held that the claim may fail where 'the payer intends that the payee shall have the money at all events, whether the fact be true or false, or is deemed in law so to intend'.[169] In *Maskell v Horner*,[170] the claimant could not recover because he had paid to avoid litigation despite being in doubt as to his liability to pay. In *Kleinwort Benson v Lincoln*[171] Lord Hope held that '[a] state of doubt is different from that of mistake. A person who pays when in doubt takes the risk that he may be wrong'.[172]

Such dicta have more recently been applied in *Brennan v Bolt Burdon (a firm)*.[173] Burrows believes that the claim should only fail if the claimant thinks the facts are *probably* as they are in truth[174] whereas Virgo would exclude recovery whenever the claimant was aware that there was a possibility that he or she was mistaken.[175] This issue arose again in the case of *Deutsche Morgan Grenfell* which suggested at first

[165] *Kleinwort Benson* (n 147) 359.

[166] ibid 391.

[167] ibid. For an opposing view see: D Sheehan, 'What is a Mistake?' (2000) 20 *LS* 518, who argues along Dworkinian lines that there is always a right answer to any question of law and thus that the claimants in *Kleinwort Benson* were mistaken. For rejection of that view, albeit in a different context, see: R Williams, 'When is an Error not an Error? Jurisdictional Review of Error of Fact and Law' [2007] *Public Law* 793–808.

[168] *Barclays Bank Ltd v WJ Simms Son and Cooke (Southern) Ltd* [1980] QB 677 (QB).

[169] ibid 695 (Robert Goff J).

[170] *Maskell v Horner* [1915] 3 KB 106 (CA).

[171] *Kleinwort Benson* (n 147).

[172] *Kleinwort Benson* (n 147).

[173] *Brennan v Bolt Burdon (a firm)* [2004] EWCA Civ 1017, [2005] QB 303.

[174] Burrows, *Law of Restitution* (n 3) 140.

[175] Virgo, *Principles* (n 9) 163.

instance that a level of uncertainty was not incompatible with mistake.[176] This was supported by Jonathan Parker LJ in the Court of Appeal who held that 'mere knowledge that the statutory provisions in question are under challenge is not to be equated with a state of doubt as to the validity of those provisions'.[177] The majority of the Court of Appeal (Rix and Buxton LJJ) preferred Lord Hope's remarks in *Kleinwort Benson v Lincoln* to the effect that a state of doubt is different from that of mistake, but in the House of Lords the majority concluded that a state of doubt was not actually inconsistent with making a mistake as long as the person who made the mistake was not taking the risk of his or her mistake at the time.[178] This kind of investigation will be inevitable in cases where mistake is the only available ground of recovery, but nevertheless adds to the reasons for using another unjust factor where that is possible. Indeed, this concern with the 'metaphysics of mistake' is another reason why Birks prefers the *sine causa* approach.[179]

The conclusion must therefore again be that the existing unjust factors are inapt to cover the particular situation, but in particular they are inapt to cover the dual public and private nature of the claims and it is this duality in particular that has led to their being stretched. In addition, commercial certainty cannot be helped by the possibility of opening transactions years after they were closed. Thus, even if there has been a mistake of law it is hardly so straightforward a reason for restitution that it could not be improved upon. By contrast, use of the public law hybrid unjust factor would again go straight to the heart of the matter; if the real problem was in fact the ultra vires nature of the swaps transactions, this could be addressed directly, as could concerns over the relevant time limit.[180] It is therefore at least unnecessary, and perhaps impossible, to base restitution on the parties' beliefs about the unlawfulness of the transaction. Instead the swaps cases, *Auckland Harbour Board* and *Woolwich* could all be aligned. In each case the public law event of ultra vires could provide the reason for restitution, while the private law concept of unjust enrichment would deal with issues of enrichment of the defendant at the claimant's expense.

Of course, one important obstacle to such an approach[181] comes from the judgment of Lord Goff in *Kleinwort Benson v Lincoln*, where he held that there was a distinction to be made between 'payments of taxes and other similar charges and, on the other hand, payments made under ordinary private transactions'.[182] The

[176] *Deutsche Morgan Grenfell v IRC* (first instance) [2003] EWHC 1779 (Ch), [2003] 4 All ER 645.

[177] *Deutsche Morgan Grenfell v IRC* [2005] EWCA Civ 78, [2006] Ch 243 [235].

[178] *Deutsche Morgan Grenfell* (HL) (n 80) [26] (Lord Hoffmann).

[179] P Birks, *Unjust Enrichment*, 2nd edn (Oxford, Oxford University Press, 2005) 113.

[180] See also: below, ch 5.

[181] The question of time limits, a second important obstacle, will be discussed in ch 4 p 74 onwards.

[182] *Kleinwort Benson* (n 147) 381. G Jones also writes that '[t]he claim of the Crown for restitution of its money improperly drawn from the Consolidated Fund is very different from its claim to retain in the Consolidated Fund money which it was never entitled to receive': G Jones, *Restitution in Public and Private Law* (London, Sweet and Maxwell, 1991) 48. However, this is in answer to the argument that it would require Parliamentary authorisation to pay *back* money received ultra vires, rather than in answer to the alignment proposed here. Thus Jones also states that 'the right of the taxpayer to recover money to which the Crown was not entitled should not be dependent upon subsequent Parliamentary authorisation': ibid.

swaps cases, he held, belonged in the latter category.[183] His distinction focused on two matters, first that in *Woolwich*-type cases the money could be recovered 'as of right, without the need to invoke a mistake of law by the payer', whereas 'cases . . . concerned with repayment of money paid under private transactions . . . are governed by the common law',[184] and second that different defences may be applicable in the two 'different' types of case. Neither assertion, however, is entirely straightforward. Once it is understood that the '*Woolwich* unjust factor' is actually the presence of an ultra vires event in public law, it is clear that that event is present in the swaps context as much as in the context of unlawful taxation, as evidenced by the fact that both sets of cases began with an application for judicial review. It then becomes difficult to see *why* recovery in the swaps context must be 'governed by the common law'. Why must a claimant demonstrate a mistake about the invalidity when recovery could be granted as of right on the basis of the invalidity itself, as in *Woolwich* or *Auckland Harbour Board*? Similarly, once it is established that recovery could be granted in the same way in all such cases there seems no basis for asserting that different defences need to be applicable to the two 'different' kinds of case. On both matters, therefore, it appears that Lord Goff's argument is the wrong way round and based on mistaken assumptions. Instead we could recognise that there is no reason in principle to distinguish between the swaps cases, *Auckland Harbour Board* and *Woolwich* and that anyone who wishes to do so must provide a positive justification for the difference.

It is clear, then, that a proper understanding of the true nature of the '*Woolwich* unjust factor' has at least one important implication; once there has been an ultra vires transfer of money it is no longer necessary to distinguish between cases like *Woolwich* in which the public body was the recipient, and cases like *Auckland Harbour Board* in which it was the payer, or the swaps cases in which it could have been either. In all three kinds of case recovery could be available as of right whenever public law has established the ultra vires nature of the payment and the defendant can be shown to be enriched at the claimant's expense in private law. Such an approach would avoid the difficulties associated with either a purely public approach or with the different reasons for restitution chosen in the course of the swaps litigation. Incidentally this also provides a final reason for rejecting the purely public approach adopted by the Supreme Court of Canada in *Kingstreet Investments*.[185] Although it was the intention of Bastarache J in that case to strengthen the law's concern for public law considerations, in one crucial respect his decision has the opposite effect. By concentrating solely on the constitutional principle that the Crown may not levy a tax without the authority of Parliament or the legislature, his judgment is inevitably limited to cases with facts like those of *Woolwich* and *Kingstreet Investments* itself. However, as has been shown here, these are not the only cases in which public law concerns arise. If instead we recognise

[183] *Kleinwort Benson* (n 147) 382 (Lord Goff).
[184] ibid 381–82 (Lord Goff).
[185] *Kingstreet Investments* (n 11).

that the public law reason for restitution applies whenever there is an ultra vires event, we can not only extend our hybrid public and private approach beyond unconstitutional *taxes* to other forms of charge and levy, we can also begin to reach cases in which the public body has made an ultra vires *payment.* This, however, is not the only important implication to follow from the hybrid nature of the public law reason for restitution.

4

A Hierarchy of Reasons for Restitution

IN THE PREVIOUS chapter it was argued that once the true nature of the public law unjust factor is understood, as outlined in chapter two, not only does this provide us with the answers to several questions about the scope and operation of that unjust factor, it also means that there is then no reason to continue to separate cases in which the public body is the defendant from those in which it is the claimant. In all cases, if there has been an ultra vires transfer of money which constitutes an event in public law, this can provide the reason for restitution in the private unjust enrichment claim. However, so far the claim has generally been a descriptive one about the capabilities of the public law reason for restitution, rather than a normative one about its proper scope of application. It will be argued here that these descriptive conclusions can have normative force: not only *can* public law provide a more straightforward reason for restitution in all such cases, the second important implication of the true nature of the public law reason for restitution is that it *should* do so.

Essentially, public bodies may become involved in unjust enrichment claims in five different sets of circumstances as follows:

(1) A public body can behave in exactly the same manner as would a private individual. In the context of contractual claims, it is suggested that public bodies should be treated the same as private individuals when all they are doing is purchasing paperclips for use in their offices.[1] Perhaps the unjust enrichment equivalent of this is restitution of the price paid for the paperclips following breach of the contract, using, for example, total failure of consideration. This brings us to the second situation.

(2) A public body can behave in a 'public' manner, for example by levying tax or raising resources under the private finance initiative, but again, the basis for the transfer may fail. This gives rise to a further distinction between two different scenarios:

  (a) A private party and a public body enter a contract, which is terminated for some practical reason, such as a failure of the private party to complete the job given to it by the public body. The validity of the initial contract is not in question.

  (b) A private party and a public body enter a contract, which is terminated because it was ultra vires the public body. The swaps cases can fall into this category.

[1] Craig gives the example of the purchase of furniture: P Craig, *Administrative Law*, 6th edn (London, Sweet and Maxwell, 2008) 26-026. It was seen in ch 1 that there are those who think such a distinction should not be drawn (see above at ch 1, pp 10–11). The point here is that such a distinction *is* drawn and that the existence of judicial review depends on it. Thus as long as it exists it should also form the basis for the distinction suggested here.

Both failure of consideration and the validity of the public body's actions are relevant.

(3) It is also possible for public bodies acting in a 'public manner' as above to become involved in a claim based on mistake of law, for example where a private party misunderstands a taxing statute and pays too much tax, or a levying public body misunderstands a taxing statute and charges too much tax, as in *British Steel plc v Customs and Excise Commissioners*.[2] In such cases, the validity of the particular decision is in question, but the validity of the underlying legislation is not. There are, of course, also cases where the whole concept of the transaction or the legislation is ultra vires, but one of the parties has paid money in the belief that it was intra vires. The swaps cases can fall into this category, as do 'mistaken *Woolwich*'[3] cases such as, apparently, *Deutsche Morgan Grenfell v IRC*,[4] where the trusting private party simply pays the tax believing it to be validly demanded.

(4) Alternatively, it is possible for public bodies behaving in a 'public' manner, as above, to become involved in a claim based on a mistake of fact, for example where a tax is charged on red-haired employees and the claimant pays, believing it has such employees when in fact it does not.

(5) Finally, a public body can behave in a 'public' manner, and then become involved in a claim in which the unjust factor used by or against it is the public law reason for restitution, involving a combination of public and private law events. *Woolwich*[5] falls into this category, as could the *Auckland Harbour Board*[6] case and the swaps cases following the re-analysis conducted in chapter three.[7]

It is assumed that in the first case, as in the parallel contract and tort cases, the claim can be viewed from an entirely private law perspective and that the claim need not be based on the public law unjust factor. At the other extreme, of course, is situation (5) in which the public law reason for restitution provides the basis for the claim, which is thus a hybrid of public law and private law reasoning. The claimant must prove that the defendant has been enriched, at the claimant's expense, and that the defendant cannot plead any of the defences to unjust enrichment (requirements of the private law event of unjust enrichment). The claimant must also prove that the enrichment was unjust (private law requirement), which

[2] *British Steel plc v Customs and Excise Commissioners* [1997] 2 All ER 366 (CA).

[3] *Woolwich Equitable Building Society v IRC* [1993] AC 70 (HL).

[4] *Deutsche Morgan Grenfell v IRC* [2003] EWHC 1779 (Ch), [2003] 4 All ER 645 (first instance), [2005] EWCA Civ 78, (2006) Ch 243 (CA) and [2006] UKHL 49, [2007] 1 AC 558 (HL). The case has been noted at: A Burrows, 'Restitution in Respect of Mistakenly Paid Tax' (2005) 121 *Law Quarterly Review* 540; G Virgo, '*Deutsche Morgan Grenfell*: the Right to Restitution of Tax Paid by Mistake Rejected' [2005] *British Tax Review* 281; R Stevens, 'Justified Enrichment' (2005) 5 *Oxford University Commonwealth Law Journal* 141; and R Williams, 'The Beginnings of a Public Law of Unjust Enrichment?' (2005) 16 *King's College Law Journal* 194. It is questionable whether *Deutsche Morgan Grenfell* does indeed belong in this category, but the presence or absence of a mistake on the facts of this case will be discussed further below.

[5] *Woolwich* (n 3).

[6] *Auckland Harbour Board v The King* [1924] AC 318 (PC).

[7] It should be noted that in cases (2)(b) (failure of consideration for ultra vires), (3) (mistake as to vires) and (5) (dual event claims) it is assumed for the moment that the claimant in unjust enrichment is also to be responsible for challenging the legality of the public body's actions. Situations in which this is not the case will be discussed below.

he, she or it does by proving that a public law event has occurred (public law, the key to this possibility, having been mistranslated in the past as transactional inequality, incapacity and so on).

In between (1) and (5) lie all the other examples in the list. The key distinguishing feature between situations (1) and (5) is the presence or absence of a public law event. It will be noted, however, that situations (2), (3) and (4) (failure of consideration, mistake of law and fact) also have the potential to contain a public law event, just like situation (5). Not all the failure of consideration cases in situation (2) do so, but it is relatively easy to distinguish between situations in which the consideration has failed for purely practical reasons (2)(a) and those in which there was an event in public law, for example where the consideration has failed because the transaction itself was beyond the powers of the public body (2)(b). Indeed, situation (2)(a), the purely practical context, could in fact be the cause of action used in the first, 'paperclip' situation (1). Situation (2)(b) (ultra vires contract terminated), on the other hand, like situations (3) and (4), also contains a public law event, albeit that this is in the background to the claim so that in each case the enrichment, the expense, the lack of defences and the unjust factor are all made out within the private law framework.

The proposal here is that instead all such situations (2)(b), (3) and (4), should be subsumed into category (5) so that the reason for restitution in all those cases is provided by the public law unjust factor. To do so is not to draw a difficult and arbitrary distinction between public and private aspects of unjust enrichment, it is simply to recognise within unjust enrichment the existence of another sphere of law which has been functioning separately for years. There are several reasons for doing this.

The Advantages of the Public Law Reason for Restitution over the Private Law Unjust Factors

First, as has already been suggested in chapter three, this is more desirable in the sense that claims by and against public bodies can thus be brought together and in each case the dual public and private nature of the claim can be addressed directly. Second, as was also seen in chapter three, it is in addition more straightforward in many cases to allow recovery on the basis of the public law illegality itself, rather than requiring the claimant to show a failure of consideration, or mistake, especially when, for example, the existence of a mistake is not wholly uncontroversial,[8] or there are other difficulties involved in classifying such a hybrid claim under one of these purely private headings.[9]

[8] See ch 3, text following n 163.

[9] See ch 2, pp 58 onwards.

However, the argument here is more than just a negative assertion that where more than one unjust factor *is* available the public law reason for restitution is coincidentally more straightforward in pragmatic terms than the private law reasons for restitution. The point is that only by regarding public law as the reason for restitution does the law gain full access to that crucial event in a manner which allows it to take the truly hybrid approach such claims require. If the action is brought on the basis of mistake or failure of consideration, the public law event may be equally crucial to the claim, but the court will be prevented from seeing the case as anything more than purely private and this is bound in turn to lead to private law mistranslations of concepts, or to the separation of cases which actually entail similar policy concerns in precisely the manner seen in the previous two chapters. It is no coincidence that a round peg fits in a round hole better than does a square peg; the public law unjust factor avoids the problems associated with the private law unjust factors for the simple reason that only it deals with the true reason for restitution. Private law unjust factors may provide *a* reason for restitution, but as Meier puts it, in most cases they simply end up mirroring the underlying reasons why the transaction was invalid in the first place.[10] Thus *even if* the claimant can frame the action in terms of a private law unjust factor, if the case involves a public law ultra vires event this should take precedence, and only the public law reason for restitution should be used. Certainly this should be the case when the alternative private law reason for restitution rests directly on the public law event (for example, where the ultra vires nature of a contract constitutes a failure of consideration or the subject of a mistake) but it is even arguable that this should be the case when the connection is more remote. For example, let us take the idea suggested above, that a tax is created which will charge companies money based on the number of red-haired employees they have.[11] Were a company to believe that it employs some red-haired people when in fact it does not, receipt by the taxing authorities of the resulting payment would be beyond its powers on two fronts: first because as a matter of fact no tax was due even if the rules are applied on their own terms[12] and second because of the patent invalidity of those rules in the first place. The former argument could alternatively be heard as an issue of mistake, but the latter could not. However, if the mistake ground were to be used, neither of the two forms of ultra vires receipt would come to light, whereas both forms would become evident if this was the focus of the investigation. If there is a public law ultra vires event of this nature, it is surely in the public interest that this be discovered as soon as possible and thus it is arguable that even here the company should have to use the public law unjust factor in preference to its alternative ground of mistake. This would also make operation of the hierarchy simpler:

[10] S Meier, 'Restitution after Executed Void Contracts' in P Birks and F Rose (eds), *Lessons of the Swaps Litigation* (London, Mansfield Press, 2000).

[11] The example is obviously taken from Warrington LJ's example in *Short v Poole Corp* [1926] Ch 66 (CA) 90–91, of a teacher dismissed for having red hair, famously cited by Lord Greene MR in *Associated Provincial Picture Houses Ltd v Wednesbury Corp* [1948] 1 KB 223 (CA) 229.

[12] See above p 71.

wherever the receipt or payment of money by a public body is ultra vires as a matter of public law, the reason for restitution of the money should be the existence of that ultra vires event. Of course, there may well be cases like the example just given where in any event the company would presumably not choose only to reclaim a few counts of tax if it had the option of challenging its liability to pay any of it. But there will also be cases in which the hierarchy proposed does not operate to the claimant's advantage.

Reasons for Restitution and Time Limits: Is a Hierarchy Possible?

In some cases,[13] the claimant may have a very good reason for trying to use the ground of mistake in preference to the public law reason for restitution. The Limitation Act 1980 does not clearly set out limitation periods for unjust enrichment actions.[14] Such cases are taken, therefore, to fall within the provisions for contract in section 5. This means that claims in unjust enrichment must be brought within six years from the date on which the defendant became unjustly enriched. However, according to section 32(1)(c), where 'the action is for relief from the consequences of a mistake', the time will not begin to run until 'the plaintiff has discovered . . . the mistake . . . or could with reasonable diligence have discovered it', and it was confirmed in *Kleinwort Benson Ltd v Lincoln CC* that this applied to the recovery of money paid by mistake of law.[15] Recently, a debate has arisen over whether it is *only* in such cases, where the mistake is the basis of the claim, that the 32(1)(c) extension will apply, or whether, as Edelman argues, it can apply in any case where the relief is *from the consequences of a mistake,* whether or not that mistake is itself the basis of the claim.[16] Obviously, if Edelman's argument is correct,

[13] The number of such cases will be fewer given the recent changes to the available time limits, see text at n 170 below, and p 134.

[14] For a detailed discussion of limitation periods in relation to unjust enrichment actions, see: F Rose, 'Lapse of Time: Limitation' in P Birks and F Rose (eds), *Lessons of the Swaps Litigation* (London, Mansfield Press, 2000) and P Birks, 'Private Law' in P Birks and F Rose (eds), *Lessons of the Swaps Litigation* (London, Mansfield Press, 2000) 41.

[15] *Kleinwort Benson Ltd v Lincoln CC* [1999] 2 AC 349 (HL). Again, the cause of action pleaded is in fact money had and received, a vehicle for unjust enrichment reasoning.

[16] In *Deutsche Morgan Grenfell* (n 4), Park J (first instance) and the CA assumed that to take advantage of s 32(1)(c), mistake had to be 'an essential ingredient of the cause of action', as had been stated to be the case by Pearson J in *Phillips-Higgins v Harper* [1954] 1 QB 411 (CA) 419. In the HL, this view was also assumed by the majority (and was expressly stated by Lord Scott at [91]–[92]). However, Lord Hoffmann held that an action could be described as being 'for relief from the consequences of a mistake' even if a mistake was not an essential element of the cause of action 'but merely one example of a case which falls within a more general principle': [8] and [22]. Similarly, Lord Walker found the views of Edelman and Burrows 'persuasive' and felt that a wider view should be taken of the section: J Edelman, 'Limitation Periods and the Theory of Unjust Enrichment' (2005) 68 *MLR* 848; and Burrows, 'Restitution in Respect of Mistakenly Paid Tax' (n 4). On this wider view, s 32 would apply equally to cases brought on the basis of the public law unjust factor as long as the claimant had in fact

then one, perhaps even the most, important objection to the proposed hierarchy is immediately removed, and thus the hierarchy might well then come about naturally on the basis that the public law reason for restitution would just be a simpler route to recovery than having to prove the same ultra vires event *plus* mistake, failure of consideration etc in any given case. However, the law currently adopts the opposite view,[17] and since this is also the approach which causes the most difficulties for the hierarchy proposed here, let us assume that this is correct and proceed on the basis that a claimant could be outside the six year limitation period applicable to the public law unjust factor, but nevertheless able to bring a claim by relying on the ground of mistake as to vires. This is possible even when the same party is responsible both for challenging the validity of the payment and for bringing the action in unjust enrichment, but it is even more likely to arise where an application for judicial review brought by Party A is successful and Party B wishes to rely on this decision to reclaim the money it paid more than six years ago. Indeed, as has already been seen (and will be seen again below when possible defences to the claims are discussed)[18] one of the most important concerns in this area is the possibility that by establishing the public law event once, the first claimant will open the 'floodgates' to a host of other claimants basing themselves, apparently, on only the private law event of unjust enrichment, as was the case in *Kleinwort Benson v Lincoln* itself (with Kleinwort relying on the *Hazell v Hammersmith* decision[19]). This was also an issue of great concern in the more recent case of *Deutsche Morgan Grenfell*,[20] where one of the key questions was whether Deutsche Morgan Grenfell should be allowed to rely on a decision of the European Court of Justice (ECJ) to evade the usual time limits in order to recover money it had paid more than six years previously.[21] Consideration of *Deutsche Morgan Grenfell* is therefore vital in making the case for the hierarchy proposed here.

Deutsche Morgan Grenfell v IRC

The Facts

Deutsche Morgan Grenfell (DMG) had paid tax to the Commissioners of Inland Revenue (IRC) in 1993, 1995 and 1996, in the manner required by the English rules. The rules were that companies whose parent was resident in England, as well as companies whose parent was not, had to pay Advanced Corporation Tax (ACT)[22]

made a mistake as well. In terms of the coherence of the s 32 rules, this may well be desirable, but it will be argued in ch 5 that in any case a specific time limit must be chosen for the public law unjust factor which will reflect both the public and private aspects of the issue.

[17] ibid.

[18] See ch 5.

[19] *Hazell v Hammersmith and Fulham LBC* [1992] 2 AC 1 (HL).

[20] *Deutsche Morgan Grenfell* (n 4).

[21] The first instance decision that the limits could be evaded was reversed by the CA and then reinstated by the HL: *Deutsche Morgan Grenfell* (n 4). See further below.

[22] ACT was subsequently abolished by the Finance Act 1988 s 31.

and Mainstream Corporation Tax (MCT).[23] The ACT was payable first, but could then be set off against the MCT paid later. Under the relevant legislation, two companies resident in the UK, one of which held at least 51% of the other could make a group income election. The result of such an election was that the subsidiary could choose not to pay ACT on dividends which it paid to its parent company. However, for companies whose parent was not resident in the UK, this election was not an option, so ACT was payable on all the distributions made by them to their parent companies. Overall, they paid no more than companies whose parent companies were resident in the UK, because the ACT they had paid was later offset against their MCT, but it did mean that in the meantime they had lost interest on the funds used to pay the ACT up front, when subsidiaries with parent companies resident in the UK would have been able to retain the money.

In 2001, two other companies that had suffered under these rules, Metallgesellschaft and Hoechst (M&H), brought a case claiming that the English rules were contrary to EC law. A preliminary reference was made to the ECJ under the procedure laid down in what is now Article 267 of the Treaty on the Functioning of the European Union (TFEU) (ex Art 234 EC) and, in another key landmark case which has since generated a plethora of further litigation,[24] the ECJ agreed that:

> [I]t is contrary to Article 52 [now Art 49 TFEU ex Art 43 EC] of the Treaty for the tax legislation of a Member State, such as that in issue in the main proceedings, to afford companies resident in that Member State the possibility of benefiting from a taxation regime allowing them to pay dividends to their parent company without having to pay advance corporation tax where their parent company is also resident in that Member State but to deny them that possibility where their parent company has its seat in another Member State.[25]

And that:

> [It] is contrary to Community law for a national court to refuse or reduce a claim brought before it by a resident subsidiary and its non-resident parent company for reimbursement or reparation of the financial loss which they have suffered as a consequence of the advance payment of corporation tax by the subsidiary, on the sole ground that they did not apply to the tax authorities in order to benefit from the taxation regime which would have exempted the subsidiary from making payments in advance and that they therefore did not make use of the legal remedies available to them to challenge the refusals of the tax authorities, by invoking the primacy and direct effect of the provisions of Community law, where upon any view national law denied resident subsidiaries and their non-resident parent companies the benefit of that taxation regime.[26]

DMG therefore wished to recover the money it had lost by paying the ACT up front.

It is thus clear that the discriminatory unavailability of the group income election was contrary to Article 49 TFEU (ex Art 43 EC), and the fact that the com-

[23] Income and Corporation Taxes Act 1988 (ICTA) s 14.
[24] As happened, for example, in *Hazell* (n 19) which led to the swaps litigation and *Woolwich* (n 3).
[25] Cases C-397/98 and C-410/98 *Metallgesellschaft and Hoechst v IRC* [2001] ECR I-1727 [76].
[26] ibid [107].

panies had not tried to make the impossible election or challenge its unavailability without paying the ACT did not block their claims. It is also clear that some form of 'remedy' for this unavailability of the election was required at national level in order to comply with the requirements of EC law.[27] This gives rise to various important questions: whether the money could be recovered on the basis of unjust enrichment at all, and if so, what should be the correct reason for restitution; or whether the money should instead be recovered as compensation for a loss.

Can the Money Be Recovered as Restitution for Unjust Enrichment at all? Or is Compensation for Loss the Only Route to Recovery?

It is true that none of the previous unjust enrichment authorities dealt with the precise question of loss of interest in this way as opposed to recovery of a principal sum. However, it is possible to draw some evidence from the dicta of Lord Goff and Lord Woolf in *Westdeutsche Landesbank Girozentrale v Islington LBC*[28] that the claim for interest should be seen as one based on unjust enrichment; that full restitution is not achieved unless the correct level of interest is paid. Alison Jones agrees with this view, citing *Harbutt's 'Plasticine' Ltd v Wayne Tank and Pump Co Ltd*[29] in support of her conclusion that interest is not only about compensating a claimant, but is also designed to strip the defendant of any unjust enrichment.[30] Certainly, although the independent source of the enrichment (such as payment of interest by a bank) may seem to cloud the issue, put this way both the 'enrichment' and 'at the expense of the plaintiff' requirements can be satisfied. These conclusions have since been confirmed by the decision of the House of Lords in *Sempra Metals Ltd v IRC*,[31] another case in the *Metallgesellschaft and Hoechst* line, which held that the measure of restitution was gain to the defendant rather than loss to the claimant.[32]

[27] On which see further p 237 onwards.

[28] *Westdeutsche Landesbank Girozentrale v Islington LBC* [1996] AC 669 (HL).

[29] *Harbutt's 'Plasticine' Ltd v Wayne Tank and Pump Co Ltd* [1970] 1 QB 447 (CA) 468.

[30] A Jones, *Restitution and European Community Law* (Oxford, Mansfield Press, 2000) 33. She also cites Mason and Carter in support of this proposition: K Mason and J Carter, *Restitution Law in Australia* (Sydney, Butterworths, 1995) 951 52.

[31] *Sempra Metals Ltd (formerly Metallgesellschaft Ltd) v Her Majesty's Commissioners of Inland Revenue and another* [2007] UKHL 34, [2008] 1 AC 561.

[32] Lord Hope, Lord Nicholls and Lord Walker held that it was the opportunity to turn the money to account during the period of the enrichment that passed from the claimants to the Revenue. Computation of the time value of the enrichment on the basis of simple interest would inevitably fall short of its true value, so the compounding of interest was the basis on which the restitutionary award due to C should be calculated. (See further ch 3 pp 44–49.) Where the actual benefit to the IRC was difficult to calculate resort would have to be had to a conventional rate of interest. Lord Mance and Lord Scott dissented on the basis that if any claim to restitution was to be recognised in relation to the use of money had and received, at common law or in equity, it had to refer to any actual benefit obtained by the recipient. In any case Lord Scott held, as he had earlier done in *Deutsche Morgan Grenfell*, that the correct claim was for compensation for state liability for breach of EC law, see further below. Lord Mance held that it would now be a step too far to reverse the common law approach to compound interest in respect of money had and received, and would have preferred to address the issue by revisiting the area of equity: ibid [235] and [236].

The more problematic question is whether the early payments of ACT (and thus the loss of interest) could also be regarded as undue, and thus unjust. Obviously the unavailability of the group income election, being a contravention of Article 49, was ultra vires the IRC. On the other hand, the ECJ's decision did not invalidate the whole ACT/MCT scheme and nor did it refer to the specific payments of ACT as being invalid. Indeed, in *Metallgesellschaft and Hoechst* the ECJ held that:

> It is important to bear in mind in this regard that what is contrary to Community law, in the disputes in the main proceedings, is not the levying of a tax in the United Kingdom on the payment of dividends by a subsidiary to its parent company but the fact that subsidiaries, resident in the United Kingdom, of parent companies having their seat in another Member State were required to pay that tax in advance whereas resident subsidiaries of resident parent companies were able to avoid that requirement.[33]

Again it reiterated that 'the breach of Community law arises, not from the payment of the tax itself but from its being levied prematurely'.[34] It could thus be argued that only the absence of the election was ultra vires the IRC. On that basis, once the election had not been made, for whatever reason, the ACT would remain payable. It was for this reason that when the issue reached the House of Lords, Lord Scott, drawing on the views of Stevens,[35] dissented from the majority decision,[36] a conclusion he reiterated in *Sempra Metals.*[37] Key to Lord Scott's decision was his finding that:

> The ECJ did not hold that subjecting resident subsidiaries of non-resident companies to the obligation of paying ACT was contrary to European law. What was unlawful was the discriminatory nature of the group income election provisions . . . The question is what effect this unlawful feature of the ACT tax regime should be held to have had on the obligation of subsidiaries, such as DMG, to pay ACT.[38]

For Lord Scott the answer to this question was that because

> the breach of Community law was the failure of the UK's ACT tax regime to provide for corporate groups with a parent company resident in a Member State other than the UK the same opportunity of postponing the payment of corporation tax by making a group income election as was available to domestic corporate groups . . . The unlawfulness of the tax regime identified by the ECJ lies not with the imposition of ACT but in the discriminatory nature of the group income election provisions.[39]

If instead the courts were to conclude that the ACT was unlawful 'then it would follow that every demand for ACT had been an ultra vires demand, that every payment of ACT had been paid under a mistake of law and that every payer of ACT

[33] *Metallgesellschaft and Hoechst* (n 25) [83].
[34] ibid [87].
[35] Stevens (n 4).
[36] *Deutsche Morgan Grenfell* (HL) (n 4).
[37] *Sempra Metals* (n 31).
[38] *Deutsche Morgan Grenfell* (HL) (n 4) [78].
[39] ibid [81]–[82].

should be entitled, subject to limitation defences, to a restitutionary remedy'.[40] Since 'there must be many domestic corporate groups which, for one reason or another, did not make a group income election and whose subsidiaries accordingly paid ACT in respect of dividends paid to their corporate shareholders'[41] this conclusion would lead to 'a remarkable state of affairs' in which such domestic corporate groups could recover the money on the basis of what Lord Scott called 'the *Woolwich* principle'. Thus, while Lord Scott agreed with the majority that 'English law does now recognise a restitutionary remedy for tax paid under mistake of law',[42] money would not be recoverable on this ground unless the mistake had also undermined the legal obligation which required the payment of the money.[43] He therefore concluded that DMG could not recover their payments of ACT on the basis of mistake because even if the mistake about the legality of denying the group income election had been a 'but for' cause of payment of the ACT, 'the ACT was paid because there was a legal obligation under a valid statutory provision for the money to be paid'.[44] Thus, if DMG were to recover at all, for Lord Scott it would have to be via a claim for compensation to recover the loss caused by the breach of EC law.[45] This would in turn mean that the extended time limit of section 32 of the Limitation Act 1980 would not be open to them, because mistake would not then be an essential element of their claim.[46]

In order to understand this point fully we should imagine three different companies.

Company A has its parent in the UK and is thus able to make an election if it wants to. It chooses for its own reasons not to do so and thus pays ACT. Under the ECJ's ruling, this receipt of ACT by the Revenue is perfectly intra vires, because the ECJ did not invalidate the whole scheme of elections, ACT and MCT.[47]

Company B is in the situation of DMG and M&H. It has its parent abroad and therefore cannot make the election, but would have preferred to do so and thus

40 ibid [81].
41 ibid.
42 ibid [83].
43 ibid [85].
44 ibid [89].
45 ibid.
46 ibid [91]. On the question of s 32 more broadly, see above n 16.
47 The system was held to be beyond the powers of the IRC in as much as it involved discrimination against companies in the situation of DMG and M&H, but Company A would still be unable to bring an action for two reasons. As a matter of public law, it is unlikely that Company A would have standing to challenge the rules which did it no harm. The first important decision on the sufficiency of interest test enacted in s 31(3) of the Supreme Court Act 1981 itself concerned a challenge to tax. The National Federation of Self-Employed and Small Businesses objected to a general tax amnesty granted by the IRC to casual workers on Fleet Street, in return for which the casuals would fill in returns for the last two years. Since the House of Lords ultimately found for the IRC even in this instance in which the claimants had some grounds for feeling at least that they had been treated unequally, it seems unlikely that standing would be granted to Company A: *R v IRC, ex p National Federation of Self-Employed and Small Businesses Ltd* [1982] AC 617 (HL). On the rules of standing generally, see also: Craig (n 1) ch 24, especially 24-036. Even if it did have standing, the receipt of ACT *from Company A* was not ultra vires because it was not the result of the unlawful discrimination, and thus it could not be recovered in an action for unjust enrichment.

does not want to pay ACT. Lord Scott's view is that since the demand for and receipt of the ACT was not ultra vires in the case of Company A, it cannot be ultra vires in the case of Company B either. With respect to Lord Scott, however, it is submitted that this does not follow and that, unlike Company A, this time the collection of the ACT is invalid and ultra vires as a matter of EU law. It is true that, as Stevens notes,[48] the ECJ did not 'say that the tax was not due'. He is also right to point out that the decision on whether UK legislation is compatible with EU law is one for the national courts.[49] However, the ECJ made it clear that what was contrary to Community law was the fact that only domestically-resident companies could '*benefit*' from the ACT/MCT system,[50] and the ability to make the group income election is of no 'benefit' at all to the company without the resulting ability to defer payments of ACT. So the ECJ's references to 'benefits' must surely refer not only to the ability to make the election but also to the ability to avoid paying the tax until later as a result of that election. It was this whole, combined process of 'affording' only resident companies 'the possibility of benefiting' that was invalid as a matter of EC law. Payment of ACT by a company which could not have made the election thus becomes invalid precisely because that company, contrary to EC law, has had no option to act differently, and therefore it does follow that because the denial of an election was unlawful, any ACT paid as a result was not due.

As ever, it is important to recognise the public law nature of this finding of ultra vires, which explains why it may have a broader scope than, for example, the setting aside of a transaction in purely private law, to which Lord Scott kept comparing it. Thus, Lord Scott argued that it would not be enough for the buyer of a horse to assert that but for his mistake about the horse's breeding he would not have entered into the contract to buy it and so would not have paid the money.[51] This may well be the case, but there is nothing to suggest that what is necessary for the setting aside of a contract in private law must be the same as what is necessary for a finding that something was beyond the powers of a public body, nor that the extent of those two invalidities must be the same.[52] Indeed, when the different policy considerations underlying the two sets of rules are considered, it would not be wholly surprising to find that the rules for setting aside contracts were the more stringent of the two. When it is recalled that, in some instances, public actions may be rendered ultra vires even though the illegality tainting the action has had no causative effect whatsoever,[53] the suggestion that an illegality which *has* had such a

[48] Stevens (n 4) 143.

[49] See further ch 8 below.

[50] Above: ns 25 and 26.

[51] *Deutsche Morgan Grenfell* (HL) (n 4) [84].

[52] The same objection can be made to the argument of R Stevens, 'Is there a Law of Unjust Enrichment'? in S Degeling and J Edelman (eds), *Unjust Enrichment in Commercial Law* (Sydney, Lawbook Co, 2008).

[53] eg: *Dimes v The Proprietors of the Grand Junction Canal* (1852) 3 HLC 759 (HL), 10 ER 301. In that case, Lord Campbell (at 793, 315) held: 'No-one can suppose that Lord Cottenham could be, in the remotest degree, influenced by the interests that he had in this concern'. Nevertheless, the fact that Lord Cottenham held shares in the respondent company meant that his decision on a case involving that company had to be set aside on grounds of financial interest and thus bias.

causative effect may have rendered a further action (here the charging of ACT) invalid, does not seem particularly strange. Indeed, in *Fleming (trading as Bodycraft) and Condé Nast Publications v Revenue and Customs Commissioners*,[54] the House of Lords, including Lord Scott himself, unanimously held that the invalidity of the relevant legislation in that case left taxpayers with an 'accrued right' even if they would not have taken advantage of it had it been available to them, let alone if, like Company B, they would have done so. Lord Neuberger's view was that the legislation in question was intended to be for the benefit of anyone who *could* take advantage of it, whether or not they in fact did so.[55] It is submitted that this is perfectly in keeping with the fact that what was being discussed was the extent, under EC law, of the Customs Commissioners' powers in public law to enact rules. Indeed, as will be seen in the discussion of Company C below, the question is not whether the public law invalidity is wide enough to cover Company B, but whether it is so wide that it covers Company C as well. To ask whether receipt of a tax can be set aside as if it were a transaction in private law is therefore, with respect, neither here nor there. The real question is whether receipt of the ACT was beyond the powers of the taxing authorities and, for the reasons given here, it was.

Stevens' concern is that this is a 'radical conclusion as it means that the effect of European Community Law is not merely to render legislation of the United Kingdom unlawful but also that it is, to an extent, a nullity'.[56] However, this is not quite the way in which EU and national law interrelate. In *Ministero Delle Finanze v IN.CO.GE.'90 Srl*,[57] the ECJ rejected the Commission's argument that a national rule imposing unlawful charges should be treated as invalid rather than inapplicable. There is therefore no question of a decision of the ECJ making national law a nullity; all it can ever do is to identify a potential incompatibility. This is then applied to the facts of the case by the national court, and if the incompatibility is found by that court to exist on the facts, it renders the national law inapplicable during that country's membership of the EU.[58] Here, given that the *denial of the benefit* of the ACT/MCT scheme was incompatible with EC law, the form of this denial (namely charging companies the ACT upfront following a refusal of the group income election option) was, as a matter of UK law ultra vires the Revenue on the basis that it contravened the will of Parliament as expressed in the European Communities Act 1972.[59]

[54] *Fleming (trading as Bodycraft) and Condé Nast Publications v Revenue and Customs Commissioners* [2008] UKHL 2, [2008] 1 WLR 195. For further discussion of the case see below p 84.

[55] ibid [97].

[56] Stevens (n 4) 144.

[57] Cases C-10-22/97 *Ministero Delle Finanze v IN.CO.GE.'90 Srl* [1998] ECR I-6307 [28], see further ch 8.

[58] Case 106/77 *Amminstrazione delle Finanze dello Stato v Simmenthal SpA* [1978] ECR 629 [17]. For a recent domestic application of this reasoning, see: the majority of the HL in *Fleming and Condé Nast* (n 54).

[59] *Factortame Ltd v Secretary of State for Transport (No 2)* [1991] 1 AC 603 (HL); *Equal Opportunities Commission v Secretary of State for Employment* [1995] 1 AC 1 (HL). The precise requirements of EU law will be discussed in more detail in chs 7 and 8.

The more difficult question, as noted above, is precisely *how* broad the scope of this finding of illegality should be. It is relatively easy to argue that, as in the case of DMG itself (ie Company B) the receipt of ACT was ultra vires where the company had wanted instead to make a group income election and was denied the ability to do so in breach of EC law. The harder case concerns Company C. This company has its parent abroad and so would not have been able to make the election, like Company B, but it would in any event have chosen not to do so, like Company A. Stevens' arguments imply that if we are to regard the ACT as undue in the case of Company B, we must also regard it as undue in the case of Company C.[60]

If the invalidity only extends to the denial of the election then it is not ultra vires the Revenue to receive money from a company which would not have made the election anyway because the payment is nothing to do with the ultra vires refusal of the election. Should the company nevertheless be allowed to use the fortuitous application of EU law to escape from what is essentially a bad bargain with the Revenue in such a case? There are good reasons why recovery in such cases should not be allowed; as Henderson J puts it in *Europcar UK Ltd v The Commissioners for HM Revenue and Customs*,[61] another of the *Metallgesellschaft & Hoechst*[62] progeny, 'if the election would not have been made, even if it was available, the claimant would have nothing to complain about'.[63] The question is therefore whether recovery is indeed automatic in the case of Company C on the argument made here. From the point of view of the private law elements of the claim, it is difficult to argue that the ultra vires denial of the group income election *caused* Company C's subsequent payment of ACT as the unjust enrichment elements of the hybrid claim would presumably require.[64]

As far as the reach of the public law through the public law unjust factor is concerned, no answer to this question was given by the ECJ and it must therefore turn on the extent of the invalidity as a matter of national public law. It may be the case that any demand for ACT which follows a denial of the group income election is ultra vires, but this will not necessarily be so. Although, as noted above, in some

[60] Stevens (n 4) 145. He does not refer specifically to the concepts of Companies A, B and C which I have developed here for the purposes of setting out the problem.

[61] *Europcar UK Ltd v The Commissioners for HM Revenue and Customs* [2008] EWHC 1363 (Ch), [2008] STC 2751 [34].

[62] *Metallgesellschaft and Hoechst* (n 25).

[63] *Europcar* (n 61) [34].

[64] eg, if the claimant intended the IRC to have the money in any event it could not be recovered. Some evidence for this may come from *Norwich CC v Stringer* (2001) 33 HLR 15 (CA). In this case a landlord continued to receive housing benefit from the local council after the tenant for whom it was paid had moved out. He accepted liability to repay the £64 benefit acquired after he realised the tenant had moved but the Council brought County Court proceedings to recover the remainder of the overpaid benefit, whereupon Mr Stringer counterclaimed for return of the £64. The Council's claim was dismissed because they had not followed the procedure for reclaiming the money contained in Part VIII of the Housing Benefits (General) Regulations 1987, but Mr Stringer's counterclaim was also dismissed on the basis that his payment of the £64 was not covered by the *Woolwich* principle. In other words, any illegality tainting the claim for the remainder of the money had not caused his repayment of the £64 because he had repaid that anyway on the basis that it was not due.

cases a public body's action can be set aside even when its ultra vires nature had no practical effect on the outcome,[65] conversely not all technical invalidities in a public body's actions will lead to the decision being overturned if the court considers that this would be inappropriate,[66] and in particular, a flaw in the public body's decision will not always be regarded as materially vitiating that decision if it would have made no difference to the outcome of the case.[67] Obviously the situation is slightly different where the question is not what effect the flaw had on the reasoning of the public body, but rather what effect it had on the reasoning of the taxpayer. Nevertheless, the materiality cases suggest that by analogy the ultra vires refusal of the election may not necessarily have tainted the collection of ACT from a non-elector like Company C. A second, interconnected, circumstance in which the decision will not be struck down occurs where there has been no 'prejudice' as a result of the public law wrong[68] and here again it is difficult to see what prejudice Company C might have suffered. Finally, and perhaps most relevantly, there are certain circumstances in which a party can waive its rights, for example, to a fair hearing. Any such waiver 'must be clear and unequivocal and made with full knowledge of all of the facts relevant to the decision whether to waive or not'.[69] Of course the decision made by Company C would have to comply with this requirement, but as long as it had been aware of the discrimination and had made the decision to pay ACT purely for its own reasons, the requirement would presumably be met. Thus, taking these three sets of rules together, it is at least possible to argue by analogy that the receipt of ACT from Company C would not be tainted with the ultra vires refusal of the election to that company and thus it would not be possible to argue that there had been a public law event capable of providing the reason for restitution in that case.

[65] *Dimes* (n 53).

[66] For other, different, reasons why recovery may be denied, see the decision of *ex p AMA* [1993] COD 54.

[67] See, for example: *R v Independent Television Commission, ex p TSW Broadcasting Ltd* [1994] 2 LRC 414 (HL); *R v Independent Television Commission, ex p Virgin Television Ltd* [1996] EMLR 318 (DC); *West Coast Wind Farms Ltd v Secretary of State for the Environment* [1996] Env LR 29 (QB); *R (Nadesu) v Secretary of State for the Home Dept* [2003] EWHC 2039 (QB Admin); *R v Epsom Justices, ex p Gibbons* [1984] QB 574 (DC); *R v Secretary of State for Education, ex p Southwark LBC* [1995] ELR 308 (QB); *Dobie v Burns International Security Services (UK) Ltd* [1985] 1 WLR 43 (CA); and *A v Kirklees MBC* [2001] EWCA Civ 582, [2001] ELR 657.

[68] *R v Aston University Senate, ex p Roffey* [1969] 2 QB 538 (DC); *R (Ghadami) v Harlow DC* [2004] EWHC 1883, [2005] BLGR 24 (QB Admin); *R v Joint Higher Committee on Surgical Training, ex p Milner* (1995) 7 Admin LR 454 (QB); *R v Panel on Takeovers and Mergers, ex p Guinness plc* [1990] 1 QB 146 (CA); *R v Liverpool Magistrates Court, ex p Ansen* [1998] 1 All ER 692 (DC); and *R v Chief Constable of South Wales, ex p Merrick* [1994] 1 WLR 663 (QB).

[69] *R v Secretary of State for the Home Dept, ex p Fayed* [2001] Imm AR 134 (CA) [84]. It should also be noted that not all rights can be waived in this manner, see also: H Wade and C Forsyth, *Administrative Law*, 9th edn (Oxford, Oxford University Press, 2004) 239–42. However, in many of the cases cited in this passage where waiver is not permitted, this may equally have been because it did not fulfil the *Fayed* requirements outlined in the quote above. It is therefore difficult in some instances to tell whether the rejection of waiver was occurring in principle or simply on the facts of the case. It is also worth noting the distinction Craig draws between waiver of the illegality and waiver of a remedy for the illegality, the latter being acceptable even when the former is not: Craig (n 1) 25-010.

On the other hand, support for the opposite point of view comes from the decision of the House of Lords in *Fleming and Condé Nast*.[70] This case concerned the introduction, without any transitional period, of a retrospective time limit for the reclaiming of VAT in a manner which was contrary to EC law,[71] and the Customs Commissioners argued that only those who could and would have made claims during a transitional period had one been available should be entitled to complain that it was not. However, as noted above, this argument was unanimously rejected by their Lordships,[72] Lord Neuberger holding that it was 'wrong in principle and inconvenient in practice',[73] while Lord Walker similarly held that

> it would be contrary to legal certainty and administratively unworkable, for the extent of disapplication to depend not only on the duration of the transitional period but also on an hypothetical question to be answered by reference to the circumstances and states of mind of the particular taxpayers.[74]

Following this logic, therefore, Company C would also be entitled to bring a claim on the basis that it would be 'unworkable' to try to distinguish between Companies B and C on the facts of a given case.

The conclusion must therefore be that the Company C dilemma simply provides us with yet another example of something which may be novel to private lawyers, but which is wholly familiar to the public law which ought also to be operating in this context, and which already contains, as outlined above, a set of tools to deal with this problem. On the one hand, allowing Company C to recover provides a more efficient result in the sense that if Company B would have made the election and therefore will have a good claim at a future point[75] it is better that the Revenue knows this as soon as possible, even if the case is brought by Company C. Otherwise the Revenue will continue to act in an ultra vires manner, opening up the possibility of further challenges, in the period before Company B claims. Also, as noted above, in principle, the whole point of imposing limits on the powers of public authorities is that correct application of the relevant rules (whether they concern time limits or the rules for levying tax in the first place) is 'intended to be for the benefit of anyone who could take advantage' of them,[76] whether or not they in fact do so, or, more broadly, whether or not the invalidity makes a practical difference to the outcome of the case.[77] However, in public law, these principles are also counterbalanced by the doctrines such as materiality and waiver discussed above. Again, therefore, it is regrettable that private lawyers are left reinventing the public law wheel, when an understanding that these cases involve both public and

[70] *Fleming and Condé Nast* (above n 54).

[71] For further details of the relevant EU law see ch 8.

[72] Lord Hope, Lord Carswell, Lord Neuberger, Lord Walker *and* Lord Scott (on other matters and in the result as a whole Lord Walker dissented from the reasoning of the majority).

[73] *Fleming and Condé Nast* (n 54) [96].

[74] ibid [64].

[75] Within the requisite time limit.

[76] *Fleming and Condé Nast* (n 54) [97] (Lord Neuberger).

[77] *Dimes* (n 53). See also: n 67 above.

private law would have allowed them to draw on the experience of a sphere of law already used to having to balance such competing concerns. Taking a hybrid approach which involved the use of public law in such cases would not avoid the dilemma, but it would provide a well established set of tools for resolving it and would allow the courts to develop their reasoning on the extent of public law invalidity in a manner which would increase both understanding and certainty in future cases.

Of course, as will be discussed further below, it may be necessary for the causal link between the ultra vires breach of EU law and the loss suffered by the claimant to be closer in the case of an unjust enrichment action than it need be for a *Francovich* and *Brasserie/Factortame III*[78] claim for state liability in damages of the kind favoured by Stevens and Lord Scott.[79] But however strict the causation rules for unjust enrichment claims may be, Company B and DMG can be regarded as falling within them, first for the reasons given above and second because there is nothing in the more recent case law on this question to suggest otherwise.[80]

Conversely, while on the question of causation an action in state liability for damages may be slightly wider than a cause of action in unjust enrichment, an action for damages still requires the existence of an ultra vires event, and it should be borne in mind that in addition, a *Francovich* and *Brasserie/Factortame III* action also requires the ultra vires action to have been a sufficiently serious breach of EU law which amounts to a manifest and grave disregard of the limits of the member state's discretion.[81] In the case of *Deutsche Morgan Grenfell* itself this could be made out fairly readily given the overt nature of the discrimination, but this need not always be the case. Indeed, in *Test Claimants in the FII Group Litigation v Commissioners of the Inland Revenue*[82] (*FII*) AG Geelhoed pointed out that not

[78] Cases C-6/90 and C-9/90 *Francovich & Bonifaci v Italy* [1991] ECR I-5357 and Cases C-46/93 and C-48/93 *Brasserie du Pêcheur SA v Federal Republic of Germany and R v Secretary of State for Transport, ex p Factortame* [1996] ECR I-1029. See further ch 8.

[79] It will be noted below, pp 110–18 that the ECJ appears to have laid down a test of 'inevitability' or at least 'directness' as the test for causation for actions in unjust enrichment as a matter of EU law. The narrowness of this particular test will be questioned, but whatever test is ultimately chosen, it is nevertheless likely that there will be some instances of loss which could be recovered via an action in state liability in damages which could not be recovered via a cause of action in unjust enrichment (such as, for example, loss caused by a drop in sales following the passing on of an unlawful tax by incorporating it in the purchase price of a product). See further ch 5 p 155.

[80] The case law in question is of course the decision in Case C-446/04 *Test Claimants in the FII Group Litigation v Commissioners of the Inland Revenue* [2006] ECR I-11753. 'FII' stands for 'Franked Investment Income'. Nothing in that decision or the subsequent decision of Henderson J in *Test Claimants in the FII Group Litigation v The Commissioners for Her Majesty's Revenue & Customs* [2008] EWHC 2893, [2008] STI 2726 suggested that the DMG's claim could not be regarded as a claim in unjust enrichment. Indeed, while it is clear that there are some cases in which the damages action will cover cases not covered by an action for restitution for unjust enrichment, nevertheless, the *FII* case concerned choices actually made by the applicants and thus it is the converse of the situations involving Companies B (ie DMG themselves) and C, where the point is that no choice could be made. In this latter instance the amounts claimed can be obtained, if at all, through an action in unjust enrichment as explained above and this would be considered preferable on the reasoning of both the AG and ECJ.

[81] *Brasserie/Factortame III* (n 78) [55]. See also the decision of Henderson J, ibid [243].

[82] *FII* (EC) (n 80).

only could actions in unjust enrichment arise in circumstances where the 'sufficiently serious breach' condition would not be fulfilled, but also, for precisely this reason, the Member State's obligation to provide an effective remedy for a breach of EU law might require it to provide 'reimbursement' instead.[83] It therefore appears that to adopt the solutions proposed by Stevens and Lord Scott would be to make life potentially harder for claimants such as DMG, with no corresponding benefits either to them or to the clarity of the law in general. This does not mean that the claim *cannot* be classified as a wrong, merely that it need not be; that, following the *FII* decision, classification as a wrong and exclusion of the unjust enrichment cause of action might be a breach of the EU principle of effectiveness, and that conversely the claim can, without undue danger, be more simply classified as an unjust enrichment. And, it should not be forgotten that it was the unjust enrichment conception of the facts that was preferred by AG Fennelly in *Metallgesellschaft and Hoechst*, the ECJ decision which gave rise, in the first place, to the issue in *Deutsche Morgan Grenfell* and other related litigation.[84] Any problems, therefore, arise not from the adoption of unjust enrichment as opposed to a cause of action based on wrongdoing. The problem, as usual, arises from a failure to understand that the approach to the claims must be a hybrid one, incorporating both public and private law. Indeed, once it is thus assumed that, at least on the facts of *Deutsche Morgan Grenfell* itself (Company B), the ACT can be regarded as ultra vires and undue, it then becomes possible to address this key question directly; the choice of unjust factor to be used for the claim and in particular the relationship between the public law reason for restitution and the private law concept of mistake.

The Reason for Restitution and the Decision of Park J at First Instance

At first instance, Park J's conclusions directly contradicted the possibility of the public law reason for restitution finding a place at the top of the hierarchy, relying on Lord Goff's dicta in *Kleinwort Benson v Lincoln*[85] to hold that there was no principle forbidding the recovery of overpaid taxes on the basis of mistake. This was particularly surprising given that in 1995 DMG had learned that M&H were pursuing their claim before the ECJ. It was therefore at least arguable that from 1995 onwards DMG knew that the tax might infringe EC law requirements and hence that it was no longer mistaken about the law when it made its third payment in 1996. Of course whether DMG was mistaken or not depends on whether the mistake concerned the lawfulness of denying the election or the lawfulness of the subsequent collection of ACT. Park J's view was that the claimant's mistake concerned the unavailability of the election, which meant that the claimant could

[83] ibid [134] (AG Geelhoed). Although the ECJ was not so explicit, it also clearly regarded the action for reimbursement as preferable to the *Francovich* action (n 78), since it only turned to consider the latter for circumstances where it had established that the former was not available: [207]–[208].

[84] See further below, ch 8.

[85] *Deutsche Morgan Grenfell* (first instance) (n 4) and *Kleinwort Benson v Lincoln* (n 15).

assert that it would not have paid ACT but for this mistake. However, if this is so then it might be thought difficult to argue, contrary to the protests of DMG's Head of Taxation, that this mistake was not affected by knowledge of M&H's action. The precise operation of such mistakes will be discussed in further detail below,[86] but it will be noted there that it is not entirely clear how far a claim grounded on mistake should be undermined by the fact that the claimant suspected the true state of affairs. Academic opinion on the matter is divided,[87] but it is at least arguable that on the facts DMG's knowledge was too great to allow it to recover for mistake if the relevant mistake does indeed concern the unavailability of the group income election. It is always difficult to apply to large companies concepts more usually applied to individuals[88] and it may therefore be that Park J was simply avoiding in a pragmatic way the difficulties of establishing whether DMG could have been said to be 'mistaken' in the usual sense of the word. On the other hand, DMG issued its claim form after the delivery of the Advocate General's opinion, which points to discovery at that point if not sooner. Also, Park J sought to shore up his decision by pointing to the fact that even if DMG had tried to take the appropriate action the Revenue would have rejected this attempt and DMG *would still have been liable to pay the tax* according to the IRC.[89] If DMG's inaction is simply evidence of their mistake then it is hard to see why the Revenue's action is relevant. The IRC's continued mistake would hardly make up for an action indicating a lack of mistake on the part of DMG.[90]

The key to Park J's decision to allow recovery must therefore be found instead in his conclusion that the ACT was, as a matter of law, payable when DMG paid it.[91] Thus for Park J, DMG's claim was not affected by DMG's knowledge of the *Metallgesellschaft and Hoechst* claim because by the time it discovered its mistake on the election it was already locked into a system which later led to a *valid* ACT payment. If the above conclusion that the ECJ invalidated receipt of the ACT, as well as the unavailability of the group income election is accepted, however, Park

[86] p 94 onwards.

[87] In *Barclays Bank v Simms*, Robert Goff J also held that the claim may fail where 'the payer intends that the payee shall have the money at all events, whether the fact be true or false, or is deemed in law so to intend': *Barclays Bank Ltd v WJ Simms Son and Cooke (Southern) Ltd* [1980] QB 677 (QB) 695. In *Maskell v Horner* [1915] 3 KB 106 (CA) the claimant could not recover because he had paid to avoid litigation despite being in doubt as to his liability to pay. In *Kleinwort Benson v Lincoln*, Lord Hope held that: 'A state of doubt is different from that of mistake. A person who pays when in doubt takes the risk that he may be wrong': *Kleinwort Benson v Lincoln* (n 15) 410. These dicta have more recently been applied in *Brennan v Bolt Burdon (a firm)* [2004] EWCA Civ 1017, [2005] QB 303. Burrows believes that the claim should only fail if the claimant thinks the facts are *probably* as they are in truth: A Burrows, *The Law of Restitution* (London, Butterworths, 2002) 140, whereas Virgo would exclude recovery whenever the claimant was aware that there was a possibility that he or she was mistaken: G Virgo, *The Principles of the Law of Restitution*, 2nd edn (Oxford, Oxford University Press, 2006) 163. See further ch 3 above, pp 64–67.

[88] See further: S Hedley, 'Tax Wrongly Paid—Basis of Recovery—Limitation' (commenting on the Court of Appeal decision in *DMG*) [2005) 64 *Cambridge Law Journal* 296.

[89] *Deutsche Morgan Grenfell* (first instance) (n 4) [28].

[90] Indeed, in circumstances very similar to these the HL in *Woolwich* had specifically rejected the application of mistake: *Woolwich* (n 3).

[91] *Deutsche Morgan Grenfell* (CA) (n 4) [21], [22] and [27].

J's reasoning will not work. On the other hand, since the precise status of the ACT collection was not wholly clear, DMG could possibly be said to have remained mistaken about that, even after discovery of the *Metallgesellschaft and Hoechst* action.

The Reason for Restitution and the Decision of the Court of Appeal

Given that the existence of a mistake on the part of DMG was therefore not wholly straightforward, it might be thought that the more likely and less revolutionary approach of the Court of Appeal could have been to examine the precise definition of the type of mistake necessary to ground a claim in unjust enrichment and to establish whether or not, on the facts as found at first instance, DMG's collective state of mind could be said to have fulfilled this requirement. Indeed, on this issue the Court of Appeal did adopt the solution proposed above, Jonathan Parker LJ holding that:

> [A]lthough under [the national] regime ACT was due and payable, the true state of the law . . . was that the regime gave rise to no obligation to pay. Thus the payments were made pursuant to an unlawful demand . . . Thus DMG's mistake lay not in its belief that a group income election was not available, but rather in its belief that the ACT was payable when, on the true state of the law, it was not. That was plainly a mistake of law.[92]

Given the relative simplicity of this aspect of their decision, the Court of Appeal's full judgment in *Deutsche Morgan Grenfell* was surprising for two reasons. First, and most significantly, although the same outcome in the appeal could have been achieved solely on this issue of mistake, all three judges chose what Jonathan Parker LJ called 'the cause of action issue' (the relationship between *Woolwich* and *Kleinwort Benson v Lincoln*) as their central ground of decision instead. Had this survived the appeal to the House of Lords it would have made *Deutsche Morgan Grenfell* extremely important, because in deciding this question the Court of Appeal did two vital and interlinked things. The first was to reiterate that there is something different about 'the *Woolwich* cause of action' that distinguishes it from all other private law reasons for restitution.[93] The second was to establish a hierarchy of the kind suggested here, at least between actions for mistake of law and *Woolwich*, such that actions for return of tax which could have been brought using *Woolwich*, or as it has been reinterpreted here, the public law reason for restitution, could not be brought using mistake of law. In other words, as Jonathan Parker LJ put it, 'the *Woolwich* cause of action effectively subsumes any cause of action which might otherwise exist for mistake of law'.[94] This support for at least a limited form of hierarchy of reasons for restitution should not be underestimated, particularly in the light of Park J's decision at first instance and

[92] ibid [231]–[232].

[93] See: *Deutsche Morgan Grenfell* (CA) (n 4) [203]–[207] (Jonathan Parker LJ), [261] (Rix LJ) and [290] (Buxton LJ).

[94] ibid [195]. See also: [261] (Rix LJ) and [291] (Buxton LJ).

the fact that in all other circumstances claimants had been thought free to pick and choose between the reasons for restitution on which they rely. As such, the decision of the Court of Appeal in *Deutsche Morgan Grenfell* had the potential to be vitally important.

The second surprising feature of the Court of Appeal's decision was that, having unusually chosen the cause of action issue in preference to the mistake issue as its central question, the court did not then decide that chosen central question using a principled analysis of the two competing reasons for restitution (public law and mistake) as I have argued above. Instead, the judges relied on interpreting the dicta of Lord Goff in the two leading cases, albeit to varying extents.

Jonathan Parker LJ's judgment exhibited this interpretation technique to the greatest extent. He took the view that 'it is clear from [Lord Goff's] comprehensive treatment of the subject matter [in those two cases] that he cannot have intended to leave over for future consideration an issue as important as [this]'.[95] This led Jonathan Parker LJ to conclude that the answer must therefore be found by scrutinising Lord Goff's dicta in each of them.

It is certainly true, as Buxton LJ puts it at the beginning of his judgment, that Lord Goff's

> speeches are no ordinary judgments. In both cases the leading authority in a particular area of the law set himself to explain developments in that law that were acknowledged to be of general significance and which, before those cases, had been feared to be beyond the reach of judicial as opposed to legislative intervention.[96]

Indeed, the proper relationship between development by the common law as opposed to statute was the issue that split the majority and the minority in *Woolwich.* However, Buxton LJ also notes that he has warned himself 'against treating Lord Goff's speeches in *Woolwich* . . . and in *Kleinwort* as if they were statutes'[97] and it is not difficult to see why. On the one hand, the advantage of development by the common law is that courts are able to proceed on an evolutionary and principled basis with the substance of particular issues before them. On the other, statutes may result in the courts' room for manoeuvre being limited, but have the weight of Parliamentary democracy behind them. Approaching this important question by analysing the judgment, even of so influential a figure as Lord Goff, as if it contained the answer to a further common law issue, could be seen as containing the worst of both these worlds. Development on a principled, evolutionary basis is excluded, and yet the text removing this flexibility is not supported by the weight of democratic legitimacy.

In addition, the greater the weight placed on interpretation, the more easily the judgment can be weakened simply by presenting an alternative interpretation. Beginning with *Woolwich*, Jonathan Parker LJ took the following passage from Lord Goff's judgment:

[95] ibid [192].
[96] ibid [265].
[97] ibid.

> [I]f there is to be a right of recovery in respect of taxes exacted by the revenue, it is irrelevant to consider whether the old rule barring recovery of money paid under mistake of law should be abolished, for that rule can have no application where the remedy arises not from error on the part of the taxpayer, but from the unlawful nature of the demand by the revenue.[98]

This was open to two possible interpretations. The first was indeed that chosen by Jonathan Parker LJ, who concluded that Lord Goff would not have allowed mistake of law as an alternative to the '*Woolwich* cause of action'.[99] It is submitted that while this result was absolutely correct as a matter of principle, it cannot be derived from the dicta of Lord Goff. The second, and arguably more persuasive interpretation of this passage arises because, as Jonathan Parker LJ himself noted,[100] Woolwich was not mistaken, so even if Lord Goff had wanted to do away with the mistake of law rule in that case, it would not have done Woolwich any good and thus another reason for restitution had to be found. Nothing in the passage can therefore be taken to indicate what Lord Goff thought should happen where the taxpayer *was* mistaken, precisely because he was considering a case in which it was not.

Furthermore, it is even less likely that Lord Goff in *Woolwich* was dealing with the relationship between that action and one based on mistake of law given that, as Jonathan Parker LJ again notes himself, once the '*Woolwich* cause of action' was established, taxpayers could recover as of right '*without the need* to invoke a mistake of law'[101] (emphasis added). This pushes the question of mistake of law further away from the subject matter at issue in *Woolwich*, because now fewer claimants need use mistake. The only circumstances in which they would want to go to the added effort of doing so are those that arose in *Deutsche Morgan Grenfell* itself, where mistake is necessary to extend the limitation period. Given how far this matter is from the context of Lord Goff's dicta in *Woolwich*, it must be at least arguable that he was not dealing with it there.

Perhaps the oddest thing about Jonathan Parker LJ's choice of interpretation is that he himself reached the opposite conclusion in considering Lord Goff's treatment of *Willis Faber Enthoven (Pty) Ltd v Receiver of Revenue*,[102] *Air Canada v British Columbia*[103] and *Commissioner of State Revenue v Royal Insurance Australia Ltd*[104] together. All three cases concerned recovery of overpayments of tax for mistake and at first instance Park J thought Lord Goff's treatment of them indicated that Lord Goff had no objection to a similar result forming part of English

[98] ibid [194]. The quote is from *Woolwich* (n 3) 176. Lord Goff was agreeing with Wilson J's dissenting judgment in *Air Canada v British Columbia* [1989] 1 SCR 1161, 59 DLR (4th) 161.

[99] ibid [195].

[100] ibid [194]: 'Thus an abrogation or relaxation of . . . the mistake of law rule would not have met . . . the plain justice of the building society's case [in *Woolwich*], hence his attraction to the approach of Wilson J in her dissenting judgment in *Air Canada*'.

[101] ibid [203].

[102] *Willis Faber Enthoven (Pty) Ltd v Receiver of Revenue* (1992) 4 SA 202 (A).

[103] *Air Canada* (n 98) 198.

[104] *Commissioner of State Revenue v Royal Insurance Australia Ltd* (1995) 182 CLR 51.

law.[105] Jonathan Parker LJ, however, disagreed with Park J's interpretation, precisely because the taxpayers in *Woolwich* were not mistaken and thus he did not believe Lord Goff's dicta in that context should be seen as deciding anything about cases in which they were.[106]

Moving on to consider Lord Goff's judgment in *Kleinwort Benson v Lincoln*, Jonathan Parker LJ reached the same conclusion; that Lord Goff did not intend mistake of law as an alternative to the right to recovery established in *Woolwich*. Again, it is certainly true (as noted above) that Lord Goff thought 'private law transactions', such as those involving swaps, could not be dealt with using the '*Woolwich* cause of action',[107] but this does not necessarily mean, conversely, that he thought that mistake of law could not be used to deal with taxes. He was not being asked to answer that question so, just as with his dicta in *Woolwich*, we cannot necessarily assume that he did.

It would be unfair to suggest that Jonathan Parker LJ's judgment was entirely based on interpretation and not principle. In particular, he was concerned that if the common law were to allow recovery for mistake alongside the statutory regime, this would undermine that regime, whereas the '*Woolwich* cause of action' operates around the regime, preserving it. However, if it is accepted that nothing Lord Goff says in *Woolwich* is intended to deal with a situation where the taxpayer was mistaken, and conversely that nothing he says in *Kleinwort Benson v Lincoln* is intended to deal with the situation where the payment is of tax, then this more principled objection also falls. If Lord Goff has not considered the relationship between *Woolwich* and mistake of law, it is unsurprising that there is no discussion of how the statutory rights of recovery should fit within that relationship. It is submitted that Jonathan Parker LJ's principal error is to regard 'cases where a payment is made to the revenue which engages the relevant statutory regime regulating recovery for mistake of law' as being cases of 'lawful' demands.[108] If instead it is considered that it is ultra vires the Revenue to receive any more tax than Parliament has given it the right to receive, whether those overpayments result from mistaken and unlawful demands by the IRC, or spontaneously mistaken overpayments by taxpayers, then none of them are lawful. The only difference is that some such unlawful receipts are governed by legislation while others are governed by the common law. Thus it is simply a matter of recognising that statutory rights must be exhausted before common law rights can be used (whatever the reason for restitution) and that the common law cannot be used to undermine the statutory framework. This may well mean that the time limits available at common law should not be used to undermine the time limits available in the statutory framework,[109] but that is a question of applicable defences and will be dealt with

[105] *Deutsche Morgan Grenfell* (first instance) (n 4) [17].

[106] *Deutsche Morgan Grenfell* (CA) (n 4) [218]–[222].

[107] A conclusion criticised in ch 3, pp 67–68.

[108] *Deutsche Morgan Grenfell* (CA) (n 4) [207].

[109] There was no danger of this in the case of *Woolwich* because, as Jonathan Parker LJ notes (ibid), s 33(1) of the Taxes Management Act 1970 provides for a six year time limit, which is identical with the normal private law time limit contained in the Limitation Act 1980. The issue only arises when an

as such in chapter five. This defences 'cart' should not come before the cause of action 'horse'.

It may seem churlish thus to criticize the reasons for the decision in *Deutsche Morgan Grenfell* when the result had the potential to achieve so much, and is so helpful to the argument made here in terms of effect, but it is submitted that by sticking so closely to the dicta of Lord Goff rather than undertaking a principled examination of the two causes of action, the Court of Appeal prevented itself from seeing the full implications of its decision. If the Court had used different reasons, its decision might have become even more right and this might in turn have made it easier for the House of Lords to realise the potential of the Court of Appeal's decision.

As noted above, although Jonathan Parker LJ relied to the greatest extent on interpreting the judgments of Lord Goff, he was not alone in doing so. Rix LJ's conclusion was relatively short, simply expressing agreement with the conclusions of his colleagues, but Buxton LJ, as the quotes above indicate, also thought that Lord Goff's dicta were central to the decision in *Deutsche Morgan Grenfell*.[110] However, his judgment is arguably to be preferred to that of Jonathan Parker LJ, because it relies less on an examination of *what* Lord Goff said and more on consideration of *why in principle* Lord Goff might have been coming to those conclusions. For example, Buxton LJ accepts that Lord Goff may not have seen *Woolwich* as an appropriate vehicle for removal of the mistake of law rule, but explains that this was not just because there was no mistake in *Woolwich*, rather it was because such mistakes are in any case inevitably irrelevant when the reason for recovery was the 'unlawful nature of the action on the part of the revenue'.[111] Similarly, he did examine the context and detail of Lord Goff's dicta on the separateness of public and 'private' law transactions in *Kleinwort Benson v Lincoln*, but concluded that he was

> unable to accept the argument of the respondents that . . . [that] crucial part of Lord Goff's judgment is in some way limited in its generality because it occurs during a discussion of the settled law defence . . . *precisely because* Lord Goff needed to set out the general structure of the law before identifying the different effect of the arguments about the settled law defence.[112] (emphasis added)

This kind of examination comes much closer to the approach I have been advocating and furthermore, having examined Lord Goff's reasons, Buxton LJ added some of his own. Far from being 'superogatory' as he feared, it is this that strengthens Buxton LJ's judgment and makes it the most important of the three, containing several important points.

One of these points is his consideration of the first characteristic he believes to be peculiar to the *Woolwich* cause of action. This is that 'although stress is laid

attempt is made to extend the latter time limit using s 32(1)(c) of the Limitation Act 1980 which did not occur in *Woolwich*.

[110] See, eg: *Deutsche Morgan Grenfell* (CA) (n 4) [267], [272] and [275]–[277].
[111] ibid [273].
[112] ibid [278].

upon the coercive power of the state, that in itself does not satisfy the requirements for restitutionary recovery on the ground of compulsion'.[113] This is extremely important. I have argued that the significance of coercive power is indeed not that it provides the reason for restitution, but that it indicates the presence of the public law, or ultra vires event, which does provide the reason.[114] The coercive powers trigger the application of public law, which then provides the relevant ultra vires action, which in turn forms the reason for restitution. Once it is thus understood that the role of the coercive powers is at a stage removed from the reason for restitution it is possible to liberate the '*Woolwich* cause of action' from the confines of fact situations in which the public body is the *defendant* and to make it a general 'public law event' reason for restitution, applicable whenever the transfer of money was caused by such an event, even if the public body is the claimant.[115]

Of course, this suggestion is directly contrary to the dicta of Lord Goff in *Kleinwort Benson v Lincoln* which were so important to the Court of Appeal in *Deutsche Morgan Grenfell.* The swaps cases provide a classic example of an ultra vires event generating a right to recover where the public body could be the claimant instead of the defendant and yet, as noted in chapter three, in *Kleinwort Benson v Lincoln* Lord Goff specifically designated them to be 'private law' cases to which the '*Woolwich*' cause of action would be inapplicable. This is precisely why a full understanding of the so-called '*Woolwich*' or 'public law event' cause of action cannot be derived simply by examining Lord Goff's previous judgments. I have argued in chapter three that Lord Goff's statement in *Kleinwort Benson v Lincoln* was itself upside-down.[116] As Buxton LJ himself points out, it is necessary to set out the general structure of the law before identifying the application of defences and yet this is exactly the opposite of what Lord Goff did in *Kleinwort Benson v Lincoln.* It is true that Buxton LJ also suggests that in the swaps cases 'the element of public interest [present in *Woolwich*] is lacking', but it is difficult to see why this is so, given the parallels between the swaps cases and *Woolwich.* And once he moves away from considering Lord Goff's dicta, there is another aspect to Buxton LJ's judgment which supports the inclusion of the swaps cases in the *Woolwich*, or public law, reason for restitution. As he puts it, it is 'inept' to try to include *Woolwich*-type cases in the definition of mistake. His concern is the difficulty of accommodating DMG's knowledge of the *Metallgesellschaft and Hoechst* decision, but it is equally difficult to accommodate the misprediction/mistake dilemma in *Kleinwort Benson v Lincoln.* In both cases, the attempts to do so are beside the point. The real question is not whether cases such as *Deutsche Morgan Grenfell can* be fitted into the category of mistake of law, but whether we really want them to belong there anyway. This is

[113] ibid [271].
[114] See ch 2, at pp 36–37.
[115] In a sense this is similar to the suggestion made by Birks, to which Buxton LJ refers: *Deutsche Morgan Grenfell* (CA) (n 4) [274]. He cites: P Birks, *Unjust Enrichment*, 2nd edn (Oxford, Oxford University Press, 2005) 134. Of course, Birks's view (at 113) was that the civilian 'absence of basis' approach was necessary in order to accommodate the swaps cases, whereas my argument is the reverse, namely that a specifically tailored reason for restitution should be adopted instead.
[116] Ch 3 pp 67–68.

what explains why the Court of Appeal chose to deal with the 'cause of action' issue rather than simply challenging Park J's definition of mistake and leaving it at that. The 'vice', as Buxton LJ puts it,[117] of both *Deutsche Morgan Grenfell* and *Kleinwort Benson v Lincoln* is the ultra vires action by the public authority. By using the public law reason for restitution that vice can be addressed directly and the specifically tailored[118] defences would then apply to all such cases, following the requirements of their specific reason for restitution, rather than vice versa. Buxton LJ was right to suggest that such an unjust factor would stand 'outside the main stream of restitution as understood in a private law context'.[119]

All this connects to a further point. Throughout his judgment, Jonathan Parker LJ referred to *Woolwich* as being concerned with taxes, or payments to the revenue specifically. Buxton LJ's language, however, was wider, since throughout his judgment he refers to 'ultra vires payments'. As I have shown in chapter three,[120] although *Woolwich* itself was only concerned with taxes, dicta at all levels in that case vary in terms of their generality and it is not possible to discern, just by looking at that case, the extent of the payments or receipts to which it might extend. However, by expanding the point above, the full scope of application of *Woolwich*, or public law, reason for restitution becomes clear. It need not be limited, as Jonathan Parker LJ suggests, just to taxes, but is in fact applicable to any payment or receipt which is the result of an action held to be ultra vires as a matter of public law.

The Court of Appeal's judgment in *Deutsche Morgan Grenfell* thus represented an important step in support of the establishment of the hierarchy I proposed, albeit that it was a step based more on the interpretation of Lord Goff's dicta than on principled reasoning of the kind outlined here. However, the decision also proved to be a high point from which the law has since receded.

The Reason for Restitution and the Decision of the House of Lords

In July 2006, *Deutsche Morgan Grenfell* finally reached the House of Lords, which gave judgment in October,[121] allowing the appeal from the Court of Appeal, by a 4:1 majority[122] and essentially restoring the judgment of Park J at first instance by a majority of 3:2.[123]

On the 'mistake issue', Lord Hoffmann, Lord Hope and Lord Walker concluded that when it paid the money, DMG had indeed been acting on the basis of a mistake. Judicial decisions, held Lord Hoffmann, do indeed change the law, but they do so retrospectively. A person whose understanding of the law (however

[117] *Deutsche Morgan Grenfell* (CA) (n 4) [284].

[118] See further ch 5 where it is argued that private law defences such as limitation periods may have to be altered to take account of public law issues, but that conversely public law defences such as fiscal disruption should not be allowed to obscure the law's access to the private law event of unjust enrichment. For examples given in *Deutsche Morgan Grenfell* (CA) (n 4) see [280] (Buxton LJ).

[119] *Deutsche Morgan Grenfell* (CA) (n 4) [272].

[120] Ch 3 at pp 52–53.

[121] *Deutsche Morgan Grenfell* (HL) (n 4).

[122] Lord Hoffmann, Lord Hope, Lord Walker and Lord Brown, Lord Scott dissenting.

[123] Lord Hoffmann, Lord Hope and Lord Walker.

reasonable and widely shared at the time) is falsified by a subsequent decision of the courts should thus, for the purposes of the law of unjust enrichment, be treated as having made a mistake.[124] It may be, he continued

> that this involves extending the concept of a mistake to compensate for the absence of a more general *condictio indebiti* and perhaps it would make objectors feel better if one said that because the law was now deemed to have been different at the relevant date, he was *deemed* to have made a mistake. But the reasoning is based upon practical considerations of fairness and not abstract juridical correctitude.[125]

This is consistent with Beatson's earlier suggestions.[126]

As for the precise nature of DMG's mistake, if any, while Lord Hoffmann agreed with the Court of Appeal that the mistake went to the question of whether DMG was liable to pay ACT—not to the availability of the group income election as suggested by Park J,[127] Lord Hope concluded that Park J's analysis was correct:

> It was the mistaken belief that group relief could not be claimed that led inevitably to the liability to pay ACT which, absent a valid claim to group relief, DMG was not in a position to dispute. That was where the mistake was made, of which the payment of ACT was a secondary consequence . . . There was an unbroken causative link between the mistake and the payment.[128]

Lord Walker concluded, apparently like Lord Hoffmann, that 'DMG paid the ACT because it mistakenly thought that it had to',[129] but nevertheless counselled against 'a nice analysis as to the precise nature of the mistake of law', in the words of Neuberger J in *Nurdin and Peacock plc v DB Ramsden and Co Ltd*.[130]

On the question of whether DMG had actually made such a mistake, the difference of opinion among their Lordships was even more noticeable, causing Lord Brown to regard himself as being 'in a minority of one'.[131] Lord Hoffmann held that when Lord Hope in *Kleinwort Benson v Lincoln* regarded a state of doubt as being different from that of mistake,[132] he did not mean that a state of doubt was 'actually inconsistent with making a mistake',[133] so much as to ask 'whether the person who made the payment took the risk that he might be wrong'.[134] Lord Hope himself agreed with this analysis, holding that the issue was 'essentially one of causation'[135] so that

[124] *Deutsche Morgan Grenfell* (HL) (n 4) [23].

[125] ibid.

[126] J Beatson, 'Unlawful Statutes and Mistake of Law: Is there a Smile on the Face of Schrödinger's Cat?' in A Burrows and A Rodger (eds), *Mapping the Law: Essays in Memory of Peter Birks* (Oxford, Oxford University Press, 2006) 163.

[127] *Deutsche Morgan Grenfell* (HL) (n 4) [32] and [144] respectively.

[128] ibid [62]. For criticism of this approach see: A Goymour, 'Premature Tax Payments and Unjust Enrichment' (2007) 66 *Cambridge Law Journal* 24.

[129] ibid [143] (Lord Walker).

[130] *Nurdin and Peacock plc v DB Ramsden and Co Ltd* [1999] 1 WLR 1249 (Ch) 1272.

[131] *Deutsche Morgan Grenfell* (HL) (n 4) [161] (Lord Brown).

[132] *Kleinwort Benson* (n 15) 410.

[133] *Deutsche Morgan Grenfell* (HL) (n 4) [26].

[134] ibid.

[135] ibid [65] (Lord Hope).

> the payer's reason for making the payment despite his doubt will have a part to play in resolving the issue as to whether the payer, who would not have made the payment had he known the true state of the facts or the law at the time of the payment, should bear the risk or can recover on the ground that he was mistaken.[136]

Lord Walker also adopted this causative approach.[137] Again, Lord Hoffmann suggested that this may indicate that the civilian system of looking for cause might be a simpler approach than the common law system of examining the state of mind of the payer, but this issue did not arise on the facts of the case because both Jonathan Parker LJ in the Court of Appeal and Park J at first instance had found on the facts that, even if a state of doubt was inconsistent with a mistake, DMG had been mistaken. The fact that 'someone with a more sophisticated approach to the law might have had doubts—might even have thought that *Metallgesellschaft and Hoechst* had a good case and that the ECJ ruling would apply retrospectively' was irrelevant since DMG (in the person of Mr Thomason, its Head of Taxation) made a mistake and could not 'with reasonable diligence' have discovered it until after the decision of the ECJ in *Metallgesellschaft and Hoechst.*[138] It was on the 'discovery' issue, however, that Lord Brown found himself in the minority. For him, 'DMG ceased to be acting under any relevant mistake of law in July 1995 when they first became aware of the *Hoechst* proceedings and recognised that there was a serious legal challenge to the legality of the UK's ACT regime under EC law'.[139] His Lordship acknowledged the difficulty of articulating 'the precise touchstone by which to determine whether a payment ought properly to be held to have been made under a mistake of law',[140] but concluded ultimately that 'as soon as a paying party recognises that a worthwhile claim arises that he should not after all have made the payment and accordingly is entitled to recover it (or, as here, to compensation for the loss of its use), he has "discovered" the mistake' so that 'if he makes any further payments thereafter, they are not to be regarded as payments made under a mistake of law'.[141] Someone who paid money knowing that he may be under no liability to do so would, for Lord Brown, not be precluded from recovering that money on another ground, such as total failure of consideration, it would simply be that he could not recover the money as having been paid under a mistake of law for the purposes of benefiting from the longer limitation period available under section 32 of the Limitation Act 1980.[142]

From the point of view of the argument here, however, by far the most important aspect of the decision in *DMG* is the fact that on the cause of action issue the

[136] ibid [65].
[137] ibid [143]–[144] (Lord Walker).
[138] Again, Lord Walker agreed with this analysis: ibid [71].
[139] ibid [162].
[140] ibid [164].
[141] ibid [165].
[142] ibid [175]. Note that a mistake would still be necessary whether one takes the view that s 32(1)(c) of the Limitation Act 1980 can only be activated when the mistake is the basis for the claim or whether one takes the Edelman view that as long as there is a mistake it can be used to activate s 32(1)(c) in reply to a Limitation Act defence whether or not it is the basis for the claim. See further above n 16.

majority of their Lordships held that, in contrast to the argument proposed here, there is no reason why the ground of mistake of law should not be used for the recovery of overpaid taxes rather than the public law reason for restitution if the claimants so chose and thus they rejected even the limited hierarchy of reasons for restitution established by the Court of Appeal.

Further Arguments against the Hierarchy

Their reasons for doing so were varied. Lord Hoffmann's judgment is principally based on precedent. As argued above, he concluded that Lord Goff's speeches in *Woolwich* and *Kleinwort Benson v Lincoln* did not have the meaning attributed to them by the Court of Appeal.[143] Nor did he think any authority for excluding recovery for mistake could be derived from section 33 of the Taxes Management Act 1973 (TMA 1973).[144] Again, this is not surprising. As noted in chapter three, where such an Act does apply it can exclude common law rights, but there is nothing in the TMA 1973 to suggest that Parliament intended to exclude recovery on the grounds of mistake.[145] The argument here, however, is not based on precedents of this kind. It has been suggested that there is some evidence from the decided cases which support it[146] and further evidence of a similar kind will be discussed shortly,[147] but the key point is precisely that no court has ever fully grasped the hybrid nature of restitution for unjust enrichment based on the public law unjust factor and that as a result, obviously, there has never been direct judicial support for according the public law reason for restitution the difference in treatment it entails. The argument here is a normative one that cases would be better decided in this manner in future, should the opportunity ever arise again.

Lord Hope and Lord Walker's reluctance to create a hierarchy, on the other hand, was based more on principled objections to doing so. Lord Hope's first concern was that the result would be to build two exceptions into the ground of recovery for mistake of law first established in *Kleinwort Benson v Lincoln*:

> The first exception would involve treating payments made under a mistake of fact differently from payments made under a mistake of law. The second would involve

[143] *Deutsche Morgan Grenfell* (HL) (n 4) [14]–[18] (Lord Hoffmann). The focus in these paragraphs is on dicta from *Kleinwort Benson v Lincoln* rather than the passage from *Woolwich* analysed above (n 72), but Lord Walker also dealt with the *Woolwich* passage in the same manner as described above: ibid [47].

[144] A similar conclusion was reached by Lord Hope: ibid [55].

[145] ibid [19] (Lord Hoffmann).

[146] Such as the coincidence of discussion of 'absence of consideration' in both the swaps cases and *Woolwich* (above ch 3 at pp 60–61), from the fact that both sets of cases contained one judicial review action followed by private law unjust enrichment actions (above ch 3), from the fact that *Woolwich* and *Kingstreet Investments* reach opposing views on the choice between the public and private approaches (see esp ch 2 pp 31–39) and, not least, from the decision of *Deutsche Morgan Grenfell* (CA) (n 4).

[147] Below pp 118–20.

> treating the Revenue differently from all other public authorities which receive payments made under a mistake of law. If this argument were to succeed it would have a significant impact on the law's taxonomy. English law has been moving step by step towards a principled statement of the law of restitution. The carving out of exceptions which are not clearly based on principle would risk reversing that process.[148]

A similar objection was voiced by Lord Walker, who argued that he could see 'no good reason' for excluding 'not only an alternative cause of action based on mistake of law, but also one based on mistake of fact'.[149] Once the true nature of the public law reason for restitution and the resulting operation of the proposed hierarchy are properly understood, these objections vanish. The hierarchy proposed here certainly *would* treat the public law unjust factor as taking preference over *both* mistakes of fact and mistakes of law. But the idea is not to carve out a random exception to one unjust factor, rather it is to place the public law reason for restitution above *all* private law unjust factors that could be used as alternatives to it. It does not entail denying a cause of action to someone who has, through his own mistake of fact, paid his or her tax twice because he forgets he has already paid.[150] In such a case, the question would be whether the Revenue had in any way exceeded its powers. If it had, the public law unjust factor would be available, but if it had not, the claimant would be free to rely on mistake if that could be made out instead. There is no suggestion that the long established grounds for restitution are somehow being swallowed up by the *Woolwich* cause of action, because there will still be instances when the reason for restitution recognised in *Woolwich* does not apply. The only suggestion made here is that when the *Woolwich* reason for restitution (as analysed in chapters two and three) does apply, it should. Nor is the proposed hierarchy, as Lord Hope fears, unprincipled. For even longer than it has been moving towards 'a principled statement of the law of restitution' the law has been moving towards a principled development of administrative law. Both these sets of developments are relevant to situations where an enrichment is rendered unjust as a result of an ultra vires event, but only by using the public law reason for restitution can this be fully recognised and addressed, and it is this that provides the principled justification for prioritising that reason for restitution over others which can only capture the issue indirectly. We need not worry, as Lord Hope does, about 'treating the Revenue differently from all other public authorities'. The whole point of the scheme proposed here is precisely to ensure that public authorities are treated the *same* as each other (that is, subject to judicial review) and differently from private entities.[151] A similar point can be made in

[148] *Deutsche Morgan Grenfell* (HL) (n 4) [44] (Lord Hope).

[149] ibid [138] (Lord Walker). A similar point was also made by Burrows, 'Restitution in Respect of Mistakenly Paid Tax' (n 4) 542.

[150] See: Burrows ibid. See also: Stevens (n 4) 147.

[151] See further above, ch 3 pp 55–56. Similarly Burrows, ibid, suggested that a tenant who paid too much rent to his public authority landlord might be able to invoke s 32(1)(c) so as to extend the normal limitation regime whereas the person who pays too much tax cannot. Once it is realised that it is an ultra vires event with which we are dealing, and the usual public/private divide, it is clear that such questions have already been answered by cases like *Wandsworth LBC v Winder (No 1)* [1985] AC 461 (HL).

response to Lord Walker's concern that 'legal certainty would require the limits of the exception to be ascertainable with a fair degree of precision'. At the beginning of chapter three, answers were given to all the remaining questions about the precise functioning of the public law reason for restitution, all of which became available immediately once the true nature of that unjust factor was understood, thereby increasing the certainty of its operation. Finally, as outlined in chapter three, the solution proposed here would not perpetuate the distinction between the swaps transactions and the payment of taxes, as criticized by Virgo.[152] It would not even focus on the nature of the defendant as he proposes instead.[153] Rather it would make use of an existing, operational scheme with which the law is already familiar. The whole point of this exercise is that it is not necessary to create such rules or limits afresh in this context. To find them, or indeed to find the answers to any such questions likely to arise in future cases, courts need only look to the rules and limits which have already been developed by administrative law.

Lord Hope's second set of objections, shared by Lord Walker,[154] centred on the principle of concurrent remedies. Citing Burrows' argument that

> in general terms now that this concurrent liability has been accepted, a claimant ought to be free to choose between causes of action and that it would be odd for one cause of action, offering an advantage to a claimant, to be knocked out by a wider cause of action which does not offer that advantage.[155]

Lord Hope concluded that, '[i]t would indeed be odd', and that he could 'think of no principle that could justify such a strange result'.[156] In *Henderson v Merrett Syndicates Ltd*,[157] Lord Goff had said that 'there is no sound basis for a rule which automatically restricts the claimant to either a tortious or a contractual remedy and that there could be no objection to his taking advantage of the remedy which was most advantageous to him'[158] and his reasoning was, for Lord Hope, 'just as compelling in this context'.[159] From the private law perspective, in the light of *Henderson v Merrett* such a proposal must indeed look 'odd', 'strange' and without a principled basis. But once it is understood that it is only the use of 'private law spectacles'[160] that is distorting the view of what is actually a hybrid private *and public* cause of action, it becomes much easier to think of a principle which would indeed justify the hierarchy in a manner which is far from strange or unusual. In chapter one it was explained that, following the decision in *Clark v University of*

[152] Virgo, 'Right to Restitution' (n 4) 283. See ch 3 pp 67–69.

[153] ibid 285. Indeed, as noted in ch 3, the scheme proposed here would apply to all public law events, whether the public body in question was the claimant or defendant.

[154] *Deutsche Morgan Grenfell* (HL) (n 4) [136]–[137] (Lord Walker).

[155] Burrows, 'Restitution in Respect of Mistakenly Paid Tax' (n 4) 542. A similar point was made by Stevens (n 4) 147.

[156] *Deutsche Morgan Grenfell* (HL) (n 4) [51].

[157] *Henderson v Merrett Syndicates Ltd* [1995] 2 AC 145 (HL).

[158] ibid 193–4.

[159] *Deutsche Morgan Grenfell* (HL) (n 4) [51].

[160] See A Burrows, 'Public Authorities, Ultra Vires and Restitution' in A Burrows (ed) *Essays on the Law of Restitution* (Oxford, Clarendon Press, 1991).

Lincolnshire and Humberside,[161] even if a case is brought using the ordinary private law procedure, the court can still give summary judgment if it is dealing with a public law issue and thinks there has been undue delay, insufficient interest in the case and so on. Thus in *Carter Commercial Developments v Bedford BC,*[162] where the claimant initiated ordinary proceedings in respect of a public law issue, the court held that use of this procedure had been a deliberate attempt to circumvent the time limits which would have applied had the public law procedure been used and thus on that basis the use of ordinary proceedings was held to be an abuse of process. On this basis, it does not seem quite so odd to suggest that a claimant should not be allowed to circumvent public law concerns by using a wholly private reason for restitution, particularly when the motivation for doing so again concerns time limits. The suggestion is not that *British Steel*[163] should be reversed and the claims sent through the judicial review procedure; cases involving private rights have long provided an exception to procedural exclusivity even when that did apply.[164] It is simply, first, that the choice between public and private law has never been regarded as depending solely on the preference of the claimant, but rather has always been decided by detailed, policy-based rules, and second that with their new, more substantive focus[165] one of those policies concerns the need for time limits to be tailored to take account of the special position of public bodies. The relevant comparators, therefore, are not *Henderson v Merrett*, but *Clark*, and its predecessor *O'Reilly.*[166]

Finally, Lord Walker's last concern with the hierarchy was that it could be in breach of EC law on the basis that:

> The domestic court must give DMG an equivalent and effective remedy, and that would not be achieved, in my opinion, if recovery were limited so as to exclude an alternative concurrent remedy which would be available in a dispute between private citizens.[167]

The precise operation of the principles of adequacy and effectiveness of remedies in EU law will be discussed in more detail in chapters seven and eight, but enough can be said here to lay Lord Walker's concerns to rest. The principle of equivalence does not require a comparison to be drawn between public law and private law. The ECJ in *Edis v Ministero delle Finanze*[168] made it quite clear that it is perfectly compatible with EU law to have different rules for public bodies from those applicable to private parties; the requirement of equivalence operates *within* each of those contexts, not between them. Indeed the hierarchy proposed here is as much about *providing* a remedy which would *not* be available in a dispute

[161] *Clark v University of Lincolnshire and Humberside* [2000] 1 WLR 1988 (CA).

[162] *Carter Commercial Developments v Bedford BC* [2001] EWHC 669 (QB).

[163] *British Steel* (n 2).

[164] See *O'Reilly v Mackman* [1983] 2 AC 237 (HL) itself as well as *Roy v Kensington and Chelsea and Westminster Family Practitioners Committee* [1992] 1 AC 624 (HL) and see further chs 1 and 3.

[165] See ch 1 p 15.

[166] *Clark* (n 161) and *O'Reilly* (n 164).

[167] *Deutsche Morgan Grenfell* (HL) (n 4) [142].

[168] Case C-231/96 *Edis v Ministero delle Finanze* [1998] ECR I-4951.

between private citizens as it is about *excluding* those which would be. The point is simply that public law occupies a different sphere from that of private law and claims which involve both spheres must be viewed in a hybrid manner. Indeed, as will be seen in more detail in the following chapter, the irony is that while the approach proposed here *is* compatible with EU law, that adopted by the government as a result of Park J's decision (now restored by the House of Lords), was held not to be. Following DMG's success at first instance, the IRC used press releases on 8 September and 11 November 2003 to announce the enactment of what became sections 320 and 321 of the Finance Act 2004, reinforced by section 107 of the Finance Act 2007 which together provide that section 32 of the Limitation Act 1980 will no longer apply to any 'taxation matter under the care and management of the Commissioners of Inland Revenue' or 'any action for relief from the consequences of a mistake of law, whether expressed to be brought on the ground of mistake or on some other ground (such as unlawful demand or ultra vires act)'.[169]

This does establish the hierarchy for which I have argued, but since the Finance Acts of 2004 and 2007 have retrospective effect,[170] and do not allow for transitional implementation periods, in the light of *Marks and Spencer plc v Commissioners of Customs and Excise*,[171] and *Grundig Italiana SpA v Ministero delle Finanze*,[172] they were held to be in breach of the principle of effectiveness required by Community law,[173] in *FII*[174] (part of the Franked Investment Income Group Litigation Order[175] which has been used to handle what Lord Hoffmann in *Deutsche Morgan Grenfell*

[169] Indeed, as Hacker has pointed out, 'on its face, *Deutsche Morgan Grenfell* dealt with a problem which no longer exists': B Hacker, 'Still at the Crossroads' (2007) 123 *Law Quarterly Review* 177, 181. Although they were originally posted on the Revenue's website, both the 8 September and the 11 November press releases are now only available by contacting the Revenue directly.

[170] Section 320 of the Finance Act 2004 provided that s 32(1)(c) of the Limitation Act 1980 (the extended time limit for mistake claims) would not apply 'in relation to a mistake of law relating to a taxation matter under the care and management of the Commissioners of Inland Revenue' brought on or after 8 September 2003. This was the date of the government's announcement of its intention to legislate to reduce the time limit in this way, but obviously the Finance Act 2004 did not come into force until later. The effect of the legislation is therefore retrospective to the date on which it was announced, rather than prospective from the date on which it came into force. Then, in the light of the HL's decision in *Deutsche Morgan Grenfell* (n 4), the government decided that s 320 of the Finance Act 2004 had not provided enough protection and thus enacted s 107 of the Finance Act 2007, which disapplies the extended time limit in s 32(1)(c) to *all* claims relating to tax and the Revenue, regardless of when the claim was brought (subject to the very limited exception that it does not apply to actions covered by decisions of the HL given before 6 December 2006, the date on which the government announced the Finance Act 2007). The section also provides that any judgment given after the legislation was announced but before the Finance Act 2007 was in force, would be treated as if s 107 of the Finance Act 2007 had already been in force and any payments made to satisfy such a judgment would be repayable. The Finance Act 2007 therefore has retrospective effect twice over: it extends the extent to which the Limitation Act 1980 is retrospectively denied effect by extending the period of exclusion back beyond 8 September 2003, and it does so in a manner which is itself retrospective to 6 December 2006.

[171] Case C-62/00 *Marks and Spencer plc v Commissioners of Customs and Excise* [2002] ECR I-6325. For the final national chapter in the case see now: [2009] UKHL 8.

[172] Case C-255/00 *Grundig Italiana SpA v Ministero delle Finanze* [2002] ECR I-8003.

[173] See further below, ch 8.

[174] *FII* (n 80). As noted there, 'FII' stands for 'Franked Investment Income'.

[175] For further detail of the order, see: *Boake Allen Ltd v Revenue and Customs Commissioners* [2007] UKHL 25, [2007] 1 WLR 1386.

referred to as 'the forensic fall-out' from the *Metallgesellschaft and Hoechst*[176] litigation).[177]

Does Mistake Provide a Broader Ground of Recovery than the Public Law Reason for Restitution?

The *FII* case itself, however, presents a further potential argument against the hierarchy which must be considered. As Henderson J puts it, at the simplest level this case concerned 'factual situations which are the opposite of those which gave rise to the questions considered in [*Metallgesellschaft and*] *Hoechst*'.[178] Whereas *Deutsche Morgan Grenfell* and *Metallgesellschaft and Hoechst* concerned UK-resident subsidiaries of foreign parent companies which were prevented from making group income elections, the FII Group Litigation concerned foreign subsidiaries of UK parent companies and the tax treatment of dividends coming into the UK from abroad. As with *Metallgesellschaft and Hoechst* and *Deutsche Morgan Grenfell*, the ECJ had held the national rules to be partly in breach of EC law[179] and so the question before Henderson J in the High Court in *FII* was how this finding should be applied to the facts of the case, and how the EC law findings should be translated into national law. However, this time, unlike *Metallgesellschaft and Hoechst*, the decision of the ECJ in *FII* gave more specific guidance on how this should be achieved.[180]

The case concerned a series of different claims. Some of these were relatively straightforwardly for restitution of the tax payments[181] which had been found to be in breach of Community law, plus compound interest to represent the time value of those payments.[182] Others, however, were less straightforward. In particular, the application of the ACT regime to UK parent companies with foreign subsidiaries tended to lead to an 'ACT mountain'[183] building up within the company. ACT would become payable on the distribution of dividends, either within the company or to its outside shareholders to a greater extent than would have been the case with a wholly UK-based company, and then, whereas a wholly UK-based company would be able to offset these ACT payments against other liabilities, the scope for UK parent companies with foreign subsidiaries to do this was very

[176] *Metallgesellschaft and Hoechst* (n 25).

[177] *Deutsche Morgan Grenfell* (HL) (n 4) [2]. See further: *Aegis Group plc v IRC* [2005] EWHC 1468 (Ch), [2006] STC 23; *Europcar* (n 61); chs 5 and 8; and M Chowdry, 'How Long can Section 80 Last?' [2004] *British Tax Review* 106.

[178] *FII* (UK) (n 80) [2].

[179] *FII* (ECJ) (n 80). The national rules in question were again the ACT regime at issue in *Metallgesellschaft and Hoechst*, which were held to be contrary to Arts 49 and 63 TFEU on freedom of establishment and free movement of capital (ex Arts 43 and 56 EC respectively).

[180] See further below, ch 8.

[181] ACT and Schedule D Case V corporation tax.

[182] *FII* (UK) (n 80) [201]–[205] and [209]–[211] (Henderson J).

[183] ibid [33] (Henderson J).

limited.[184] As a result, companies in this position, such as the test claimants in *FII* tended to regard ACT not as *advance* corporation tax at all, but rather as an absolute and final form of liability with which they were stuck.[185] In order to minimise this, especially when ACT was abolished and 'shadow ACT' was introduced in its place, the claimants wanted to use up their surplus ACT as far as they could and as fast as they could, lest they should lose the chance to do so altogether. They thus waived (or 'disclaimed') capital tax allowances for three years, thereby increasing their liability to MCT, against which they could then set off some of the surplus ACT. However, the ACT could only ever discharge a proportion of this MCT, so in *FII* the claimants also sought to claim loss of use of the additional MCT thus paid. The claimants also set off their surplus ACT against 'Case V corporation tax', which was itself one of the taxes which was unlawful as a matter of EC law. Finally, the claimants also sought to make use of their ACT mountain through what was known as the 'FID regime'.[186] UK-based companies distributing foreign profits to their shareholders could elect to treat them as 'Foreign Income Dividends' or 'FIDs'. The ACT paid on FIDs was in principle repayable and so the payment of dividends in the form of FIDs would substantially reduce the group's overall tax burden. Because there was virtually no other way in which surplus ACT could be used within the group, the claimants opted to make use of the 'FID regime'. However, FID elections had to be made on an all or nothing basis. A company could not elect to pay FIDs for recipients liable to UK income tax but not exempt shareholders; an election could only be made in respect of all the dividends on the same class of share. Also, shareholders could not receive tax credits for dividends paid under the FID system. Since 40% of the claimants' shareholders were 'exempt shareholders', that is, those who would have received partial or full tax credits on normal dividends, they were resistant to the idea of FID dividends.[187] As a result, the claimants issued what became known as 'enhanced FIDs' made up of the original amount of the distribution, topped up to compensate the

[184] The main reasons for this were first that a UK resident company making a qualifying distribution to another UK-based company would be entitled to a tax credit. The total of the distribution and the tax credit was called Franked Investment Income (FII). The company would then only be liable to pay ACT to the extent that its dividends and the ACT referable to them exceeded the FII tax credit. However, a UK resident company receiving a distribution from a foreign company was not entitled to this credit. The amount of ACT payable in the first place would therefore be greater than that payable by a wholly UK-based company. In addition, companies were entitled to set this ACT off against MCT, but where a company received credit for foreign tax, this reduced the amount of MCT liability against which ACT could be set off. Thus UK-based companies with foreign subsidiaries would both accrue more ACT and have less use to make of it than wholly UK-based companies. See further: ibid [19]–[23] (Henderson J).

[185] ibid [32], quoting from the witness statement of Mr K Hardman, Head of Tax at BAT industries, the group from which the test claimants were drawn.

[186] ibid [15], [164]–[191], [208] and [273]–[302].

[187] Though as Shiers notes, companies could actually pay both an ordinary dividend and a FID at the same time and often did so. It would only pay a FID to the extent necessary to avoid incurring additional surplus ACT, and would otherwise pay a normal dividend. See further R Shiers and R Williams, 'The *FII GLO* and *F J Chalke*: Tax and Restitution Developing Hand-in-Hand' 2009 *British Tax Review* 365 n 32.

shareholders for the resulting loss of tax credit.[188] In *FII*, the claimants argued that had it not been for the unlawful ACT and FID system, they would not have paid 'enhanced FIDs', and that by compensating the recipient shareholders for the lack of repayable tax credits, they had enriched the Revenue by relieving it of its obligations in respect of those tax credits.

At the European level, AG Geelhoed reiterated that the classification of such claims under English law was a matter for the domestic courts rather than the ECJ, but he nevertheless went on to hold that with one exception, the claims brought should be 'considered equivalent to claims for the recovery of sums unduly paid, that is to say, claims for recovery of charges unlawfully levied',[189] rather than as claims based on state liability for damages.[190] Also, as noted above, where such a reimbursement claim could be brought, he pointed out that it was the duty of the national court to provide 'an effective remedy' even where a claim for state liability in damages might not succeed.[191] The 'one exception' to this decision concerned the claim for the FID enhancements, which he held were not necessarily 'a direct consequence of the UK's unlawful failure to grant an equivalent credit to the shareholders'.[192] The direct consequence was the extra tax levied on those shareholders, not the efforts made by the companies to alleviate this. However, he left it for the national court to determine whether this was correct on the facts.

The ECJ agreed with the Advocate General that it was not for the ECJ itself to assign a legal classification to the actions brought before the national court,[193] but likewise, it nevertheless reiterated the *San Giorgio*[194] principle, according to which the right to a refund of unlawful charges is 'the consequence and complement of the rights conferred on individuals'[195] by EU law and 'where a Member State has levied charges in breach of the rules of Community law, individuals are entitled to reimbursement not only of the tax unduly levied but also of the amounts paid to that State or retained by it which relate directly to that tax'.[196] However, unlike the Advocate General, the ECJ thought that *two* of the claims would fall outside this principle. One, as with the Advocate General, concerned the issue of enhanced FIDs, and the other was the waiver of tax credits in order to increase the liability to MCT against which ACT could then be offset. According to the ECJ:

[188] Though Shiers notes that tax-exempt shareholders would typically not in fact be better off overall receiving an 'enhanced' FID dividend than if they had received a 'normal' FID dividend. This was because, since all shareholders received the 'enhanced' FID dividend, the effect was to reduce company reserves which would depress the share price. The exempt shareholders' income stream would thus be maintained at the expense of capital growth. Shiers, ibid, n 33.

[189] *FII* (ECJ) (n 80) [132].

[190] For further detail on both causes of action, see below, ch 8.

[191] *FII* (ECJ) (n 80) .

[192] ibid [133].

[193] ibid [201].

[194] Case 199/82 *Amministrazione delle Finanze dello Stato v San Giorgio* [1983] ECR 3595. See further below, ch 8.

[195] *FII* (ECJ) (n 80) [202].

[196] ibid [205].

> Such waivers of relief or increases in the amount of dividends are the result of decisions taken by those companies and do not constitute, on their part, an inevitable consequence of the refusal by the United Kingdom to grant those shareholders the same treatment as that afforded to shareholders receiving a distribution which has its origin in nationally-sourced dividends.[197]

That being the case, it was for the national courts to decide whether these last two claims should instead succeed on the basis of state liability in damages for breach of EC law.[198]

When the case returned to the domestic level, Henderson J noted what he called the width of 'the *San Giorgio* principle'[199] on the basis that it covers all 'direct consequences' of the unlawful levying of tax, but at the same time he also noted that this test for causation was strict, requiring a direct and unbroken causal link[200] (hence the exclusion of the FID enhancements and the waiver of credit issues). However, somewhat oddly, Henderson J also concluded that 'the *Woolwich* principle' could not alone provide a matching UK remedy for claims which as a matter of EC law fall under this *San Giorgio* principle. His reason for doing so was that 'the Court of Appeal in *NEC Semi-Conductors*[201] has strictly confined the ambit of the *Woolwich* cause of action to cases where the tax in question was itself unlawfully demanded'.[202] This was not to say, on the other hand, that such claims could not fall within the scope of an unjust enrichment claim at all. On the contrary, he held that 'the UK cause of action in mistake-based restitution is also needed in order to provide an effective UK remedy for many *San Giorgio* claims'.[203] He therefore concluded that '[w]here mistake is present . . . a restitutionary claim based on the mistake is likely to cover all the ground that a *Woolwich* claim could cover, but also has the potential to extend considerably further'.[204] Dealing with these points in reverse order, there is no question, as noted above, that in the light of the House of Lords decision in *Deutsche Morgan Grenfell* at present, in practical terms, 'the *Woolwich* cause of action is likely to play a subsidiary role'.[205] The argument here is that when the true nature of these cases is better understood, that such order should be reversed. Again, as noted above, the point of doing so

[197] ibid [207]. See also: Case C-201/05 *Test Claimants in the CFC and Dividend Group Litigation* [2008] STC 1513 [2008] ECR I-2875; and Case C-524/04 *Test Claimants in the Thin Cap Group Litigation* [2007] ECR I-2107.

[198] ibid [207]. In the event, notwithstanding that HMRC's general approach had been one of 'insular insouciance', Henderson J concluded that there had been no sufficiently serious breach of EC law and thus a key element of the action for state liability in damages had not been made out. *FII* (UK) (n 80) [400]–[4].

[199] *FII* (UK) (n 80) [227].

[200] ibid [235].

[201] *Boake Allen and NEC Semi-Conductors v The Commissioners for Her Majesty's Revenue and Customs* [2006] EWCA Civ 25, [2006] STC 606. The case was also known and subsequently heard in the HL as *Boake Allen* (HL) (n 175).

[202] *FII* (UK) (n 80) [260].

[203] ibid.

[204] ibid.

[205] ibid [260].

certainly would be to recognise the particular concerns associated with transactions involving public bodies such as the Revenue, but, as a result of the decision in *Edis*,[206] to do so would not in any way fail to fulfil our obligations under EU law to provide an effective remedy, and indeed a failure to recognise this, as happened in the *Deutsche Morgan Grenfell* case itself, could lead to the use of other techniques which *are* in breach of EU law for limiting the effects of such decisions instead.[207]

As for the argument that the '*Woolwich* principle' cannot provide a cause of action in such cases whereas a cause of action based on mistake could do so, there are four arguments which can be made. The first is to point out that 'the *Woolwich* principle' has never been fully understood by the case law as representing what has been referred to here as 'the public law reason for restitution'. It is therefore entirely possible that while, as a matter of unreflective and piecemeal case law development, 'the *Woolwich* principle' may not be able to provide recovery, the properly-understood and fully developed 'public law reason for restitution' could. Thus, for example, in *NEC Semi-Conductors and Boake Allen*,[208] on which Henderson J relied, Sedley LJ held if a taxpayer brings a successful appeal against his liability to tax

> [this] does not mean that the Revenue has made an unlawful demand in the *Woolwich* sense of relying on ultra vires powers of recovery and enforcement. It means simply that the taxpayer's liability is less than the Revenue claims, and that if he has overpaid he can have his money back with whatever interest the law allows him.[209]
>
> True enough, the relationship between the taxpayer and the Crown, in whose right taxes are levied, is governed by fiscal laws, so that any impermissible taxation can be said to be based on a mistake of law. But it is not a relationship in which either party can relevantly be said to have been unjustly enriched by an underpayment or overpayment of tax . . . A body collecting revenue on behalf of the state is required to disgorge unlawful imposts if, and only if, an independent appellate tribunal . . . holds that it has no entitlement to the money. By parity of reasoning, the taxpayer is not called upon to make restitution of underpayments which the Revenue has failed at the proper time to demand. Failing such a decision, taxes are to be treated as properly levied. Arguably there has in such a situation been no relevant mistake of law and no unjust enrichment of the Crown or—in the latter example—the taxpayer. What would attract the remedy of restitution is a failure by the Crown to disgorge overpaid tax after an appellate ruling in the taxpayer's favour.[210]

Similarly, Mummery LJ did not engage with the claimants' argument that even if the tax itself was valid they had misunderstood the scheme, holding simply that any demands made by the taxing authorities in the case were lawful.[211] It is true

[206] See above, n 168 and surrounding text.
[207] See above pp 101–102.
[208] *Boake Allen* (CA) (n 201).
[209] ibid [90].
[210] ibid [95].
[211] ibid [147]. The decision of the CA in *Boake Allen and NEC Semiconductors* took place between the decision of the (differently constituted) CA in *Deutsche Morgan Grenfell* and the decision of the HL

that some of the cases listed by Sedley LJ in the passage quoted above may well not fall literally within the terms of the *Woolwich* judgment itself,[212] since in that case the tax rules themselves were invalid, rather than just the understanding of them adopted by the IRC or *Woolwich.*[213] But as was noted in chapter three, *British Steel*[214] established that misinterpretation of a valid statute was also included in the *Woolwich* unjust factor, and indeed in *Deutsche Morgan Grenfell* itself, the House of Lords did not hold that the '*Woolwich* principle' could *not* be used, merely that a cause of action based on mistake of law was both necessary and available in order to trigger the operation of the section 32(1)(c) time limits.[215] Once the reason for restitution at issue in all these cases is fully understood as the existence of a public law ultra vires event, it does not seem particularly difficult to characterise a mistaken overcharge, or receipt of a mistaken overpayment as being, literally, beyond the powers of the taxing authority at the time of the payment, even if this fact is only pointed out later by the decision of a court or tribunal.[216] Indeed, given that the whole point of the *San Giorgio* principle is that it applies to taxes which are beyond the powers of the public body as a matter of public law, *San Giorgio* claims are by definition a subset of claims in which the reason for restitution is public law. The only difference between *San Giorgio* claims and *Woolwich* claims thus interpreted is that the latter incorporates situations in which the payment or receipt of money was beyond the powers of the body as a matter of domestic public law as well as incorporating *San Giorgio* claims in which the receipt was beyond the powers of the body as a matter of EU law. Whatever the source of the limit on the public body's powers, the taxing authority can be regarded as having been enriched by the receipt of the payment in circumstances when it was beyond its powers to do so, and all the relevant criteria are present for the *prima facie* operation of the public law reason for restitution. It is of course the case that, as Sedley LJ points out, the reverse would not be true; a taxpayer cannot be unjustly enriched by holding onto a payment which the Revenue has failed at the proper time to demand. It may well be enriched by the extra time value of the money (for example interest) that it receives as a result, and the failure to charge the tax may well have been beyond the powers of the public body, but the law of unjust enrichment is so far confined to dealing with cases where there has been some

in that case. The CA in *Boake Allen* seems to have taken the view that the decision of that court in *DMG* operated in a similar fashion to the old 'mistake of law bar' idea: not only were the claimants not to rely on the mistake to provide their cause of action, apparently they could not even use the mistake to explain why the receipt of the tax was invalid. As explained in ch 3, once the public law reason for restitution is properly understood, there is no need for such a restrictive view to be taken.

212 *Woolwich* (n 3).

213 See further above, ch 2.

214 *British Steel* (n 2). See also *Hillsdown Holdings plc v IRC* [1999] STC 561 (Ch); *Mallusk Cold Storage Ltd v Dept of Finance and Personnel* [2003] NIQB 58 (QB); *Carvill v IRC (No 2)* [2002] EWHC 1488 (Ch), [2002] STC 1167; *British Sky Broadcasting Group plc v Customs and Excise Commissioners* [2001] EWHC 127 (QB), [2001] STC 437; and *Waikato Regional Airport Ltd v AG* [2003] UKPC 50.

215 *Deutsche Morgan Grenfell* (HL) (n 4). For discussion of whether it was indeed necessary, see: (n 16).

216 See further above, ch 3, 'What Sort of Invalidity Triggers this Unjust Factor?'

form of action or transfer, not those where the whole point is that nothing at all has happened.

Second, it is not clear that the decision of the Court of Appeal in *Boake Allen and NEC Semiconductors* did in fact narrow the scope of even the '*Woolwich* principle' in a way that would prevent it from fulfilling the role required by the *San Giorgio* principle. On the facts of the case in *Boake Allen*, the Court of Appeal concluded, and the House of Lords confirmed,[217] that the tax in that case was in any event lawful. There was therefore simply no ultra vires event on the facts of the case to raise either the '*Woolwich* principle' or the public law reason for restitution proposed here, whether narrow or wide. At the Court of Appeal level, the claimants did argue in the alternative that they had made their payments on the basis of a mistake of law,[218] but this was not a more general, additional mistake of a *British Steel* kind which would give rise to an unauthorised over-receipt on the part of the taxing authorities even if the basic legislation was held to be valid. Had it been so, and had the Court of Appeal held that this more general form of unauthorised over-receipt could not be recovered by the claimants using the *Woolwich* principle, there might have been something to support Henderson J's conclusion in *FII*[219] that *Boake Allen and NEC Semiconductors* had narrowed the '*Woolwich* principle' in a manner which prevented it from matching at domestic level the requirements of the ECJ *San Giorgio* principle. But this was not the case. Instead, the mistake raised by the claimants in *Boake Allen* was simply an alternative route to claiming that the tax was itself unlawful[220] which would thus fall, along with the argument based on the '*Woolwich* principle' as soon as the tax was held not to be unlawful at all.[221] Further confirmation of this comes from the fact that no remedies were considered by the House of Lords in *Boake Allen* once it had decided that the tax was lawful, even though by that stage the House had also given judgment in *Deutsche Morgan Grenfell* and a cause of action based on mistake would have been available had it had any role to play.[222] Similarly, although Henderson J seems to regard *Boake Allen and NEC Semiconductors* as requiring proof of a 'demand' in a manner that would reduce the scope of the '*Woolwich* principle', as discussed in chapter three,[223] even Mummery LJ (who, of the Court, devoted the most attention to the question of demands) merely held that on the facts of the case, even if there had been a 'demand', it had been lawful.[224] The *Boake Allen* decision does not, therefore, generate any examples of actions on the part of public bodies which would be invalid as a matter of EU law, thus giving rise to a *San Giorgio* claim,

[217] *Boake Allen* (HL) (n 175).

[218] *Boake Allen* (CA) (n 201) [148].

[219] *FII* (UK) (n 80).

[220] ibid [161] (Mummery LJ).

[221] Even once the cause of action in mistake became available following the decision of the HL in *Deutsche Morgan Grenfell* (HL) (n 4), as it was not at the time of the CA's decision in *Boake Allen and NEC Semiconductors*, (CA) (n 201).

[222] *Boake Allen* (HL) (n 175).

[223] pp 40–41.

[224] A view upheld in *Boake Allen* (HL) (n 175).

which could be recovered using a cause of action based on mistake but not one based on the invalidity itself using the public law reason for restitution.

Third, in more general terms, it is not surprising that this is the case. The only potential difference between the public law reason for restitution as properly understood and a cause of action based on mistake of law when the validity of a public body's rules or actions is also at issue[225] relates, as discussed above, to the question of time limits.[226] Otherwise the mistake of law cause of action is simply the public law reason for restitution (that is, the ultra vires nature of the action or rule as a matter of public law) plus a requirement that the claimant demonstrate that he, she or it mistakenly thought it was intra vires. Or, as Mummery LJ put it in *Boake Allen and NEC Semiconductors*:

> [a]n even more fundamental criticism can be advanced against the whole enterprise of searching for a mistake of law on the part of the taxpayer on which to found the restitutionary claim. It can be argued that the true foundation of the restitutionary claim in such cases [ie cases such as *Deutsche Morgan Grenfell* and *Boake Allen* itself] lies in the absence of a basis for the payment rather than in the making of a mistaken payment.[227]

It is not therefore so remarkable that a cause of action with an *extra* requirement should not cover more ground than a simpler cause of action without that extra requirement. If anything the opposite seems more likely, as was evidenced by the *Woolwich* decision itself.

Fourth, if the cause of action in mistake is chosen instead, all that happens is that the court then has to take such a broad view of what constitutes the relevant mistake that it might as well have chosen the ultra vires nature of the event anyway. Thus in *FII* Henderson J ends up preferring to 'identify the mistake at a fairly general level'[228] later holding that:

> the mistake of law in the present case should be identified as a mistake as to the lawfulness of the ACT regime or the Case V charge, and it is probably not helpful to try to express it in more precise terms.[229]

[225] Described as situation 3b in the list of options at the beginning of this chapter.

[226] See discussion above. Of course *DMG* also concerned a breach of EC law, but obviously even if it had not done so, once an extended time limit had become available in principle for unjust enrichment cases dealing with unlawful taxation schemes, it would in any event have had to apply to EC claims under the principle of equivalence laid down in Case 33/76 *Rewe-Zentralfinanz GmbH v Landwirtschaftskammer für das Saarland* [1976] ECR 1989, especially [5]. Thus for the time being at least, it is probably the case that *San Giorgio* claims do require use of mistake of law as well as *Woolwich* where the claims relate to events more than six years ago. But first it should be noted that these are not the reasons given by Henderson J for rejecting the match between *Woolwich* and *San Giorgio* claims (indeed it seems that Henderson J did not regard the claims falling outside the six year limit as being *San Giorgio* claims at all, see below p 137) and second, it will be argued further in ch 5 that in any event the issue of time limits should be dealt with in a manner specific to the hybrid nature of such claims and that such treatment would be perfectly compatible with our obligations to provide an equivalent remedy under EU law as a result of the decision in *Edis* (n 168).

[227] *Boake Allen* (CA) (n 201) [161]. It will be remembered from chs 2 and 3 that 'absence of basis' in this context can be seen as a private law mistranslation of the public law *ab initio* voidness of an ultra vires action or decision.

[228] *FII* (UK) (n 80) [261].

[229] ibid [262].

For the reasons outlined in the paragraph above, this is an odd choice to make. Either the concept of mistake should do some real work in the claim, in which case it should be specifically defined and made out, with the attendant danger that, as in *Kleinwort Benson*[230] and *Deutsche Morgan Grenfell*[231] differences of opinion will arise over how the required kind of mistake should be defined and whether such a mistake has in fact been made in a given case. Or, as Mummery LJ points out,[232] the mistake is only a proxy for the public law reason for restitution anyway, in which case we should make use of that reason directly. For the reasons given here, the latter option is preferable.

Further evidence in support of this point comes from the fact that in the subsequent case of *F J Chalke Ltd and AC Barnes (Wokingham) Ltd v The Commissioners for Her Majesty's Revenue and Customs*,[233] Henderson J arguably broadened the concept of mistake even further, permitting recovery on the basis of mistake notwithstanding the fact that the claimants in that case accepted that they had continued to make payments for some two years after the mistakes had been discovered.[234] In Henderson J's view 'it was reasonable' for Chalke to continue to make payments after discovery of the mistake and these payments 'were still made as a consequence of that mistake, in the sense that but for the original mistake they would not have been made'.[235] In other words, the concept of mistake was stretched so widely that it could apply even when in fact there was no actual mistake.

How Wide are the Effects of the Public Law Reason for Restitution?

In chapter three, many of the general parameters of the public law unjust factor were established, but discussion of the extent of its operation was held over to this point so that it can now be examined in the light of the facts of the decided cases.[236] Doing so now reveals that there are in fact two aspects to this problem.

How Wide is the Finding of Ultra Vires?

One such aspect is the same as in *Deutsche Morgan Grenfell*, namely how far the finding of ultra vires can be taken to extend. After all, if the acceptance of the

230 *Kleinwort Benson* (n 15).

231 *Deutsche Morgan Grenfell* (n 4). See further below, n 286 and surrounding text.

232 *FII* (UK) (n 80) [161] (Mummery LJ).

233 *F J Chalke Ltd and AC Barnes (Wokingham) Ltd v The Commissioners for Her Majesty's Revenue and Customs* [2009] EWHC 952 (Ch). For an account of the facts see Shiers and Williams, n 187.

234 ibid [137]–[8], citing as support the dicta of Robert Goff J in *Barclays Bank v Simms*, n 87.

235 ibid [138].

236 p 55.

money on the part of the taxing authorities can be found to be beyond its powers then the public law reason for restitution will be made out, and the money would then be recoverable in the normal way. It was argued above that this was in fact the case in *Deutsche Morgan Grenfell*; that since the ECJ held that the 'benefit' of the GIE scheme should have been extended to the claimants, it was beyond the powers of the taxing authorities to receive the advance payment of ACT on the facts of the case, even though it would not have been unlawful to receive it in the case of a company which chose for its own reasons not to make an election even though that course of action was open to it (Company A).[237] However, it was pointed out that the question would be more difficult in relation to Company C which would not have had the option to make the election, but would in any case not have chosen to make it anyway. In relation to this company, it was noted then that public law already has tools for balancing the constitutional need to intervene to remove the ultra vires action even when the invalidity has made no difference to the facts of the case, against, on the other hand, the more practical desirability of recognising such issues of materiality or allowing claimants to waive the invalidity,[238] and it was argued that with recognition of the hybrid nature of claims based on the public law reason for restitution these tools could be used equally well in the unjust enrichment sphere.

However, the *FII* case[239] raises further questions in this regard. Here, Henderson J faced the opposite situation to that raised by *Deutsche Morgan Grenfell* because in *FII* the problem was not that the invalidity may have made no difference in some cases, but rather that it had had a whole series of effects, and the question was which of these consequential losses could be recovered on the basis of unjust enrichment via the public law reason for restitution.

The Advocate General and the ECJ, as noted above, regarded the *San Giorgio* principle, that is the EU law obligation to refund charges levied in breach of EU law, as extending to all 'direct consequences' of the unlawful levying of tax[240] and counsel for the claimants sought to argue that the 'but for' test ought to be adopted as the basis for establishing which consequential losses ought to be recoverable on the basis of the unjust enrichment claim.[241] Henderson J, however, resisted this 'siren call'.[242] Like the ECJ, he held that the actual payments of the unlawful taxes[243] together with associated claims for interest and time value of ACT were recoverable as a claim in unjust enrichment.[244] However, he was not prepared to go any further than this.[245] As a result his judgment is the narrowest of the three. The Advocate General had held that the *San Giorgio* principle could found all the

237 See above.
238 See further above, text to notes 53 and 66–69.
239 *FII* (UK) (n 80). For the facts of the case see the section above.
240 *FII* (ECJ) (n 80) [132] (AG Geelhoed) and [205] (ECJ). See also: ibid [231] (Henderson J).
241 ibid [264]. Of course the basis of the claim was at this stage a cause of action in mistake of law.
242 ibid.
243 ACT and Case V Corporation tax.
244 *FII* (UK) (n 80) [267]–[269] and [275].
245 ibid [270].

claims except for those concerning the 'FID enhancements'. The ECJ's view was narrower than this, exempting from *San Giorgio* both the 'enhanced FIDs' and the reliefs from MCT waived in order to increase the amount of MCT liability against which surplus ACT could be offset. However, Henderson J's judgment appears to exempt three categories of case from the scope of recovery on the basis of unjust enrichment. In addition to the 'FID enhancements' and waived credits, he also regarded as beyond the scope of the unjust enrichment principle the 'consequential steps that were taken within the group to utilise surplus ACT, for example by setting it off against unlawful Case V corporation tax'.[246]

As far as the public law question of the extent of ultra vires is concerned, it is clear that this can play no further role in the claim involving the FID enhancements, since in this instance there was no additional receipt of money by the Revenue which could count as an ultra vires action on the basis of which the money should have been recovered. The Revenue was, as explained in detail below, saved a necessary expense, but this took place passively from the Revenue's point of view, without any further action, or even failure to act, on their part which could be described as being beyond their powers. Whether or not the enhanced FID claim can be recovered on the basis of the public law unjust enrichment action therefore depends entirely on the extent to which consequential loss is recoverable as a matter of the private law of unjust enrichment. The claim can receive no additional assistance in the form of a consequential finding of ultra vires.

Conversely, it is relatively clear that acceptance of ACT against the unlawful Case V corporation tax should straightforwardly be regarded as having been beyond the powers of the IRC. As will again be explained further below, it is difficult to see why this claim should not have been treated in exactly the same way as if the companies had paid the Case V corporation tax in money.

However, the situation involving the waived or disclaimed MCT tax credits is more difficult. It is certainly true that had the claimants not had an ACT mountain to reduce they would not have disclaimed their MCT tax credits, but as far as the public law reason for restitution is concerned, the receipt of the MCT was not itself part of what the ECJ had held to be invalid in the way that the inability to benefit from the group income election had been held to be a breach of EC law in *Metallgesellschaft and Hoechst*.[247] On the other hand, it is at least arguable that since the waiver was the result of the companies' attempts to mitigate the loss to them caused by the IRC's unlawful discrimination against them it was equally unlawful for the Revenue to receive the benefit of those constrained choices. On this basis it is to be distinguished from the inheritance tax example discussed by Henderson J;[248] if the choice to waive the tax credits had been the result of mistakenly choosing an option it was perfectly open to them to take, and perfectly within the powers of the Revenue to offer, then it would not be beyond the powers of the Revenue to receive the money paid as a result, whereas, on the other

[246] ibid [273].
[247] *Metallgesellschaft and Hoechst* (n 25).
[248] *FII* (UK) (n 80) [257].

hand, if it was held to be beyond the powers of the Revenue to receive the waivers and increased liability to MCT then recovery would be straightforward. Administrative law has not yet really had to grapple with the question of how far the invalidity of a particular action extends, being far more familiar with the opposite question of whether the action was void at all, or whether it could have partial or interim validity.[249] Indeed, the chance for public law to discuss and decide this question is a further dimension of the public body unjust enrichment cases which has been lost as a result of the failure to recognise their hybrid public and private nature and in a future case it would be preferable for these questions to be addressed outright, as they could be if public law were the reason for restitution.

How Far does a Claim in Unjust Enrichment Extend into Consequential Loss?

Just as public law therefore provides one aspect of the 'width of invalidity' issue, the second aspect of this issue arises from the other, private law half of the claim and, as noted above, in *FII* this aspect of the issue is crucial.

FII is the first case really to address the chain of causation in unjust enrichment in terms of problems with consequential loss.[250] Here, as noted above, the three claims excluded from the scope of unjust enrichment by the ECJ, Advocate General and/or Henderson J were all found to fall outside it on the basis that they were not the 'inevitable' or 'direct' consequence of the IRC's initial unlawful action in discriminating against the claimant companies, but rather were the result of choices made by those claimant companies (although in some of the claims there is the additional complication of having to establish whether or not the Revenue was also enriched).

Taking each of these exemptions in turn, it is certainly the case that but for the existence of an unlawful ACT mountain the claimants would not have made their distributions in the form of FIDs which had to be enhanced before they would become palatable to the recipient shareholders. It is also clear that the Revenue was not enriched by receipt of the enhancements, because this amount was received by the shareholders. However, the claimants argued that by compensating the recipient shareholders for the lack of repayable tax credits, the ultimate parent company thereby enriched the Revenue by relieving it of its obligations in respect of the tax credits.[251] In other words, had the claimants not had an ACT mountain to try to get rid of, they would not have paid their distributions as FIDs, and if they had not done so the Revenue would have had to give tax credits on these distributions to the tax

[249] See, eg: Wade and Forsyth (n 69) 300–7.

[250] Questions of causation in the past have tended to centre on matters such as 'interceptive subtraction'; whether the enrichment was really received *at the claimant's expense*, as opposed to the expense of a third party. See also: Burrows, *Law of Restitution* (n 87) 31–41 and ch 5, and the question often raised in the defence of passing on.

[251] *FII* (UK) (n 80) [208].

exempt shareholders. The Revenue was therefore saved this necessary expense by the use of the FID scheme. Henderson J rejected this claim, holding that the FID enhancements could not be regarded as having discharged a liability to which the Revenue would otherwise have been subject[252] because even if the FID scheme breached EC law in that the FIDs should have carried tax credits on the whole or part of their value, the Revenue was not itself obliged to pay the credits together with the dividends, but only to allow the recipient shareholders to make use of the credits in due course and to repay them, upon a claim being made for that purpose, if the recipient was exempt or a non-taxpayer. Henderson J also held that this was the case even assuming that the loss of the tax credits should be regarded as having been suffered by the claimants rather than the recipient shareholders.[253] However, in addition to finding that the Revenue had not been enriched, Henderson J also agreed with the ECJ's reasoning[254] that the FID enhancements had not been directly caused by the breach of EC law, but had instead been the result of a 'decision taken' by the claimants which was thus not an 'inevitable consequence' of the invalidity.[255]

With respect, neither argument is wholly convincing. As far as the enrichment point is concerned, the matter would obviously have to be decided on the facts, and may involve difficult questions of causation[256] but it was apparently known that around 40% of the shareholders were exempt.[257] If in these circumstances it could be shown that the recipient shareholders *would* have made use of the credits in due course, it is difficult to see that the Revenue was not enriched in the circumstances.[258]

As far as the reasoning of the ECJ is concerned, as noted above, the question of causation in unjust enrichment has not previously been addressed so directly. On the one hand, adoption of a simple 'but for' test would certainly have the potential to increase the liability of public bodies and such an approach should not therefore be taken lightly. However, on the other hand, first, it should be borne in mind that the decision to make distributions in the form of enhanced FIDs was not a wholly voluntary decision on the part of the claimants. Rather it was a decision they were constrained to take by the unlawful discrimination against them practised by the Revenue. Thus recovery could be granted in this context without laying down the rule that *no voluntary* choice would be capable of breaking the

252 ibid [273].
253 ibid [274].
254 ibid [274].
255 *FII* (ECJ) (n 80) [207].
256 Since a large number of the major exempt shareholders are claiming payment of the tax credits directly from HMRC in the *FID/Manninen Group Litigation* it is possible that the courts will deal with this question more thoroughly in that context and it is to be hoped that they do so at some point.
257 *FII* (UK) (n 80) [298].
258 On saved expense as an enrichment, see, eg: *Exall v Partridge* (1799) 8 TR 308 (KB), 101 ER 1045 and *County of Carleton v City of Ottawa* [1965] SCR 663, (1965) 52 DLR (2d) 220. There is of course an underlying theoretical question here about whether the existence of a tax credit represents an expense on the part of the Revenue, or whether it simply reduces the amount the Revenue is entitled to claim in the first place. It is certainly arguable that the former interpretation is correct and thus that the Revenue was enriched by the payment of the enhanced FIDs.

chain of causation in the manner envisaged by the ECJ, Advocate General and Henderson J, and as noted above, the situation can be distinguished from the inheritance tax example discussed by Henderson J.[259] Second, the problem with the 'inevitable consequences' test as opposed to the 'but for' test of causation, is that almost *nothing* can be held to be an *inevitable* consequence, since it will almost always be the case that another option would be available. For example, if here the claimants had not enhanced the FID payments and a claim had then been brought by the recipient shareholders that the Revenue had been unjustly enriched by failing in breach of EC law to pay the tax credits,[260] their loss would not have been *inevitable* either, since the recipient shareholders could instead have lobbied the claimants to enhance the FIDs (as in fact they did).[261] It seems, then, as if, rather than a strict test of 'inevitability', the ECJ may be tending towards something like a test of directness or straightforwardness; an amount can be reclaimed under the *San Giorgio* principle if the enrichment and expense have been allowed to lie where they fell. This in turn is an odd policy decision to make. It may well be the case that there is no *duty* to mitigate loss in relation to an unjust enrichment claim as a matter of EU or indeed national law[262] and it may even be as a matter of national law that mitigation of loss will not operate as a defence even when it does occur.[263] However, that is obviously not the same thing as *forbidding* mitigation of loss, in the sense that steps taken to mitigate will count as 'decisions taken' which prevent the unjust enrichment from being an 'inevitable consequence' of the unlawful action and deprive the *claimant* of an action in unjust enrichment. Indeed, as a matter of efficiency it is surely preferable that claimants should not be thus dissuaded from mitigating the expense to them, even if they are not positively required to do so, and if anything that approach is supported by the rule that it will not deprive the claimant of an action against the defendant if it succeeds in mitigating the loss,[264] whereas conversely the *FII* case is a strong deterrent to companies considering attempting to mitigate. As a matter of both EU and national

[259] *FII* (UK) (n 80) [257].

[260] As they are also in fact doing, see: Henderson J's reference to the FID Group Litigation Order (GLO) in *FII* (UK) (n 80) [273].

[261] Admittedly in this example the avoidance of the loss to the recipient shareholders depends on the action of a third party, namely the claimants, and it might therefore be argued that there was nothing else the recipient shareholders could have done themselves to reduce their expense, but it is not difficult to imagine other scenarios in which this would not be the case, for example see further below in relation to the discussion of disclaimed credits to MCT.

[262] See further ch 8, text to note 198.

[263] *Kleinwort Benson Ltd v Birmingham CC* [1997] QB 380 (CA). See also: Burrows, *Law of Restitution* (n 87) 593; and Virgo, *Principles* (n 87) 719–20.

[264] Where the mitigation takes the form of the passing on defence this is particularly important since it will be argued in ch 5, first, that if the passing on has been successful it would still be more efficient for the initial claimant to receive restitution and then in turn to have to account for it to the third parties to whom the expense was successfully passed, see, also: ch 5 and Burrows ibid 595–96. Second, it will be argued that in any case in such circumstances the mitigation itself almost inevitably causes further loss. So, eg, a company may attempt to pass on an unlawful tax in the price of its sales but it may then suffer a drop in sales as a result of the increased price. Any separate claim for this loss is so difficult to separate from the original claim in unjust enrichment that it may be thought simpler just to prevent the passing on defence from operating; see also: ch 5.

law, therefore, it is not wholly clear that the 'inevitable consequence' test is preferable to a 'but for' test of causation. It is therefore doubly significant, first that the 'inevitable consequence' test has so far been chosen over the 'but for' test and second, that this choice was not made by the national court but came to it from the ECJ's decision. The importance of this should not be underestimated and will be discussed further in chapter eight. It is also worth noting first, that since it is an EU law test it may not necessarily apply in wholly domestic situations and second, that there is a sharp contrast between this strict approach to causation in the context of *San Giorgio* claims and the much looser approach to causation in mistake adopted by Henderson J in *F J Chalke*.[265] Given Henderson J's view that *San Giorgio* claims would themselves require a cause of action based in mistake in some circumstances,[266] the potential for confusion is evident and, it is submitted, provides further evidence in favour of a rationalisation of causes of action of the kind advocated here.

As for the decision to waive or disclaim tax credit in order to increase MCT liability against which ACT could then be offset, the ECJ held that

> neither the reliefs waived by a taxpayer in order to be able to offset in full a tax levied *unlawfully*, such as ACT, against an amount due in respect of another tax . . . can form the basis of an action under Community law for the reimbursement of the tax unlawfully levied.[267] (emphasis added)

In his own judgment, Henderson J stated that he was 'puzzled by the reference to unlawfully levied ACT. If the ACT was levied unlawfully, it can be recovered in any event'.[268] It appears, however, that the further claims under this head are in fact concerned with loss of the additional MCT paid, since as Henderson J explains,[269] ACT discharges only a proportion of MCT liability and so by increasing their liability to MCT in order to use ACT against some of it, the claimants also increased their liability to (lawful) MCT. If this latter interpretation were correct, it would explain the confusion over the use of the term 'unlawfully' since whether or not the ACT set off against the MCT had been lawful or unlawful and whether or not it was recoverable on its own terms, the increased liability to lawful MCT would remain. Taking this latter issue first, there has certainly been an enrichment of the Revenue, but as far as any reasons for restitution are concerned, the ECJ again held that there is a break in the causal chain between the unlawfulness of the UK rules and the payment of the MCT by the claimants. In *Deutsche Morgan Grenfell*, once the group income election had been unlawfully denied to the claimants, the payment up front of ACT and consequent loss of its time value were inevitable; they were not the result of a further choice by the claimants in that case. Also, as discussed above, it was this direct denial of the benefit of the GIE which was itself

[265] *F J Chalke* (n 233) [138]. See above pp 109–10.
[266] *FII* (n 203).
[267] *FII* (ECJ) (n 80) [207]. See also: *FII* (UK) (n 80) [233]–[234] (Henderson J).
[268] *FII* (UK) (n 80) [271].
[269] *FII* (UK) (n 80) [206].

the breach of EC law in this instance. As regards the Test Claimants in *FII*, however, discrimination in the taxing rules which led to the creation of the ACT mountain was in breach of EC law, but the increased liability to MCT did not follow inevitably from this in the same way that liability to pay ACT up front followed inevitably from the unlawful denial of the GIE in *Deutsche Morgan Grenfell*.[270] However, for the reasons given above in relation to the enhanced FID payments, it is not clear that the 'direct or inevitable consequences' test is wholly preferable to the 'but for' test of causation, as a matter either of practice or of policy. Indeed, here the argument against inevitability is even stronger, since the choice between allowing the ACT mountain to pile up unused and the decision to waive or disclaim tax credits in order to increase liability for MCT lay solely with the claimants. Had they taken the former option, they could have claimed for recovery of the time value of the ACT but could then have been met with the argument that this expense was not an inevitable result of the invalid tax rules, because they could always have waived their tax credits, increased their liability to MCT and thus set off ACT against it as on the facts they did. Again, the problem seems to be that the ECJ has moved from reasoning that mitigation of loss is not required to a position in which it is positively discouraged, since steps taken to mitigate loss will tend to break the chain of 'inevitable consequences' while letting the loss lie where it falls in the absence of self-help seems more likely to lead to recovery on the basis of unjust enrichment.[271] Thus even though the case certainly *can* be distinguished from *Metallgesellschaft and Hoechst* and *Deutsche Morgan Grenfell*, it is not clear that it should be, though again, this is really a result of the reasoning of the ECJ in the case, rather than that of Henderson J.

If this is true of the increased liability to MCT when this was paid directly, it must also be true of the tranche of MCT against which ACT was offset. If the ACT was itself unlawful, as Henderson J points out, that would be recoverable anyway on its own terms, and there is no distinction between use of lawful ACT to offset extra MCT liability and the payment of that liability directly as discussed above. Thus however the 'disclaimed MCT' issue is interpreted, the conclusion must be the same; that according to Henderson J, under neither EC nor English law would the increased liability to MCT be recoverable as unjust enrichment. It would be recoverable, if at all, only as state liability in damages under the *Francovich* and *Brasserie/Factortame III* rules.[272] This conclusion can be questioned for the reasons given above.

This leaves the claim for ACT set off against unlawful 'Case V corporation tax'. Here Henderson J's reasoning is as follows:

[270] *Deutsche Morgan Grenfell* (n 4).

[271] Also, as noted above and as is made evident in the case of *FII* itself, unjust enrichment may well be the only route to recovery since the criteria for state liability in damages may well not be made out. See above and *FII* (UK) (n 80) [404].

[272] *Brasserie/Factortame III* (n 78). In the event, as noted above, n 198, Henderson J held that the claims would not succeed on this ground either.

If lawfully paid ACT was used to offset an unlawful liability to Case V corporation tax, the result was that the company concerned did not pay corporation tax which, if it had done so, it would admittedly now be able to recover. If the Revenue was enriched at all, it was certainly not by the receipt of unlawfully levied corporation tax but rather as a result of the group then having less ACT available to use for other purposes. An enquiry into whether (and if so how) such ACT would otherwise have been used within the group can in my judgment only form part of a claim for consequential loss. I do not see how it could be said that the Revenue was immediately and directly enriched at the group's expense by an amount equal to the ACT so used.[273]

It is extremely difficult to see why this should be. In principle, the right to set off ACT against other taxes was just a kind of asset[274] and it is therefore difficult to see why the use of that asset should be treated differently from a payment of money. If the claimants had paid the unlawful Case V corporation tax in cash it would not have been thought remotely relevant to ascertain any other purposes to which they would otherwise have put it. Obviously money, being a credit against a third party treasury, is inherently enriching in a way that ACT is not, but as Henderson J himself points out it is certainly not impossible to argue that the Revenue was enriched as a result of the group's credit against it, in the form of ACT, diminishing. There could, of course, be difficult questions of valuation; unlike an enrichment of £100 cash, where a statutory relief is used to eliminate liability of £100 the enrichment of the Revenue at the taxpayer's expense is probably only equal to the net present value of the relief, discounted by reference to the likely period of time until it was used, and also for the risk that it never would be used.[275] But these are issues of quantification, not liability, and are not insurmountable. Given his acceptance that the Case V corporation tax was otherwise recoverable as an unlawful tax, it is therefore difficult to see why Henderson J did not draw the same line as the ECJ and hold that these payments could constitute instances of unjust enrichment, just like the payment of unlawful tax in the *Woolwich* case. Nevertheless, even though he did not reach the same decision on the facts as the ECJ on this point, it is clear that his decision is the result of trying to follow the ECJ's 'direct' or 'inevitable consequences' test.[276] Both this test and Henderson J's extension of it to Case V corporation tax issue are, for the reasons given, undesirable.

Evidence for the Hierarchy and the Issue of 'Closed' Swaps

Finally, it should not be thought that the special nature of the public law reason for restitution has gone entirely unnoticed elsewhere, and indeed Lord Goff himself

[273] *FII* (UK) (n 80) [270].

[274] See, eg: the evidence given by the head of tax at BAT, the group from whom the test claimants were largely drawn: ibid [33].

[275] Shiers (n 187).

[276] ibid [271].

has in other circumstances provided some support for it. On the issue of 'closed' swaps, Birks had argued that 'after the execution of the supposed contract the force of this type of mistake is spent'.[277] This argument was considered and rejected by Lord Goff and Lord Hope in *Kleinwort Benson v Lincoln*. In particular, Lord Goff held that:

> [I]t is incompatible with the ultra vires rule that an ultra vires transaction should become binding on a local authority simply on the ground that it has been completed. Moreover the ultra vires rule is not optional; it applies whether the transaction in question proves to have been profitable or unprofitable. If the argument in Professor Birks' footnote is right, the result would be that effect would be given to a contract which public policy has declared to be void.[278]

It will be remembered that Birks also believed that completion of the swaps transactions would rule out the unjust factor of failure of consideration, but the Court of Appeal rejected this argument in *Guinness Mahon*,[279] and its reasoning was upheld in *Kleinwort Benson v Lincoln*.[280] The words used by Morritt LJ are very similar to those of Lord Goff cited above:

> If, as the Council contends there is no claim for money had and received in the case of a completed swap then practical effect will be given to a transaction which the doctrine of ultra vires proclaims had no legal existence.[281]

But why should this matter? It is true that a case based on mistake as to vires requires the claimant to prove the public law event of ultra vires, but the reason for restitution, it should be remembered, is still the private law unjust factor of mistake (vitiated intention). Similarly, a case based on absence of consideration due to the voidness of the contract in public law requires proof of the ultra vires event, but again, the reason for restitution is still the private law unjust factor of failure of consideration. Why should we care that this leads to a conflict with the ultra vires finding in the background of the case, if that finding was only necessary in order to prove that the claimant was in fact mistaken or that the consideration failed? If the force of the particular private law reason for restitution is spent, why is a denial of recovery problematic? Certainly if the closure of the swap were to bar claims based on either failure of consideration or mistake this would be further evidence that where these grounds overlap with the public law unjust factor they are rendered redundant, since their more stringent rules can be evaded by use of that unjust factor. Indeed, Birks had argued that precisely for this reason the 'policy' unjust factor (which he describes as having 'never been fully explicated',

[277] P Birks, 'No Consideration: Restitution after Void Contracts' (1993) 23 University of Western Australia Law Review 195, 230, fn 137.

[278] *Kleinwort Benson* (n 15) 387. See also: J Convery, 'Lord Goff's Swansong: Restitution, Mistake of Law, and the Retrospective Effect of Judicial Decisions' (1999) 3 *Edinburgh Law Review* 202, 214, quoting A Burrows, 'Swaps and the Friction between Common Law and Equity' (1995) 3 *Restitution Law Review* 15, 29.

[279] *Guinness Mahon and Co Ltd v Kensington and Chelsea RLBC* [1999] QB 215 (CA).

[280] *Kleinwort Benson* (n 15).

[281] *Guinness Mahon* (n 279) 229.

but which has been developed here into the public law unjust factor) may be the only choice for claimants in closed swaps cases.[282] However, this potential redundancy does not really go to the heart of what it is that concerns Lord Goff and Morritt LJ.

Arguably the answer is that they want the public law event to play a greater role than this so that, as suggested here, when a case contains a public law event, *even if* a claim can be formulated in private law, with the public law event playing only a background role, the public law reason for restitution should nevertheless prevail. Otherwise it is difficult to understand their concerns.

From the secondary literature, further evidence of a different sort in favour of the hierarchy comes from Crerar, who argues that:

> Given collective action problems, coupled with the imprecision and inadequacy of traditional joinder rules, such unjust enrichment will usually go unchecked. The class action legislation [for which he argues, on the other hand] empowers individuals to recoup their loss. It serves in turn as a regulatory mechanism, deterring the unjustly enriched from illegal collections.[283]

In ordinary circumstances this would be an unusual argument. The sorts of cases with which he is concerned are those in which an unlawful charge has affected a large number of people, but only to a very small extent each. Indeed, he suggests the restitutionary class action as a solution for cases where the party who initially paid the money is unable to recover, having passed on the expense to many of his/her customers. At present, therefore, it is not worth each of the potential claimants exercising their right to recover the money. Under normal circumstances surely we would not care whether individuals exercised the rights they had or not. If they had only suffered to a very small extent, too small for it to be worth their while claiming, surely we would see that as a good reason why the court should not be concerned with their case? But the situation here is obviously different, and Crerar argues that we should promote claims in order to 'deter' and 'check' illegality. As suggested above, not only would this indicate a preference for the public law reason for restitution over those such as mistake of law and failure of consideration in which the public law illegality plays a background role, it would also suggest that a private party who had obeyed an ultra vires request through mistake of fact (for example, by paying tax on more red-headed employees than it actually had) should use the public law reason for restitution in preference to relying on that mistake of fact too.

[282] Birks, 'Private Law' (n 14) 19–21.

[283] D Crerar, 'The Restitutionary Class Action' (1998) 56 *University of Toronto Faculty of Law Review* 47, 98.

Conclusion

Ultimately, then, the series of appeals in *Deutsche Morgan Grenfell* represents a missed opportunity. The judgments of the Court of Appeal had the advantage of recognising that there was indeed something special about the public law unjust factor which ought to allow it to take precedence over other purely private reasons for restitution. Unfortunately, their decisions were based less on principled analysis and more on their interpretations of Lord Goff's speeches. This left them exposed to the possibility that the House of Lords could take a contrary interpretation without also having to deal with any principled objections to doing so. As for the judgments of the House of Lords, it is clear that their Lordships' reluctance to maintain the hierarchy begun by the Court of Appeal stems largely from a failure to understand why such a hierarchy should exist or how it should operate. Had their Lordships had the advantage of a pair of public law spectacles as well as their private law ones, the justification for and functioning of the proposed hierarchy would, it is submitted, have become much clearer and more appealing and incidentally this would also have enabled them to avoid their unsurprising differences of opinion concerning the nature and existence of the mistake, if any, made by DMG.[284] A situation in which the House of Lords splits 4:1 over whether a mistake can be made at all in such circumstances, 3:2 over whether in fact DMG was labouring under a mistake when it made the relevant payments, and suffers a further 2:1 split among that majority concerning the content of the mistake, to say nothing of differences between the three levels of court, or between different courts in different branches of the post *Metallgesellschaft and Hoechst* litigation,[285] can hardly be regarded as a successful and clear method of dealing with the facts of the case.[286] It is true that those facts were complicated, but the extra complexity added by the mistake issue would be rendered entirely unnecessary if the true nature of the case was fully understood. By far the most important reason for giving preference to the public reason for restitution as suggested here, however, is that only by doing so can the law adequately address and respond to the concerns arising in both private and public law. As seen in this chapter, this means principally that as well as dealing with the existence of an enrichment at a claimant's expense, the law also needs access to the public law illegality as rapidly as possible and in a context which will allow it to address that illegality in the way thought most appropriate in administrative law. In other words, by using the public law

[284] See also: Hedley (n 88) 298–99.

[285] See, eg: Mummery LJ in *Boake Allen* (CA) (n 201) [161], quoted above, n 227 and the odd uses of relatively unspecific mistake by Henderson J in *FII* (UK) (n 80) and *F J Chalke* (n 233). The confusion between this broad use of mistake and the narrow test for causation in *San Giorgio* claims discussed in *FII*, added to Henderson J's view that the former cause of action is necessary for upholding claims of the latter kind should also be borne in mind (text to ns 265 and 266).

[286] For a detailed analysis of the complexity of different treatments of mistake in *Deutsche Morgan Grenfell*, see also: C Mitchell, 'Mistaken Tax Payments' (2007) 15 *Restitution Law Review* 124.

unjust factor in the private law claim, private law must pass the reason for restitution over to administrative law for definition of its precise nature and extent, rather than distorting administrative law concepts by squeezing them into the categories of private law.[287] Had the House of Lords thus taken the opportunity to do this provided by *Deutsche Morgan Grenfell*, the law would then have been set up for more straightforward application in all the other related cases such as *FII*, where, for example, the opportunity for public law to consider the extent of the invalidity in the consequential loss claims could potentially have made an important contribution. However, the balance between the requirements of public and private law must also be struck later in the claim, and it is this issue to which we now turn.

[287] Thus we should not, for example, try to mistranslate 'jurisdictional error of fact and law', or their suggested replacements, into 'mistake of law' and 'mistake of fact' in unjust enrichment. Nor should we mistranslate the existence and extent of a public law illegality by trying to analogise it to the setting aside of a contract like Lord Hope (see above), any more than we should try to mistranslate that public law illegality into '*ab initio* voidness' in the manner attempted in *Woolwich* and the swaps cases (see ch 3 above).

5

Defences

What General Implications does the Hybrid Nature of the Reason for Restitution have for Defences?

ONE IMPORTANT DIFFERENCE between the core public law 'remedies' of declaration, injunction, certiorari, prohibition and mandamus on the one hand, and restitution, contractual responses, responses to torts and habeas corpus on the other, is that the former are discretionary, and the court can withhold them if it thinks fit.[1]

Birks argues that we should move away from using the word 'remedy', motivated in part by his abhorrence of what he identified as the fifth potential meaning of the word, discretionary remedialism, which he argues would lead to 'rightlessness'.[2] Nevertheless, even in private law, as Birks notes, '[m]any judicial orders are weakly discretionary'.[3] However, the rules for the exercise of that discretion have been developed over many years.[4] The same is true of public law. The court does have a discretion whether to grant any of the possible responses such as certiorari, but it is not nonsense to speak of the claimant having a 'right' to them, and public law does not contain this state of 'rightlessness' any more than private law.[5] Indeed, Wade and Forsyth have been judicially approved in arguing that discretion should be *limited* to the sphere of 'remedies',[6] further evidence that 'remedies' in public law can be equated with 'responses'.[7]

[1] H Wade and C Forsyth, *Administrative Law*, 9th edn (Oxford, Oxford University Press, 2004) 700. See also: T Bingham, 'Should Public Law Remedies be Discretionary?' [1991] *Public Law* 64 and R Cooke, 'The Discretionary Heart of Administrative Law' in C Forsyth and I Hare (eds), *The Golden Metwand and the Crooked Cord: Essays in Honour of Sir William Wade* (Oxford, Clarendon Press, 1998).

[2] P Birks, 'Rights, Wrongs and Remedies' (2000) 20 *Oxford Journal of Legal Studies* 1, 22–24.

[3] ibid 16.

[4] ibid.

[5] Lord Bingham's view is that the discretion should remain: (n 1) 75, 'probably, in some cases, up to a point, provided the discretion is strictly limited and the rules for its exercise clearly understood'. This is supported by Lord Cooke (n 1).

[6] Wade and Forsyth (n 1) 701, citing *Bugg v DPP* [1993] QB 473 (DC) 499 (Woolf and Pill LJJ) and *R v Wicks* [1998] AC 92 (HL) 121 (Lord Hoffmann), where their views were quoted.

[7] Wade and Forsyth contrast the discretionary 'remedies' of declaration, injunction, certiorari, prohibition and mandamus with 'remedies in tort, contract or restitution' (and habeas corpus), the 'remedies' which may be claimed as of right: ibid 700. This proposition is supported by Lord Bingham's analysis of this judicial discretion as the choice of 'what is the fair and just thing to do or order in the instant case': Lord Bingham (n 1) 67.

Various factors operate to determine whether the public law 'remedies' will be granted.[8] For example, in *R v Secretary of State for Social Services, ex p Association of Metropolitan Authorities* (*ex p AMA*),[9] relief was withheld because there would be serious public inconvenience in upsetting the impugned order. Such considerations can, then, be seen as the corollary to the *ex p Datafin* criteria discussed in Chapter 1.[10] On the one hand, public bodies wield a different kind of power from that held by private parties. Such power can be monopolistic but must be used for the public good.[11] On the other hand, however, any responses granted by the law in cases involving public parties can have immediate implications for the public good in a way that responses granted to private parties cannot. It is true that a change in private law precedent can have 'public policy' implications and can raise concerns about the opening of 'floodgates' but when it is private money which will flow through these floodgates, the concerns are different from those which apply to public revenue. A decision taken under public law, supposedly in the interests of the public at large, cannot simultaneously be allowed to harm those interests. The same reasoning does not apply in private situations.

This explains why it is that the public law responses are discretionary. The fact that the private law responses are so much less so is again, it is submitted, due to the Diceyan orthodoxy. If a public body was behaving purely privately in contracting, doing wrong, or becoming unjustly enriched, then according to this orthodoxy there is no need for the response to take account of public law considerations.[12] However, it has been established here that this 'purely private' account is not satisfactory when there are two events contained within the cause of action, one of which is public. A practical example of this comes from the fact that very different concerns are raised by those who have considered the 'swaps' cases from the public law point of view. Largely they focus on the *Hazell v Hammersmith and Fulham LBC*[13] decision, and the original finding of invalidity. They suggest that this case has stifled the private finance initiative, and made it harder for local authorities to deal with banks, as a result of the commercial uncertainty generated by *Hazell* and the subsequent litigation.[14] However, these arguments necessarily extend also to the 'mopping up' process performed by the grant of restitution in

[8] See: P Craig, *Administrative Law*, 6th edn (London, Sweet and Maxwell, 2008) ch 25 and 26-055.

[9] *R v Secretary of State for Social Services, ex p Association of Metropolitan Authorities (ex p AMA)* [1993] COD 54 (QB).

[10] See ch 1 above, especially text at n 81 onwards.

[11] See: *R v Tower Hamlets LBC, ex p Chetnik Developments Ltd* [1988] AC 858 (HL).

[12] The reasoning behind the non-discretionary nature of habeas corpus is, it is submitted, different. Here the argument is not that there is nothing public about the party's actions but, that the interest at stake is personal liberty, and as Lord Cooke has pointed out, 'personal liberty being at stake, the courts would not excuse an irregularity except for most compelling reasons': Lord Cooke (n 1) 211. There is thus not the same discretion because of the limited number of things that can be weighed against personal liberty.

[13] *Hazell v Hammersmith and Fulham LBC* [1992] 2 AC 1 (HL).

[14] See, eg: R Clutterbuck, editorial, (1991) *Journal of Business Law* 105; J Convery, 'Lord Goff's Swansong: Restitution, Mistake of Law, and the Retrospective Effect of Judicial Decisions' (1999) 3 *Edinburgh Law Review* 202, especially 'Coda' at 216; and M Loughlin, 'Innovative Financing in Local Government: the Limits of Legal Instrumentalism—Part II' [1991] *Public Law* 568.

these cases, and suggest that if restitution were to be a public law response alongside the prerogative remedies it might not, under the *ex p AMA* decision, have been granted.[15]

A further suggestion for future reform is therefore that, once the public law reason for restitution is given precedence over other unjust factors, the availability of the restitutionary response in such cases should be different from purely private single event cases. In other words, the hybrid nature of the claims and the consequent hierarchy of unjust factors suggested here may have important implications for the operation of defences and other related arguments.

Two sets of such defences and related arguments must be considered. On the one hand, the ordinary private law defences such as passing on or change of position can potentially play the same role here as in any other part of the law of unjust enrichment. However, there is also a series of defences and related matters which may be relevant as a result of the public law nature of the claims, or possibly of one of the parties. These include: the defence of 'fiscal disruption'; prospective overruling; subsequent legislation; and the Law Commissions' special defence of 'failure to exhaust the statutory remedies'.[16]

All the defences can be altered either in favour of the public body, or in favour of legality. For example, the defence of 'fiscal disruption' could apply whenever a public body is a defendant in any kind of unjust enrichment claim. Or on the other hand, this defence could be rejected, and even the usual defences could be restricted in their application, when there is a public law unjust factor claim, in order to promote legality. The argument here is, first, that it is the hierarchy of unjust factors and the consequent monopoly of the public law reason for restitution which should affect the application of the defences. The variation of private law defences and the introduction of public law defences should only take place when public law is the reason for restitution and, as has been argued here, when it can be made out on the facts this unjust factor will be used in preference to any other. As a result, since public law unjust factor cases include *Westdeutsche*, *Woolwich* and *Auckland Harbour* type situations, it is also proposed, second, that in many cases alterations to existing defences, or creation of additional defences, should apply uniformly whether the public body is the defendant or the claimant.

Third, while the choice between altering the defences in favour of the public body and altering them in favour of legality may be a new choice for unjust enrichment lawyers,[17] it should be noted this is a familiar problem for public lawyers.

[15] Most local authorities wished to fulfil their contracts. None had speculated on the scale of Hammersmith. In most authorities, the losses were relatively small, and these authorities had generally made provision within their budgets to continue to make payments. They would not therefore be taken by surprise if required to do so. Furthermore, some authorities remained net gainers in their transactions. More generally, many local authorities felt that they were honour-bound to maintain these deals. Finally, there was a fear within local government that, if they were not allowed to make these payments, credit would become more expensive for the entire sector. For further details, see: Loughlin ibid 572.

[16] Law Commission (n 54) [9.19]–[9.20], [10.7], [10.42]–[10.43].

[17] It is, of course, true that alteration of defences for reason of public policy is perfectly familiar to unjust enrichment lawyers, but this form of alteration is different. Chen-Wishart argues that the relevant unjust factor can be an important indicator of the application of the change of position defence:

Very similar questions arise in relation to the discretionary nature of public law responses, illustrated by *ex p AMA* above,[18] and there are several factors which will mean that when a private party applies for a public law response through judicial review the response may be denied. These are: waiver; bad faith; the premature nature of the application; the absence of any injustice; the impact on third parties; the impact on the administration; the fact that the same decision would have been reached in the absence of the public law event; the ongoing best efforts of the respondent authority to be legally compliant; the fact that the error is substantially cured; the fact that the problem is now moot; and, as noted above, serious public inconvenience in upsetting the impugned order. Craig argues in addition that since we are willing to qualify the ultra vires principle *against* the individual in such circumstances, we should also be willing to qualify it in favour of private parties when they have suffered loss through relying on an ultra vires representation.[19] These matters are an important part of public law, but should now also be borne in mind when examining the defences available to unjust enrichment claims involving public bodies. The important thing is that in public law there are reasons why the response may be denied entirely, or in part. Similarly, in the specific public law unjust enrichment cases at issue here, the response to the ultra vires event may be denied entirely, or in part, depending on the precise method of application, if any, of each of the defences.

It is necessary here to make it clear exactly how and why the above alterations to these defences, if accepted, would apply. First, it should be noted that the two considerations outlined above, legality and protection of public bodies, will not always conflict. Protection of public bodies against disruption contrary to the greater public interest will always favour the public body, but promotion of legality can favour either party. Thus where the public body is the claimant, it could potentially claim that the defences should be altered in its favour for both reasons. Where it is the defendant, on the other hand, the public body will only be able to claim disruption, and the private party could potentially argue that the defences should be altered in its favour for the promotion of legality. Second, it should be noted that while the promotion of legality can therefore favour either party, it will always favour the disapplication of defences.[20]

Thus it is necessary to examine whether, and if so how, each of the defences needs to be altered in order to strike the correct balance between the public and

M Chen-Wishart, 'Unjust Factors and the Restitutionary Response' (2000) 20 *Oxford Journal of Legal Studies* 557. The view here supports that result, but extends it to all defences and does so not as a 'tailoring' of the law of unjust enrichment so much as through the operation of public law. Similarly, Chen-Wishart adopts the public policy alteration conception of defences in *Woolwich* whereas, just as I have rejected the general 'public policy' analysis of the reason for restitution in *Woolwich* in favour of the more specific 'public law event' analysis, what I am discussing in relation to defences is not private law public policy alteration but the specific application of public law rules.

[18] *ex p AMA* (n 9).

[19] Craig (n 8). See also: Wade and Forsyth (n 1) 700–3.

[20] Thus Jones suggests that it would be 'odd' for those who support the disapplication of change of position in these cases to grant other defences that are more generous to the public body (such as short limitation periods): G Jones, *Public and Private* (n 60) 28.

private aspects of the dual event claims. The operation of each of the private law defences suggested by the unjust enrichment event must be compared with the reasons why discretion may be exercised against the grant of a response in public law. In other words, the 'qualifications to the ultra vires principle', which arise in pure public law must be compared with those which arise in the public law unjust enrichment dual event cases through the existing private law defences to unjust enrichment. The reverse inquiry must then be conducted in relation to the specialised defences applicable only to public law reason for restitution cases. The question here will be whether the public law defences unduly restrict the law's access to the private event of unjust enrichment.

One case which has come close to examining some of these questions is *R v Tower Hamlets LBC, ex p Chetnik Developments Ltd.*[21] In this case, the applicants had redeveloped a site to provide two warehouse units. It was a condition of the requisite building construction consent issued under the London Building Acts 1930–1939 that the buildings should not be occupied until consent to the proposed user had been obtained, and for a while the buildings were not occupied. During this time the applicants paid rates on the buildings, despite the fact that General Rate Act 1967 provided that 'no rates . . . [would] be payable . . . for . . . any period during which (a) the owner is prohibited by law from occupying the hereditament or allowing it to be occupied'.[22] Obviously, this would have exempted the applicants from such payments. However, unlike the other cases discussed in this investigation, the applicants did not bring an action based on the common law of unjust enrichment.[23] Instead, they had to apply under section 9 of the General Rate Act 1967, which gave the rating authority discretion to refund the whole or part of the money, a discretion which the rating authority refused to exercise in the applicants' favour.[24] This case is therefore not one which should, on the argument made here, be considered as a dual event case. The recovery in *ex p Chetnik* is based on statute rather than on the common law event of unjust enrichment, so that there are in fact two sequential public law events: the mistaken payment and therefore receipt of the money, followed by the refusal to exercise the discretion to repay, rather than two simultaneous events, one a public law event and the other a private law event of unjust enrichment. However, it was clear, at least to Lord Goff, that the General Rate Act 1967 created 'a statutory remedy of restitution, in the circumstances specified by the section, to prevent the unjust enrichment of the rating authority at the expense of the ratepayer'.[25]

It is submitted that when his Lordship states that 'the general principles of the law of restitution can provide useful guidance in these cases',[26] put into my terms he is actually suggesting that two events are relevant: the public law event of the

[21] *ex p Chetnik Developments* (n 11).

[22] General Rate Act 1967 Sch 1[2].

[23] ie an action for money had and received.

[24] In particular, the applicants relied on s 9(1)(e) which provided for situations where 'the person who made a payment in respect of rates was not liable to make that payment'.

[25] *ex p Chetnik Developments* (n 11) 882 (Lord Goff). His Lordship is referring to s 9.

[26] ibid 883.

rating authority's refusal to exercise its discretion in favour of the ratepayers; and the private law event of unjust enrichment. This still does not parallel the case exactly with the dual event cases considered here, because the right of recovery was still to be derived from section 9 of the 1967 statute. Nor was it the case that the court was considering public law as the reason for restitution; indeed the only relevant 'unjust factor' considered was mistake of law.[27] However, their Lordships did consider factors which could influence the exercise of the statutory discretion to repay and to this extent the case is relevant to the current investigation and should be considered under the appropriate headings below.

Time Limits

One key application of these suggestions, and a matter which bridges both private and public law defences and related issues, is the question of the time limits applicable to claims involving public law events. Where the public law reason for restitution overlaps with another unjust factor, it has been argued that the former should prevail, but it has also been seen that some cases can only use mistake of law because only then can they take advantage of a longer time limit.[28] Yet even in those cases the arguments in favour of recognising the public law nature of the claim through the public law reason for restitution still apply. This suggests that rather than interpreting such cases controversially as involving mistakes of law in order to evade the usual statutory protection for legal certainty, thus losing sight of their public law nature and implications, it would be better to have one time limit applicable exclusively to all claims where a charge or payment is found to be beyond the powers of a public body and either the same claimant or another wishes to rely on that fact to reclaim money. In other words, it would be better to tailor the time limit to the relevant cause of action, rather than allowing that cause of action to be driven in an inappropriate direction by time limit concerns. In one sense this has already happened. On 8 September and 11 November 2003, the IRC announced not only that it would appeal the *Deutsche Morgan Grenfell* decision,[29] but also that it would introduce a Finance Bill which will stop section 32 of the Limitation Act 1980 from applying to any 'taxation matter under the care and

[27] ibid 869, 870 and 874–77 (Lord Bridge).

[28] Above ch 4 at 74 onwards. It was noted there that there is a dispute over the precise implications of s 32(1)(c) of the Limitation Act 1980, and in particular whether mistake must be the cause of action before the extension of the six year time limit is available, ch 4 note 16.

[29] *Deutsche Morgan Grenfell v IRC* [2003] EWHC 1779 (Ch), [2003] 4 All ER 645 (first instance); [2005] EWCA Civ 78, (2006) Ch 243 (CA); and [2006] UKHL 49, [2007] 1 AC 558 (HL). The CA decision has been noted at: A Burrows, 'Restitution in Respect of Mistakenly Paid Tax' (2005) 121 *Law Quarterly Review* 540; G Virgo, '*Deutsche Morgan Grenfell*: the Right to Restitution of Tax Paid by Mistake Rejected' [2005] *British Tax Review* 281; R Stevens, 'Justified Enrichment' (2005) 5 *Oxford University Commonwealth Law Journal* 141; and R Williams, 'The Beginnings of a Public Law of Unjust Enrichment?' (2005) 16 *King's College Law Journal* 194.

management of the Commissioners of Inland Revenue'. It stated that the Bill would apply to 'any action for relief from the consequences of a mistake of law, whether expressed to be brought on the ground of mistake or on some other ground (such as unlawful demand or ultra vires act)'.[30]

This was duly enacted as sections 320 and 321 of the Finance Act 2004, and further reinforced by the Finance Act 2007 opening the way for the hierarchy of unjust factors to be fully established: where the public law unjust factor overlaps with another ground of restitution the former should prevail and there would be no cases involving public law events where the public law reason for restitution is unavailable and yet another could be used. However, the problem was that these provisions were not compliant with EC law. When time limits are applied to cases involving questions of EU law, they must not prevent the remedy from being effective to protect the relevant EU legal rights and must be equivalent to the rules applicable in purely domestic situations.[31] It seems likely in the light of the decision in *Edis v Ministero delle Finanze*[32] that a six year general time limit would comply with these requirements. However, the problem was that the 2004 legislation announced on 8 September 2003 and the 2007 Finance Act both had retrospective effect and did not contain any transitional provisions.[33] Thus, in the light of *Marks and Spencer plc v Commissioners of Customs and Excise*[34] and *Grundig Italiana SpA v Ministero delle Finanze*,[35] these factors were held in the *FII* case to create a breach of the duty to provide an effective remedy as a matter of EC law.[36] It would, of course, be possible to provide for this category of claimants in transitional provisions and as long as their time limit was not 'too short' this ought to comply with the requirement of effectiveness. Certainly, it would be possible to introduce legislation which would apply the six year time limit across the board to charges yet to be paid, because this would be wholly prospective.

Marks and Spencer and *Deutsche Morgan Grenfell* are not the only instances, of course, in which the Revenue has sought to impose a retrospective time limit. After *Woolwich*[37] itself, the government enacted section 53 of the Finance Act 1991

[30] Originally the press releases were available on the IRC's website, but they are now only available by contacting the Revenue directly.

[31] On which see ch 8 below.

[32] Case C-231/96 *Edis v Ministero delle Finanze* [1998] ECR I-4951. In that case, a three year time limit for reclaiming sums paid but not due was held to be adequate even though this was a special rule applicable to public bodies which was not applicable between individuals. The court held that 'the position would be different only if those detailed rules applied solely to actions based on Community law for the repayment of such charges or levies': ibid [37].

[33] For an explanation of the retrospective nature of the provisions see ch 4, n 170.

[34] Case C-62/00 *Marks and Spencer plc v Commissioners of Customs and Excise* [2002] ECR I-6325. For the final national chapter in the case, see: [2009] UKHL 8, [2009] 1 All ER 939 (HL).

[35] Case C-255/00 *Grundig Italiana SpA v Ministero delle Finanze* [2002] ECR I-8003.

[36] *Test Claimants in the FII Group Litigation v The Commissioners for Her Majesty's Revenue and Customs* [2008] EWHC 2893 (Ch), [2009] STC 254. See further ch 8, *Aegis Group plc v IRC* [2005] EWHC 1468 (Ch), [2006] STC 23; *Europcar UK Ltd v Revenue and Customs Commissioner* [2008] EWHC 1363 (Ch), [2008] STC 2751 [2]; ch 4, ch 8 and M Chowdry, 'How long can section 80 last?' [2004] *British Tax Review* 106.

[37] *Woolwich Equitable Building Society v IRC* [1993] AC 70 (HL).

retrospectively to validate the *Woolwich* tax, save in respect of anyone who commenced proceedings before 17 July 1986. On 16 July 1992, section 64 of the Finance (No 2) Act 1992 entered into force, providing, with retrospective effect, that the Treasury orders 'shall be taken to be and always to have been effective'. Many felt this legislation was unfair, especially since, as Jordan notes, calls for retrospective legislation in the swaps cases where the defendants were public bodies 'fell upon deaf ears . . . Depending how one looks at it, this may or may not be viewed as consistent behaviour'.[38]

Three building societies excluded by this legislation, the National and Provincial, the Yorkshire and the Leeds, therefore challenged its validity, this time in Strasbourg, alleging violations of Article 1 of Protocol 1 to the ECHR (because the effect of the legislation was to deprive them of their possessions); of Article 6(1) (because it deprived them of a fair hearing before a court); and Article 14 (because they had been subjected to discriminatory treatment). The Commission held (by 13 votes to 3) that while the building societies did have 'possessions', the fair balance between the demands of the general interest of the community and the protection of the fundamental rights of the applicants had not been upset.[39] Nor had there been a violation of Article 14 (14 votes to 2) because Woolwich alone had incurred the costs and run the risks of challenging the regulations, so there was an objective and reasonable justification for treating the applicants differently. Finally, there had been a violation of Article 6(1) (9 votes to 7), because the rights at issue in both the restitution and judicial review proceedings were 'civil', and the subject matter was clearly pecuniary. The state had thus intervened through the legislature in a manner that was decisive to ensure that the proceedings were resolved in its favour, and had deprived the applicants of their right to obtain a determination of their civil rights and obligations following a fair hearing before a court.

The European Court of Human Rights (ECtHR), however, found against the building societies.[40] On 23 October 1997, the ECtHR agreed that there had been no violation of Article 1 of Protocol 1, or of Article 14, but it also held that there had been no violation of Article 6(1). While the ECtHR was mindful of the dangers of retrospective legislation, the authorities had not interfered with pending legal proceedings to which they were a party. The applicant parties must reasonably be considered to have anticipated that the Treasury would seek Parliament's permission to cure the defects in the Regulations, and the three building societies had been trying to pre-empt this. The extinction of the restitution proceedings was a significant consequence of the legislation, but the applicant societies were not its particular targets. Finally, while section 64 was intended to bring an end to the proceedings brought by the three societies, these proceedings were really the next stage in the effort to frustrate the original intention of Parliament, and the applicants could not really expect the Treasury to remain inactive. Nor had the judicial

[38] N Jordan, 'Retrospection and Restitution: The Woolwich Building Society Rulings' (1991) *Butterworths Journal of International Banking and Financial Law* 481, 483.

[39] European Commission of Human Rights: 25 June 1996 (Merits) [1997] 1 EHRLR 111.

[40] [1998] 2 EHRLR 236.

review proceedings reached the stage of an *inter partes* hearing.[41] It is thus clear that the ECHR places fewer limitations on the government's power to enact time limits than does the EU.

Turning to the public law context, two sets of provisions cover the time limits for applications for judicial review. Rule 54.5(1) of the Civil Procedure Rules (CPR) provides that the claim form must be filed promptly and in any event not later than three months after the grounds to make the claim first arose, though even shorter time limits can be set out in specific contexts (rule 54.5(3)). This limit can only be extended by the court pursuant to a general power contained in CPR 3.1(2)(a).[42] Section 31(6) of the Supreme Court Act 1981 provides that where the High Court considers that there has been undue delay in making an application for judicial review, the court may refuse to grant leave for making the application, or any relief sought on the application, if it considers that the granting of the relief sought would be likely to cause substantial hardship to, or substantially prejudice the rights of, any person or would be detrimental to good administration. It is clear that a claim can fail for lack of promptness even if it is brought within three months,[43] though it has been argued that this leads to uncertainty over the exact time limit in any case and that this could breach the ECHR.[44] Where the claim is not prompt enough for the purposes of CPR 54.5(1)(a) it will also fail for undue delay under section 31(6) of the Supreme Court Act 1981,[45] even if the court has extended the time under CPR 3.1(2)(a). The court will then have to decide whether to refuse permission to bring the claim (if not yet granted) or relief at the substantive hearing of the claim, taking into account hardship to third parties and detriment to good administration. However, where third party interests are insufficient to tip the balance the other way, the interests of good administration suggest that the abuse of power should be corrected and the claim should be allowed.[46] In contrast to these short public law time limits, as was noted above,[47] the time limit for purely private unjust enrichment actions is six years and this can be further extended because the time will not begin to run until a decision reveals the ultra vires event.

If we are to have a new, universally applicable time limit which cannot be evaded through denial of the public law elements in favour of the private law aspects of the claim, then it must fall between these two extremes. There are various arguments to be considered in choosing the new limit. On the one hand, it might not be appropriate simply to split the difference between the two time limits and

[41] ibid.

[42] Which it will exercise taking into account whether there was a reasonable objective excuse for late application, the possible impact on third party rights and the administration, and the general importance of the point raised: *R v Secretary of State and Industry, ex p Greenpeace* [2000] 2 CMLR 94 (QB).

[43] *Hilditch v Westminster CC* [1990] COD 434 (CA).

[44] *R v Hammersmith and Fulham LBC, ex p Burkett* [2002] UKHL 23, [2002] 1 WLR 1593.

[45] *R v Dairy Produce Quota Tribunal for England and Wales ex p Caswell* [1990] 2 AC 738 (HL).

[46] See generally: *R v Lichfield DC ex p Lichfield Securities Ltd* [2001] EWCA Civ 304, (2001) 3 LGLR 35 and Craig (n 8) 26-045-26-048.

[47] See text at n 16, ch 4.

choose 33 months as the new limit, because this would not be to give due weight to the extreme shortness of the public law limits and measuring the limit in years could thus have the effect of favouring the private law viewpoint. It is also arguable that while other defences relate to the unjust enrichment claim as a whole, or to an aspect of that claim other than the unjust factor, the time limit is more closely related to the reason for restitution than it is to any of the other, private, aspects of the claim. After all, it is the emergence of the reason for restitution that will prompt the construction of the claim as a whole. Thus, while it may be necessary in purely private cases to allow more time for the parties to realise that the consideration has failed, or that their consent has in some way been vitiated, any party transacting with a public authority knows that they are dealing with a limited-capacity entity and ought, therefore, to check before or immediately after the transaction that the tax was validly levied, the grant validly paid, the contract validly entered into, etc. Further support for short time limits comes from La Forest J in *Air Canada v British Columbia*,[48] and the idea was contemplated by Lord Goff in *Woolwich*.

On the other hand, Lord Goff concluded that 'such draconian time limits [as those found in German law] may be too strong medicine for our taste'.[49] Certainly, against a particularly short limit it should be noted that the current public law rules are the subject of criticism. Craig argues that before 1977, the longer time limits did not cause problems and that in fact the short time limits can lead to an *increase* in litigation as claimants hurriedly submit applications for judicial review, lest they should run out of time by considering their action more carefully.[50] He concludes that there are other techniques (as will be discussed below[51]) which can promote legal certainty and suggests that a discretion on the part of the court is perhaps a better solution than an absolute time limit, since, as Virgo points out, any such time limit will inevitably be somewhat arbitrary.[52] Such 'fact-sensitivity' would also be more likely to comply with the requirements of the ECHR as being a more proportionate approach to balancing the requirements of legal certainty against the rights of the claimant,[53] provided that the discretion only operated in favour of the claimant to extend the time limits.

The Law Commission originally favoured the existing six years for its statutory scheme,[54] but in a later Consultation paper[55] it set out five basic options for a new

[48] *Air Canada v British Columbia* [1989] 1 SCR 1161, (1989) 59 DLR (4th) 161.

[49] *Woolwich* (n 37) 174.

[50] See, eg: Craig (n 8) 26-047.

[51] Such as prospective overruling.

[52] See: Craig (n 8) 26-047; and G Virgo, 'The Law of Taxation is not an Island—Overpaid Taxes and the Law of Restitution' [1993] *British Tax Review* 442, 461.

[53] See: P Sales and B Hooper, 'Proportionality and the Form of Law' (2003) 119 *Law Quarterly Review* 426, especially 433–34.

[54] Law Commission, 'Restitution: Mistakes of Law and Ultra Vires Public Authority Receipts and Payments' (Law Com No 227 Cm 2731, 1994) [10.41].

[55] Law Commission, 'Limitations of Actions' (Law Com Cons Paper No 151, 1998).

core regime. Of these, it favoured a general limitation period of three years to run from when the claimant knows, or ought reasonably to know, that he has a cause of action.[56] There would also be a 'long-stop' of 10 years from the date of the act or omission giving rise to the claim, regardless of discoverability. However, this regime would apply to claims in contract, tort and for restitution,[57] which would mean that a set limitation period applied equally to all possible unjust factors,[58] and to 'actions against public authorities'[59] as well as private parties, whereas it has been argued here that special considerations might apply to situations where the unjust factor is a public law event and this should at least be considered before a universal time limit is created.

Alternatively, there is some academic commentary currently in favour of a limit of two years.[60] This idea of a two to three year time limit which begins to run from the date of payment and, like the public law time limits, is only extended in exceptional circumstances, would certainly provide one solution. Of course, such a time limit would ultimately be subject to the EU principle of effectiveness, and of course all such proposals are somewhat dependent on the future development of that principle. However, it does not appear as if at present this suggestion would contravene EU law. The applicable rules will be discussed further in chapter eight,[61] but there is no suggestion that a two to three year time limit proposed here would be imposed retroactively[62] and it would not be specifically targeted at the effects of a particular decision of the ECJ.[63] Nor does there seem to be any reason to conclude that two to three years is too short a period to be 'effective' in principle. In *Edis*,[64] a three year time limit was held to be reasonable for reclaiming charges

[56] The other options are: either a short period from discoverability or a longer period from the accrual of the cause of action; a period from the accrual of the cause of action; a period from the date of the act or omission giving rise to the cause of action; or the date of accrual of the cause of action for contract claims and the date of discoverability for tort claims.

[57] As well as breach of trust and related actions; actions on judgments or arbitration awards; and actions on a statute.

[58] As well as to restitution for wrongdoing.

[59] Scottish Law Commission (n 55) [13.153].

[60] See: Virgo, 'Taxation is not an Island' (n 52). Collins agrees with this figure, and adds that a 'vigorous application of the doctrine of laches could achieve the same result': R Collins, 'Restitution from Government Officials' (1984) 29 *McGill Law Journal* 407, 435. See also: F Toube, 'Restitution for Public Lawyers' [1996] *Judicial Review* 92. Jones also believes that 'it may well be appropriate to enact a stringent time limitation': G Jones, *Restitution in Public and Private Law* (London, Sweet and Maxwell, 1991) 43.

[61] Below p 239–41.

[62] And indeed this in itself is not fatal as long as there are adequate transitional provisions, see also: *Marks and Spencer* (n 34) and *Grundig* (n 35) and see also: below pp 239–41.

[63] As forbidden by: Case 309/85 *Barra v Belgium* [1988] ECR 355; and Case C-343/96 *Dilexport Srl v Amministrazione delle Finanze dello Stato* [1999] ECR I-579. See also: *Marks and Spencer* (n 34) [36]: '[N]ational legislation curtailing the period within which recovery may be sought of sums charged in breach of Community law . . . must not be intended specifically to limit the consequences of a judgment of the Court to the effect that national legislation concerning a specific tax is incompatible with Community law'.

[64] *Edis* (n 32).

paid but not due as a matter of EC law, and in *Recheio-Cash and Carry*[65] the Court held that nevertheless it followed from *Edis*

> and the Court's settled case-law that the Member States remain at liberty to fix longer or shorter periods for repayment of sums paid though not due, on condition that they do not render virtually impossible or excessively difficult the exercise of rights conferred by the Community legal order.
>
> In this instance, a period of 90 days reckoned from the end of the period allowed for voluntary payment of the charges must be considered to represent a sufficient length of time to enable the taxpayer to take the decision to bring an action for annulment in full awareness of all the facts and for that purpose to gather all the matters of fact or law required.[66]

Thus, a three year time limit certainly appears to be compatible with EU law on the basis of *Edis*, and a two year limit may also be acceptable. However, while it is possible to have a time limit this short, in the light of Schedule 39 of the Finance Act 2008, it seems likely that a limit of four years would be preferable. According to that schedule, from the point of view of the private claimant,[67] measures came into effect from 1 April 2009 to standardise the general time limits across income tax, capital gains tax, corporation tax, VAT, and stamp duty land tax, at four years. A similar long stop of four years is contained in section 100 and schedule 52 of the Finance Act 2009 and will come into effect from 1 April 2010. This demonstrates that a four year time limit can be operated without undue hardship to public finances and thus suggests that it would not be undesirable to extend it across all public body claims of the kind discussed here. If a shorter time limit could be considered to be compatible with EU law then it certainly seems likely that this longer four year limit would be without problems on that front. Finally, while of course tax cases in which the public body is the defendant are only one context in which the public law reason for restitution may arise, this proposed consistency between the statutory tax context and the common law would be advantageous, since it would tend to reduce the impetus to seek one method of redress rather than another, and thus perhaps lead to an increase in efficiency and a decrease in litigation over the appropriate route for recovery.[68]

In terms of the date from which the time limit begins to run, it is true that in *Preston v Wolverhampton Healthcare NHS Trust*[69] the ECJ held that where the

[65] Case C-30/02 *Recheio-Cash and Carry SA v Fazenda Publica/Registo Nacional de Pessoas Colectivas* [2004] ECR I-6051.

[66] ibid [20]–[21].

[67] From the point of view of the Revenue there are exceptions to this rule such as might arise in the event of negligence (careless error) or fraud (deliberate error), in which cases the time limits for the Revenue to discover that tax has been underpaid would become six and twenty years respectively.

[68] For this reason it would also be desirable to have a consistent time limit regardless of the specific factual context and regardless of whether the public body was the claimant or the defendant. A uniform time limit would thus be preferable to the 'time limit plus exceptions' approach of Schedule 39 of the Finance Act 2008.

[69] Case C-78/98 *Preston v Wolverhampton Healthcare NHS Trust* [2000] ECR I-3201.

claimants were employed under temporary contracts, a time limit which ran for six months from the end of each contract rather than from the point at which that series of contracts (and thus the ongoing stable employment relationship) was interrupted, rendered the exercise of the Treaty right excessively difficult and was therefore precluded by EC law. Similarly, in *Manfredi v Lloyd Adriatico Assicurazioni SpA*[70] the Court held that:

> A national rule under which the limitation period begins to run from the day on which the agreement or concerted practice was adopted could make it practically impossible to exercise the right to seek compensation for the harm caused by that prohibited agreement or practice, particularly if that national rule also imposes a short limitation period which is not capable of being suspended.
>
> In such a situation where there are continuous or repeated infringements, it is possible that the limitation period expires even before the infringement is brought to an end, in which case it would be impossible for any individual who has suffered harm after the expiry of the limitation period to bring an action.[71]

It might thus be suggested that any national time limit could only begin to run from the date of the judgment invalidating the relevant tax or charge, since otherwise here too the limitation period could 'expire even before the infringement was brought to an end'. Ultimately, as noted above, this would be a matter for decision by the ECJ, but on the other hand, it does not seem impossible that a national time limit could begin to run sooner than that. In *Recheio-Cash and Carry*, the limitation period was permitted to run 'from the end of the period allowed for voluntary payment of the charges',[72] and in *Edis*, the permissible period ran from the date of payment itself. It may therefore be that the keys to the *Manfredi* judgment were, first, the specific findings that the time had been allowed to run from the date on which the *illegality first occurred*, second that this was 'particularly' problematic 'if that national rule also imposes a short limitation period which is not capable of being suspended',[73] and third that as a result of the time beginning to run from the date on which the agreement was concluded, it would be possible for individuals to suffer 'harm after the expiry of the limitation period to bring an action'.[74] On the other hand, the time limit imposed here would run, not from the date on which the tax was imposed, but the date of payment. Second, as explained above, it would not be excessively short by the ECJ's own reasoning, and third, there would be no question of any 'individual suffer[ing] harm after the expiry of the limitation period to bring an action', because the suffering of the harm would itself be the event triggering the running of time. It therefore appears that the limit proposed here would be compatible with EU law, though the decision ultimately would rest with the ECJ.

[70] Case C-295–298/04 *Manfredi v Lloyd Adriatico Assicurazioni SpA* [2006] ECR I-6619.
[71] ibid [78]–[79].
[72] *Recheio-Cash and Carry* (n 65) [21].
[73] *Manfredi* (n 70) [78].
[74] ibid [79].

Private Law Defences

Change of Position

In English law this defence was introduced in *Lipkin Gorman v Karpnale Ltd*[75] by Lord Goff who held that:

> In these circumstances, it is right that we should ask ourselves: why do we feel that it would be unjust to allow restitution in cases such as these? The answer must be that, where an innocent defendant's position is so changed that he will suffer an injustice if called upon to repay or to repay in full, the injustice of requiring him so to repay outweighs the injustice of denying the plaintiff restitution.[76]

In order to establish the precise scope of the defence in relation to the cases at issue here, it is necessary to clarify six points: whether the defence can be used by public bodies at all; whether its operation upsets the balance between the public and private law aspects of the claim; the causal link required between the claimant's payment and the defendant's disenrichment; whether it matters that the public body can in any event simply raise taxes to recover the money it must pay out; the required chronology of the enrichment and change of position; and finally, the role of good faith or fault.

The first question only concerns some of the relevant claims, because *Lipkin Gorman* itself established that the defence can be used by private parties. However, it is important to determine whether it can also be used when the defendant is a public entity.[77] It is true that in *ex p Chetnik* their Lordships in the end concluded that the statutory equivalent of the change of position argument should not succeed in a public body context. However, it is clear from Lord Bridge's judgment that he did not think *section 9 of that particular statute* permitted him to allow such an argument and the court was not examining whether change of position should be a defence to dual event public law unjust enrichment claims of the kind investigated here. It was considering whether change of position reasoning was a relevant consideration to be taken into account by the rating authority in the exercise of its statutory discretion to refund rates. Far from being an authority against the suggestion made here that change of position reasoning could apply to public law unjust enrichment cases, *ex p Chetnik* arguably provides support for that argument. Lord Bridge thought the argument deserved 'anxious scrutiny' and admitted that he was 'initially much impressed by this . . . line of argument'.[78] In

[75] *Lipkin Gorman v Karpnale Ltd* [1991] 2 AC 548 (HL).

[76] ibid 579. See generally: R Goff and G Jones, *The Law of Restitution*, 7th edn (London, Sweet and Maxwell, 2007) ch 40.

[77] Any issues regarding the use of the defence by a private party in the context of an ultra vires event will instead relate to question five; whether or not the defence upsets the balance between public and private law.

[78] *ex p Chetnik Developments* (n 11) 880.

a common law public law unjust enrichment case, therefore, free from the constraints of that particular statute, the courts could in principle apply the defence and indeed in *Westdeutsche* both Hobhouse J and Lord Goff made it clear that the defence of change of position is capable of applying against a claimant who seeks restitution *from* a public authority, provided that it is made out on the facts.[79]

Similarly, in *FII*,[80] Henderson J held that he could 'see no reason in principle why the defence of change of position should not be available to the Revenue, or indeed to any other category of defendant',[81] and confirmed that it would apply to some of the claims in that case, albeit that it is not wholly clear from the judgment which these were.[82] It is apparent that he may have had in mind claims arising more than six years previously, since HMRC's concession on the change of position defence in *FII* only extended to so-called *San Giorgio* claims for tax paid (or other enrichments) within the previous six years. However, it is arguable that even these earlier claims ought to be regarded as falling under *San Giorgio*. Given the principle of equivalence laid down in *Rewe-Zentralfinanz GmbH v Landwirtschaftskammer für das Saarland*,[83] if national law provides a means of recovering taxes or other enrichments paid more than six years previously, it would be difficult to argue that EU law did not require the same 'remedy'. It is particularly odd that these earlier claims, relying on mistake of law to extend the time limit, should not be regarded as *San Giorgio* claims, when the whole essence of the mistake of law was that the tax had been lawful when in fact, as a matter of EC law, it was not.[84] Even more strangely, it was Henderson J himself who had held that the *San Giorgio* principle required use of the mistake of law ground and that the *Woolwich* principle alone could not found recovery, and yet the only circumstances in which this is true are those in which it is necessary to rely on the extended time limit under the Limitation Act 1980. It is hard to see, therefore, how any of the claims in *FII* could be regarded as falling outside the *San Giorgio* principle and thus, by implication, outside HMRC's concession.

If the defence is thus available in principle we reach the second question: whether it unduly restricts the law's access to and reversal of the ultra vires event. This broader question arises whether or not the defendant is the public body and can apply equally where the public body has made an ultra vires payment which it

[79] *Westdeutsche Landesbank Girozentrale v Islington LBC* [1994] 4 All ER 890 (QB) at 946–954 (Hobhouse J) and [1996] AC 669 (HL) 688, where Lord Goff referred to 'any available restitutionary defences'. Obviously, the situation will be more difficult where the public authority knew that the tax was illegal but coerced the claimant into paying anyway, see: G Jones, *Public and Private* (n 60) 37–39. This is a matter for the investigation into the bona fide requirement of the defence, which applies generally, whether the defence is used by a public or private party, see also: below, issue six.

[80] *FII* (UK) (n 36).

[81] ibid [336].

[82] He held that the defence would still be available for all those claims he had not classified as '*San Giorgio*' claims: ibid [304].

[83] Case 33/76 *Rewe-Zentralfinanz GmbH v Landwirtschaftskammer für das Saarland* [1976] ECR 1989.

[84] Given the decision in Case C-231/96 *Edis v Ministero delle Finanze* [1998] ECR I-4951 it would of course have been perfectly lawful for the House of Lords in *Deutsche Morgan Grenfell* (n 29) and thus Henderson J in *FII* to hold that *San Giorgio* claims could be dealt with exclusively through the cause of action in *Woolwich* and that the extension of the time limit using the 1980 Act was not permissible.

now seeks to reclaim from a private party. By analogy with the statutory context of *ex p Chetnik*, could a court decide that to allow the defence would defeat the purpose of the ultra vires rule in a particular context?[85] One such context is obviously a situation in which the relevant charge was beyond the powers of the public body as a matter of EU law. This issue was considered in the *FII* case,[86] which concerned tax provisions which had been found to be in breach of the EC free movement rules.[87] As Henderson J noted, the argument was novel in that case in that there had been no previous case in which the Revenue or any other government department had sought to rely on the defence,[88] thereby providing further support for the argument made above that *ex p Chetnik Developments* does not constitute binding authority on this point. However, the matter was not fully argued in *FII* either, because the Revenue had accepted that the defence could not apply in relation to '*Woolwich*-based' claims and Henderson J took this concession as applying to any other reason for restitution on which the claim was based instead.[89] The reason for this concession was that the change of position defence was thought to be a breach of the requirement to provide an effective remedy for breach of EC law,[90] but it is not clear that the Revenue should have given in so easily on this matter. Henderson J's grounds for accepting the point were first, that while EU law does allow for the setting of reasonable time limits for claims and for the defence of passing on

> there is, however, no precedent for a defence of this nature in a case involving direct taxation and breach of one of the fundamental freedoms, and the court has adopted a robust approach in holding that conflicting rules of national law must be disregarded if they would prevent full recovery of an unlawful tax. So, for example, in *Hoechst*[91] the ECJ expressly ruled that the so-called *Pintada*[92] principle of English domestic law, as it was then understood, could not bar recovery on the footing that at the date of issue of the

[85] As will be seen, this was the reasoning behind the decision in *South Tyneside MBC v Svenska Intl plc* [1995] 1 All ER 545 (QB). It was thought that to allow anticipatory reliance would be to allow reliance on the ultra vires transaction and would thus be contrary to policy. This decision was confined to its specific facts in *Dextra Bank and Trust Co Ltd v Bank of Jamaica* [2002] 1 All ER 193 (PC). However, that Court also noted the criticism of the *Svenska* decision even on these specific facts [39]. It has been argued that the PC in *Dextra Bank* was correct to point out that the reliance, albeit anticipatory, is on the payment, not on the transaction (below n 144 and surrounding text). On this basis, it is possible to argue that the defence should have operated even in *Svenska*.

[86] *FII* (UK) (n 36).

[87] See further ch 4 p 102 onwards.

[88] ibid [303].

[89] ibid [304]. Henderson J had previously held that the reason for restitution in *FII* would have to be mistake of law rather than what he called 'the *Woolwich* principle'. It is submitted that within that internal logic he must have been correct to hold that if change of position was not available for the former it could not be available for the latter basis of claim either, but of course it has been argued here that the public law reason for restitution based on the *Woolwich* case should have been used as the basis for the claim instead of mistake, see also: ch 4.

[90] On which see further below, ch 8.

[91] Cases C-397/98 and C-410/98 *Metallgesellschaft and Hoechst v IRC* [2001] ECR I-1727. See also: chs 4 and 8.

[92] As Henderson J puts it, 'for the coup de grâce now delivered by the House of Lords to the *Pintada* principle see *Sempra Metals*': *FII* (UK) (n 36) [307]. The full citation is: *Sempra Metals Ltd (formerly Metallgesellschaft Ltd) v IRC* [2007] UKHL 34, [2008] 1 AC 561.

> writ no principal sum was outstanding . . . Similarly, in a Danish case,[93] the ECJ held that Denmark could not refuse to make a repayment on the basis of a settled law defence available under Danish law.[94]

He later confirmed this view in *F J Chalke Ltd and AC Barnes (Wokingham) Ltd v The Commissioners for Her Majesty's Revenue and Customs*,[95] holding that 'to allow the defence would not recognise, but would infringe, the principle of effectiveness',[96] and pointing to the statement in *Weber's Wine World v Abgabenberufungskommission Wien*[97] that there was 'only one exception' to the obligation to make repayment,[98] namely the passing on defence.

Examining each of these arguments in detail, first, while it may be true that the ECJ has 'adopted a robust approach in holding that conflicting rules of national law must be disregarded if they would prevent full recovery of an unlawful tax', there is a clear distinction between the change of position defence on the one hand and, on the other, the settled view of the law defence and the *Pintada* principle, in that change of position does not prevent recovery altogether, it simply reduces it. Indeed, even on this front, as Henderson J himself points out, the ECJ still permits the defence of passing on, which can completely prevent recovery, as long as the burden of proof is not placed on the claimant to disprove that the charge has been passed on.[99] It is therefore difficult to see why the *partial* defence of change of position should be so objectionable to the principle of effectiveness when this potentially full defence is not. Second, while *FII* may involve direct taxation and breach of one of the fundamental freedoms, the fundamental freedoms were no less at stake in the cases on passing on, and indeed if anything direct taxation is still thought to remain more within the competence of the Member States than other areas.[100] Third, it is also clear that, as Henderson J notes, in addition to the passing on defence EU law permits the setting of time limits provided that they are reasonable and non-wholly-retroactive.[101] As noted above, the reasoning behind the setting of a time limit is essentially the same as that behind the change of position defence; both are concerned with promoting legal certainty. When they apply, time limits also provide a complete defence to the claim.[102] Again, therefore, it is

[93] Case C-188/95 *Fantask A/S v Industriministeriet* [1997] ECR I-6783, see also: ch 8.
[94] *FII* (UK) (n 36) [307].
[95] *F J Chalke Ltd and AC Barnes (Wokingham) Ltd v The Commissioners for Her Majesty's Revenue and Customs* [2009] EWHC 952 (Ch).
[96] ibid [176].
[97] Case C-147/01 *Weber's Wine World v Abgabenberufungskommission Wien* [2003] ECR I-11365.
[98] ibid [94].
[99] Case 811/79 *Amministrazione delle Finanze dello Stato v Ariete* [1980] ECR 2545; and Case 199/82 *Amministrazione delle Finanze dello Stato v San Giorgio* [1983] ECR 3595. See also: ch 8.
[100] See, eg: C Barnard, *The Substantive Law of the EU: The Four Freedoms*, 2nd edn (Oxford, Oxford University Press, 2007) 296 fn 92.
[101] *FII* (UK) (n 36) [421].
[102] It is true that, unlike a 'settled view of the law' defence, the defences of passing on, time limits and the *Pintada* principle will allow some claimants to succeed, but where these latter defences apply they are still complete defences and those who are out of time, have passed on the burden of the charge or had no principal sum outstanding would fail altogether. Though on the *Pintada* principle, see: *FII* (UK) (n 36) [307] (Henderson J).

difficult to see why a partial defence for the promotion of legal certainty should be objectionable when a full defence for that purpose is not. It is perhaps surprising, then, that the Revenue did not even ask for an Article 267 TFEU (ex 234 EC) reference to be made to the ECJ on the compatibility of the change of position defence with the principle of effectiveness, especially given first, that other references will in any case need to be sent concerning the *FII* case,[103] and second, that so much of the claim is now based on explicit dicta from the ECJ.[104] Indeed it is not impossible that the reason that passing on (and time limits) represent the 'only exception(s)' to the obligation to repay is simply because the ECJ has so far not been asked to rule on the change of position defence.

Finally, further evidence for the ECJ's commitment to legal certainty comes from the reverse fact situation (in which the public body is the claimant and the private party the defendant) in the form of the legitimate expectations doctrine. Legitimate expectations are closely related to the concept of estoppel, as is the defence of change of position, as will be seen immediately below. All have a common root in the promotion of legal certainty, and the prevention of retroactivity.[105] It is thus submitted that the idea that change of position should be allowed to qualify the ultra vires principle need not be peculiar to private law, and the application of this defence is thus not an example of the private law event restricting the law's access to the public law event, or of a national rule being permitted to breach the EU principle of effectiveness. It is true that currently in English administrative law, ultra vires representations will not generate legitimate expectations,[106] unless, for example, the representation was intra vires the body as a whole but just ultra vires the particular agent who made it.[107] However, the same is not true of other systems, and in particular the EU does allow legitimate expectations to be upheld even where this would limit the reversal of the ultra vires action,[108] and it is arguable that

[103] See, eg: *FII* (UK) (n 36) [138].

[104] In ch 8 the extent to which the parameters of the claim are now a matter for EU, rather than national, law will be further noted. Given that the case is so directly governed by EU law it is therefore doubly surprising that the ECJ is not being given the opportunity to rule on this aspect of the case as well.

[105] This point will be developed further in ch 8 when German law will be considered in relation to the EU system. See M Jewell's comparative comments on this defence: 'The Boundaries of Change of Position—a Comparative Study' (2000) 8 *Restitution Law Review* 1. Of course, for a successful legitimate expectation claim it is not absolutely necessary that the applicant demonstrate that he or she relied on the expectation in question: *Minister for Immigration and Ethnic Affairs v Teoh* (1995) 3 CLR 1 (HCA), reaffirmed in the UK in *R v Secretary of State for Education and Employment, ex p Begbie* [2000] 1 WLR 1115 (CA). Nevertheless, as Peter Gibson LJ puts it in *ex p Begbie*, 'it would be wrong to understate the significance of reliance in this area of the law. It is very much the exception, rather than the rule, that detrimental reliance will not be present when the court finds unfairness in the defeating of a legitimate expectation': ibid 1124.

[106] *Western Fish Products Ltd v Penwith DC* [1981] 2 All ER 204 (CA).

[107] See also: *South Buckinghamshire DC v Flanagan* [2002] EWCA Civ 690, [2002] 1 WLR 2601; and Craig (n 8) 20-031-20-052.

[108] Unlike in English law, legitimate expectations can in EU law be based on an ultra vires representation. See, eg: Cases 42 and 49/59 *SNUPAT v High Authority* [1961] ECR 53 and Case 14/61 *Hoogovens v High Authority* [1962] ECR 253.

this should be the case in England too.[109] Thus, where the public body is the claimant there is nothing unusual, at least as a matter of EU law, about allowing the need for legal certainty to qualify the need to correct the unlawful action and, as will be seen in chapter eight, precisely this reasoning has already been accepted by the ECJ in unjust enrichment cases.[110] There is thus no reason in principle why this reasoning should not be applied more generally, in English law and to situations where the public body is the defendant. Finally, given that at all times Henderson J made it clear that the change of position remained 'live' in relation to all the claims in the case which did not fall under the EC *San Giorgio* principle,[111] the result of his decision is to set up precisely the same kind of disparity between EU and domestic claims that Lord Goff was so keen to avoid in the *Woolwich* decision.[112]

However, it will be remembered that in part this reasoning that change of position is compatible with EU law depends upon change of position being a partial defence. It is true that the ECJ has also accepted some total defences in this context, but none of these are directly analogous to a complete defence based on change of position. Time limits share change of position's occupation with legal certainty, but they do allow for some recovery during the running of the relevant time. Similarly, legitimate expectations could potentially be a complete defence based on legal certainty, but as noted above, this tends to operate against public bodies rather than for their benefit. While passing on can in principle constitute a complete defence, as will be noted further below, it is very difficult to prove and does not prevent *any* claim from being brought, only the claim brought by that particular claimant rather than those to whom the charge was passed on. If change of position were on the facts to provide a defence to the whole of the claim brought, it is not impossible that the ECJ would accept this by analogy with its reasoning based on legitimate expectations, but there is no question that this situation would come closer to the defences the ECJ has previously rejected, such as a

[109] This is not the place for a full discussion, but, for example, it is sometimes argued that were legitimate expectations to be upheld this would involve the perpetuation of illegality on the part of the public body. This is true, but of course exactly that kind of perpetuation is allowed as a result of the short time limits discussed above. If legal certainty is thus allowed to defeat the prohibition of ultra vires actions *for* the public body, it seems only fair that legal certainty should also be allowed to defeat that principle in favour of the private party too. There is little risk that such a rule would encourage actors deliberately to make ultra vires representations solely in order to extend their powers, since most of the existing cases involved representations made in the belief that they were intra vires. Finally, although the courts are often regarded as choosing between legality and illegality in such cases, in reality their choice is between *two* evils; uphold the rule of law and the ultra vires representation or remove the ultra vires representation but infringe the rule of law. Put thus, the case for automatic failure of ultra vires representations to found legitimate expectations loses much of its force. See also: Craig (n 8) ch 20 and P Craig and G de Búrca, *EU Law, Text, Cases and Materials*, 4th edn (Oxford, Oxford University Press, 2008) 558.

[110] As will be seen in more detail in ch 8 p 265 onwards. It will be noted there (pp 247–48) that there is an exception to this rule in the case of state aid, but this is because, as will also be explained in ch 8, recovery of state aid is governed not by the general principle of unjust enrichment or '*San Giorgio* claims' but by legislation.

[111] *FII* (UK) (n 36) [304], though, as noted above, it is hard to see which claims these are.

[112] *Woolwich* (n 37) 177.

defence based on the view of the law being settled or prospective overruling where this has been refused on the facts of a given case.[113] Thus although the defence is in principle perfectly compatible with the EU principle of effectiveness, whether or not it is compatible in practice will depend on its application to the facts of a given case, and the precise extent to which it would deny the claim in that case. Should it operate to deny the claim completely it would be much more likely to be incompatible with EU law.

This in turn relates directly to the third issue, that of the causal link between the enrichment and the change of position. The narrowest potential view of this link comes from the Canadian Supreme Court in *Rural Municipality of Storthoaks v Mobil Oil Canada Ltd*[114] and confines the result of the defence to specific matched items of income and expenditure. However, as the Law Commission points out:

It will always be difficult for a public authority, and especially for the Crown, to show that it has undertaken items of expenditure other than those which it would in any event have undertaken on the strength of a particular tax receipt. The spending plans of revenue raising public authorities, and particularly those of the Crown, are generally decided in principle several years in advance of the taxation year to which they relate.[115]

In general, academic opinion supports the view that this will be the result of the rule,[116] although the argument can be turned around, so that while it is unreasonable to expect a private individual to keep receipts in order to establish the defence, it is much more reasonable to expect this of a large body such as a public authority.[117] It was this problem which gave rise to the second approach, developed by the Irish Supreme Court in *Murphy v AG*,[118] where Henchy J held that

> it is beyond question that the State in its executive capacity received the moneys in question in good faith, in reliance on the presumption that the now-condemned sections [of the (Irish) Income Tax Act 1967] were favoured with constitutionality. In every tax year from the enactment of the . . . Act . . . until the institution of these proceedings in March

[113] Though in this context, it should be noted that Henderson J's quotation from the *Fantask* decision is somewhat selective since the reference to the settled view of the law defence was not the ultimate ground for decision. Instead, the ECJ actually upheld the public body's claim on the basis that the national time limit was compatible with the principle of effectiveness, see further: *Fantask* (n 93); and *FII* (UK) (n 36) [308] (Henderson J).

[114] *Rural Municipality of Storthoaks v Mobil Oil Canada Ltd* [1976] 2 SCR 147, (1975) 55 DLR (3d) 1. According to Robert Walker LJ, this restrictive approach is also applied, apparently, in Canada and some states of the US: *Scottish Equitable plc v Derby* [2001] EWCA Civ 369, [2001] 3 All ER 818 [33]. See also: *David Securities Pty Ltd v Commonwealth Bank of Australia* (1992) 175 CLR 353 [18]–[19], noted in Goff and Jones (n 76) 819.

[115] Law Commission (n 54) [11.12].

[116] See J McCamus, 'Restitutionary Recovery of Moneys Paid to a Public Authority under a Mistake of Law: *Ignorantia Juris* in the Supreme Court of Canada' (1983) 17 *University of British Columbia Law Review* 233; P Mitchell, 'Restitution, "Passing On" and the Recovery of Unlawfully Demanded Taxes: Why *Air Canada* Doesn't Fly' (1995) 53 *University of Toronto Faculty of Law Review* 130, 142; and P Butler, 'Restitution of Overpaid Taxes, Windfall Gains, and Unjust Enrichment: *Commissioner of State Revenue v Royal Insurance Australia Ltd*' (1995) 18 *University of Queensland Law Journal* 318.

[117] G Borland, 'Change of Position in Scots Law' *Scots Law Times* (10 May 1996).

[118] *Murphy v AG* [1982] IR 241 (SC).

> 1978, the State justifiably altered its position by spending the taxes thus collected and by arranging its fiscal and taxation policies and programmes accordingly.[119]

As the Law Commission points out, this is not a 'pure change of position defence' because it depends on a time limit, rather than any demonstrated inequity that would result from repayment following a change of position.[120] Arguably such a defence also contains elements of 'fiscal disruption' reasoning and thus should be considered further under that heading below.

Somewhere in between these two approaches, though much closer to the first than to the second, is the decision of the High Court in *Phillip Collins Ltd v Davis*.[121] In dealing with the 'relaxed and philosophical attitude'[122] of two musicians to their financial arrangements over a time in which they had received periodical mistaken overpayments of royalties, Jonathan Parker J held that a 'broad approach'[123] should be taken to the question of change of position, so that although he was

> unable to find that any particular item of expenditure was directly referable to the overpayments of royalties . . . [g]iven that the approach of the defendants to their respective financial affairs was, essentially, to gear their outgoings to their income from time to time . . . it is . . . open to the court to find [and he did find] that the overpayments caused a *general change of position* by the defendants, in that they increased their level of outgoing by reference to the sums so paid.[124] (emphasis added)

Thus the defendants were required to show an unusual form of expenditure in line with the first formulation of the defence, but it was not necessary for them to show that any specific expenditure was the result of the overpayments. This leniency was accepted by the Court of Appeal, affirming the judgment of Harrison J, in *Scottish Equitable*.[125] Robert Walker LJ confirmed the requirement of a 'but for' causal link between receipt of the enrichment and the change of position[126] but continued that he

> would readily accept that the defence is not limited . . . to specific identifiable items of expenditure. I would also accept that it may be right for the court not to apply too demanding a standard of proof when an honest defendant says that he has spent an overpayment by improving his lifestyle, but cannot produce any detailed accounting . . . But the court must proceed on the basis of principle, not sympathy, in order that the defence of change of position should not 'disintegrate into a case by case discretionary analysis of the justice of individual facts, far removed from principle'.[127]

[119] ibid 319–20.
[120] Law Commission (n 54) [11.14].
[121] *Phillip Collins Ltd v Davis* [2000] 3 All ER 808 (Ch).
[122] ibid 829.
[123] ibid 830.
[124] ibid 829–30.
[125] *Scottish Equitable* (CA) (n 114).
[126] ibid [31].
[127] Robert Walker LJ, ibid, citing A Burrows, *The Law of Restitution*, 1st edn (London, Butterworths, 1993) 426 and *Phillip Collins* (n 121).

This is perhaps important in the present context, since whatever reason there may be for leniency towards haphazard musicians, it is not unreasonable to suggest that it is at least as justifiable to be lenient towards bodies whose funds are public and which have more complicated financial processes than any individual. Thus in *FII*, Henderson J pointed out that 'to state the obvious, taxation is not imposed for its own sake, but in order to fund government expenditure'.[128] He therefore accepted that while 'as a matter of causation, no precise link can be demonstrated between particular receipts and particular items of government expenditure', 'common sense' would suggest that departmental budgets and expenditure would be based on the availability of tax receipts.[129] He ultimately concluded that 'it would be inequitable to require repayment in such circumstances'.[130] It should be noted in passing that while this argument was made in relation to situations in which public bodies are the defendants, the same argument can be made in situations involving, for example, the payment *by* a public body of social security allowances to an individual.[131] In any event, it is clear that on the facts of the *FII* case this wide characterisation of the defence was chosen by Henderson J on the premise that even if the defence was available in general 'the claimants have a perfectly good separate *San Giorgio* claim for repayment of the unlawfully levied tax itself, free from any change of position defence'. It was argued above and in chapter four that for various reasons this premise is incorrect,[132] though of course it is true that such a wide view of the defence as Henderson J took would not be compatible with EU law, because it effectively turns change of position into a complete defence, which, as noted above, may well bring it into conflict with the EU principle of effectiveness.[133]

Closely connected to this point is the fourth question. In reaching his decision on the degree of causal link necessary for a successful defence of change of position, Henderson J rejected an argument that the necessary causal link was not made out because the government could always have raised money in a different

[128] *FII* (UK) (n 36) [344].

[129] ibid.

[130] ibid.

[131] Exactly this argument is made by Voirin in the context of social security payments in French law and will be discussed further in ch 6 at p 201. P Voirin, *Droit Social* 1964 p 61; 1966 p 663 and 1969 p 66. A similar view may have been taken by the government in deciding not to reclaim public sector pension overpayments worth millions of pounds: 'Thousands face pension cut after overpayment blunder' *The Times* (16 December 2008).

[132] First, in ch 4 it was argued that *San Giorgio* claims should be seen as being a subset of *Woolwich* claims, not separate from them. Thus if the change of position defence applies, it applies to both *Woolwich* and *San Giorgio* claims. Second, it was argued above that in any event it is difficult to regard any of the claims in *FII* as falling outside the *San Giorgio* principle, see further above p 137. Third, it was argued that Henderson J was wrong to assume, without more, that the EU rules of effectiveness automatically rule out the application of the change of position defence, see further above pp 138–42, though they will usually do so in practice.

[133] It is less likely that this would be the case where the payment was by rather than from a public body, in the light of the ECJ's case law on payments by National Intervention Agencies (see further ch 8 at 265–69), although, as noted (n 110) the defence is not permitted in the legislatively-governed recovery of state aid.

way, on the basis that this missed the point. What really mattered, in Henderson J's view, was not whether the government could raise more money, but rather 'the existence of a causal link between the tax revenues which were in fact received and the expenditure which was actually made'.[134] It is true that the causal link and the ability to recover the money by other means are separate issues, but this does not in itself mean that the latter is irrelevant; that is something which must be decided as a matter of principle.

On the one hand, parity of reasoning with the situation of the claimant would suggest that the ability to avoid the loss should not operate as a defence. If mitigation of the claimant's loss does not reduce the validity of his or her claim,[135] it is difficult to see why the defendant's mitigation of his or her loss should have any greater effect on the validity of his or her defence.

Conversely, in *Oelmühle Hamburg AG v Bundesanstalt für Landwirtschaft und Ernährung*,[136] the ECJ heard an argument that the defendants had passed on the benefit of a payment found to be in breach of EC law and replied that there could only be a defence in such circumstances if the defendants could show that it would not be possible for them to recover the benefit from those on whom it had been conferred.[137] This would militate against Henderson J's conclusions.

Oelmühle also appears to be in keeping with the view of Lord Templeman in *Lipkin Gorman*,[138] Burrows[139] and Virgo[140] that if D retains the property he or she bought with the overpayment, he or she remains enriched to the extent of the resale value of that property. In other words, if D has spent £1000 on a car, (s)he may have changed his or her position to some extent, but if the car can be resold for £800, in their view that money should be returned to the claimant and the change of position defence should apply only to the extent of the remaining £200. Admittedly, selling the property bought with the overpayment or retrieving the overpayment from its ultimate recipients may be different from raising the equivalent level of money from a different source, but on the other hand, since a public body can arguably raise more money without even the inconvenience suffered by a private party required to sell property, the reasoning of Lord Templeman, Burrows and Virgo would tend, a fortiori, to deny the defence in such public body situations.

It is clear, therefore, from consideration of the last two issues that the defence of change of position cannot necessarily operate in the same way in public law claims as it does in purely private ones, because by definition, some public payments such as social security are made precisely because the recipients will need to spend them

[134] ibid [345].

[135] See further below, *Passing On*.

[136] Case C-298/96 *Oelmühle Hamburg AG v Bundesanstalt für Landwirtschaft und Ernährung* [1998] ECR I-4767.

[137] ibid [34]. For further discussion of other aspects of the case see ch 8.

[138] *Lipkin Gorman* (n 75) 560.

[139] A Burrows, *The Law of Restitution*, 2nd edn (London Butterworths 2002) 521.

[140] G Virgo, *The Principles of the Law of Restitution*, 2nd edn (Oxford, Oxford University Press, 2006) 695–6.

when they could not otherwise have spent the same money, and conversely public bodies, unlike private parties, do spend on the basis of their income and yet they can always raise more money to replace that income. In this latter case, then, despite Henderson J's perfectly correct efforts to try to keep the change of position defence separate from that of 'fiscal disruption',[141] when pleaded by a public body in practice the two become very difficult to separate, as the *Murphy* decision demonstrated.[142] The conclusion must therefore be that private parties certainly can use the defence and, in the event that a public body can show both that it has clearly acted differently in reliance on receipt of a particular income, that it would now be impossible or very difficult to recoup that loss from elsewhere and, perhaps that on the facts of the particular case the defence would only be partial, there is no objection in principle, and certainly not as a matter of EU law, to the defence being available to a claim based on the public law reason for restitution. However, situations where these requirements can be fulfilled and the public body is the defendant will probably be extremely rare or non-existent.

Nevertheless, because such situations may exist, and because the defence may also be used in situations where the public body is the claimant, it is necessary to go on to answer the fifth question concerning the chronology of the payment and change of position. In *South Tyneside MBC v Svenska Intl plc*[143] the court held that the specific expenditure had to occur *after receipt* of the payment. In other words, the defendant must have relied on the validity of the payment, not the validity of the agreement, a result convincingly criticised in academic commentary on the case.[144] In *National Westminster Bank plc v Somer Intl (UK) Ltd*[145] lack of argument to the contrary led the court to assume that this was correct[146] but the Privy Council in *Dextra Bank & Trust Co Ltd v Bank of Jamaica*[147] held that it was

> difficult to see what relevant distinction can be drawn between (1) a case in which the defendant expends on some extraordinary expenditure all or part of a sum of money which he has received from the plaintiff, and (2) one in which the defendant incurs such

[141] *FII* (UK) (n 36) [347]. For further discussion of the 'fiscal disruption' defence see below at pp 157–59.

[142] *Murphy* (n 118).

[143] *Svenska* (n 85).

[144] See: Goff and Jones (n 76); P Birks, 'Private Law' in P Birks and F Rose (eds), *Lessons of the Swaps Litigation* (London, Mansfield Press, 2000); Burrows, *Law of Restitution* (n 139) 518; A Jones, 'It's a Fair Swap' (1995) 59 *The Conveyancer* 490; M Jewell, 'Change of Position' in P Birks and FD Rose (eds), *Lessons of the Swaps Litigation* (London, Mansfield Press, 2000); R Nolan, 'Change of Position in Anticipation of Enrichment' (1995) 3 *Lloyds Maritime and Commercial Law Quarterly* 313; and P Key, 'Change of Position' (1995) 58 *The Modern Law Review* 505. There is an interesting contrast here with the recent decision of Judge Chambers QC in *Papamichael v National Westminster Bank* [2003] EWHC 164, [2003] 1 Lloyd's Rep 341 in which the defence failed in the opposite direction. Here the prima facie position was that the bank did not have any right to deal as it liked with the money received. Receipt of the money was therefore not only necessary before the defence could operate, it was not even sufficient. Nor was it enough that a third party had represented to the bank that it could so deal with the money because this person did not have and had not been given the authority to make such representations.

[145] *National Westminster Bank plc v Somer Intl (UK) Ltd* [2001] EWCA Civ 970, [2002] QB 1286 (CA).

[146] ibid [47].

[147] *Dextra Bank* (n 85). See also: Burrows, *Law of Restitution* (n 139) 517–19.

> expenditure in the expectation that he will receive the sum of money from the plaintiff, which he does in fact receive. Since *ex hypothesi* the defendant will in fact have received the expected payment, there is no question of the defendant using the defence of change of position to enforce, directly or indirectly, a claim to that money. It is surely no abuse of language to say, in the second case as in the first, that the defendant has incurred the expenditure in reliance on the plaintiff's payment or, as is sometimes said, on the faith of the payment.[148]

It is submitted that this is true regardless of the claim at issue, but it should be noted that since the Privy Council held that the exclusion of anticipatory reliance in *Svenska* depended on the exceptional facts of that case, on such facts the rule must still apply.[149]

On the sixth matter, the role of the defendant's good faith or fault, in *Dextra* the court rejected an approach based on weighing up the relative fault of the claimant and defendant, holding that this would be too uncertain. Instead a simple requirement of good faith would be sufficient. This approach was applied by Moore-Bick J and in principle approved by Clarke LJ in *Niru Battery Manufacturing Co v Milestone Trading Ltd*,[150] though his description of bad faith as being 'capable of embracing a failure to act in a commercially acceptable way and sharp practice of a kind that falls short of outright dishonesty as well as dishonesty itself' may soften the test away from the *Dextra* position.[151] This rule was also applied by Judge Chambers QC in *Papamichael v National Westminster Bank*[152] who held that, while the concept of good faith would need to be worked out on a case by case basis, he was 'content to proceed upon the basis of a requirement of actual knowledge where good faith is concerned. This would include wilfully and recklessly failing to make such inquiries as an honest and reasonable man would make'.[153]

Obviously, this makes the situation more difficult for a public authority that knew the tax was illegal but coerced the claimant into paying anyway.[154] Further, it is by no means impossible, given the difficulty of applying concepts such as 'bad faith' or 'dishonesty' to corporate entities, that in a future case the defence could

[148] ibid [38].
[149] ibid [39].
[150] *Niru Battery Manufacturing Co v Milestone Trading Ltd* [2002] EWHC 1425 (Comm); [2003] EWCA Civ 1446 (CA) [135] and [164].
[151] ibid [164]. See also: P Birks, 'Change of Position: The Two Central Questions' (2004) 120 *Law Quarterly Review* 373, especially 377.
[152] *Papamichael* (n 144).
[153] ibid [209].
[154] See also: G Jones, *Public and Private* (n 60) 37–39.

[148] ibid [38].
[149] ibid [39].
[150] *Niru Battery Manufacturing Co v Milestone Trading Ltd* [2002] EWHC 1425 (Comm); [2003] EWCA Civ 1446 (CA) [135] and [164].
[151] ibid [164]. See also: P Birks, 'Change of Position: The Two Central Questions' (2004) 120 *Law Quarterly Review* 373, especially 377.
[152] *Papamichael* (n 144).
[153] ibid [209].
[154] See also: G Jones, *Public and Private* (n 60) 37–39.

simply be denied to a public body from the point at which it had notice that the claimants were challenging their liability to provide it with the income in question. Indeed, in *FII* Henderson J wanted to go much further than this in cases where the public body is the defendant. His view was that:

> The Revenue should not be entitled to rely on change of position as a defence to a *Woolwich* claim, because such a claim is founded on the unlawful levying of tax and therefore on the commission of a legal wrong, but that the defence should in principle be available to the Revenue when restitution is sought of overpaid tax on the basis of mistake. The critical distinction is that the unlawfulness of the tax forms no part of the cause of action in mistake. It is therefore irrelevant, just as the club's conversion of the banker's draft was irrelevant in *Lipkin Gorman.*[155]

With respect, this conclusion is wrong on three counts. The first is the argument that the change of position defence is unavailable in '*Woolwich* claims' but available where the claim is based on mistake. If the mistake was wholly unrelated to the lawfulness or otherwise of the decision, this might be plausible, but since the whole essence of the mistake was the belief that the tax was lawful when in fact it was not, it is difficult to see why the unlawfulness of the tax 'infects' the *Woolwich* or public law claim, but not the mistake claim. For either cause of action, the claimants would have to base themselves on the unlawfulness of the tax and it would be in response to this that the Revenue would raise the change of position defence. Henderson J rejected this response on the basis that it contained 'neither logic nor justice'[156] but it contains both and Henderson J gives no reasons for his conclusion that it does not.

The second count is that discussed in chapter one. It appears in the passage quoted above that Henderson J is equating the 'unlawfulness' of the tax with the tort of conversion but, as ever, this is to miss the point that while conversion is a tort in private law, the tax in *FII* was 'unlawful' in the very different sense that it was beyond the scope of the powers of the Revenue as a matter of public law. It was noted in chapter one[157] that it would be perfectly possible to regard all public law ultra vires events as 'wrongs', but that to do so would be first to blur the important distinction between public and private law established by the development of a separate discipline of administrative law, and second that such a move would also blur important distinctions within developing administrative law itself, such as, for example, the difference between voiding a decision for bias as opposed to voiding it for misunderstanding of the relevant legislation or facts. Once these important distinctions are realised, it becomes obvious that while private law may have developed the rule that change of position should not be available to 'wrongdoers', there is no automatic reason why this should be extended to the very different category of public law defendants in a case involving an ultra vires event. As for Henderson J's argument that:

155 *FII* (UK) (n 36) [339], citing *Lipkin Gorman* (n 75).
156 ibid [342].
157 pp 12–13.

> The proposition that the Revenue should not be able to rely on change of position as a defence to a *Woolwich* claim gains further support . . . from the fact that no suggestion to this effect was made by Lord Goff in the *Woolwich* case itself, even though it was decided not long after *Lipkin Gorman*[158]

it should be remembered that, on the other hand, the change of position defence did receive support from Lord Goff and Hobhouse J in *Westdeutsche*,[159] another case in which the transaction undertaken by the public body was held to be ultra vires. If the defence was in principle available in *Westdeutsche*, there is no reason why it should not be available in a case such as *FII*.

The third objection to Henderson J's reasoning is then that, unsurprisingly in the circumstances, it misses the point that the existence of a public law ultra vires action was in that case already factored into the availability of the defence or otherwise as part of issue two, discussed above, namely whether, particularly as a matter of EU law, the defence would restrict to too great an extent the law's ability to reverse the ultra vires action. Only the issue of knowledge that the income should not be relied upon is relevant here.

Estoppel

This defence is closely related to that of change of position, and indeed, it was not clear whether it continued to exist following the introduction of change of position in *Lipkin Gorman*. Closely connected to this question is that of the exact operation of the defence, it being assumed by many, including Key,[160] that estoppel should not continue to exist because of its absolute, rather than pro tanto nature. In *Scottish Equitable v Derby*[161] Harrison J held that it would be 'unconscionable or clearly inequitable to allow the defendant to keep the whole of the overpayment . . . when his detriment is limited to [only part] of that amount'.[162] This was cited with approval in *Phillip Collins*,[163] where Jonathan Parker J held that, as he read the relevant authorities 'the law has now developed to the point where a defence of estoppel by representation is no longer apt in restitutionary claims where the most flexible defence of change of position is in principle available'.[164]

However, since the Court of Appeal held in *Somer Intl*[165] that estoppel by representation could be limited to the extent of the defendant's detriment, it may be that estoppel is not wholly inflexible. Similarly it is clear that although he had not

[158] *FII* (UK) (n 36) [340].
[159] *Westdeutsche Landesbank Girozentrale* (n 79).
[160] P Key, 'Exercising Estoppel by Representation as a Defence to Restitution' (1995) 54 *The Cambridge Law Journal* 525.
[161] *Scottish Equitable Ltd v Derby* [2000] 3 All ER 793 (QB) (affirmed in *Scottish Equitable* (CA) (n 114)).
[162] ibid 806.
[163] *Phillip Collins* (n 71).
[164] ibid 826.
[165] *Somer Intl* (n 145).

heard sufficient argument to make more than 'tentative observations' on the matter, for Robert Walker LJ in *Scottish Equitable*, the relationship between the two defences remained interesting and not wholly settled. Some academic response to the first instance decision in *Scottish Equitable* also suggested that estoppel should be available concurrently with change of position.[166] It is unsurprising therefore that Clarke J expressed the hope that the House of Lords would have the chance to consider both of these issues. In any case, however, the same arguments apply to this defence as were outlined above in relation to the defence of change of position.

Bona Fide Purchase

Various views on this defence exist. If the House of Lords was right to hold as it did in *Foskett v McKeown*[167] that it is a defence to proprietary claims, then it will not in any case apply to personal claims based on the public law unjust factor. On the other hand, Birks has suggested that while it is explicable as a protection for the exception to the *nemo dat* rule, it can also be seen as 'no more than a special manifestation of disenrichment' (which he sees as being the basis of change of position).[168] Other views are held by Key (who argues that bona fide purchase is separate from change of position)[169] and Burrows.[170] However, even though Burrows argues that, unlike change of position, bona fide purchase is not a 'disenrichment' defence, even to him it is a defence based on security of receipt because it protects contracts entered into by indirect recipients of the enrichment, and therefore the same arguments apply here as were outlined in relation to the defence of change of position, above.

Impossibility of Counter-Restitution

This defence, if it applies,[171] can act as a qualification to the ultra vires principle in one of two ways; first, because the claimant has also received a benefit as a result of the public law event, which cannot be returned to the defendant (for example because it was a service or perishable goods). The defendant can therefore use this defence to avoid returning the money received as a result of the ultra vires event and the effects of the ultra vires thus remain. Alternatively, the claimant may be allowed to make counter-restitution in money terms, but this may have the effect of perpetuating the ultra vires event. For example, Toube cites *McShane v Manitoba* in which service fees were paid under an ultra vires statute. It was held

[166] See: E Fung and L Ho, 'Change of Position and Estoppel' (2001) 117 *The Law Quarterly Review* 14.

[167] *Foskett v McKeown* [2001] 1 AC 102 (HL). See also: Virgo, *Principles*, above n 140 656–61.

[168] P Birks, *Unjust Enrichment*, 2nd edn (Oxford, Oxford University Press, 2005) 208–23 (on the defence of change of position) and 240–45 (on the specific issue of bona fide purchase).

[169] See: P Key, 'Bona Fide Purchase as a Defence in the Law of Restitution' (1994) 3 *Lloyd's Maritime and Commercial Law Quarterly* 421.

[170] Burrows, *Law of Restitution* (n 139) 585–91.

[171] Its application is supported in principle: Birks, 'Private Law' (n 144) 35–36.

that although the fees were prima facie recoverable, where the services had actually been provided, the fees were not recoverable. Toube argues that 'restitution of the money's worth of the services could have been made',[172] but it appears that either in this case, or in other similar cases, paying for the services could perpetuate the illegality to some extent. Should this qualification be allowed to stand, or is this an example of a private law defence restricting the law's access to the public law event? It is submitted that this defence is in fact based on the same considerations of legal certainty and non-retroactivity as those considered above. It is in that sense a simultaneous change of position, where the detrimental reliance takes place at the same time as receipt of the ultra vires payment. If this is true, then the qualification is as familiar to public law as it is to private law, and the defence does not harm the balance struck between public and private law and it should be considered alongside the discussion of change of position itself, above.

Submission to an Honest Claim[173]

It is possible that this defence does not apply to the public law reason for restitution, since Hill argues that it operates to deny the particular unjust factors of mistake or duress.[174] It was rejected as a defence by the House of Lords in *Kleinwort Benson v Lincoln*:

> [I]t would be most unwise for the common law, having recognised the right to recover money paid under a mistake of law on the ground of unjust enrichment, immediately to proceed to the recognition of so wide a defence as this which would exclude the right of recovery in a very large proportion of cases. The proper course is surely to identify particular sets of circumstances which, as a matter of principle or policy, may lead to the conclusion that recovery should not be allowed . . . before so novel and far-reaching defence [sic] as the one now proposed can be recognised, a very strong case for it has to be made out; and I can discover no evidence of a need for so wide a defence as this.[175]

Hedley also points this out[176] and, in general, academic opinion seems to be against its application.[177] The little support it receives is only for its application in true cases of contractual agreement,[178] or waiver, such as *ex p Chetnik* in which

[172] F Toube, 'Restitution for Public Lawyers' [1996] *Judicial Review* 92, 96 (citing *McShane v Manitoba* [1993] Manitoba Suit No SC 93-01-40538).

[173] See: Goff and Jones (n 76) 10-052–10-056.

[174] T Hill, 'Restitution from Public Authorities and the Treasury's Position: *Woolwich Equitable Building Society v IRC*' (1993) 56 *The Modern Law Review* 856, 861.

[175] *Kleinwort Benson Ltd v Lincoln CC* [1999] 2 AC 349 (HL) 385 (Lord Goff).

[176] S Hedley, 'Restitution—Mistake of Law—Reform in Haste, Repent At Leisure' (1999) 58 *Cambridge Law Journal* 1, 21.

[177] Hill (n 174); E McKendrick, 'Restitution of Unlawfully Demanded Tax' (1993) *Lloyd's Maritime and Commercial Law Quarterly* 88, 99; and Virgo, 'Taxation is not an Island' (n 52) 457.

[178] See: A Burrows, 'Restitution from Public Authorities' (1993) 4 *King's College Law Journal* 97, 99; McCamus (n 116) 272; and Law Commission (n 54) [10.34]. Jones suggests that, 'the right of recovery should not be absolute but should be subject to defences, such as that the payment was voluntary': G Jones, *Public and Private* (n 60) 43.

Lord Goff, quoting Lord Bridge, stated that a payment made 'in full knowledge of a possible ground on which to contest liability and in consequence of a deliberate decision not to do so would be irrecoverable'.[179]

In any case, such a defence would not be alien to, or offend, the public law point of view. It will be remembered that waiver was one of the factors cited above,[180] which will be considered by the courts in deciding whether to grant the discretionary response in a purely public law situation. Thus even if it did apply, nothing in this defence upsets the balance achieved so far in relation to the public law unjust factor dual event cases.

Ultra Vires

This defence (usually associated with *Sinclair v Brougham*[181]) is obviously inapplicable to the public law unjust factor cases, since the whole purpose of such cases is to respond to the public law event of illegality as well as the private law event of unjust enrichment.[182] There is thus no question of the law's response to the unjust enrichment infringing the ultra vires principle. Indeed, it is the defences, the restrictions on the law's response, which are being dealt with as qualifications to the ultra vires principle in this context.

Passing On[183]

In *Kleinwort Benson Ltd v Birmingham CC*,[184] Evans LJ did not think the rules on passing on would necessarily apply to the swaps cases:

> In my judgment, the taxation cases are of limited assistance in addressing the question of general principle which is raised by the present appeal. There is a public law element involved in them . . . and a further question, akin to agency, which is whether the taxpayer should be regarded as having collected tax from his customers on behalf of the taxing authority.[185]

It was argued in chapter three, in contrast to the views expressed by Lord Goff in *Kleinwort Benson v Lincoln*, that cases like those involving the swaps trans-

[179] *ex p Chetnik Developments* (n 11) 881.

[180] See above, text at n 18.

[181] *Sinclair v Brougham* [1914] AC 398 (HL). The HL held in that case that to allow an action for money had and received would indirectly contradict the ultra vires bar by producing the same result as if the contract had been valid.

[182] In any case, it obviously could not apply to a case such as *Woolwich* and it was rejected by Hobhouse J in *Westdeutsche Landesbank Girozentrale* (n 79) 915.

[183] This defence, as will be seen to some extent, is a difficult and controversial one. As such it continues to be the subject of research and debate in its own right. While interesting and important, continuation of this research is not directly relevant to the present investigation, which will focus solely on the implications of the hierarchy argument for the defence.

[184] *Kleinwort Benson Ltd v Birmingham CC* [1997] QB 380 (CA).

[185] ibid 389 (Evans LJ).

actions should be regarded as being just as 'public' as those involving tax such as *Woolwich*.[186] We thus need at least to begin by asking whether the defence of passing on ought to apply to any claims which contain such a 'public law element'.

However, this will depend to a large extent on which of two very closely related forms the defence in fact takes. On the one hand, it could be seen as an issue of mitigation of loss; if the claimant has managed to recoup the loss from somewhere then why should he or she still be able to bring a claim against the defendant? On the other hand, in its more literal sense it could be seen as relating to the correct identification of the claimant in an unjust enrichment situation; if C1 literally 'passed on' the charge to be paid to C2 then it is C2 that should be able to make the claim. The money will no longer have been received at C1's expense. The former version can obviously apply regardless of whether the public body is the claimant or the defendant, whereas the second version of the defence is obviously only likely to arise in situations where the public body is the defendant, and then often in tax cases. Not because, contrary to the views of Lord Goff and Evans LJ, only such cases are public, or because they are different in principle from other instances of the public law reason for restitution, but simply because in practice it is most likely that the facts necessary to raise the defence will arise in such cases.

As for the first version of the defence, it is clear that any idea of 'mitigation of loss' has been rejected by the Court of Appeal in *Kleinwort Benson v Birmingham*. In this swaps case, so-called 'hedging' contracts had been entered into by the bank and it was argued that since these 'back-to-back' contracts had enabled it to recoup some of the money it had paid to the local authority this should limit its claim. Evans LJ, approving Hobhouse J at first instance, stated that '[w]hat contracts or other transactions or engagements the plaintiffs may have entered into with third parties have nothing to do with the principle of restitution'.[187] Similarly Saville LJ held that '[t]he payee has been unjustly enriched by receiving and retaining money he has received from the payer . . . He does not cease to be unjustly enriched because the payer for one reason or another is not out of pocket'.[188] Thus, any subsequent recouping of the loss by the claimant was irrelevant to the situation between the claimant and the defendant.[189]

In *Kingstreet Investments v New Brunswick (Finance)*,[190] Bastarache J was equally dismissive of the defence of passing on, rejecting its application in the context of recovery of *ultra vires* taxes[191] for three reasons. First, it was inconsistent with the

[186] See ch 3, pp 67–68.

[187] *Kleinwort Benson Ltd v South Tyneside MBC* [1994] 4 All ER 972 (QB) 984–87, quoted in *Kleinwort Benson v Birmingham* (n 184) 391 (Evans LJ). See also: ibid 398 (Morritt LJ).

[188] ibid 394 (Saville LJ).

[189] Unlike, of course, any actions for compensation based on the wrong of breach of EU law under the *Francovich* principle, see: *Pirelli Cable Holding NV v IRC* [2006] UKHL 4, [2006] 1 WLR 400. Indeed, it was argued in ch 4 that if anything, the decision in *FII* (UK) (n 36) is a positive deterrent to mitigation since the steps taken to mitigate loss in that case had the result of taking the relevant claims outside the principle of unjust enrichment and into the principle of state liability in damages with its correspondingly higher threshold of 'sufficiently serious breach', above p 115.

[190] *Kingstreet Investments Ltd v New Brunswick (Finance)* [2007] SCC 1, [2007] 1 SCR 3.

[191] ibid [42].

basic premise of restitution law, on the basis that 'as between the taxpayer and the Crown, the question of whether the taxpayer has been able to *recoup its loss* from some other source is simply irrelevant'.[192] This seems to make perfect sense and is very like the reasoning of the Court of Appeal in *Kleinwort Benson v Birmingham.* However, if instead we were to turn to the second potential version of the defence and say that 'as between the claimant and the Crown it is irrelevant that the charge may in fact have been at someone else's expense', that conclusion might not be so immediately acceptable. In the case of the swaps contracts, it is clear that the hedging contracts did form a system of loss mitigation, but from the dicta quoted above it is not clear that they constituted a passing on of the cost in the more direct, literal sense. As Evans LJ puts it, 'the hedge contracts, even if they were perfect matches, were market transactions independent of the swaps contract'.[193] In tax cases, on the other hand, the second, literal form of passing on can arise as follows. A retailer sells units costing £1 each, on which it would expect to make 20p per unit profit. An ultra vires tax is charged of 10p per unit. In order to cover this charge the retailer raises the price of the units to £1.10, in order to maintain the profit margin of 20p. In these circumstances it is at least arguable that the tax has not been paid at the expense of the retailer at all, but at the expense of each purchaser of the units. It is, of course, equally possible that whereas at £1 per unit the retailer would have sold 10 units, by putting up the price it has reduced its number of sales to eight. In this situation the customers of the retailer will have paid tax of 80p (8 × 10p), which will have been received by the taxing authorities, but at the same time the retailer will have suffered a loss of profit of 40p (2 × 20p). However, this 40p loss will not have been received by the taxing authorities and it does not alter the fact that none of the 80p tax received by the authorities was received at the expense of the retailer. Even if English law does not and should not require the enrichment received by the defendant to equate with the subtraction from the claimant,[194] the key cases of non-correspondence are all the inverse of the situation here and in each of them the non-correspondence arises because the *claimant* is able to recover more than his or her *loss.* For example, a claimant can recover more through quantum meruit or quantum valebat than the services or goods actually cost.[195] In the tax situation outlined above, on the other hand, the question is in fact whether the *defendant* should be liable to pay back more than the *enrichment* (£1.20 rather than 80p in the example given above). Even if the taxing authority has to pay out £1.20, only 80p of that sum will be paid as restitution to

[192] ibid [45], citing P Maddaugh and J McCamus, *The Law of Restitution* (Aurora: Ont, Canada Law Book 2004, updated 2005) 11–46.

[193] *Kleinwort Benson v Birmingham* (n 184) 391.

[194] This issue has been the subject of debate, most recently between Birks, *Unjust Enrichment,* ch 4, 1st and 2nd edn (Oxford, Oxford University Press, 2003 and 2005) and M McInnes, 'Interceptive Subtraction, Unjust Enrichment and Wrongs—A Reply to Professor Birks' (2003) 62 *Cambridge Law Journal* 697. See also: Burrows, *Law of Restitution* (n 139) 28–29; and Virgo *Principles* (n 140) ch 5. From a different perspective, see also: *Sempra Metals* (n 92) holding that the measure of restitution should be the defendant's enrichment rather than the claimant's loss.

[195] Burrows, ibid.

the purchasers. The remaining amount (if any, and however much) will be payable as damages for the wrong done to the retailer.[196] It is also possible, therefore, to take issue with Bastarache J's second, 'economic misconception' argument. If indeed taxpayers have suffered a loss due to the increase in prices necessary to pass on the tax, their claim should actually be one for compensation for loss, not a claim in unjust enrichment. In the EU context, where passing on has been frequently discussed,[197] this would require such taxpayers to bring a *Francovich*[198] action for state liability in damages rather than a *San Giorgio*[199] claim for the return of the tax.

It is therefore not impossible that in relation to the 80p tax paid by the purchasers, the defence of passing on could still exist in English law; indeed it exists in a number of English tax statutes such as those dealing with the recovery of overpaid VAT[200] or excise duty,[201] and it has been shown that the instinctive appeal of the defence is that it seems to answer the 'at the expense of' requirement, so it is not possible to dismiss it quite so easily. It is similarly less obviously correct to adopt Bastarache J's conclusion that '[r]estitution law is not concerned by the possibility of the plaintiff obtaining a windfall precisely because it is not founded on the concept of compensation for loss',[202] when instead of referring to 'windfalls' and 'compensation for loss', it is pointed out that taxpayers who receive a refund of a tax they did not initially pay may themselves be unjustly enriched at the expense of a third party. Indeed the majority of the Supreme Court of Canada had previously adopted the defence in *Air Canada*[203] precisely on the basis that, in La Forest J's words, 'the law of restitution is not intended to provide windfalls'.[204] Ultimately, we may still conclude that it is more important that the public body be stripped of the *ultra vires* tax than that the tax ends up in the right hands, but that would entail a positive policy decision. It is not an obvious assumption that follows by default from 'the basic premise of restitution law'.[205]

[196] This matter has arisen particularly frequently in the European context, as will be seen below in ch 8 and it will be shown there that while the tax is claimed as restitution, the claim for loss of profit should in principle be brought against the state in the form of an action for state liability in damages under the authorities: C-6/90 and C-9/90 *Francovich and Bonifaci v Italy* [1991] ECR I-05357 and Cases C-46/93 and C-48/93 *Brasserie du Pêcheur SA v Federal Republic of Germany and R v Secretary of State for Transport, ex p Factortame* [1996] ECR I 1029. Often it is not. Whether or not this loss of profit can be claimed depends on the rules applicable to the claim and non-contractual/tort liability of public authorities gives rise to damages much more easily in EU law than in national law: Wade and Forsyth (n 1) 778–80.

[197] See, eg: *San Giorgio* (n 99); and Case 68/79 *Hans Just I/S v Danish Ministry for Fiscal Affairs* [1980] ECR 501.

[198] *Francovich* (n 196).

[199] *San Giorgio* (n 99).

[200] Value Added Tax Act 1994 s 80, as amended by the Finance Act 1997 s 47, applied in *Marks and Spencer plc v Customs and Excise Commissioners* [2000] STC 16 (CA).

[201] Customs and Excise Management Act 1979 s 137A, as inserted by the Finance Act 1995 s 20 and as amended by the Finance Act 1997 s 50 and sch 5.

[202] *Kingstreet Investments* (n 190) [47].

[203] *Air Canada* (n 48).

[204] ibid 193.

[205] *Kingstreet Investments* (n 189) [44].

On the other hand, Burrows argues strongly that the statutory versions of the defence should be repealed on the basis that they are 'cynically designed by the Revenue authorities to override the taxpayer's legitimate right to restitution so as not to disrupt a public authority's finances'.[206]

Certainly if the defence is really a disguised 'fiscal disruption' defence then, it should be recognised as such and will be subject to the arguments made below.[207] It is true that the retailer does not have as good a claim to the 80p as the purchasers, but it is not impossible to argue that the defendant taxing authority has no right at all to retain the money and so the enrichment should still be transferred to the retailer because it is being transferred away from the defendant.[208] However, even then, care must be taken not to tip too far in favour of these public law considerations against the private law requirement that the enrichment be received at the expense of the claimant, as did Wilson J in her dissent in *Air Canada*. She began, as suggested here, by holding that '[w]here the payments were made pursuant to an unconstitutional statute there is no legitimate basis upon which they can be retained'.[209] However, she did so by holding also that '[i]n terms of [La Forest J's majority] analysis, the [airlines] are unable to show that the unjust enrichment of the province was at their expense. In my view there is no requirement that they be able to do so'.[210]

On the contrary, there is such a requirement and its result is that the best right of all belongs to the purchasers who ought in turn to be able to bring a claim against the retailer. Mason CJ in *Commissioner of State Revenue v Royal Insurance Australia Ltd*[211] and Burrows[212] argue that on receiving the repayment the retailer should become a constructive trustee for the purchaser. This possibility survives *Kleinwort Benson v Birmingham*, and even if the rules on constructive trusts were to be altered, the retailer should at least be on notice of the purchasers' claim so that it should not have the defence of change of position to any unjust enrichment claim brought by them against it. The possibility that the recovery of the charge will in any event be passed on in this way was also noted by AG Geelhoed in considering the defence at the European level.[213] Perhaps the best answer, then, would be to circumvent these two actions in as many cases as possible through the use of class actions by the purchasers as suggested by Crerar.[214] In some circumstances, this is currently prevented

[206] Burrows, *Law of Restitution* (n 139) 595.

[207] See 'Fiscal Disruption' below.

[208] In support of such a proposition, see: Case C-129/00 *Commission of the European Union* [2003] ECR I-14637.

[209] *Air Canada* (n 48) 170.

[210] ibid.

[211] *Commissioner of State Revenue v Royal Insurance Australia Ltd* (1995) 182 CLR 51 (HCA).

[212] Burrows, *Law of Restitution* (n 139) 595–96.

[213] Case C-129/00 *Commission v Italy* [2003] ECR I-14637 [79]. For further discussion of AG Geelhoed's decision more generally, see: ch 8 p 258.

[214] D Crerar, 'The Restitutionary Class Action' (1998) 56 *University of Toronto Faculty of Law Review* 47.

by statutes which only allow refund of taxes to those who immediately paid them[215] and it would be desirable to amend the statutes accordingly.

Nevertheless, there is one further point in favour of the disapplication of the defence even in this form, which is Bastarache J's third objection to it; the difficulty of proving that the charge has actually been passed on.[216] In the context of the EU, the ECJ held, in *San Giorgio*, that where a tax is contrary to European law, making recovery of that tax dependent on proof that it has *not* been passed on renders recovery of it 'virtually impossible' and thus insufficient to fulfil the state's obligation to provide a 'remedy' for breach of European law.[217] Yet it is difficult to see how, without the use of presumptions in one direction or another, the defence can ever be proved. Even were a retailer, immediately following imposition of the tax, to put up the price of its products by exactly the same amount per unit as the tax, it could always argue that this was merely chance and the result of what AG Mancini in *San Giorgio* referred to as 'the innumerable variables which affect price formation in a free market', leading to 'the consequent impossibility of definitively relating any part of the price exclusively to a certain cost'.[218] Thus while the relationship of this defence to the 'at the expense of' requirement of the unjust enrichment claim suggests that it ought in principle to be recognised, and there is much to be said for the approach of Mason CJ, Burrows and Crerar regarding its operation, the difficulties of applying such a rule in any given case may in practical terms be insurmountable.

Special Defences in Public Law Unjust Factor Cases

Having considered the application of the existing private law defences, it is now necessary to turn to other specific defences (in addition to particularly short time limits, considered above) which would only apply, if at all, to hybrid, public law unjust factor situations. Since these defences are principally public defences, the question here is whether their application is too restrictive of the law's access to the private law event of unjust enrichment.

Fiscal Disruption

Although this consideration was clearly important to Lord Keith in *Woolwich*,[219] the Law Commission rejected this defence for several reasons. Two of these,

[215] Section 80 of the Value Added Tax Act 1994 provides that claims can only be brought by those who paid the tax to the VAT Commissioners, and since s 80(7) provides that the Commissioners are only liable to make restitution through the statute it is not possible for the customers to bring a common law *Woolwich* claim either.

[216] See: G Virgo, 'Restitution of Overpaid VAT' [1998] *British Tax Review* 582.

[217] *San Giorgio* (n 99).

[218] ibid 3629.

[219] '[T]he question of possible disruption of public finances must obviously be a very material one': *Woolwich* (n 37) 161.

inability to frame a statutory defence with any degree of precision and lack of support for such a legislative provision on consultation, relate specifically to the adoption of such a defence by legislation. The third applies equally whether the source of the defence is statute or the common law:

> [F]undamental questions of fairness to taxpayers must be addressed before such a provision could be recommended. If an individual taxpayer, whether large or small, has paid tax in circumstances where the law gives a right of recovery, it is a substantial investment of discretion in a tribunal or court to afford it power to deny that right on the basis of expediency.[220]

It is possible that in very restricted circumstances this defence could be the equivalent of the *ex p AMA* 'serious public inconvenience in upsetting the impugned legal order' discretion. However, it seems likely that this would be tantamount to choosing the public law wholly discretionary response route which has already been rejected above[221] as tilting the balance too far in favour of the public law event, against the private law one. Further support for this rejection of the defence comes from Lord Bridge in *ex p Chetnik Developments*, where he held that in exercising its section 9 discretion the 'financial constraints to which the authority are subject in providing much needed services for the residents in their area' and the fact that it was an 'indigent, rate-capped authority' were 'irrelevant to the justice or injustice of retaining rates mistakenly overpaid in the circumstances of any particular case and therefore irrelevant in the exercise of the discretion under section 9'.[222]

It is apparent that the discretion open to the rating authority under section 9 is, if anything, wider than the discretion open to a court in deciding whether to grant a public law response to a public law event under cases such as *ex p AMA*. Despite this, the fiscal disruption arguments were still not considered relevant to the exercise of the section 9 discretion because they were 'irrelevant to the justice or injustice of *retaining rates mistakenly overpaid*'[223] (emphasis added), in other words, because this would be to prioritise public law arguments over the private law event of unjust enrichment and the court was not prepared to make that choice.

A similar view was taken by Legatt LJ in the Court of Appeal in *Westdeutsche*, approved by Waller LJ in *Guinness Mahon*:

> The parties believed that they were making an interest swaps contract. They were not, because such a contract was ultra vires the local authority. So they made no contract at all. [The council] say that they should receive a windfall, because the purpose of the doctrine of ultra vires is to protect council taxpayers, whereas restitution would disrupt [the council's] finances. They also contend that it would countenance 'unconsidered dealings with local authorities'. If that is the best that can be said for refusing restitution, the sooner it is enforced the better. Protection of council taxpayers from loss is to be dis-

220 Law Commission (n 54) [11.6].
221 Above ch 2.
222 *ex p Chetnik Developments* (n 11) 879.
223 ibid (Lord Bridge).

tinguished from securing a windfall for them. The disruption of [the council's] finances is the result of ill-considered financial dispositions by [the council] and its officers. It is not the policy of the law to require others to deal at their peril with local authorities, nor to require others to undertake their own inquiries about whether a local authority has power to make particular contracts or types of contract. Any system of law, and indeed any system of fair dealing, must be expected to ensure that [the council] do not profit by the fortuity that when it became known that the contract was ineffective the balance stood in their favour. In other words, in circumstances such as these they should not be unjustly enriched.[224]

It is in any case unlikely that it would be easy for a public authority to be able to argue that the situation passed the *ex p AMA* test, or the EU law test of effectiveness[225] especially if Wilson J's view of the defence is adopted:

> I find it quite ironic to describe such a person as 'asserting a right to disrupt the government by demanding a refund,' or 'requiring a new generation to pay for the expenditures of the old'. By refusing to adopt such a policy the courts are not 'visiting the sins of the fathers on the children'. The 'sin' in this case (if it can be so described) is that of government and only government and government has means available to it to protect against the consequences of it. It should not, in my opinion, be done by the courts and certainly not at the expense of individual taxpayers.[226]

It will be remembered that if Wilson J's judgment can be criticised it is for prioritising the public law event over the event of unjust enrichment rather than regarding them as equally relevant.[227] If the defence of fiscal disruption should thus not operate when the public law event is given priority, in other words in a pure *ex p AMA* situation, then there is surely even less justification for it when both events are recognised as being relevant. It is also difficult to see that it would really operate as a defence at all, rather than a complete bar to all such claims. Public bodies specifically raise money in order to spend it in the public interest and could therefore always argue that return of the money would upset their finances.[228]

The Law Commission's 'Special' Defence of Exhaustion of the Statutory Mechanism[229]

Again, this argument is entirely familiar to public lawyers,[230] but would it restrict the law's ability to respond to the private law event of unjust enrichment? Arguably it would not: the defence does not prevent a response to the unjust enrichment, it merely governs the procedure for obtaining such a response and indeed it already

[224] *Westdeutsche Landesbank Girozentrale* (n 79) 967 (Leggatt LJ) cited in *Guinness Mahon and Co Ltd v Kensington and Chelsea RLBC* [1999] QB 215 (CA) 233 (Waller LJ).
[225] On which see further ch 8.
[226] *Air Canada* (n 48) 169.
[227] See text following n 208 above, in relation to the passing on defence.
[228] For further reasoning to this effect see the discussion of the change of position defence, above.
[229] Law Commission (n 54) [9.19]–[9.20], [10.7], [10.42]–[10.43].
[230] See: Craig (n 8) 26-056–26-059.

operates in the statutory context, where rights of appeal on tax matters must be exhausted before a judicial review of the decision can be brought.[231]

Prospective Overruling

There are English dicta which support this defence,[232] as well as dicta from the Irish Supreme Court in *Murphy*[233] and the ECJ in *Defrenne v Sabena*.[234] Craig also suggests it as an alternative to shorter time limits for judicial review.[235] There are arguments both for and against the application of this defence. On the one hand, it is a means of preventing fiscal disruption from the outset, and it prevents the opening of the floodgates to huge numbers of other claims. As such, it is arguably preferable to the legislative response to the *Woolwich* and *Deutsche Morgan Grenfell* cases discussed above.[236] It is also arguable that the existence of the defence would leave a court free to examine the illegality unperturbed by questions of the impact of its finding on public bodies and finances and nothing in the defence would distort the public and private nature of the claim because it would only affect the extent of the ultra vires finding which establishes the unjust factor in the first place. However, it is submitted that the defence should be very restrictively applied, as indeed is the ECJ's current approach.[237] In general it is submitted that a finding of ultra vires should be just that. If a public body has acted beyond its powers, then this should normally be recognised, and the actions should be void *ab initio*. The illegal action should be 'mopped up' to the greatest extent possible. We have already seen that if the *defence* of ultra vires exists, it does so to prevent unlawful actions taking effect through another route. It surely then makes little sense to uphold them without there even being such another route. At present there is a further argument against this defence. In considering the legitimate expectations of a claimant in purely public law situations, it was noted above that if a substantively ultra vires representation is made to a private party it

[231] See, eg: *Preston v IRC* [1985] AC 835 (HL) 852 (Lord Scarman); *Autologic Holdings plc v IRC* [2005] UKHL 54, [2006] 1 AC 118; and *Boake Allen and NEC Semiconductors v Revenue and Customs Commissioners* [2006] EWCA Civ 25, [2006] STC 606.

[232] See, most significantly, the obiter 'never say never' approach of the HL in *National Westminster Bank plc v Spectrum Plus Ltd* [2005] UKHL 41, [2005] 2 AC 680. See also: *R v National Insurance Commissioner, ex p Hudson* [1972] AC 944 (HL) 1026 (Lord Simon); *Miliangos v George Frank (Textiles) Ltd* [1976] AC 443 (HL); and *Aries Tanker Corp v Total Transport Ltd* [1977] 1 WLR 185 (HL) 194. However, in *Miliangos*, his Lordship believed that this approach would require statutory authority (490). In *Kleinwort Benson v Lincoln* Lord Goff held that it had 'no place in our legal system': *Kleinwort Benson* (n 175) 379. Arden has nevertheless argued that 'there may be a certain amount of territory where prospective overruling might be productive of justice and properly employed' (citing *Royal Bank of Scotland v Etridge (No 2)* [2001] UKHL 44, [2002] 2 AC 773 as a recent non-statutory, non-constitutional law example): M Arden, 'Prospective Overruling' (2004) 120 *Law Quarterly Review* 7, 11.

[233] *Murphy* (n 118).

[234] Case 43/75 *Defrenne v Sabena* [1976] ECR 00455. See also: AG Jacobs in Case C-475/03 *Banco Popolare di Cremona v Agenzia Entrate Ufficio Cremona* [72]–[88] opinion of 17 March 2005.

[235] Craig (n 8) 26-047.

[236] pp 100–102 and 128–31.

[237] *Defrenne* n 234

currently cannot found a substantive legitimate expectation.[238] Estoppel and legitimate expectations cannot operate to validate an ultra vires act, even though such an expectation would only apply to rights already accrued and the illegality could be 'mopped up' from that point onwards. From the point of view simply of reciprocity, there is thus at present a clear case against allowing prospective overruling. If this were to be changed, as it was argued that it should be, prospective overruling is still subject to at least the same criticisms as the fiscal disruption defence considered above; while in general it may appear more fact-sensitive and discretionary than the application of a time limit, in the specific case in which prospective ruling were to be applied it is actually a blunt tool which prohibits recovery altogether and does not even have the merit of the 'fiscal disruption' label. It is also less certain and predictable in its operation than a time limit. These arguments do not rule out the application of the defence altogether, as is clear from the ECJ's case law,[239] but, as suggested at the outset, they do suggest that in practice it ought to be applied sparingly.

Conclusion

In conclusion, then, there are several private and public defences available to a claim based on the public law reason for restitution. In working out which of these defences should apply, the key points in all cases are first, that the alteration of existing defences or application of special public defences should be tied to the use of the public law reason for restitution in all claims involving dual public law and unjust enrichment events, and second, that however those defences are adjusted or applied, in each case the law must be allowed sufficient access to both the relevant events. In practice, once this approach is taken it becomes apparent that the application of most of the defences discussed above will be relatively restrictive. There seems little danger in requiring claimants to exhaust the statutory mechanisms for recovery before bringing an unjust enrichment action, but other defences are difficult to apply to the facts of specific cases, may have too great an adverse impact on the law's access to one or other of the two relevant events, are likely to breach the EU law principle of effectiveness,[240] or some combination of the three. It is therefore clear that the key defence is the one with which this chapter began; the setting of an appropriate time limit which balances the concerns of both public and private law, and which is applied prospectively, with an adequate transitional period for its implementation. Then, as outlined in chapters two to four, all cases in which there has been an enrichment as the result of a public law ultra vires event, whether the public body is the claimant or the defendant, should be brought on the basis of the public law unjust factor subject to this time limit, set specifically for such claims.

[238] See: *Western Fish Products* (n 106) and text.
[239] (n 237).
[240] See further ch 8.

Conclusions and further implications

THE STUDY OF claims in unjust enrichment involving public bodies occurs at the intersection between two relatively recently-developed areas of law; administrative law and unjust enrichment. Neither area is free of controversy, but each deals with different kinds of 'events' to which the law responds. The key to understanding the cases outlined here is that each contains events from *both* these spheres; they are 'dual event' claims. Thus, when the investigation commenced with an examination of the decision in *Woolwich EBS v IRC*[1] it became apparent that none of the existing private law 'unjust factors' could supply a good reason for restitution precisely because this reason was simply the operation of public law. Thus elements of inequality and pressure, illegality, lack of basis and incapacity were all relevant, but had previously been mistranslated into their private law equivalents, rather than being recognised for what they really were; public law ultra vires events in which a body with inherently greater and more limited power exceeds the boundaries of that power, thus rendering its actions void *ab initio*. Neither a purely private approach such as that suggested in *Woolwich*, nor a purely public approach such as that adopted by the Canadian Supreme Court in *Kingstreet Investments*[2] could hope to deal adequately with an issue which instead requires a *hybrid* approach, in other words, an approach which deals with both the relevant events.

Identification of the true reason for restitution in this way then has four important consequences. First, it removes cases such as *Woolwich* from an uncertain and undefined category of 'policy-based' reasons for restitution. Whereas the House of Lords in *Deutsche Morgan Grenfell*[3] felt that this category lacked precision and had the capacity to create arbitrary distinctions, in Chapter 3 it was seen that as soon as the correct nature of the reason for restitution is understood, the pieces of the jigsaw fall easily into place. The answers to the Law Commission's post–*Woolwich* questions and any others can then be answered, not by creating rules or limits afresh, but by using an existing, operational scheme with which the law is already familiar; that of administrative law. Second, this also clears the way for extension of the use of the public law unjust factor to cases where the public body is the potential *claimant*, as well as those in which it is the defendant. Thus cases such as

[1] [1993] AC 70.

[2] *Kingstreet Investments Ltd v New Brunswick (Finance)* 2007 SCC 1, [2007] 1 SCR 3.

[3] [2006] UKHL 49, [2007] 1 AC 558.

Auckland Harbour Board[4] or those involving the swaps transactions, can all be brought together with a simpler solution than that provided by, for example, the 'metaphysics of mistake'.[5] Third, once it is understood that the public law unjust factor is thus the only reason for restitution which is properly tailored to the requirements of both events, public and private, it can be suggested that this reason for restitution should always be used in preference to those which cannot do so good a job. A hierarchy of unjust factors could then be created to ensure that the law is given access to both the relevant events in such claims, and again, this would be nothing outside the ordinary once it is considered that such a hierarchy already exists between public and private law following *O'Reilly v Mackman*[6] and *Clark v University of Lincolnshire and Humberside.*[7] Finally, as with other aspects of the claims, lack of clarity regarding the reason for restitution has led to confusion about precisely which defences can and should apply to such claims. Again, once it is understood that private law defences must not restrict access to the ultra vires event any more than public law defences should restrict the law's ability to respond to an unjust enrichment, many of these questions can be far more easily resolved. Not only does it become clear how such adjustments to defences should operate, it is also clear *when* this should happen; when there are two events to which the law responds using the hybrid public law unjust factor in preference to other one-dimensional reasons for restitution. In particular the need to adopt an equally hybrid time limit becomes particularly apparent. This in turn strengthens the case for a hierarchy and for ensuring that dual event claims are dealt with in a way that recognises both of those events.

None of these claims is uncontroversial. Indeed, the argument concerning the hierarchy has in practical terms largely been excluded by the decision of the House of Lords in *Deutsche Morgan Grenfell.* At the same time, these suggestions have never been directly considered by a court or legislature. Conversely, if they are to be wholly dismissed then we will be left with a lot of coincidences. Is it really just chance that both tax and swaps cases currently entail some form of judicial review (national or European) followed by a series of cases in unjust enrichment? Or is it that in fact there is a link between both kinds of case precisely because both contain these two events? Is it coincidence that both Lord Goff and Morritt LJ were instinctively concerned that the rules governing a private law reason for restitution might prevent the law's ability to deal with an ultra vires event? Is it just coincidence that when faced with an unnecessary choice between a purely public law approach and a purely private one, the vote of two supreme courts can be split 50:50; the Supreme Court of Canada choosing the public approach in *Kingstreet Investments* while the House of Lords chose the private approach in *Deutsche Morgan Grenfell.* Finally, is it only coincidence that in both areas the courts have found themselves using the terminology of absence of basis and a threatened shift

[4] *Auckland Harbour Board v the King* [1924] AC 318.

[5] P Birks, *Unjust Enrichment,* 2nd edn (Oxford, Oxford University Press, 2005) 113.

[6] [1983] 2 AC 237.

[7] *Clark v University of Lincolnshire and Humberside* [2000] 1 WLR 1988 (CA).

towards the civilian approach? Or is it rather that the public law ultra vires event (which was void *ab initio*) needed more recognition than could be provided by a purely private reason for restitution?

Finally this analysis of claims involving public bodies has obvious implications for Birks' more recent argument that a change to the civilian 'no basis' approach is necessitated by the swaps cases.[8] His first concern is that 'three analyses were possible in the interrupted swaps, absence of basis, failure of contractual reciprocation, and mistake. With hindsight, these multiple analyses can be seen to be unsound'.[9] Once the argument made here is adopted it becomes clear that the triple analysis can be removed without resort to the civilian system. It is therefore not necessary to adopt Birks' view in order to explain the public body cases or in order to cope with the fact that they cannot easily be analysed using the existing private law tools. This does not, on the other hand, mean that on its own terms his approach is wrong and indeed it is important to understand how civilian systems might deal with such claims. It is therefore to the French system that we now turn.

[8] The relationship between the two approaches was discussed in general above p 36.
[9] P Birks, *Unjust Enrichment*, 2nd edn (Oxford, Oxford University Press, 2005) 112.

Part 2

Unjust Enrichment and Public Law in France

6

Public Body Unjust Enrichment Claims in France; Lessons for England and Wales

IT MIGHT BE thought that the solution proposed in the previous chapters is too elaborate. After all, it will be remembered that in his final book Birks argued that the swaps cases necessitated a change to the civilian 'no basis' approach,[1] and this might therefore be thought to be a simpler and hence preferable alternative. Certainly it is true that it is in public body cases that the English courts have come closest to adopting such an approach,[2] and for this reason alone it would be worth examining a system which does follow this 'absence of basis' model, albeit that this has not been the result of conscious reflection of the Birksian kind. However, there is a second variable which also makes the French system a useful comparator to add to the investigation of public body unjust enrichment cases in England. In France, the division between public and private law could be found even in the *Ancien Régime*, and the Conseil d'Etat was founded as a check upon the administration by Napoleon in 1799. Thus, unlike the English system which came to the idea of such a distinction only recently, in France the distinction between public and private law has long been well established.

The Public/Private Divide in France

Under the *Ancien Régime* in France, there early on appeared jurisdictions specialising in certain categories of administrative litigation, such as the *bureaux de finances* for fiscal matters. Although the monarchy attempted to forbid the ordinary courts (Parlements) from dealing with administrative affairs, this instruction 'remained something of a dead letter'.[3] Following the Revolution, the Assemblée constituante responsible for fixing the rules of administrative litigation was thus faced with the decision whether, in the light of the poor reputation enjoyed by the

[1] P Birks, *Unjust Enrichment*, 2nd edn (Oxford, Oxford University Press, 2005) 113–14. The relationship between the two approaches was discussed in general in ch 1.

[2] See above pp 24–26 and 58–61.

[3] Jean-Marie and Jean-Bernard Auby, *Institutions Administratives*, 7th edn (Paris, Dalloz, 1996), para 120.

administrative courts under the *Ancien Régime*, it should create new courts of this genre or not. It decided that the active administration itself would decide administrative cases and in order to preserve this jurisdictional monopoly it passed the *Loi* of the 16–24 August 1790, of which Title II, Article 13 declares that the functions of the ordinary courts are distinct from the administrative functions. The principle of the separation of the administrative and judicial authorities was completed by a decree of the 16 *fructidor*[4] *an III*.[5] However, it was soon realised that some judicial check was needed upon the administration and this was supplied by the creation of the Conseil d'Etat by Napoleon in 1799. Originally the Conseil d'Etat, which took over from the pre-revolutionary Conseil du Roi, was a more bureaucratic body, providing expert advice on the drafting of laws and regulations. However, it also had the duty of 'resolv[ing] difficulties which might occur in the course of the administration'[6] and in time this enabled it to build its independence as a true court, though its jurisdiction as such was not recognised until the beginning of the Third Republic (1870–1940).[7] Thus, ultimately, there were two separate branches of courts; the *ordre administratif* (administrative courts) and the *ordre judiciaire* (the ordinary courts).[8] During the nineteenth century the lower administrative courts developed and the *juges judiciaires*, or the ordinary judges, began to judge certain types of administrative litigation. In 1872 the Tribunal des Conflits was established to resolve questions of jurisdiction arising between the Conseil d'Etat and the Cour de cassation[9] (the highest level ordinary court). The relationship between the jurisdictional divide and the consequently different rules applicable in each system has something of a chicken and egg quality to it, but nevertheless Auby et al argue that the duality of jurisdiction is maintained because of the difference between the rules of public and private law and the need for judges to be expert in one or the other.[10] Indeed the training is different for public law judges from that for civil or criminal law judges; they have a placement in the administration and practical experience of active administration.[11]

The result of this jurisdictional division is that, whereas in England the starting point was to follow the Diceyan orthodoxy (to examine the rules concerning restitution and unjust enrichment and then to apply them to public bodies in the same way as to private parties), in France the starting point is the reverse. The first

[4] *Fructidor* is the 12th month of the French Republican calendar, August–September.

[5] Auby(s) (n 3), point 120. See also C Dadomo and S Farran, *The French Legal System*, 2nd edn (London, Sweet and Maxwell, 1996) 46–48.

[6] N Brown and J Bell, *French Administrative Law*, 5th edn (Oxford, Clarendon Press, 1998) 47.

[7] See generally Brown and Bell, ibid 44–50.

[8] This being a further implication of the separation of powers, on which see Dadomo and Farran (n 5) 46–50.

[9] A West et al, *The French Legal System*, 2nd edn (London, Butterworths, 1998) 19–20. The Tribunal des Conflits is comprised of equal numbers of judges from the highest public law and private law courts, with the casting vote held by the Minister of Justice (*Garde des Sceaux*).

[10] Auby(s) (n 3) para 121.

[11] J Bell, S Boyron and S Whittaker (eds), *Principles of French Law*, 2nd edn (Oxford, Oxford University Press, 2008) 177.

relevant division, taking the French legal system as a whole, is between public and private law just as was suggested in relation to the English system.[12]

Today the central characteristic of French public law is the presence of the administration as one of the parties to the dispute,[13] but the converse does not hold; the administration can be party to a case which falls within the jurisdiction of the ordinary courts, as will be seen below.[14] The term 'administration' includes not only the national government, but also local authorities, public agencies, public enterprises, public services (ranging from port authorities to universities, railways and other commercial activities) and quangos (*autorités administratives indépendantes*).[15] For instance, as a close parallel of the English discussion, the regulatory functions of the French Conseil de la Concurrence (Competition Council) are public services controlled by public law.[16]

However, as well as this organic separation there is also a functional separation between public and private law; indeed Debbasch and Ricci describe the public private divide in France as 'oscillating' between these 'two poles'.[17] The distinctive feature of public law was held in *Blanco* to be the presence of 'public service', though this has since undergone radical transformation to the point where certain authors have referred to it as a 'pseudo-criterion' devoid of real value.[18] In principle it contains various sub-criteria. The public service must satisfy a public need; the activity in question must be carried on by a public authority (though as in England the line between public and private bodies has become very blurred in recent years) and 'the authority must have recourse to methods and prerogatives which would be excluded in relations between private parties, that is *des prérogatives exorbitantes du droit commun*'.[19] This leads Vedel and Delvolvé to answer

[12] Though, as will be noted again below, the quasi-contracts in their application to public bodies nevertheless derive from the Civil Code. Chapus refers to them as 'enfants adoptifs'. R Chapus, *Droit administratif général* (Tome I), 15th edn (Paris, Montchrestien, 2001) 1394.

[13] Bell, Boyron and Whittaker, *Principles* (2008) 38. See also O Kahn Freund, C Lévy and B Rudden, *A Source Book on French Law* (Oxford, Clarendon Press, 1991) 14–15, citing J-M Auby and R Ducos-Ader, *Droit Public* vol 1 (Paris, Dalloz, 1976) 1–7. NB there are certain exceptional legislative circumstances in which the administrative courts have competence to hear specific claims between private parties (such as between the Banque de France and its agents or members) and in addition a private party charged with a *mission de service public* raises the competence of the administrative courts when the person in question acts within the framework of that *mission public*. See also: C Debbasch and J-C Ricci, *Contentieux Administratif*, 8th edn (Paris, Dalloz, 2001) 45–46.

[14] In particular in relation to social security pay-offices. It is for this reason that the division between public and private law should not be thought to be perfect in French law any more than it was seen to be in English law in chs 1–5. See further n 19 and ch 1.

[15] Bell, Boyron and Whittaker (n 13) 38 and 172–73. See also Kahn-Freund, Lévy and Rudden (n 13) 14–19.

[16] Bell, Boyron and Whittaker, ibid 173. The reference here is of course to *R v Panel on Takeovers and Mergers, ex p Datafin*, [1987] QB 815 (QB).

[17] Debbasch and Ricci (n 13) 182.

[18] See Brown and Bell (n 6) 129–135, citing M Waline, *Droit Administratif*, 9th edn (Paris, Sirey, 1963) 72.

[19] Brown and Bell, ibid especially 132. In fn 14 they refer the reader to the terminology of the European Court of Justice in Case C-188/89 *Foster v British Gas* [1990] ECR I-3313, which is of particular interest given the discussion of that case as part of the public/private divide in EU law, below at 241. As an example of the blurring of the line between public and private entities they give the example of

complaints that the public service criterion is nebulous by suggesting that, rather than looking for one single distinguishing feature, one should look instead for the presence of a more general concept of *puissance publique* (public authority or power).[20] Their statement that French public law is characterised by the existence of the administration's simultaneously greater and lesser powers brings us back to the same definition of the public/private divide as was chosen in chapter one.[21]

Thus, as with our 'paper clips' example in English law[22] it is not the mere fact that a body is public, but rather the public interest in the activity undertaken by it, which attracts the operation of the public law rules in France. This means that in France, even more so than in England[23] it is the activity itself and the question whether that activity is performed in the public interest under a separate legal regime that can be relevant.[24] For example, in another two parallels with England, France has had problems with defining the role of sports' regulatory bodies[25] and citizens may raise the illegality of an administrative decision as a defence to a criminal action (collateral challenge).[26]

Once the relevant competence has been established, it is nevertheless possible that an accessory question may arise which, if it were the principal question, would raise the competence of the other branch of jurisdiction. There are two categories of such accessory question, *questions préalables*, which may be resolved by the judge hearing the principal question and *questions préjudicielles*, which may not and which must then be sent to the competent judge. Accessory questions of private law raised before the administrative judge always constitute *questions préjudicielles* and must therefore be sent to the ordinary judges. As for the competence of the ordin-

social security *caisses*, which they translate as 'provident societies' and which are discussed below, n 120 and accompanying text.

[20] G Vedel and P Delvolvé, *Droit Administratif, Tome 1*, 12th edn (Paris, Presses Universitaires de France, 1992) 126–27, cited by Brown and Bell, ibid 135.

[21] «Comme l'a souligné à juste titre J Rivero, la puissance publique ne se caractérise pas seulement par des dérogations en plus au régime juridique des simples particuliers, mais par des dérogations en moins. Autrement dit, à côté des prérogatives de l'Administration, il y a des sujétions que ne connaissent pas les simples particuliers.» Vedel and Delvolvé, ibid 36, citing J Rivero, 'Existe-t-il un critère du droit administratif?' (1953) *Revue du Droit Public et de la science politique* 279. See generally: Vedel and Delvolvé, *La notion de puissance publique* at 35–36. They give as examples the fact that private persons can make decisions for any reason of their choice; interest, generosity, caprice, as long as it is not immoral or illicit. The Administration, on the other hand, can only make decisions in the public interest. Similarly the rules are different for public as opposed to private employers.

[22] See p 70.

[23] Under the rules of *Datafin* (n 16), in England the starting point is to establish whether the body is statutory or not, and only when it is not will the courts examine whether the function in question is nevertheless public.

[24] Bell, Boyron and Whittaker (n 11) 172–74. This means that while in England it tends to be the provider of the service that affects the nature of the service (state or private company) in France it is the activity itself and the question whether that activity is performed in the public interest under a separate legal regime which is relevant.

[25] ibid 178. Such bodies are considered to be public in French law, since the Minister's approval is necessary for bodies to regulate national championships.

[26] ibid 177. Contrast this with the English case of *DPP v Hutchinson* [1990] 2 AC 783 (HL). See also: *Boddington v British Transport Commission* [1998] 2 WLR 639 (HL).

ary courts in administrative matters, issues of interpretation of administrative regulations are *questions préalables*, whereas interpretation of individual acts are *questions préjudicielles*, except where competence has been expressly granted by legislation. Matters of assessment of legality of administrative acts, whether regulatory or individual, are all *questions préjudicielles*, except in relation to regulations that inflict grave harm on individual liberty or property rights. What would be known in England as preliminary references to the ECJ under Article 267 TFEU (ex 234 EC) are deemed to be *questions préjudicielles* from either branch of court.[27] The existence of this system exemplifies clearly the point made in relation to the English system that it is not always possible to fit the concerns of a case exclusively into either a public *or* a private law event, and that expertise from two different fields may sometimes be necessary in order to decide a particular case.[28]

The French Law of Unjust Enrichment

As for its rules on unjust enrichment, in France the most relevant area is that of the quasi-contracts, three of which are covered by Title IV of the Civil Code. There are some who would argue that these quasi-contracts are unified by the principle of '*enrichissement sans cause*',[29] but as compared to the French rules on contract and delict they do not have much of a common '*régime*'; only their rules on capacity, prescription periods and proof are shared.[30] Indeed, the category of quasi-contracts may be open to additions which have little to do with the concept of unjust enrichment or enrichment without cause as it is understood in the English

[27] Ph Foillard, *Dictionnaire de Droit Public* (Paris, Centre de Publications Universitaires, 2000) (verbo «questions accessoires»). This is the term used for preliminary references under art 267 in the French text of the EU Treaties.

[28] Though of course the fact that England does not have such a separate court structure for administrative law should, if anything, facilitate the use of a hybrid public and private approach in a given case, without the need for any system equivalent to that of *questions préjudicielles*. As was noted in ch 3, there is no reason why both aspects of the claim should not be heard in the same case by the same court. The key point is that both aspects are heard in the first place.

[29] Ph Le Tourneau, *Encyclopédie Dalloz*, "Quasi-Contrat" para 50. Though he describes *enrichissement sans cause* as the 'quasi-contract *par excellence*' he points out that the quasi-contract of *gestion d'affaires* 'rebels against' this classification. See also J Flour, JL Aubert and E Savaux, *Les Obligations*, vol 2, *Le fait juridique*, 17th edn (Paris, Colin, 2005) Title 1, para 2: «Partant de l'idée selon laquelle les deux institutions reposent sur le souci d'éviter qu'une personne s'enrichisse sans cause aux dépens d'une autre, doctrine et jurisprudence ont estimé possible de généraliser ces dispositions: de faire, de l'enrichissement sans cause, une source d'obligation» ('starting from the idea according to which the two institutions rest on a concern to avoid people being able to enrich themselves at the expense of others, doctrine and jurisprudence have thought it possible to generalise these provisions: to make a source of obligations from enrichment without cause'). See also J Flour, JL Aubert and E Savaux, *Les Obligations*, vol 1, *L'acte juridique*, 12th edn (Paris, Armand Colin, 2006), para 59.

[30] See A Bénabent, *Droit Civil, Les Obligations*, 10th edn (Paris, Montchrestien, 2005), para 450; Le Tourneau (n 29) para 24 and C Aubert de Vincelles, 'L'autonomie de l'action en répétition de l'indu: fin d'une divergence au sein de la Cour de Cassation' (2002) *D* 2433, text to note 38.

system. For example, in 2002 it may have acquired a new member[31] in the form of *pseudo-gain* or 'pseudo-wins'. This arose from a case involving the well-known practice of mail-order companies who include in their mailings notices indicating that the recipient, addressed by name, has won a sum of money. In this particular case the recipient sent off the requisite slips only to discover that this merely granted him entry to a pre-draw from which the winners would subsequently be drawn. The Cour d'Appel had rejected his claim in delict for the winnings on the basis that they did not represent his loss, but a mixed chamber of the Cour de cassation held that in rejecting his claim the Cour d'Appel had violated Article 1371 of the Code, the article concerning quasi-contracts, and the lottery organisers were thus held to be liable for the winnings they had originally indicated.[32]

Although the whole category of quasi-contracts cannot therefore be regarded as matching the English conception of unjust enrichment or even as forming a unified category of 'enrichment without cause', there are nevertheless three quasi-contracts which do seem more closely related to it, two of which are particularly relevant in examining claims similar to those considered in the previous chapters.[33]

Enrichissement Sans Cause

Of the quasi-contracts it is certainly *enrichissement sans cause* which bears the most resemblance to the English law of unjust enrichment. This quasi-contract has Roman roots, and has become known as the action *de in rem verso*. However, Flour and Aubert warn against assuming that this term has exactly the same import as in Roman law.[34] The most striking aspect of this quasi-contract is that it is not laid out in any one article of the Civil Code[35] (though there are several disparate articles that can be explained on this basis)[36] but instead, and very unusually for French law, it became an autonomous source of obligations through jurisprudence. It was in the *arrêt Boudier* (*Boudier* judgment) of 1892 that this development took place and the action *de in rem verso* became a separate cause of action. Although the

[31] Academic opinion on the question is mixed: Bénabent regards it as an independent quasi-contract (ibid para 511) but Terré, Simler and Lequette think the *théorie de l'apparence* is a better basis (F Terré, P Simler and Y Lequette, *Droit Civil, Les Obligations*, 9th edn (Paris, Dalloz 2005) 1029–31) although Bénabent in any case considers the *théorie de l'apparence* as a quasi-contract.

[32] Ch mixte 6 Sept 2002. See J Mestre and B Fages, (2003) RTD civ 94; (2002) *JCP* 2002.II.10173, note S Reifergeste.

[33] For a detailed account of the French quasi-contracts written in English, see S Whittaker in Bell, Boyron and Whittaker (n 11) 417–452. Only the relevant elements of the quasi-contracts will be outlined here. The quasi-contracts are also, along with the whole of the law of obligations, the subject of an *Avant-projet de réforme* edited by P Catala (ed) *Avant-projet de réforme du droit des obligations et de la prescription* (Paris, La Documentation Française, 2005).

[34] Flour, Aubert and Savaux (n 29) vol 2 para 35, citing C Aubry and C Rau, *Droit Civil Français*, Tome IX, 6th edn by E Bartin (Paris, Litec, 1953), para 578, note 7 and Tome VI, 7th edn, number 314, note 4, with references to F Goré, *L'enrichissment aux dépens d'autrui* (Paris, Dalloz, 1949). On the action *de in rem verso* generally, see R Zimmermann, *The Law of Obligations, Roman Foundations of the Civilian Tradition* (Oxford, Clarendon Press, 1996) 878 ff, especially 884.

[35] Flour, Aubert and Savaux (n 29) vol 2 paras 34–35.

[36] ibid.

ambit of the claim as first conceived was extremely wide, subsequent case law has narrowed it, at first severely and then in a more balanced and moderate way, so that now there are three 'material elements' and four 'jurisprudential elements' to the claim. The material elements are that the claimant should have been impoverished[37] (indeed he or she is generally known as the *appauvri*); that the defendant should have been enriched (hence *enrichi*)[38] and that there should have been a causal link between these two elements,[39] though if the enrichment has passed through the *patrimoine* of a third party, as in the *Boudier* case itself, this will not block the claim. Of the four negative 'jurisprudential elements' the first, as the name of the action implies, is that there must have been no legal cause of the enrichment.[40] Most frequently a cause is constituted by a contract between the *enrichi* and the *appauvri*, but contracts between the *enrichi* and third parties can also count as causes of the enrichment, provided that they give the *enrichi* the right to hold on to the benefit.[41] The cause can also be a legal rule,[42] a legal decision or the intention to give (*l'intention libérale*).[43] The second negative requirement is that of 'subsidiarity', which originally meant that the action in *enrichissement sans cause* would not be available to the claimant if he or she had any other cause of action, even if that cause of action was blocked for some reason.[44] This requirement derived directly from the concern that the new quasi-contract would allow the existing rules of law to be overturned or bypassed, and in this sense could be regarded as another instance of the French rule of *non-cumul des responsabilités*[45],

[37] See Bénabent (n 30) para 487; Flour, Aubert and Savaux (n 29) vol 2 para 40; Terré, Simler and Lequette (n 31) para 1067 and P Malaurie, L Aynès and P Stoffel-Munck, *Droit Civil, Les Obligations*, 2nd edn (Paris, Defrénois, 2005) 1064.

[38] Enrichments include saved expenses or use of a thing as well as more direct enrichments, see Bénabent (n 30) para 488; Flour, Aubert and Savaux (n 29) vol 2 para 39; Terré, Simler and Lequette, ibid, and Malaurie, Aynès and Stoffel-Munck, ibid at 1063.

[39] See Bénabent (n 30) para 489; Flour, Aubert and Savaux (n 29) vol 2 para 41; Terré, Simler and Lequette, ibid, and Malaurie, Aynès and Stoffel-Munck (n 37) para 1065.

[40] See Bénabent (n 30) paras 491–3; Flour, Aubert and Savaux (n 29) vol 2 paras 41–50; Terré, Simler and Lequette (n 31) para 1068 and Malaurie, Aynès and Stoffel-Munck (n 37) paras 1069–70.

[41] An interesting comparison can be drawn here with the English case of *Pan Ocean Shipping Co v Creditcorp Ltd, The Trident Beauty* [1994] 1 All ER 470 (HL). See A Burrows, *The Law of Restitution* (London, Butterworths, 2002) 347–50; 'Restitution from Assignees' (1994) *Restitution Law Review* 52 and K Barker, 'Restitution and Third Parties' [1994] *Lloyds Maritime and Commercial Law Quarterly* 305.

[42] Such as the rule under art 1341 of the Civil Code which will not uphold the right of lenders to reimbursement without written proof of the loan, see Flour, Aubert and Savaux (n 29) para 48. In that sense the 'legal rule causes' might alternatively be regarded as bars to the exercise of the action.

[43] But this must be a genuine intent to give, so that where a son or daughter goes beyond the requirement of 'filial piety' in providing for their parents, the parents (or their estate) will count as having been enriched without cause: Civ (1) 23 January 2001, D2001.746. Their moral duty did not constitute an *intention libérale* or a cause in its own right. See also Whittaker (n 11) 436.

[44] See Bénabent (n 30) para 495; Flour, Aubert and Savaux (n 29) vol 2 paras 52–56; Terré, Simler and Lequette (n 31) paras 1073–81 and Malaurie, Aynès and Stoffel-Munck (n 37) para 1071.

[45] Bell, Boyron and Whittaker explain that according to this rule 'a party to a contract may not sue the other party for damages in delict as long as the facts from which the delictual responsibility would otherwise arise are governed by one of the contract's obligations. While sometimes the rule is supported by reference to the binding force of contract, its real reasons lie in a juristic preference for keeping legal categories distinct, the need to protect both the terms and the rules of contract from the invasive effect of the extraordinary general liability based on fault, and as part of the means of control

but it is perhaps here that the law has relaxed most in recent cases. For example, where the principal claim would have been brought against a third party who is insolvent, it is now possible for the claimant to bring a claim in *enrichissement sans cause* against the *enrichi* instead, though the *appauvri* must prove the insolvency.[46] The third technique for containing the action in *enrichissement sans cause* was to block it when the enrichment and impoverishment were due to the fault of the *appauvri*.[47] Traditionally the fault of the *appauvri* deprived him of any claim,[48] but some more recent judgments of the Civil Chambers of the Cour de cassation have shown the increasing flexibility common to all the jurisprudential elements, holding that the claim of the *appauvri* will succeed but he or she will also have to indemnify the *enrichi* for any harm caused to him or her.[49] Finally, if the *appauvri* has acted even slightly in his or her own interest in addition to the interest of another, he or she will not be able to bring an action in *enrichissement sans cause*.[50] When the action succeeds it is subject to a 'double ceiling' on recovery and the claimant can only recover the lesser of his impoverishment and the defendant's enrichment.[51]

Répétition de l'indu

This quasi-contract, also based on Roman Law (this time the *condictio indebiti*)[52] deals with situations where a legal subject has received a sum or benefit which is not due to him,[53] most often as a result of an error.[54] The recipient-defendant is

ling the overweening tendencies of delictual liability for the "actions of things"', (n 11) 328–29, citing Malaurie, Aynès and Stoffel-Munck (n 37) 542ff; Civ 11 Jan 1992, S.1924.1.105, note R Demogue; see also: R Rodière, 'Etude de la dualité des régimes de la responsabilité—la combinaison des deux responsabilités', (1950) I *JCP* 868; and A Weir, 'Multiple Grounds of Claim', *International Encyclopaedia of Comparative Law* (Tubingen, Mohr Siebeck, 1982) Vol XI, chs 12, 28.

[46] Com 10 October 2000, (2000) *D* 409, obs V Avena-Robardet.

[47] See also the discussion of fault of the solvens in *répétition de l'indu* and the discussion of fault liability in both actions in relation to the change of position defence, below. See generally: Bénabent (n 30) para 494; Flour, Aubert and Savaux (n 29) vol 2 para 51 and Terré, Simler and Lequette (n 31) para 1071.

[48] Indeed the Chambre commerciale of the Cour de cassation seems to maintain this position: Com 18 May 1999, (2000) *D* 609 note J Djoudi.

[49] Civ 1re 11 March 1997 (1997) *D* 407 obs M Billiau. See also: G Viney, (1998) II *JCP* 10102 commenting on Civ (1) 3 June 1997.

[50] For example, the action will not be open to someone who has had an electric cable run to his own house even if this facilitated a branch of the cable being run to his neighbours' property: Civ (1), 19 October 1976, *Bull civ*, I, no 300, p 241. See: Bénabent (n 30), para 493 for other examples.

[51] Bénabent (n 30) paras 496–97; Flour, Aubert and Savaux (n 29) vol 2 paras 59–60; Terré, Simler and Lequette (n 31) paras 1074 and 1074–81 and Malaurie, Aynès and Stoffel-Munck (n 37) paras 1066–68.

[52] On which see generally Zimmermann (n 34) 848 ff. His discussion of the requirement of error in the *condictio indebiti* is of particular interest given the discussion here.

[53] See generally Bénabent (n 30) ch 2, paras 468 ff; Flour, Aubert and Savaux (n 29), ch 2, paras 19 ff; Malaurie, Aynès and Stoffel-Munck (n 37) Title II, para 1041 ff and Terré, Simler and Lequette (n 31) ch 2, paras 1048 ff.

[54] Art 1376 provides: «Celui qui reçoit par erreur ou sciemment ce qui ne lui est pas dû s'oblige à restituer à celui de qui il l'a indûment reçu» ('Someone who receives by error or deliberately something which is not due to him is obliged to restore it to the person from whom he unduly received it'). The

known as the *accipiens* and the payer-claimant as the *solvens*. According to Article 1235 of the Civil Code 'every *paiement* supposes a debt: that which has been paid without being due is subject to recovery'.[55] However, in this context, '*paiement*' has a very narrow meaning,[56] so that receipt of services will not give rise to a claim for *répétition de l'indu*. Obviously, restitution could be made of their value,[57] but the obstacle to doing so may be that it is 'repetition', rather than 'restitution', that is required. Arts 1376 and 1377 of the Code also distinguish between objectively and subjectively undue sums,[58] in the sense that if a sum is objectively undue there was no obligation to pay at all, whereas if it is only subjectively undue, a sum of that nature was owed, but it was either owed by someone other than the *solvens*, or it was owed to someone other than the *accipiens*. Such instances of *répétition de l'indu subjectif* therefore tend to arise in situations involving three parties, the *solvens*, the *accipiens* and the true debtor/creditor, and recovery in such situations is not always as straightforward as in situations of *répétition de l'indu objectif*.[59] Although there are some aspects of *répétition de l'indu* which do not reflect unjust enrichment reasoning (such as the absence of recovery for services noted above, or the fact that it is not necessary to prove overall enrichment or impoverishment in order to bring a claim),[60] Mazeaud and Chabas refer to *répétition de l'indu* as being

first half of art 1377 provides «Lorsqu'une personne qui, par erreur, se croyait débitrice, a acquitté une dette, elle a le droit de répétition contre le créancier» ('When a person who, by error, believes himself to be a debtor, has paid a debt, he has a right to repayment against the creditor').

55 «Tout payement suppose une dette: ce qui a été payé sans être du, est sujet à répétition.»

56 A particular difficulty is caused in the context of *répétition de l'indu* by the fact that whereas English only uses the term 'payment', which is neutral as to the reasons or justifications for the action, French contains two words, '*paiement*', which means the voluntary execution of an obligation and '*versement*', a slightly more neutral form of '*paiement*'. See: P Chauvel, (1998) *D* 570, and S Whittaker, 'Performance of Another's Obligation', in D Johnston and R Zimmermann (eds), *Unjustified Enrichment* (Cambridge, Cambridge University Press, 2002) 433–36. Conversely, outside the context of quasi-contracts the word '*paiement*' can have a wider meaning than the English 'payment', see further Whittaker (n 11) 427.

57 See: Bénabent, (n 30) para 469.

58 Thus art 1376 provides for 'someone who received by error or deliberately *something which is not due to him*' (objectively undue sums) whereas art 1377 provides for 'a person who, *by error, believes himself to be a debtor*' (subjectively undue sums). The distinction was rendered official by a decision of the Assemblée Plénière of the Cour de cassation on 2 April 1993 (*Bull civ*, AP, no 9, (1993) *D* 373; (1993) II *JCP* 22051, concl M Jeol). See also: the seminal articles by J Ghestin, 'L'erreur du solvens, condition de la répétition de l'indu' (1972) *D* ch 277; I Defrénois-Souleau, 'La répétition de l'indu objectif' (1989) 88(2) *RTD civ* 243; A Sériaux, 'Beaucoup de bruit pour rien', (1993) *D* 229 and J Kamdem, 'L'évolution du régime de l'action en répétition de l'indu objectif' (1997) I *JCP* 1997, 4018. See further Whittaker in Bell, Boyron and Whittaker (eds) (n 11) 428–29. Since public body cases were at the heart of this evolution, it will be discussed in further detail below.

59 The Cour de cassation has held in the context of claims by insurers that where the *solvens* can claim against the true debtor (s)he cannot claim against the *accipiens* to whom (s)he mistakenly paid the money, on the basis that it is the true debtor who really benefited from the payment: Civ (1) 9 Mar 2004, *Bull civ* no 81, (2004) I Défrenois 996 note R Libchaber; Civ (1) 23 Sep 2003, (2004) *D* 3165 note A Harmand-Luque. Both commentators are critical of this decision, as is Whittaker, ibid 431, on the basis that it goes against the plain wording of art 1377 itself.

60 See P Chauvel, above n 56, commenting on Com 10 February 1998, para 8 of his comment on CA Versailles 19 December 1997.

'tinged with'[61] *enrichissement sans cause*, and the two quasi-contracts intertwine in three-party cases.[62] Certainly there seems to be enough of a relationship between the two for cases of *répétition de l'indu* involving public bodies to provide a further parallel with the cases examined in the previous chapters. Importantly, however, the absence of a need to show enrichment or impoverishment means that the French defence of passing on (*répercussion*) cannot apply and thus when this cause of action is used in order to reclaim invalid taxes or customs duties it is not necessary for the claimant to show that it bore those charges personally.[63]

Gestion d'affaires

Gestion d'affaires (based on the Roman *negotiorum gestio*) on the other hand, does not provide such an apt parallel, either for unjust enrichment in general or for the cases under investigation here. Article 1372 of the Code Civil states that:

> When one voluntarily manages the affairs of another, whether or not the owner knows of the management, the manager contracts the tacit agreement to continue the management that he has begun, and to complete it until the owner is in a position to make provision for it himself; he [the manager] must equally concern himself with all the appurtenances of this same matter. He subjects himself to all the obligations which result from an express mandate given to him by the owner.[64]

Gestion d'affaires thus differs from the English conception of unjust enrichment in that it leads to reciprocal obligations; the manager (*gérant*) must for his or her

[61] «Teinté d'enrichissement sans cause . . .» H Mazeaud and others, *Leçons de Droit Civil*, Tome II, vol 1, *Obligations, théorie générale*, 9th edn (Paris, Montchrestien, 1998) para 668. Flour, Aubert and Savaux also note that *répétition de l'indu* is more clearly linked to *enrichissement sans cause* than is *gestion d'affaires* (n 29), vol 2 para 19. («Beaucoup plus nettement que la gestion d'affaires, l'action en répétition de l'indu se rattache à l'enrichissement sans cause».)

[62] Note, for example, the reasoning of the Cour de cassation referred to above (n 59), which clearly focuses on identifying which party in a case of *répétition de l'indu subjectif* has actually been enriched, despite the fact that in principle a claim in *répétition de l'indu* should be available without regard to that question. Also, in 2001 the Cour de cassation held that when the *solvens* follows the enrichment and claims from the true debtor, rather than the recipient of the money, the basis of this action will be *enrichissement sans cause*: (Civ (1) 4 Apr 2001, (2001) *D* 1824 note Billiau, (2002) I *JCP* 134 note Barthez; Civ (1) 23 Sep 2003, *Bull Civ*, I, no 185.) Perhaps most importantly, in doing so the Cour de cassation ruled that in addition to the normal requirements for a claim in *enrichissement sans cause* the claimant must show that (s)he paid by mistake, a condition usually required only for *répétition de l'indu* (see further above, text to n 58 and Whittaker (n 11) 430–431).

[63] *Fils Henri Ramel c Administration des douanes et droits indirects*, decision of the first civil chamber of the Cour d'Appel de Lyon 30 November 1978, (1979) *D* 371, note C-J Berr. This of course strengthens the argument that the point of the passing on defence is to deny the 'at the expense of' requirement of the common law unjust enrichment claim.

[64] «Lorsque volontairement on gère l'affaire d'autrui, soit que le propriétaire connaisse la gestion, soit qu'il l'ignore, celui qui gère contracte l'engagement tacite de continuer la gestion qu'il a commencée, et de l'achever jusqu'à ce que le propriétaire soit en état d'y pourvoir lui-même; il doit se charger également de toutes les dépendances de cette même affaire. Il se soumet à toutes les obligations qui résulteraient d'un mandat exprès que lui aurait donné le propriétaire» (Civil Code, art 1372).

part complete the undertaking and everything dependent on it,[65] taking the care of a *bon père de famille.* In addition, even though the action brought by the manager appears to be closer to unjust enrichment reasoning than those brought by the master ('*maître*' or, inelegantly, '*géré*'), there are also occasions where it applies when the master has not really been enriched at all (for example repairs are carried out by the manager on a house which then burns down)[66], and in any case the amount of recovery is governed by the expenses incurred by the manager.[67] Conversely, unjust enrichment and *enrichissement sans cause* are largely concerned only with the existence of the enrichment, whereas the rules on *gestion d'affaires* are also concerned with the circumstances in which any enrichment came about, in the sense that it must have been intended for the benefit of the master.[68] Indeed, rather than being based on unjust enrichment or enrichment without cause, it appears that the best justification for the quasi-contract of *gestion d'affaires* is just that someone who has proved his altruism should have his expenses 'reimbursed . . . it is . . . a matter of encouraging useful initiatives and of discouraging those which are impetuous'.[69]

As for cases involving public bodies, while of course it is possible that a case of *gestion d'affaires* could involve a public body,[70] French lawyers regard it as a particularly inapt quasi-contract for the public law context.[71]

Enrichment without Cause and Public Bodies

How, then, have the two key variables of the long-standing public/private divide and the 'without cause' approach of French law affected its treatment of cases parallel to those considered in the first five chapters? And what lessons are there for the English system which does not share these variables?

[65] Art 1373 provides that «Il est obligé de continuer sa gestion, encore que le maître vienne à mourir avant que l'affaire soit consommée, jusqu'à ce que l'héritier ait pu en prendre la direction» ('he is obliged to continue his management, notwithstanding the fact that the master has died before the matter is finished, until the heir has been able to take over its direction').

[66] Bénabent (n 30) para 458; Flour, Aubert and Savaux (n 29) vol 2 para 12 and Terré, Simler and Lequette (n 31) para 1041.

[67] Bénabent (n 30) para 465; Flour, Aubert and Savaux (n 29) vol 2 para 15; Terré, Simler and Lequette (n 31) para 1047 and Malaurie, Aynès and Stoffel-Munck (n 37) para 1033.

[68] Although of course the existence of fault on the part of the *appauvri* in causing the enrichment can also affect liability for recovery in *enrichissement sans cause*, see above (n 47) and surrounding text and below.

[69] «[I]l est juste que celui qui a fait preuve d'altruisme soit indemnisé de ses dépenses . . . Il s'agit . . . d'encourager les initiatives utiles ou opportunes et de décourager celles qui seraient intempestives» Flour, Aubert and Savaux (n 29) para 4.

[70] See further below pp 178–79.

[71] «En fait, la gestion d'affaires s'est mal acclimatée en droit administratif, malgré l'attention que la doctrine lui a portée» ('in fact, *gestion d'affaires* is not well adapted to administrative law, despite the attention which *la doctrine* (academic writers) have given it') Chapus (n 12) 1395.

Quasi-Contracts are Automatically Adjusted in their Application to Public Bodies

The first, and most obvious lesson is that whereas in England the whole aim of part one was to argue for the different treatment of unjust enrichment claims involving public law events, in France the sphere of public law already contains separate administrative versions of each of the private law quasi-contracts.[72] These separate versions of quasi-contract are of course inspired by their counterparts in the civil code, to the extent that Chapus refers to them as '*enfants adoptifs*' in administrative law,[73] but they are nevertheless distinct enough for Moderne to state that he is able to study them independently, without referring to private law except for the purposes of comparison.[74]

Of the three basic quasi-contracts, *gestion d'affaires* is, as noted above, applied least often in administrative law. Once it is recalled that this cause of action most often applies in situations where the manager has to act because the master is absent, the reason becomes obvious; 'the administration is never absent'.[75] In addition to this, while French law may generally be less concerned with individuality and subjective devaluation than English law, there is every reason not to tolerate the interference of unqualified third parties in public affairs for which the administration is responsible.[76] Given the very specialist nature of public services and division of competence between public bodies there are, furthermore, scarcely any examples of *gestion d'affaires* where the claimant is a public body that has managed the affairs of another public body.[77] In many cases the Conseil d'Etat therefore prefers to appeal to the more general principle of *enrichissement sans cause*, and only in rare cases where this is not possible is the theory of *gestion d'affaires* invoked. It is particularly interesting that in criticising this tendency, Delacour accuses the administrative judges of 'confusing the particular case with the genre'.[78] This is correct in French terms, since, as noted above, in private law *enrichissement sans cause* is still separate from the other quasi-contracts as a result of its subsidiarity, but it is

[72] See generally F Moderne, *Les Quasi-Contrats Administratifs* (Paris, Dalloz, 1995).

[73] Chapus (n 12).

[74] «La présente étude . . . ne se référera au droit privé qu'à titre de comparaison» F Moderne (n 72) para 1. It should also be borne in mind that there is a sharp division between academics of public and of private law in France, which may tend to reinforce such ideas of separation.

[75] Moderne, ibid, para 32, citing M Waline. It is possible to claim damages for assisting in the public service in circumstances where a private individual performs an act in place of a public authority. Thus for instance in *Commune de Batz-Sur-Mer c Tesson* (CE 29 September 1970) there was no lifeguard on a stretch of beach but the *commune* which should have provided one was held liable to the widow of a citizen who drowned while rescuing a child. However, such actions are usually for damages for personal injury and thus do not have a direct bearing on the current discussion. See further Brown and Bell (n 6) 194–95.

[76] «Il y a lieu de ne pas tolérer en principe l'immixtion de tiers non qualifiés dans les affaires publiques dont l'administration a la charge» Moderne (n 72).

[77] Moderne, ibid.

[78] «Confondre «l'espèce» (qu'est l'enrichissement sans cause) avec le «genre» (qu'est le principe général de non-enrichissement aux dépens d'autrui)» ('confusing the particular case (which is *enrichissement sans cause*) with the genre (which is the general principle that noone should enrich themselves at the expense of another') E Delacour, 'La gestion d'affaires en droit administratif', (1999) D ch 295.

interesting that administrative law adopted the quasi-contracts after their initial development in private law and in doing so it has moved closer to the English position, 'amalgamating', in Delacour's opinion, the three quasi-contractual sources 'to the profit of *enrichissement sans cause*'.[79]

Répétition de l'indu, on the other hand, has been used far more often since the decision of the Assemblée Plénière[80] on 1 December 1961, in *Société Jean Roques*[81] and in the other branch of courts the Cour de cassation has declared that '*répétition de l'indu*' is an institution common to private law and to internal public law'.[82] Amselek notes that: '[I]n this domain one observes, over the long term, a remarkable, as if inexorable tendency of public law to align itself progressively with private law'.[83]

As in English law,[84] the areas of application of *répétition de l'indu* have been expanded as a result of EC law and the case of *Café Jacques Vabre*[85] (concerning restitution of wrongly-paid import duties on soluble coffee extracts) is well-known in France as being the first case in which first the Cour d'Appel of Paris and then the Cour de cassation checked a national law for compatibility with Article 90 (ex Art 95) of the Treaty of Rome, holding the law inapplicable in the case as a result of the incompatibility.

Unless specific procedural rules apply, whenever the case in *répétition de l'indu* is brought by a private party against a public body the administrative procedure is used.[86] The general exceptions to this rule are of course *questions préjudicielles*,[87] and there are other specific exceptions.[88] Within the administrative procedure, *répétition*

[79] «Amalgamant celle-ci au profit de l'enrichissement sans cause» Delacour, ibid.

[80] The highest formation of judgment of the Conseil d'Etat, the Assemblée de contentieux (litigation), composed of all those with the rank of Conseillers d'Etat, coming from both the litigation and administrative sections, which deals with the most important new questions.

[81] CE 1 December 1961 *Rec CE* 675.

[82] eg Cass Comm 16 Décembre 1980, *Bull civ* IV no 423, p 399.

[83] «Dans ce domaine . . . on observe sur le long terme une tendance remarquable et comme inexorable du droit public à s'aligner progressivement sur le droit privé»: P Amselek, 'La répétition de l'indu payé aux personnes publiques' in *Mélanges René Chapus: droit administratif* (Paris, Montchrestien, 1992) 5. Obviously, as noted above, the starting point of the rules for each of the quasi-contracts is the same in both the public and private spheres; the Civil Code, and thus any differences between the two, are in that sense the result of the public law quasi-contracts moving *away* from their private roots. However, what Amselek is of course referring to here is the extent to which, despite having taken root in their new home, the quasi contracts have nevertheless developed in public law in a manner parallel to the developments in private law which have taken place since that transplantation.

[84] Where, for instance, Lord Goff referred in *Woolwich Equitable Building Society v IRC* [1993] AC 70 (HL) to the fact that such a case as that brought by the Woolwich would have led to recovery had it arisen under EU law rather than under domestic law, see further below pp 207–208.

[85] Trib d'inst du 1er arondissement de Paris, 8 Janvier 1971, Cour d'Appel de Paris, 7 July 1973: (1974) *D* 159; Cour de cassation Ch mixte 24 mai 1975; (1975) *D* 497.

[86] *Société Sucre-Union*, another case in which it was Community law which rendered the sums undue: *Rec CE* 31 July 1992, 312.

[87] For a definition of *questions préjudicielles* see above at pp 170–71.

[88] eg: art L 332-6 of the Urbanism Code (mentioned below, n 156) and actions brought by users or future users of industrial or commercial public services (Tribunal Administratif de Paris 19 December 1972, *SARL Sagrino c EDF*, (1973) *CJEG*64; Nice Tribunal Administratif 9 July 1980, *Mendelson c EDF*, (1980) *CJEG*146) or by those who have been subject to an indirect expropriation go to the ordinary courts (Bordeaux Tribunal Administratif, 3 November 1989, *Commune de Mareil-Marly*, Req no 97). See: Moderne (n 72) para 23.

de l'indu is a *recours de pleine juridiction*,[89] meaning that the annulment of a decision is sought and the court has full power to replace the challenged decisions with a decision of its own and to require the administration to pay money to the claimant.

In addition to this use of the administrative procedure for *répétition de l'indu* in the administrative context, the burden of proof is reversed. This contrast with private law is less marked in practice since the claimant (*solvens*) no longer has to prove that he, she or it paid in error in cases of *répétition de l'indu objectif*,[90] but nevertheless its existence in principle demonstrates the general system of modifying the public law conceptions of these private law events. It should finally be noted that the dispute over whether *répétition de l'indu* is simply a specific instance of *enrichissement sans cause* exists in administrative law as well as in private law.[91] Despite its later pre-eminence among the administrative quasi-contracts, *enrichissement sans cause* was, in Moderne's view, originally not popular because the concern that it would overturn existing rules was even greater in administrative law than it had been in private law.[92] However, it was eventually introduced in *Ministre de la Reconstruction et du Logement c Société Sud-Aviation*.[93] Just as in private law, saved expenses can constitute enrichment,[94] but the conditions here are slightly different; there must be a real utility of the enrichment (which appears to be largely left to the discretion of the administrative judge)[95] and the public body must have 'assented' to it. This is relatively easily satisfied since it can be found in the mere 'tolerance' of the work by a public body,[96] and because, according to Furet, public interest and general utility are more important in public law than the existence of a profit of the kind that would be required in the private sphere.[97] Instead, the idea behind these requirements is that the administration

[89] Moderne, ibid, para 25.

[90] See Kamdem (n 58) para 19. Indeed it will be seen below pp 192–201 that this abandonment actually grew out of a reversal of the burden of proof in cases involving public bodies before the ordinary courts.

[91] Moderne (n 72) paras 18, 31 and 54.

[92] See Moderne, ibid, para 50. An alternative explanation could of course simply be its lack of popularity with claimants.

[93] (1961) II *JCP* 12255, note J de Lanversin, (1961) RDP 655. It is not clear that this would be considered to be a case of unjust enrichment in English law, because it is not clear that there would have been any unjust factor open to the claimants. The work in question did not appear to have been performed under a mistake of a kind that would entitle the claimants to restitution for unjust enrichment. Nor is there any evidence that there was any illegality on the part of the French authorities such that the public law unjust factor would be available, or of a failure of basis or duress. It appears, however, that the *Conseil d'Etat* found the *enrichment* of the state to be without cause even though the *impoverishment* caused by the work was not.

[94] Moderne (n72) para 88.

[95] Moderne, ibid, para 64.

[96] Moderne, ibid, paras 95–97.

[97] «S'il s'agit en effet d'un processus qui se fonde uniquement sur les notions de perte et de profit, on ne pourra, sans les nuancer, en transposer les règles dans le domaine des activités de la puissance publique. Car si le profit en tant que tel est un but en soi pour les personnes privées, il ne saurait l'être de la même façon pour les personnes de droit public. L'objectif fondamental de l'Etat c'est en effet la défense de l'intérêt public, de l'utilité générale, et non la réalisation d'un profit.» (If it were indeed a process which was based solely on ideas of loss and profit one would not be able to transpose its rules without alteration into the domain of activities of public power. Because if profit as such is a goal in

cannot be enriched without knowing it; it must be able to know and to control all forms of intervention in matters within its competence and guard against the interference of individuals where necessary.[98] As such it is only the equivalent of free acceptance as a rejoinder to subjective devaluation of non-monetary benefits,[99] and merely appears to be unusual in the French system because as a whole that system is less receptive to this form of individualism.[100] It is true that these requirements only apply in situations where the public body is the defendant, whereas it has been argued here that claims involving public law events should be treated consistently regardless of whether the public body is the claimant or defendant. However, the rule could perhaps be explained simply on the basis that public entities and private parties are, as Furet notes,[101] likely to value things differently. *Enrichissement sans cause*, like *répétition de l'indu* is a *recours de pleine juridiction* within the competence of the administrative courts, unless it relates to supply, when it will be presumed to be within the competence of the ordinary courts unless something about the situation 'endows it with an administrative character'.[102] The principle of subsidiarity of the action in *enrichissement sans cause* is also more nuanced in administrative law than in civil law so that it only applies in certain circumstances, but these include preventing claimants from bringing actions too easily against solvent public body debtors when they may have other options elsewhere.[103]

If Courts Have to Choose Between Two Events, Both of which are Actually Relevant to the Basis of the Claim, Some Courts Will Choose One, and Others the Other

In England, of course, this choice was not initially made. In both *Woolwich*[104] and the swaps cases there were two relevant actions; one for judicial review and one in unjust enrichment. It was only when the two actions were condensed into one hearing[105] that the courts chose to view the whole issue from the private law perspective alone. If this initial existence of two actions was not enough to show the

itself for private entities, the same is not true for public entities. The fundamental objective of the state is indeed the defence of public interest, of general utility, and not the realisation of a profit.) M-F Furet, 'L'enrichissement sans cause d'après la jurisprudence administrative' (1967) D ch 265, at 266.

[98] G Bayle, *L'enrichissement sans cause en Droit Administratif* (Paris, Librairie générale de droit et de jurisprudence, 1973) 121–22.

[99] On which see P Birks, *Introduction to the Law of Restitution* (Oxford, Clarendon Press, 1985) 114–116; A Burrows, *The Law of Restitution* 2nd edn (London, Butterworths, 2002) 11–14; and R Goff and G Jones *The Law of Restitution* 6th edn (London, Sweet and Maxwell, 2004) 18–22 and 26.

[100] As the very existence of *gestion d'affaires* shows.

[101] Furet (n 97).

[102] *Templier c Commune de Sempigny*, Tribunal des Conflits Rec, p 544; (1928) *S* 129, note M Hauriou.

[103] See the conclusions of O Dorion, *EDF c Commune de Talant* Tribunal Administratif de Dijon 7 April 2005, (2005) *AJDA* 1962.

[104] *Woolwich* (n 84).

[105] See *British Steel plc v Customs and Excise Commissioners* [1997] 2 All ER 366 (CA).

relevance of both events, an exercise in comparative law has already shown,[106] even without considering the French experience, that if faced with a choice between the two, it is not surprising that some systems should choose the public approach while others choose the private; this is simply the inevitable result of the fact that the choice is itself misleading. From this point of view the fact that much of the French experience is closer to that of Canada, and the opposite of England, is only further evidence in the same direction.

In France, as has recently been the case in England,[107] the reason for choosing between the two events has been the time limits applicable to each of them. The first set of cases to consider here concerns taxes on alcohol manufacture[108] and a tax known as the '*supervignette*' imposed on vehicles greater than 16 CV.[109] Both sets of taxes were declared by the ECJ to be contrary to Community law. In a series of cases brought before the Chambre Commerciale of the Cour de cassation, the court (and in particular in the *supervignette* cases Advocate General Michel Raynaud) held that when the ECJ has held a fiscal charge to be contrary to Community law, all actions for reimbursement consequently brought by taxpayers concerned must be considered as a pure civil action for *répétition de l'indu*, which does not raise any preliminary question of fiscal law. No question of the extent of the taxpayer's fiscal obligations or the basis of the tax is raised. As a result the special rules of fiscal *contentieux* (litigation) such as the rules on time limits from the book of fiscal procedures are not applicable.[110]

So far the cases are exactly parallel to *Woolwich* where the two events were similarly split. Unlike in England, in the French system it was then decided that when the nullity of the tax had not yet been established, the case was essentially fiscal, even though the taxpayer was claiming restitution of a sum which he claimed to have paid unduly. The restitutionary claim was seen as being accessory to the principal issue of validity, the argument being that the questions to be decided by the judge are exactly the same as if the taxpayer had not yet paid the amount, and so the fiscal rules should apply to the case.[111]

[106] See the discussion of the Canadian decision *Kingstreet Investments v New Brunswick* (2007) SCC 1, ch 2 above pp 31–35.

[107] See, eg: the time limit issue in the *Deutsche Morgan Grenfell* litigation: [2003] EWHC 1779; [2003] 4 All ER 645 (QB); [2005] EWCA Civ 78; [2006] Ch 243 (CA), noted A Burrows [2005] *Law Quarterly Review* 540; G Virgo (2005) *British Tax Review* 281; R Stevens (2005) 5 *Oxford University Commonwealth Law Journal* and R Williams, (2005) *King's College Law Journal* 194; [2006] UKHL 49, [2007] 1 AC 558 (HL). Above p 74 onwards.

[108] See J Huglo, 'La répétition de l'indu communautaire dans la jurisprudence de la Cour de cassation française', (1995) 31(1) *RTD eur* 2–3, citing decisions of the 12 February 1980 (Com *Bull civ* IV no 77 p 60); 3 January 1985 (Com *Bull civ* IV no 5 p 4); 17 January 1989 (*Bull civ* IV no 25 p 15); 2 June 1992 (Com *Bull civ* IV no 221 p 155).

[109] See Amselek (n 83), 15–16, citing Com 7 November 1989, 17 judgments, (1989) *RJF* 751, conclusions by JP Raynaud p 682 ff, as well as the judgments cited above by Huglo, ibid.

[110] Com 7 November 1989, ibid.

[111] Amselek (n 83) 16 citing Com 11 July 1988, (1989) *RJF* 324; 7 November 1989, ibid. Huglo (n 108) 2, citing judgments of the 11 July 1988 (*Bull civ* IV no 242 p 167) 2 June 1992, *Bull civ* IV no 221, p 155) and 9 February 1993 (*Bull civ* IV no 54 p 35).

Thus initially the French experience fell half way between that of Canada and England; cases in which the invalidity has already been established follow the latter, while cases in which the invalidity is at issue follow the former. However, the subsequent intervention of the administration tends even further towards the Canadian model. On 29 December 1989 Article 36 of the Financial Law of that date amended Article L190 of the book of fiscal procedures to provide that:

> The rules of this chapter are to apply to the investigation and judging of all actions dealing with the discharge or the reduction of a tax, or to the exercise of rights of reduction founded on the non-conformity of a rule of law which has been applied, with a superior rule of law.
>
> When this non-conformity has been revealed by a court decision, the action for restitution of sums paid or in payment of rights of deduction not exercised or the action for reparation of prejudice suffered can only bear on the period subsequent to 1 January of the fourth year before that in which the decision revealing the non-conformity took place.[112]

At first sight these two paragraphs might be thought to maintain the distinction, but this was not how the administration chose to interpret them. In its instruction of 10 May 1990,[113] it held that Article 36 also subjects the cases mentioned in the second paragraph to the fiscal procedure. Amselek strongly objects to this 'refiscalisation' of the cases, and suggests that the Cour de cassation and Conseil d'Etat might not always fully apply them in situations where they 'restrain abusively, to the profit of the State, the paying parties' right to restitution'.[114] He also argued that these rules were contrary to the jurisprudence of the European Court of Justice on the obligation of Member States to provide equivalent and effective remedies for breaches of EC law,[115] though the French courts have subsequently held that they are not.[116]

It is certainly easy to understand why the four year time limit of Article 36 might be thought abusive when compared to the default private law time limit of 30 years, and in addition, as was argued in relation to Canada this absolute prioritisation of

[112] «Sont instruites et jugées selon les règles du présent chapitre toutes actions tendant à la décharge ou à la réduction d'une imposition ou à l'exercice de droits à déduction fondées sur la non-conformité de la règle de droit dont il a été fait application à une règle de droit supérieure.

Lorsque cette non-conformité a été révélée par une décision juridictionnelle, l'action en restitution des sommes versées ou en paiement des droits à déduction non exercés ou l'action en réparation du préjudice subi ne peut porter que sur la période postérieure au 1er janvier de la quatrième année précédant celle où la décision révélant la non conformité est intervenue.»

'*Instruction*' is the process of investigation of the case, during which the parties present their statements and proof to the court, and the court makes its own investigation into the case in order to allow it to pass judgment. Depending on the procedure operating (civil, administrative, penal), the investigation is done by either a '*rapporteur*' or by the judge him/herself.

[113] Feuillets Rapides Francis Lefebvre 1990 32–90, cited Amselek (n 83) fn 40.

[114] «Elles restreignent abusivement, au profit de l'Etat, le droit à répétition des parties versantes» Amselek, ibid, 19–20 at 19.

[115] See further below, p 237 and Amselek, ibid, 20–33.

[116] Decision of the Cour de cassation Ch Commerciale 13 December 1994, *Abelsohn*, (1995) *RJF* 284, concl JP Raynaud, and 19 October 1999 *Société Nationale des Ets Piot* and *Société Sologest*: (2000) *RJF* 137.

the public law aspects of the case over the private law issues is just as undesirable as the reverse prioritisation chosen by the English courts.[117] It was also argued that the law should not adopt one rule for cases where the public body is the defendant and another where it is the claimant.[118] However, if, as suggested in chapter five, all public body cases involving unjust enrichment were to be subject to a special time limit of this kind which represented a compromise between the short time limits currently applicable in English public law and the six year time limit applicable in private law, the four years available in the *supervignette* cases would not actually be so problematic.

In addition to the tax context, a similar choice to prioritise nullity over the rules of *répétition de l'indu* occurred in the context of social security payments. In France, the office of social security is known by the acronym *URSSAF*.[119] Although this is an entity responsible for a *mission de service public*, its pay-offices, or *caisses* are more like our provident societies and have traditionally been regarded as private bodies.[120] Claims involving the *caisses* are therefore brought in the civil branch of the courts, but can nevertheless be subject to a special procedure. Thus Article 42 of the *décret* No 58-1291 of 22 December 1958 provides for a one month time limit to apply to certain claims brought by employers concerning social security payments. Consequently the social chamber of the Cour de cassation held that where a health insurance pay-office had fixed a tariff of payment and this had not been challenged by an employer within these time limits, the matter could not be reopened by way of a later action in *répétition de l'indu* to reclaim the social security payments (*cotisations*) in question.[121] Clearly, then, here too the French courts have prioritised the issue of nullity and its applicable time limits over the payment of an undue sum in a manner which is the reverse of that ultimately chosen by the English courts.

Given their attitude to nullity in these instances, it is interesting, therefore, that faced with the issue of *contractual* nullity, the French administrative courts have aligned themselves with the approach taken in England, distancing themselves from the approach of the private law courts in situations of purely private contractual nullity.

On 24 September 2002 the first civil chamber of the Cour de cassation held that restitution between the parties to a failed contract is not dealt with by the law of

[117] See further p 94 onwards.

[118] Above p 56 onwards.

[119] Union de Recouvrement des cotisations de Sécurité Sociale et d'Allocations Familiales.

[120] Brown and Bell write that '*caisses* (or, as we would say, provident societies) are the basic local organizations administering the social insurance system. Traditionally, these societies have always been regarded as private law, not public law, bodies. Without departing from this view, the Conseil d'Etat held that these private bodies were engaged in providing a public service and accordingly fell within the competence of the administrative courts.' Brown and Bell (n6) 131, citing a decision of the Conseil d'Etat of 13 May 1938, *Caisse Primaire 'Aide et Protection'*. Nevertheless they can, as seen in this section, also be subject to the jurisdiction of the ordinary courts, providing evidence of the blurring of the public/private boundary as discussed above.

[121] Cass Soc 12 July 1990, *Bull civ* V no 367; (1990) *D* 203.

quasi-contracts, but by the 'rules of nullity' themselves.[122] This meant that instead of the 30 year time limit for *répétition de l'indu* applying to restitution under annulled contracts the court applied the five year time limit applicable to the action for annulment. In administrative law, on the other hand, it is the quasi-contracts which perform this role. Thus in *Société Citécable Est*[123] the Conseil d'Etat famously held that if a contract with the Administration is annulled,[124] the co-contractor has the right to reclaim from the Administration the reimbursement of its '*dépenses utiles*', (the useful enrichment as described above) on the basis of *enrichissement sans cause.* Not only can a claimant use *enrichissement sans cause,* it can also sue for fault-based damages following the annulment of a contract, as long as the total reclaimed under these two heads does not exceed what it would have received if the contract had been enforced. Even more strikingly (for French lawyers at least)[125] the parties have the right to bring such claims regardless of the stage that the proceedings have reached ('including for the first time on appeal')[126], and despite the fact that the rules of *enrichissement sans cause* do not belong to the set of rules known as being *d'ordre public,* ie of such importance that they can be raised by either of the parties or the judge at any time in this way.[127] Only expenses specially incurred for the purpose of completing the contract can be reclaimed; even if a company has been founded solely for the purpose of carrying out a public contract, the company's ordinary everyday expenses will not qualify. However, the burden of proving the *lack of* utility of the work or expenses rests on the public body.[128] According to Guglielmi, in principle both the amounts claimed on the basis of *enrichissement sans cause* and through fault-based liability ought to be reduced to take account of the fault of the claimant, and he consequently criticises a decision of the Tribunal Administratif de Bordeaux for having reduced only the amount of fault-based damages in a case where the claimant company had agreed to conclude the contract in the knowledge that it was illegal.[129] Moderne also notes that some authors dispute the necessity for the

[122] Civ (1) 24 Sept 2002, (2003) *D* 369, note J-L Aubert. It should be noted that French law accepts that both annulment and *resolution* of contracts revest title to property transferred under the contract in its transferor, subject to a condition of identification of that property (rather than its substitute or proceeds) and provided that it constitutes *corps certain.* See further Whittaker (n 11) 442 and 450.

[123] (2001) 17(2) *RFD adm* 359 concl H Savoie. But see also Conseil d'Etat 8 December 1995, (1996) *AJDA* 448, note V Haïm; TA de Bordeaux 10 June 1999, *MB2 (Sté) c Communité Urbaine de Bordeaux,* Tribunal Administratif de Bordeaux 10 June 1999, (2001) *D* 1048 note G J Guglielmi and Conseil D'Etat 16 November 2005, (2006) *Gaz Pal* 2043; J no 138, 18 May 2006 p 18, note P Graveleau and Cour Administrative d'appel de Marseille 30 March 2004, *Carlson Wagonlit* note S Hul, (2004) *AJDA* 1648.

[124] Although Baux suggests that this rule may only apply to *travaux publics,* ie to public building projects, see A Baux, (2007) *AJDA* 146.

[125] See, eg: S Hennette-Vauchez, commenting on the subsequent case of *Société Fly International Service,* Cour administrative d'appel de Paris, 25 June 2002, (2002) *AJDA* 1195.

[126] «y compris pour la première fois en appel», and earlier «en tout état de cause» ('at any stage of the proceedings'), ibid.

[127] See further Hennette-Vauchez (n 125) 1197.

[128] MB2 (Sté) c *Communité Urbaine de Bordeaux* (n 123).

[129] Guglielmi, ibid.

public body's assent in cases of annulment, pointing out that if the contract has been annulled *ab initio* it is difficult to say that assent has not also been annulled.[130]

Enrichissement sans cause, of course, applies not only to annulled contracts,[131] but also to situations where contracts have not been validly concluded, and where the contractor has exceeded its initial contractual framework in conditions which cannot give rise to contractual liability.[132] It could also be the case that the work required by the contract has turned out to be more onerous than was anticipated,[133] or is seen as being supplementary to the contract.[134] Such supplementary work is usually the result either of the initiative of the contractor or of an order given by the administration.[135] However, there cannot be recovery if the schedule of the contract requires the contract to be unchanged, or if certain formalities for changing it are not followed[136] and it is difficult to see these 'supplementary work' cases as being wholly based on *enrichissement sans cause* because the work done must be totally remunerated.[137]

Indeed it is unclear exactly why the annulment of public contracts should be dealt with using *enrichissement sans cause* when other contractual issues are not, nor why the rules concerning public contracts should have diverged from both the private law and cases concerning taxes or social security payments. It seems unlikely to be because the quasi-contract rejected in all those other cases was *répétition de l'indu*,[138] whereas here administrative law has used *enrichissement sans cause*,[139] although the latter is certainly a more general quasi-contract able to deal with the conferral of benefits through work and services. There are, however, three potential answers which may go some way to explaining the choice to use *enrichissement sans cause* in relation to public contracts.

One is that in fact public and private law may not, after all, have diverged to such a great extent. Commenting on the decision to reject the operation of *répétition de l'indu*, Aubert argues that the Cour de cassation was simply concerned to

[130] Moderne (n 72) para 96.

[131] See further Moderne, ibid, paras 105–8.

[132] See Moderne, ibid, paras 103 and 108 respectively.

[133] Moderne, ibid, para 112.

[134] Moderne, ibid, paras 114–17.

[135] Moderne, ibid, paras 121 and 123 respectively.

[136] Moderne, ibid, para 124.

[137] Moderne, ibid, para 134.

[138] See above n 122.

[139] In such instances it would be likely to be *répétition de l'indu objectif* that would apply, since there would have been no contract and thus no obligation to confer the benefit on the public body in the first place. This form of *répétition de l'indu* is, it is submitted, the closest other quasi-contract to *enrichissement sans cause*, since it no longer requires the *solvens* to prove that (s)he/it paid in error. The only remaining real difference, therefore, seems to be that *répétition de l'indu*, unlike *enrichissement sans cause*, cannot apply to services. In addition, Kessler argues that the decision of the 24 September 2002 meant that «les restitutions sont ainsi distinguées de l'enrichissement sans cause *et* du paiement de l'indu» ('restitution [following nullity of a contract] is thus distinguished from *enrichissement sans cause and* from payment of undue sums') (emphasis added). G Kessler, 'La contrariété de l'indemnité de jouissance aux principes gouvernant la nullité et la résolution' (2004) I *JCP* 154.

ensure that restitution cannot be claimed without prior annulment of the contract and thus this annulment must occur first, within its own (shorter) time limits. On his reasoning there would therefore be no bar to the operation of *répétition de l'indu* in a situation where the contract had previously been annulled,[140] and the difference between public and private law would then not be so great, because the cases in the *Citécable Est* line all refer to co-contractors whose contracts are already null.[141]

An alternative possibility is that if the law has diverged that is simply a coincidence. Chapus asks whether of the three quasi-contracts *enrichissement sans cause* has produced the most abundant jurisprudence in administrative law because it is not specifically referred to by the Civil Code,[142] and it may just be that the jurisprudential and less rigidly-defined nature of *enrichissement sans cause* has allowed the administrative courts to develop their own version of it more independently of civil law concerns than they felt able to do in the case of *répétition de l'indu*, for example. In addition, the administrative courts may have felt that they could avoid the application of Article 1304 of the Civil Code[143] when they did not feel that they could equally avoid the application of the more specific Article 42 of the Social Security *décret* or Article L190 of the *Livre des Procédures Fiscales* in the other nullity cases discussed above. The explanation for the different treatment of contracts when compared with the tax and social security cases could be that this is just a further illustration of the same unsurprising split as occurred between the Canadian and English courts; both the nullity and the enrichment[144] are relevant, so if courts must choose between them, some will choose one and others will choose the other.

A slightly more radical alternative would be to see the different choices made by the public and private courts as reflecting different understandings of the nullity involved. It is evident that both branches of court regard annulled contracts as being void *ab initio*, and thus as effectively never having existed,[145] but it is nevertheless the case that the five year prescription period applicable in private law courts comes from Article 1304 of the Civil Code, and only concerns the nullity of 'conventions'.[146] To some extent, therefore, paradoxically, the non-existent convention is still allowed to determine the time limits applicable to the declaration of its own non-existence. However, for the Conseil d'Etat in *Citécable Est*, the nullity of the contract meant that a decision to resile from it could not be annulled, because that decision could not have existed in the first place, and further that

[140] See above n 122.

[141] eg, in *Citécable Est* itself (n 123), the key part of the judgment begins «le cocontractant *dont le contrat est entaché de nullité* est fondé à réclamer . . .» (emphasis added).

[142] R Chapus (n 12) 1223.

[143] Dealing with the time limits for establishing nullity of a contract.

[144] Whether this is regarded as being unjust, undue or without cause.

[145] See the conclusions of H Savoie and the Conseil d'Etat in *Citécable Est* (n 123) and compare F Terré, P Simler and Y Lequette, *Droit Civil, Les Obligations* (n 31) 424–25.

[146] Civ (2), 18 November 1987, *Bull civ* II no 232; 8 October 1987, *Bull civ* II no 245; 3 October 2002, *Bull civ* II no 206; (2003) *D* 1596, note M Lehot.

recovery was governed by the wholly independent concept of *enrichissement sans cause*. At least in terms of principle, then, the nullity applied by the Conseil d'Etat in *Citécable Est* appears to be more absolute, and therefore more in keeping with the *ab initio* voidness discussed in part one[147] than the rules of nullity used in the Cour de cassation's decision of 2002.[148]

As for the practical effects of these two approaches, however, it seems that the difference between a simple unravelling of the contract and an action in *enrichissement sans cause* is the quantity of recovery on the part of the claimant.[149] The rules of nullity used by the civil law are objective and literal, so that the parties have to return everything they still hold, and where they cannot make specific restitution they have to return the value of the thing at the date it was transferred with, in some cases, an allowance for its use in the interim.[150] With *enrichissement sans cause*, however, recovery is only of the lesser of the *appauvri*'s loss and the *enrichi*'s gain, measured in terms of 'useful expenses' in the case of public bodies. Oddly, the loss is measured at the time it occurred, whereas the enrichment is measured at the time of the claim (unless the *enrichi* was in bad faith) so that if the *appauvri* has done the work but it is destroyed, damaged or lost before the claim is brought, the *enrichi* will not be regarded as having been enriched at the time of the claim and thus the *appauvri* will be unable to recover.

In a sense, then, conversely, the rules of nullity used by the civil law actually represent a more literal unravelling and reversal of the annulled contract, and more effort is focused on returning the parties to the position they would have been in had the contract not existed there than under the rules of *enrichissement sans cause* used by the Conseil d'Etat. On the other hand, once it is acknowledged that this unravelling is largely going to be impossible when the enrichment constitutes work done by the *appauvri*, it is possible that the rules of *enrichissement sans cause* are actually more consistent with the purpose of annulling the contract in the first place. For example, taking the facts of *Citécable Est*, if the contract is simply void for procedural reasons, as in that case itself[151] the work will presumably still have counted as being useful to the public authority, whereas if the contract related to something the public authority was not permitted to do in the first place[152] then it may not be so easy to argue that the result was 'useful' to that public authority and

[147] See above p 36.

[148] This still makes it hard to explain why the social security and tax time limits applied, since the charges were presumably equally void in those cases. On the other hand, art 42 of the social security law does provide that it should apply to certain actions under the social security code, rather than to *cotisations*, and art L190 of the *Livre des Procedures Fiscales* does state that it applies to 'the exercise of rights to deduction based on the non-conformity of the rule that was applied with a superior rule of law', rather than supposing the existence of a '*taxe*' or '*impôt*'.

[149] For a comparison of recovery under the rules of nullity with those of *répétition de l'indu*, see Aubert (n 122). The comparison here is of course between the rules of nullity and those of *enrichissement sans cause*.

[150] See further Whittaker (n 11) 443 and Kessler (n 139).

[151] See the conclusions of Savoie (n 123) 364.

[152] This potential reason for invalidity is also taken from the conclusions of Savoie, ibid.

therefore that it constituted an enrichment. Recognition of the relevance of *enrichissement sans cause* could therefore prevent the public body from paying for something it should not have contracted to receive, in circumstances where the whole point of annulling the contract was to prevent such an exchange from taking place, whereas the rules of nullity would require the public body to pay the private contractor the value of anything that it could not return specifically, despite the fact that paying for such work was precisely what the annulled contract required it to do. Indeed if the value of the work and goods transferred had gone up in price, the public body could actually end up paying *more* for those goods and services than it had contracted to do under the annulled contract. Obviously, however, such a conclusion would depend on the courts' precise definition of 'usefulness' in *enrichissement sans cause* claims, and in any case it runs the risk that the public body could be left with the work without having to pay for it, to the detriment of the private contractor, though this in turn could be seen as an incentive for private contractors to ascertain carefully the power of the public body to enter the contract in the first place.

So far, then, the French system has provided two important discoveries which further support the arguments made in Part 1. Actions which involve unjust or baseless enrichment resulting from the nullity of a public action could be based on either of those two relevant issues. The Supreme Court of Canada in *Kingstreet Investments* and the French tax and social security cases have chosen the nullity, while the House of Lords in *Deutsche Morgan Grenfell* and the French courts dealing with the nullity of public contracts have chosen the latter. That there is an almost 50:50 split in this way is not surprising once the relevance of both issues is accepted, but it does neatly illustrate that assuming only one of the two events to be relevant gives a distorted view of the situation.

In addition, looking at the quasi-contracts as a whole, it is clear that in France there are differences between the application of the quasi-contracts in private and in public law, and that at least in the case of their essential core features these differences are usually the result of modifying their requirements so that they are better adapted to the public law context. In keeping with the argument in Part 1, there is therefore a significant lesson here for English law with its relatively recently developed system of administrative law. Of course, England and Wales still do not share the French court structure, but while we have a separate doctrine of administrative law with its own procedural rules, we should at least ask ourselves whether we can continue to apply the rules of private law as if the presence of a public body made no difference, when that approach has been clearly rejected by other systems with longer standing experience in this regard (albeit that the precise causes of action and consequent adaptations remain specific to each jurisdiction).

However, while these first and most basic lessons can thus be drawn from the French experience, this does not mean that the treatment of such claims in France has been wholly unproblematic. The difficulty is that having such a separate regime of quasi-contracts is only the first step; it does not ensure that any given case falls within the specialised rules,[153] and in the cases which fall outside these rules, there are other lessons for England.

As well as Adjusting its Quasi-Contracts to Take Account of Public Bodies, French Law Also Distinguishes between Public Law Rules and Public Law Procedure, so that even within the Private Procedure Adjustments can be Made to Take Account of the Public Nature of one of the Parties to the Claim

In part one a distinction was drawn between the procedure used to hear a claim and the particular rules applicable to it. It was not suggested that the decision in *British Steel v Commissioners of Customs and Excise*[154] be reversed so that unjust enrichment claims involving public bodies would fall within the public law procedural rules,[155] but it was argued that within the private law procedure the courts should take account of the public law event in the rules applicable to the claim. In certain contexts French law does exactly this.

For example, the 'refiscalisation'[156] of actions brought under Article L190 of the Book of Fiscal Procedures[157] means that in addition to altering the applicable time limits, such actions for restitution are subject to fiscal rules concerning the way the claims are brought before the courts, the method used to investigate them and the court procedures followed. However, this set of rules applies regardless of the court system hearing the claim (within fiscal cases there is a division between direct and indirect taxes,[158] the former going to the administrative courts, the latter to the ordinary courts).

[153] See, eg: F Moderne, commenting on *Commune de Vaulx-en-Velin c Commune de Vulleurbanne*, Conseil D'Etat 18 June 1976, (1976) *AJDA* 570, at 574 who points out that given the differences between the civil and administrative branches on the question of *enrichissement sans cause*, regrettable distortions can occur when charges for the consumption of water go to the *competence judiciaire* (private courts) while cleansing charges go to the administrative courts.

[154] British Steel (n 105).

[155] See further ch 3 pp 49–52.

[156] Amselek (n 83) 19. See also: Moderne (n 72), paras 13–15. Art L332–30 of the Urbanism Code also imposes a five-year time limit on other forms of tax and personal housing aid and is subject to its own regime governed by art L351–14 of the Construction and Habitation Code. These cases go to the administrative courts.

[157] Livre des Procédures Fiscales. See further above p 183.

[158] This is a «distinction dont le principe est difficile à définir rigoureusement, mais dont le droit positif consacre l'existence par les effets qu'il lui attache. Deux critères principaux sont avancés. Critère administratif: est direct l'impôt recouvré par les agents naguère appelés percepteurs, généralement par voie de rôle. Critère économique: est direct l'impôt établi directement à la charge de celui qui doit en supporter le prélèvement; est indirect l'impôt qui, payé par un assujetti, est ensuite répercuté par lui sur un tiers qui est le contribuable effectif» (R Guillien, J Vincent, S Guinchard and G Montagner, *Lexique de Termes Juridiques*, (Paris, Dalloz, 2003) (verbo «Impôts directs, indirects») (distinction whose principle is difficult to define rigorously, but whose existence is consecrated by positive law through the effects which are attached to it. Two principal criteria are advanced: an administrative criterion: direct taxes are those recovered by the agents formerly known as *percepteurs* [collectors], generally through the means of a *rôle* [annual list of taxpayers and the tax to which they were subject for that year]. An economic criterion: a direct tax is that established directly to the responsibility of

Also, as seen above, this is not the only context in which the relevant time limits, (particularly those relating to *répétition de l'indu*) are adjusted, regardless of the court system.[159] Nor should it be thought that the adjustments relate only to time limits, indeed it appears that the rules on interest have been as contentious in France as they were in *Woolwich*.[160] In simple private law situations Arts 1153 and 1378 of the Civil Code in combination mean that someone who is bound to make restitution of a sum unduly levied must pay interest from the date of the claim (*demande*) if he or she is in good faith, but from the date of the payment (*paiement*) if he or she is not in good faith.[161] However, the French rules become more restrictive when the case is one of restitution of an undue sum which is either fiscal or related to customs, since in such cases the payer cannot claim interest even on the basis of Arts 1378 and 1153. Indeed, whereas in England 'one should be taxed by law, and not be untaxed by concession'[162] so that 'constitutional principles' *required* the granting of interest in *Woolwich*, in France very similar 'constitutional principles' seem originally to have prevented it. Instead of it being the case that taxes could not be *levied* without the consent of Parliament,[163] it appears that in France taxes could not be changed in *either* direction without the consent of Parliament. Thus the Cour de cassation held that:

> [T]he customs tariffs, which are attached to the system of taxes charged in France, cannot, like all other taxes, be augmented, diminished or modified except by a Loi; in consequence the customs administration cannot be condemned to pay interest on sums unduly charged and of which restitution has been ordered.[164]

Similarly the *Conseil d'Etat* held that: '[N]o legislative provision gives taxpayers who benefit from a rebate in the matter of taxes the right to claim interest on the sums from which they have obtained a discharge'.[165]

someone who must support its levy; a tax is indirect if, its being paid by a taxpayer, is then passed on to another party who is the effective taxpayer). Since VAT is however classed as a direct tax, it appears that the administrative criterion is perhaps a better guide. This criterion could also explain why it is that such taxes go to the administrative courts while indirect taxes go to the ordinary courts; only in the case of direct taxes is there an administrative act that can be challenged.

[159] See the *URSSAF* cases and M Douchy-Oudot, *Encyclopédie Dalloz*, 'Répétition de l'indu', paras 82–86.

[160] *Woolwich* (n 84).

[161] «Il résulte de la combinaison des art. 1153 et 1378 c. civ. que celui qui est condamné à restituer une somme indûment perçue doit les intérêts du jour de la demande s'il était de bonne foi et du jour du paiement s'il n'était pas de bonne foi.» Code Civil, 107th edn (Paris, Dalloz, 2008) Art 1378 '1, *Point de départ des intérêts*' at 1503. In English law s 35A of the Supreme Court Act 1981 provides that simple interest can run for all or any part of the period between the date when the cause of action arose and (a) in the case of any sum paid before judgment, the date of the payment; and (b) in the case of the sum for which judgment is given, the date of the judgment.

[162] *Vestey and others v Inland Revenue Commissioners* [1979] Ch 177, 197 (Ch) (Walton J).

[163] Art 4 of the Bill of Rights 1688, see further *Woolwich* (n 84).

[164] «Les tarifs de douane, se rattachant au système des impôts perçus en France, ne peuvent, comme tous autres impôts, être augmentés, diminués ou modifiés qu'en vertu d'une Loi; en conséquence l'administration des douanes ne saurait être condamnée au paiement des intérêts des sommes indûment perçues et dont la restitution est ordonnée.» Civ 21 May 1924, (1926) I *DP*147; 10 July 1928, (1928) *DH* 462; 17 June 1931, (1931) *DH* 445. See also: Amselek (n 83) 10.

[165] «aucune disposition législative ne donne aux contribuables qui bénéficient d'un dégrèvement en matière d'impôts le droit de réclamer les intérêts des sommes dont ils obtiennent décharge» Conseil

However, as Amselek points out, under the influence of EC law subsequent legislation and case law has altered them,[166] so that, for example, in *Fils Henri Ramel*[167] the court upheld a claim for interest on the repayment of an import '*taxe*'[168] on wine, without even requiring the claimant to prove bad faith on the part of the public authority, as would have been required had the claim been purely private. Thus, although the particular direction of variation has changed over time, the variation of the rules to take account of public bodies in one way or another has not.

It is clear, then, that the two branches of court contain different substantive rules concerning the quasi-contracts, but that even within the judicial (private) branch, matters such as interest and time limits can be adjusted to take account of public bodies. However, for an exact parallel with the situation in England and Wales, the key question is what happens when a claim brought within the private law courts needs to take account of the public nature of one of the parties to the claim in relation to the substance of the claim itself. It is here that we learn two particularly interesting things from the French system.

The 'Absence of Cause' Approach does not Necessarily Provide a Better Solution for Public Body Enrichment Cases

It was argued in part one that England and Wales do not need to adopt the 'absence of basis' or 'without cause' approach in order to accommodate claims involving public bodies,[169] but this of course leaves open the question whether such a move would be desirable on its own terms. The French experience, however, suggests that it would probably make little difference and could even have some unwanted side effects.

It was noted above that there are two forms of *répétition de l'indu*; '*subjectif* and '*objectif*', the former relating to situations in which the sum is owed, just not by that particular *solvens* or not to that particular *accipiens*, whereas the latter relates to situations in which no sum was due at all. Originally both forms of *répétition de l'indu* would only allow recovery if the *solvens* could prove that (s)he/it had paid in error. However, somewhat oddly, proof of pressure would be admitted as an

d'Etat 17 June 1932, *Bertharion*, (1934) III *DP* 49; Conseil d'Etat 15 May 1857, *Robert*, (1860) III *DP* 45; 31 August 1863, *Lecq*, (1864) III *DP* 9; 25 June 1868, *Bécharet*, (1869) III *DP* 62. See also: Amselek, ibid 10–11.

166 Amselek, ibid 11–15.

167 Decision of the Cour d'appel de Lyon of the 30 November 1978 (1re Ch Civ) (1979) *D* 371, note C-J Berr.

168 '*taxe*' normally signifies individual sums, as opposed to the global '*impôt*', although the terminology does not always entail legal consequences, so that, for example, VAT (*taxe sur la valeur ajoutée*) is treated legally as an '*impôt*'.

169 See above, p 36 and P Birks, *Unjust Enrichment*, 2nd edn (Oxford, Oxford University Press, 2005) pt 3.

alternative to proof of error.[170] Thus although the quasi-contract of *enrichissement 'sans cause'* lived up to its name of applying without cause, *répétition de l''indu'* did not. The sum must have been paid in error or under pressure as well as having been undue.

Before the decision of the Cour de cassation of 24 September 2002[171] the only exception to this rule was for situations of *répétition de l'indu objectif* in cases of nullity.[172] Given this exception, one might have anticipated that at least *répétition de l'indu objectif* would, from the start, move closer to its neighbouring quasi-contract *enrichissement sans cause*, focusing on the nullity and the consequently undue nature of the payment, rather than on specific reasons for restitution such as mistake and pressure. If it had done so this might well have appeared preferable, at least to the *Kleinwort Benson v Lincoln*[173] approach of trying to determine whether it is possible to be mistaken about something which was only revealed to be null by a later court decision, if not to the solution proposed in Part 1. However, the French courts did not in fact move in this direction.

In part this may have been because the option of nullity was not open to everyone. For example, in *URSSAF du Calvados c Quidel et Roy*[174] the Quidel and Roy company had paid social security contributions which were later revealed to have been unnecessary, but the Chambre Sociale of the Cour de cassation held that since Quidel and Roy had not been a party to the case in which the new interpretation was given, it could not now rely on that new interpretation in order to bring into question payments that it had voluntarily made in the knowledge that there was a divergence of opinion over the correct interpretation of the text at issue.

However, even in cases where the nullity could have been used to justify their decision, the courts often tended to focus on the issue of constraint in order to justify recovery instead.[175] For example, the case of *Fils Henri Ramel*,[176] as noted above, concerned the recovery of import charges on wine which had been held to contravene EC law in a preliminary reference requested by the claimant company itself. Nevertheless, the Cour d'Appel of Lyon did not use nullity as the basis of its decision; instead it held that error was not a condition of restitution since the claimant had been constrained to pay the amounts in order to retain the unduly taxed merchandise. As Amselek puts it:

[170] eg: Amselek cites cases of the Conseil d'Etat of 2 November 1888, *Rupp*, Lebon p 782 and of the 7 February 1890, *Massboeuf*, (1892) III *S* 61. See: Amselek (n 83) 8 and fn 9.

[171] Civ (1) 24 Sept 2002 (n 122). This decision as noted above established that the rules of nullity would apply to annulled contracts, rather than the rules of *répétition de l'indu.*

[172] «En rattache les restitutions consécutives à toute annulation au domaine général de la répétition de l'indu et on rattache la répétition de l'indu au domaine général de la nullité des actes juridiques» (restitution following all annulments is attached to the *répétition de l'indu* and one attaches the *répétition de l'indu* to the general domain of the nullity of the legal acts'): I Defrénois-Souleau (n 58) para 3, p 244. See also: Amselek (n 83) 6 and A Sériaux (n 58) para 4.

[173] [1999] 2 AC 349.

[174] Decision of the Cour de Cassation, Ch Soc 24 May 1973, (1974) 20 *RDS* 365, note J Ghestin.

[175] See also: Amselek (n 83) 8.

[176] *Fils Henri Ramel* (n 166).

> When a public entity claims a sum from an individual and that individual pays it, even in the knowledge that he is not bound to do so, it is not generally with the intention to give, but through fear of the trouble that the administration has the power to cause him in forcing execution of the payment, in inflicting sanctions upon him, in subjecting him to various obstacles or nuisances. This is particularly so in the case of taxes, customs charges or similar levies: the condition of error of the *solvens* is set aside since he has paid under the threat of administrative pressure.[177]

Nevertheless, although in some cases even the threat of a legal action would constitute sufficient pressure[178] this was not held to be sufficient in the case of *Quidel et Roy*[179] because, as Ghestin puts it, there was no threat of 'illegitimate violence', even though, as he points out, criticising the result in the case, failure to pay on time could have led to a 10% increase in the fine for each trimester that it did not pay.[180]

So far, then, there are two important points of similarity between the English experience and the French. First, there is the instinctive desire of the courts to link the reason for granting the claim to the inequality between the powers of the public body and the inability to resist on the part of the private entity. Indeed even the very early cases assimilating pressure to error for the purposes of an action in *répétition de l'indu* come from the Conseil d'Etat.[181] Second, at the same time the French courts, like the English, have found it difficult to consider that this pressure was illegitimate, since this is precisely how the relationships of public entities and private parties are supposed to work.[182] Connected to this point is a further, and perhaps more significant, parallel with the English system.

There is, of course, no reason why French law should not in principle accept pressure as an alternative to error in a list of reasons for restitution. Indeed, there would be no need to stop at only these two 'vitiations' (for example, Ghestin cites a case in which grief was expressly assimilated to error on the part of the *solvens*),[183]

[177] «Lorsqu'un organisme public réclame une somme à une particulier et que celui-ci le paye même en sachant qu'il ne la doit pas, ce n'est pas généralement dans une intention libérale, mais par crainte des ennuis que l'administration a le pouvoir de lui causer en recourant à l'exécution forcée, en lui infligeant des sanctions, en lui faisant subir diverses gênes ou désagréments. C'est le cas, en particulier, en matière des impôts et droits de douane ou prélèvements assimilés: la condition d'erreur du *solvens* est écartée dès lors qu'il a payé sous la menace d'une contrainte administrative» Amselek (n 83) 8.

[178] Thus Amselek's quote, ibid, 177 continues «à la suite d'une mise en demeure ou, *a fortiori*, d'actes de poursuites».

[179] *Quidel et Roy* (n 173).

[180] ibid 368. See also Defrénois-Souleau (n 58) 264 ff.

[181] (n 169).

[182] See also: ch 2.

[183] «Un arrêt de la Chambre des requêtes du 5 décembre 1932 admet la répétition du règlement de fournitures d'une entreprise de pompes funèbres. Pour cela il assimile expressément à une erreur du solvens «la douleur causée par la mort de la personne à l'inhumation de laquelle on procédait» qui ne lui avait pas laissé «la liberté d'esprit de discuter, ni d'accepter dans leur nature et leur étendue» les fournitures litigieuses» ('A judgment of the Chambre des Requêtes of the 5 December 1932 admits repayment of the payment for supplies from a funeral directors' firm. For this it assimilates expressly to an error on the part of the solvens "the grief caused by the death of the person whose burial they were arranging" which did not leave [the claimant] "the freedom of mind to discuss or to accept in their nature and extent" the litigated supplies') (S 1933.1.61) J Ghestin, 'L'erreur du solvens, condition de la répétition de l'indu' (n 58). Obviously in England to be an action for unjust enrichment it would be necessary to prove that the situation was not governed by contract.

or indeed to limit the reasons for restitution to vitiations of consent, when absence and qualification of consent and policy-motivated restitution are also possible.[184] However, to do so would be to replicate exactly the English system, and to adopt the *unjust* enrichment approach, rather than the approach of *enrichissement sans cause* or *répétition de l'indu*. This is thus the exact mirror-image of the argument made in the English system; that it would be perfectly possible for England to adopt the 'absence of consideration' approach, but that to do so would require a complete change in the whole structure of the subject, and the development of many more rules in order to complete the new system in either case.

Thus just as the English courts' struggle to accommodate both the public and private law events led them to examine 'transactional inequality' and then to resort to the civilian language of absence of basis, so in France the struggle to use the existing private law rules to deal with illegal charges by public bodies led the courts first to use the alternative of pressure and then to begin, even in private law situations, to list 'vitiations of consent' that could be used to ground recovery, rather than focusing directly, as they ultimately did,[185] on the absence of cause itself. So whether one starts from the specific unjust factors approach or from the civilian absence of cause approach the problem is the same; attempting to deal with hybrid public and private claims solely through the rules of private law has a tendency to put more strain on that system than it can bear and in turn this can lead to a distortion of the structure of that law itself. Indeed, it even appears that the situation in France may have been exacerbated by a confusion of terminology similar to that which occurred in England. In England, references to the absence of cause approach in the case law appear at least in part to have sprung from confusion over the word 'consideration',[186] and in France, Defrénois-Souleau argues, the tendency to resort to vitiations of consent appears also to have resulted in part from a misunderstanding relating to the issue of 'cause'.[187] The problem is, she argues, that '*paiement*' of an objectively undue sum is misunderstood as an '*acte juridique*', (a manifestation of the will which is intended to have legal effects) when in fact it can only be a '*fait juridique*' (a legal event, other examples including death, accidents, etc). As a result of this assumption, she explains, there is a tendency to ask whether the *paiement* was null for absence of cause. In France, '*cause*' can mean not only an objective counter-obligation such as a debt, but also the debtor's motivation in taking on the debt,[188] which in turn inevitably leads the courts to examine whether or not this motivation was vitiated in some way. Instead, she argues, the courts should recognise that it is impossible to analyse the *paiement* of an objectively undue sum as being null for absence of cause for the good reason that

[184] eg: in the purely private context see J Carbonnier, *Droit Civil, Tome 4, Les Obligations*, 22nd edn (Paris, Presses Universitaires de France, 2000) p 537–47 para 304, where he cites a payment made on the basis of a marriage which never transpires as an equivalent to cases where the cause is subsequently annulled.

[185] See further below, p 198 onwards.

[186] Above pp 58–64.

[187] Defrénois-Souleau (n 58) 259 para 33.

[188] See also: Defrénois-Souleau, ibid 259 and Whittaker (n 11) 317 ff.

an undue *paiement* is not a *paiement.*[189] They would then realise that such a *paiement* is in fact a *fait juridique* and thus that the absence of any debt would itself found recovery in the case of *répétition de l'indu objectif.*

Clearly, then, although the French system might have been expected to tend more naturally towards focussing on *un*due sums, or enrichment *without cause*, this did not prevent it from going through a process very similar to that experienced in England as it tried to accommodate public law claims in the private law context, as far as claims *from* public bodies were concerned. However, while these claims were thus tending towards the common law approach of identifying specific vitiations of consent, claims *by* the *URSSAF* pay-offices were indeed heading in the more expected direction.

First, the courts recognised that an *erreur-bévue*, a blunder caused by inadvertence or inattention, could count as an error for the purposes of *répétition de l'indu objectif*, rather than the claimant having to show that it acted in complete ignorance of the truth.[190] As Defrénois-Souleau puts it, the courts would regard the error as being proven by the fact that the money had been unduly paid and it was sufficient that the payment was objectively erroneous, without the courts having to analyse the will of the URSSAF *solvens.*[191] Originally this leniency applied to both URSSAF pay-offices and banks on the basis that both were engaged in multiple complex and often (newly) computerised transactions. However, in 1977 the Chambre Sociale held that while negligence would not constitute an obstacle to a claim for restitution of *répétition de l'indu* in the social security context,[192] where only a 'gross error' would prevent recovery,[193] banks would lose their right to restitution even in the event of negligence. The basis for this was that such negligence would constitute a professional fault which gave the defendant a right to reparation, albeit that this would require more than a simple *erreur-bévue* of inadvertence or inattention.[194] In 1965 the gap widened, and the Cour de cassation reversed the burden of proof in a social security case, so that the pay-office could recover unless the *assuré-accipiens* could prove an *intention libérale* on the part of the pay-office,[195] which is of course exactly the technique used by the public law courts in *répétition de l'indu.*[196] This was reinforced in *CPAM de la Région Parisienne c Jardry,*[197] where the pay-office had mistakenly paid a medication allowance to which the recipient was not entitled on six separate occasions and this

[189] «Il est impossible, à notre sense, de l'analyser comme un paiement nul pour absence de cause, pour la bonne raison que ce paiement de l'indu n'est pas un paiement» Defrénois-Souleau, ibid para 34.

[190] Soc 3 Nov 1972, (1974) II *JCP* 17692, obs J Ghestin; Soc 4 July 1984, *Bull civ* V no 290; Soc 9 December 1987, *Bull civ* V no 716.

[191] Defrénois-Souleau (n 58) 249–250, paras 13–14.

[192] Soc 8 Nov 1977, *Bull civ* V no 603.

[193] Soc 4 Dec 1975, *Bull civ* V no 595, following earlier decisions of Soc 24 Nov 1971 and 13 April 1972, (1973) II *JCP* 17343.

[194] Defrénois-Souleau (n 58) 250, para 14.

[195] Defrénois-Souleau, ibid para 17, citing a decision of the 2nd Civil Chamber of the 16 July 1965, *Bull civ* II no 661.

[196] See above p 180.

[197] Soc (1974) II *JCP* 17692.

was not held to be sufficient to imply an *intention libérale* on the part of the pay-office. The pay-offices could thus simply assert an error on their part, which could include any form of inadvertence whatsoever, and the burden of proof would then shift to the *accipiens*. This development was well received by *la doctrine* (academic writers)[198] but in the case law it remained limited to cases of claims made by social security pay-offices. It was thus not possible to decide whether it was intended to be limited in this way or whether it was a more general move towards dispensing with the requirement of error in cases of *répétition de l'indu objectif*. Ghestin, writing in 1973 immediately after *Jardry*, noted the specifically public law-type considerations which could have motivated the Cour de cassation,[199] but which he did not consider sufficient to justify this difference in treatment between cases in which the pay-offices are the claimants and those in which they are the defendants.[200] This viewpoint is of course in keeping with the argument in part one that the presence of a public body should make a difference to the claim regardless of whether it is in the role of claimant or defendant, and indeed eventually, three decisions of 1984,[201] 1986[202] and 1987[203] in the private law context moved away from the requirement of error in cases of *répétition de l'indu objectif* so that a savings bank could recover overpayments it had made to its staff by using the wrong information in a computer program; a buyer failed to reclaim his deposit and a company failed to recover overpayments it had made to its former president, without the courts ever investigating the presence of an error on the part of the *solvens* in any of the three cases. Finally in 1993 the circle was completed and the Jeumont-Schneider company was able to recover social security overpayments from an URSSAF pay-office 'without having to prove anything else' beyond the fact that the payments were undue, and indeed, departing from the decision in *Quidel et Roy*, it was not even necessary for the company to show that it had been a party to

[198] See Defrénois-Souleau (n 58) 251 para 18.

[199] «Une appréciation purement statistique [de la jurisprudence de la Cour de cassation] pourrait faire croire que celle-ci est sensible à l'équilibre financier, assez précaire, de la Sécurité sociale. En effet, elle semble accorder à celle-ci la répétition de l'indu plus facilement qu'aux assujettis qui ont versé des cotisations dont ils n'étaient pas tenus» ('A purely statistical assessment [of the jurisprudence of the Cour de cassation] could allow one to believe that the court is sensitive to the fairly precarious financial equilibrium of Social Security. It seems to grant it repayment more easily than it does to those subjected to charges who have paid contributions which they were not obliged to pay') J Ghestin, 'La réparation du dommage résultant du reversement de prestations de sécurité sociale payées par erreur' (1973) I *JCP*.2528 para 2. See also Ghestin's note on *Quidel et Roy* (n 174) and 'L'erreur du solvens, condition de la répétition de l'indu' (n 58).

[200] «La mission de service public et la fonction sociale des organismes de sécurité sociale ne pourraient évidemment justifier une telle discrimination» ('the mission of public service and the social function of the organisms cannot evidently justify such a discrimination') Ghestin, note on *Quidel et Roy*, ibid 366. In fairness this is not a feature shared by England and Wales. It is true that *Auckland Harbour Board* preceded *Woolwich* by nearly 70 years, but in recent cases such as *Deutsche Morgan Grenfell* (n 107), the tendency has been to lean in favour of the private entity against the interests of the public body, eg on time limits.

[201] Civ 1re 17 July 1984, *Bull civ* I no 235, (1985) *D* 298, note P Chauvel (1985) *RTD civ* 577, obs J Mestre, *Rép Defrénois*, 1985 art 33535, no 49, obs J-L Aubert.

[202] Civ 3re 19 March 1986, *Bull civ* III no 36, (1987) *RTD civ* 543, obs J Mestre.

[203] Com 27 February 1987, (1987) *D* 244, note A Bénabent, (1987) *RTD civ* 543, obs J Mestre.

the case revealing their undue nature.[204] This broad interpretation of the case was not universally welcomed or accepted, but even its sceptic Sériaux[205] accepts that the first Advocate General, M Jéol had intended it to have this effect and that 'one does not refer to the highest formation of the Cour de cassation for small fry'.[206] Certainly all textbooks now state that *répétition de l'indu objectif* does not require the *solvens* to prove that (s)he/it paid in error.[207] For *répétition de l'indu subjectif*, on the other hand, error is still required for recovery, but pressure will operate as an alternative and often does so when the case concerns pressure of a public kind such as a court decision.[208] However, in the predominantly three-party situations which give rise to subjectively undue sums there is an increased chance that the pressure will not have been directed at the claimant and if that is the case (s)he/it may not be able to recover.[209]

Thus, even if the courts did not initially take the opportunity to move in the direction of aligning *répétition de l'indu* with *enrichissement sans cause*, since 1993 they have done so,[210] at least in cases of *répétition de l'indu objectif*. Can we then conclude that since 1993 the 'absence of cause' approach has worked better in the context of handling claims involving public bodies than would an approach based on a specific reason for restitution? The answer is that in practice the two approaches are not really so different, and that the distinction in fact only seems to locate the burden of proof. For example, in his conclusions on the *Jeumont-Schneider* case Advocate General Jéol argued that there were two reasons in favour of the decision reached by the court in that case; the treatment of the social security pay-offices as claimants and the principle that the payment of an undue sum was a payment without cause. While these two approaches were theoretically distinct, he noted, on the basis that the first approach presumed the presence of an error while the second approach did away with it altogether,

[204] «que, dès lors, les cotisations litigieuses n'étant pas dues, la société Jeumont-Schneider était en droit, *sans être tenu à aucune autre preuve* d'en obtenir la restitution» *URSSAF de Valenciennes c Sté Jeumont-Schneider* Cour de Cassation, Assemblée Plénière 2 April 1993; (1993) II *JCP* 22051, concl M Jéol.

[205] See Sériaux, 'Beaucoup de bruit pour rien' ('A lot of fuss about nothing') (n 58), in which he argued that the case should be seen as falling under the original exception that applies to cases where the money becomes undue after the payment, rather than as abandoning the requirement of error altogether.

[206] «on ne saisit pas la plus haute formation de la Cour de cassation pour du menu fretin» ibid.

[207] See eg Flour, Aubert and Savaux (n 29) vol 2 para 22; Terré, Simler and Lequette (n 31) 1054 and Malaurie, Aynès and Stoffel-Munck (n 37) 1043.

[208] See, eg: *SNTM CNAN c Sté Comasud*, Decision of the Cour de cassation Commercial Chamber 5 May 2004 no 723: Juris Classeur Contrats, Concurrence, Consommation 2004 no 123 note L Leveneur.

[209] See, eg: *Centre hospitalier de Marc Jacquet de Melun c M et Mme X*, Decision of the Cour d'Appel de Paris of 20 October 2004, concl B Folscheid, (2005) *D* 416; (2005) *AJDA* 222 note D Peljak.

[210] For an explicit parallel between the two, see the conclusions of M Jéol (n 203) 189: «en d'autres termes, le paiement de l'indu est un paiement *sans cause*, et le véritable fondement de la répétition, en même temps que la seule condition, est l'absence du cause du paiement, indépendement du vice du consentement» ('In other words, payment of an undue sum is a payment *without cause*, and the true foundation of restitution, as well as its only condition, is the absence of cause of the payment, independently of any vitiation of consent') and Chauvel commenting on the decision of the Cour de cassation of 16 March 1984 (n 200) 302.

> in practice they end up with the same result: the solvens who claims restitution . . . does not have to prove his error, he need only establish the inexistence of the obligation which deprives his payment of cause; as for the accipiens, he has, in both cases, the possibility of proving that, if the debt did not exist, the payment had another cause, such as the intention to make a gift.[211]

Thus in either case it appears likely that arguments in litigation will centre around lists of positive factors, whether in the common law system these are reasons for restitution, or in the civilian system they are positive 'causes' of the payment (such as the intention to make a gift) which can be used to rebut the presumption that apparently undue sums should be repaid. There is even scope under the civilian system for the list of vitiations of consent to re-emerge; the *solvens* argues that the sum was undue and ought therefore to be repaid, the *accipiens* responds that in fact it was paid with the intention of making a gift and the *solvens* could then resort to showing that his/her/its consent had been vitiated in some way in order to deny this. Indeed Defrénois-Souleau[212] points out that in any case proof of error will remain the 'queen of proofs', in other words the most straightforward way in which to demonstrate the undue nature of a sum. In the public body context, the *solvens* could reclaim unduly paid money from the public body only for the public body *accipiens* to respond, along the lines of *Quidel et Roy*, that the *solvens* had paid in the knowledge that the law was disputed and thus that it had intended to settle the issue which in turn provided an alternative cause for the payment.[213] Again, the claimant would then have to show that this consent was not present or vitiated in some way in order to recover.

However, arguments that a settlement has been reached may not always be accepted following the reasoning adopted by Advocate General Jéol in the *Jeumont-Schneider* case. He argued that it is possible to dispute whether doubt over the precise implications of the law need necessarily be exclusive of the possibility of an error on the part of the *solvens*[214] but that it is preferable to ask instead whether the error itself, in law or in fact, is a condition of repayment when the *solvens* has paid a debt which does not exist at all.[215] The problem is that these are two different things; the sum may have been undue but there may also have been doubt as to the state of the law, and if the payment was made to settle such an issue, that settlement would be undermined if it could subsequently be recovered when the payment did turn out to be undue. Conversely, it is difficult to see how one

[211] «en pratique, ils aboutissent au même résultat: le solvens qui demande la répétition de ce qu'il a versé indûment n'a pas à prouver son erreur, il doit seulement établir l'inexistence de l'obligation qui prive de cause son paiement; quant à l'accipiens, il a, dans les deux cas, la possibilité de prouver que, si la dette n'existait pas, le paiement avait une autre cause, tell que l'intention de faire une libéralité»: Jéol, ibid. Along similar lines see also Defrénois-Souleau (n 58) 265.

[212] «la reine des preuves», Defrénois-Souleau, ibid 262, para 40, cited with approval by Kamdem (n 58) para 7.

[213] As for whether or not such a settlement should be effective, in the English context see the discussion of 'waiver' ch 4, text to note 69.

[214] An issue not unlike that in *Kleinwort Benson v Lincoln* (n 172) and *Deutsche Morgan Grenfell* (n 107). See: pp 65–67, 94–96 and 121.

[215] *Jeumont-Schneider* (n 203) 188.

could uphold such a settlement without also examining the intentions of the *solvens* at the time of payment. In doing so, as noted in chapter three, the courts must be careful to avoid equating an absence of protest with an intent to give or to settle. In examining the previous approach based on vitiation of consent, Defrénois-Souleau pointed out the importance of entering a reservation at the time of payment in cases where the obligation to pay is disputed,[216] but such a requirement can obviously be criticised on the basis that it is likely to prioritise those who, as Ghestin puts it, are either more audacious or better advised.[217] Shifting the burden of proof to the *accipiens* to establish the intent to give or settle certainly helps in this regard, but it does not do away with the problem altogether.

Thus even in a system based on the undue nature of the payment, or an absence of cause, it is clear that vitiations of consent are likely to enter the picture at some stage, even if it is to deny an intent to give or to settle rather than to justify the recovery of the sum in the first place. Even if they reverse the burden of proof, the civilian rules do not seem to remove the purely private perspective rejected in Part 1. Thus in that sense, not only are the civilian rules likely to be little different from those in the common law, they also, perhaps unsurprisingly, appear to be *less* well adapted to the public body context than a reason for restitution which takes account not only of the absence of full and free consent (in identifying the public power of one of the parties) and the voidness of the transaction or payment, but also the public law event which gave rise to these considerations. In other words, the importance of the French system's approach to public body cases lies not so much in the fact that it focuses on the *absence* of cause for the payment, but rather in the further adjustments of the kinds listed above[218] that it makes to accommodate those bodies. It can therefore be concluded that not only is the 'absence of cause' approach unnecessary, as proposed in part one, it is also arguably less desirable than an approach which is able to take account of both the private and public aspects of the claim at the stage of establishing the reason for return of the money.

However, this is not the only lesson to be drawn from examination of the URSSAF cases; not only have they provided an opportunity to examine the absence of cause approach, they have also demonstrated a further commonality between the experience of England and France in this context:

The Need to Accommodate Public Bodies in Private Claims has a Tendency to Change the Rules of Private Law Itself

Thus, just as in England, the catalyst for many developments (such as, for example, the acceptance of mistake of law as a ground of restitution in *Kleinwort Benson v Lincoln*)[219] has been the presence of a public body as a party to the claim, so in

[216] Defrénois-Souleau (n 58) 263, para 41.
[217] Ghestin (n 173) 365.
[218] See pp 178–81 and 190–92 in particular.
[219] *Kleinwort Benson v Lincoln* (n 172).

France the *URSSAF* cases have led to two developments in private law. One obviously concerns the abandonment of the requirement of error in cases of *répétition de l'indu objectif*, described above, but the other, also alluded to in that context,[220] concerns the role of fault as a defence to a claim.

Although, as noted above,[221] the pay-offices were ultimately treated more leniently than banks in terms of their fault in making the payments in the first place, Voirin argued that the restitution by their recipients of periodic payments should be at least related, if not assimilated, to restitution of fruits and interest, which is not required where the *accipiens* is in good faith.[222] In other words, it is necessary for the *accipiens* to have more security of receipt in such cases because the whole point of social security payments is that they are to be spent. In this sense the role of fault by the payer in making the payment as a defence to the claim plays a role not dissimilar to the arguments concerning change of position in England,[223] though of course the two principles operate differently. Voirin's argument was accepted by a first instance social security commission which refused restitution because 'it would be inequitable to make the interested party bear the cost of the reimbursement of sums which it had charged in all good faith',[224] but this was overruled by the Second Civil Chamber of the Cour de cassation, which recalled that the texts 'exclude the notion of good faith of the *accipiens* in that which concerns the restitution of the capital even if it was paid without being due'.[225]

In 1968 the Chambre Sociale of the Cour de cassation (without specifically referring to Voirin's arguments) did set aside an action for restitution brought by a pay-office, citing the fault of the pay-office as its reason, and Voirin welcomed this result,[226] but not long afterwards it appeared that the court had returned once more to the reasoning of the Second Civil Chamber, since in December 1969 the Social Chamber overruled a decision which had refused restitution as a result of the 'inexcusable error' of the pay-office. Ghestin suggests that this was because the total exclusion of restitution was seen as being a drastic result that the courts immediately felt compelled to mitigate. They did so, Ghestin believes, by

[220] p 196 onwards.

[221] ibid.

[222] «Il observe, en effet, que les prestations périodiques versées par la caisse de Sécurité sociale ou d'allocations familiales constituent, comme les fruits et revenus, des sommes d'argent affectées à des dépenses courantes» ('He observes, in effect that periodic payments made by the social security pay-office or family allowances constitute, like fruits and revenues, sums of money allotted to current expenses') Ghestin, 'La réparation du dommage' (n 198), para 7, citing P Voirin (1964) *Droit Social* 1964 p 61; 1966, 663 and 1969, 66.

[223] Where the same argument was made in relation to public body income, see: ch 5 p 144 and text to n 131.

[224] «il serait inéquitable de faire supporter à l'intéressé le remboursement de sommes qu'il a perçues en toute bonne foi» cited by Ghestin, ibid para 7.

[225] «. . . excluent la notion de bonne foi de l'accipiens en ce qui concerne la restitution du capital même de ce qui a été payé sans être du» Ghestin, ibid para 7, citing a judgment of 14 January 1965, (1965)1 *Gaz Pal* 216.

[226] Ghestin, ibid para 8, citing a decision of the 19 July 1968, *Bull civ* IV p 329 no 403, Droit social 1969 p 66 obs P Voirin.

'appealing to the notion of public service and referring implicitly to the jurisprudence of the Conseil d'Etat in the matter of *répétition de l'indu*'.[227]

Thus instead of completely refusing restitution, the Cour de cassation held that the pay-offices would be liable to pay *dommages-intérêts* (damages and interest). Although the Second Civil Chamber readily adopted this solution, the approach of the Social Chamber was more restrictive, requiring a 'gross error in the execution of the public service incumbent upon it',[228] a requirement directly derived from administrative law.

This set of developments is particularly interesting given the conclusions drawn in relation to defences at the end of chapter five. It was argued there that where a public law event is relevant to an otherwise purely private law cause of action in unjust enrichment, the public law unjust factor should apply and this should trigger at least a reconsideration of the applicable defences, so that the law's access to both of the relevant events could be ensured. In adopting the requirement of 'gross error' the Social Chamber was apparently trying to do exactly this, even though it applied only to situations in which the public body was the claimant. Ultimately, however, the requirement of gross error seems to have been abandoned and simple error will suffice, and the principle of recovering damages and interest now applies across private law, at least to *répétition de l'indu objectif*.[229]

Conclusion

There are therefore five important lessons that the English system can learn from an examination of the French experience in this context. First, that a mature division between public and private law seems to entail an understanding that private law claims cannot be applied to public entities in the same way as between private individuals, without any adjustment. Second, that the choice to prioritise the private law enrichment event[230] over the public law nullity is not inevitable; indeed an examination of Canada, France and the UK produces an almost 50:50 split on that question. At the very least, then, it can be concluded that the public law event is relevant, even if the claim is brought primarily in private law. Following on from this it is important to note, third, that this question of how the claim is brought should not be thought to end the matter; particular rules applicable to

[227] «Après avoir admis, sans restrictions, dans un premier temps, la responsabilité des caisses, conduisant à écarter en fait la répétition, la Cour de Cassation, aujourd'hui s'efforce de limiter cette responsabilité. Elle fait alors appel à la notion de service public et se réfère implicitement à la jurisprudence du Conseil d'Etat en matière de répétition de l'indu» Ghestin, ibid para 14.

[228] 24 November 1971, overruling a decision of the Commission of first instance at Nancy, because there was not a gross error on the facts. See Ghestin, ibid para 16.

[229] For *répétition de l'indu subjectif* it is suggested that fault will still block the claim altogether, see Whittaker (n 11) 433.

[230] Whether the rest of the event is based on this enrichment being regarded as 'unjust' or 'without cause'.

public bodies can be applied regardless of whether the claim is brought through private or public law channels. Fourth, an adoption of the civilian 'without cause' approach does not necessarily provide a more straightforward means of dealing with public body cases than does the common law approach of ascertaining specific reasons for restitution. The availability of such an approach elsewhere in French law did not prevent the Cour de cassation in cases of *répétition de l'indu* from flirting with a move towards the common law system, just as the difficulties presented by public body cases led the English courts to begin to use the terminology of 'absence of consideration'. When the French courts did finally move towards the 'absence of cause' approach, at least for *répétition de l'indu objectif*, this did not seem to differ much from the common law approach in anything other than burden of proof; investigations will still tend to focus on positive factors, whether these are reasons for repaying the money or reasons for denying repayment, and indeed both sets of factors seem likely to require an investigation into the intentions of the payer-claimant. Certainly, the absence of cause approach taken on its own does nothing to address the public as well as the private law aspects of the claim; that is done by other adjustments of the kind mentioned earlier. Finally, as well as demonstrating a need to adjust private law in its application to public bodies, in both systems the process of accommodating public claims in both systems has ultimately led to changes which affect private law itself.

However, while Amselek agrees that cases involving public bodies have thus certainly had an effect on the structure of the private law, at least in relation to *répétition de l'indu*, he in fact argues that the process has often started one stage beyond that, with EU law bringing so much depth and enrichment to the general theory of *répétition de l'indu* in its applications to public bodies that it is now public law which informs private law, rather than the other way round.[231] Not only do the French courts regard *répétition de l'indu* as a principle common to public and private law,[232] they have also stated that it is a principle common to public, private and EC law.[233] It is clear, then, from both the English and French experiences that what is now EU law has played a crucial role in the development of the law relating to unjust enrichment and quasi-contracts respectively. In order to complete the picture, therefore, it is necessary to consider the relationship of EU law with unjust enrichment in more detail.

[231] «le droit communautaire a conduit à des approfondissements et à des enrichissements de la théorie générale de la répétition de l'indu dans ses applications aux personnes publiques,—de sorte que c'est aujourd'hui le droit public qui apporte ici des enseignements au droit civil!» Amselek (n 83) 36.

[232] (n 82).

[233] «La répétition de l'indu est un principe commun au droit privé et au droit public internes, ainsi qu'au droit communautaire» Com 3 January 1985, *Bull civ* IV no 5; 17 Jan 1989, (1989) RJF 192.

Part 3

Unjust Enrichment and Public Law in the EU

7

Unjust Enrichment and the EU Institutions

IT WAS NOTED at the end of the last chapter that the French courts have referred to *répétition de l'indu* as a principle common to public, private and what is now European Union (EU) law,[1] and that no picture of claims involving unjust enrichment and public bodies would be complete without an investigation of the impact of the EU on such claims. There are three obvious reasons for this. First, as far as the EU-Member State relationship is concerned, the EU's free movement and anti-discrimination rules have provided an important source of nullity in the sense that the power of Member States' public bodies are limited not only by domestic law but also by the requirement to comply with EU law. Thus the reason why a particular contract, tax or levy may be beyond the powers of a public body in a particular case may well be provided by EU law rather than by domestic public law. In addition, and more directly, the European Court of Justice (ECJ) has laid down criteria which must be fulfilled by the national courts when providing a remedy in such cases. The influence of these two factors on French law was seen clearly in the cases discussed in chapter six such as *Café Jacques Vabre*[2] and *Fils Henri Ramel.*[3] Similarly, in England, one of Lord Goff's reasons[4] for allowing recovery in *Woolwich Equitable Building Society v IRC*[5] was:

[1] «la repetition de l'indu est un principe commun au droit privé et au droit public internes, ainsi qu'au droit communautaire» Cass Com 3 January 1985, *Bull civ* IV no 5; 17 Jan 1989, RJF 1989, 192. Of course the reference at that stage was to European *Community* law, but in line with the Lisbon Treaty the term EU is used here, as explained in the preface.

[2] Trib d'inst du 1er arondissement de Paris, 8 January 1971, Cour d'Appel de Paris 7 July 1973: *D* 1974.159; Cour de Cassation 24 May 1975; *D* 1975.497.

[3] Decision of the Cour d'appel de Lyon of the 30 November 1978 (1re Ch Civ) *D* 1979.371, note C-J Berr.

[4] In addition to general motivations based on constitutional principles and justice, Lord Goff cited six further reasons for granting recovery in *Woolwich.* Four of these were relatively pragmatic dealing with the limited practical effect of the judgment in this particular case, the fact that the opportunity to make a similar decision would not arise again, the fact that the issue was at the time under active consultation by the Law Commission and the fact that if any action were to be taken it would have to be taken by the courts, because it would obviously not be in the Treasury's interest for the government to initiate legislation along the same lines: *Woolwich Equitable Building Society v IRC* [1993] AC 70 (HL) 176–77. Two, however, were more conceptual, and related to ideas of parity with other contexts. As seen above (pp 56–69) one of these was the ability of the Crown to obtain restitution in cases like *Auckland Harbour Board v The King* [1924] AC 318 (PC), but the other was the comparison with the situation in cases involving EU law noted here.

[5] *Woolwich*, ibid.

> the decision of the European Court of Justice, in *Amministrazione delle Finanze dello Stato v SpA San Giorgio*,[6] which establishes that a person who pays charges levied by a member state contrary to the rules of Community law is entitled to repayment of the charge, such right being regarded as a consequence of, and an adjunct to, the rights conferred on individuals by the Community provisions prohibiting the relevant charges . . .[7] I only comment that, at a time when Community law is becoming increasingly important, it would be strange if the right of the citizen to recover overpaid charges were to be more restricted under domestic law than it is under European law.[8]

In the same way, the decision of the ECJ in *Metallgesellschaft and Hoechst v IRC* was of course the catalyst for several important English cases such as *Deutsche Morgan Grenfell v IRC*,[9] *Sempra Metals Ltd (formerly Metallgesellschaft Ltd) v IRC*,[10] and *The Test Claimants in the FII Group Litigation v The Commissioners for Her Majesty's Revenue & Customs (FII)*.[11] For all these reasons, then, it is important to understand the precise relationship of EU and Member State law on questions involving unjust enrichment and public bodies,[12] and in particular what happens when there is an EU law element in the cases as well as the national public law and unjust enrichment elements discussed so far. Does EU law simply provide an imperative for national courts to reach a particular outcome in a particular case, regardless of the national mechanism chosen to do so, or has EU law begun to develop its own conceptions of those mechanisms? Such questions are important enough in their own terms, but become even more so when combined with investigation into the possibilities of codifying European private law,[13] or matters concerning the conflict of laws. However, in addition to these issues relating to the

[6] Case 199/82 *Amministrazione delle Finanze dello Stato v San Giorgio SpA* [1983] ECR 3595.

[7] At this point he cited: *San Giorgio*, ibid [12].

[8] *Woolwich* (n 4) 177.

[9] *Deutsche Morgan Grenfell v IRC* [2003] EWHC 1779 (Ch), [2003] 4 All ER 645 (first instance); [2005] EWCA Civ 78, (2006) Ch 243 (CA); and [2006] UKHL 49, [2007] 1 AC 558 (HL). The CA decision has been noted at: A Burrows, 'Restitution in Respect of Mistakenly Paid Tax' (2005) 121 *Law Quarterly Review* 540; G Virgo, '*Deutsche Morgan Grenfell*: the Right to Restitution of Tax Paid by Mistake Rejected' [2005] *British Tax Review* 281; R Stevens, 'Justified Enrichment' (2005) 5 *Oxford University Commonwealth Law Journal* 141; and R Williams, 'The Beginnings of a Public Law of Unjust Enrichment?' (2005) 16 *King's College Law Journal* 194.

[10] *Sempra Metals Ltd (formerly Metallgesellschaft Ltd) v IRC* [2007] UKHL 34, [2007] 3 WLR 354. It is also worth noting that in Case 212/94 *FMC v Intervention Board for Agricultural Produce* [1996] ECR I-389, the ECJ held that the old English rule preventing restitution where there was a mistake of law 'manifestly failed to satisfy' the EC remedy requirements (on which see further ch 8) and was 'liable to prejudice effective protection of the rights conferred on the traders in question by Community law': [72]. Thus had the HL not removed the rule in *Kleinwort Benson v Lincoln CC* [1999] 2 AC 349 (HL), it would almost certainly have been required to do so eventually in the interests of complying with its obligations under European law.

[11] *The Test Claimants in the FII Group Litigation v The Commissioners for Her Majesty's Revenue & Customs* [2008] EWHC 2893 (Ch), [2008] STI 2726.

[12] For similar comments, see: Lord Slynn's Introduction to A Jones, *Restitution and European Community Law* (London, Mansfield Press, 2000).

[13] See, eg: Commission (EC), 'Communication to the Council and the European Parliament on European Contract Law' COM (2001) 398 final, 11 July, to the Council and European Parliament on *European Contract Law* [2000] OJ C 255/1; the Study Group on a European Civil Code (www.sgecc.net); the *Principles for International Commercial Contracts* (PICC), prepared by UNIDROIT ('Institut pour l'unification du droit privé', www.unidroit.org); and the *Principles of European Contract Law* (PECL)

EU-Member State relationship, the third reason for examining unjust enrichment in the EU is of course that the public body involved in the claim may not be a domestic body at all, but one of the institutions of the EU itself. It is this issue with which the rest of this chapter will be concerned.

An EU Law of Unjust Enrichment?

Relatively early on in the development of the European Economic Community (EEC), it became clear that it would not be possible for the ECJ to avoid questions relating to unjust enrichment, and given that those working in the court had started their careers as lawyers in their respective national systems, it is hardly surprising to find them using reasoning familiar to those national systems. In *Mannesmann AG v High Authority*,[14] for example, a payment was made by the Imported Ferrous Scrap Equalisation Fund, as part of the compulsory EC scheme on the equalisation of ferrous scrap established under Article 53 of the European Coal and Steel Community (ECSC) Treaty. The Community's internal resources in ferrous scrap were not sufficient to cover the requirements of the scrap-consuming undertakings (SCUs), and imported scrap was much more expensive than Community scrap. The equalisation scheme was thus set up to ensure an orderly supply of scrap at reasonable prices for all SCUs. The fund would pay out the difference between the price of Community scrap and imported scrap on each consignment of the latter purchased, but in order to do so it needed certification of the origin of the imported scrap. In Germany, the regional office for the administration of this scheme was known as the DSVG. Rather than paying the money to the SCUs (who would then have to pay it to their scrap suppliers), the DSVG paid it directly to the supplier for the account of the SCUs. In one such contract, Hansa (a scrap supplier) provided the certificates required for the payment of the equalisation money and named the applicant SCU as the undertaking entitled to receive the scrap in question. However, it turned out that there were mistakes in the certificates, so that the equalisation payments made by the DSVG were made in error. The High Authority asked the applicant SCU (Mannesmann) for the repayment of these sums, but Mannesmann refused, and so the High Authority took decisions ordering them to repay. These decisions were enforceable under

prepared by the Commission on European Contract law ('the Lando group' (www.cbs.dk/departments/law/staff/ol/commission_on_ecl)). See further Editorial, (2002) 39 *Common Market Law Review* 219; and W van Gerven, 'Codifying European private law? Yes, if. . .!' (2002) 27 *European Law Review* 156, especially 164 ff. In any case, the principal area for discussion is contract law, but it is clear that this cannot be entirely divorced from the law relating to wrongs and to unjust enrichment, and indeed some work has been done on the codification of these areas too. See: Commission (EC), Communication, [13] and the draft unjust enrichment articles of the Study Group on the European Civil Code, available on the website above).

[14] Cases 4 to 13/59 *Mannesmann AG v High Authority* [1960] ECR 113.

Article 92 of the Treaty, and the applicant challenged the validity of these decisions. The ECJ upheld Mannesmann's claim and in annulling the High Authority's decision for infringement of the rules of law relating to the application of the ECSC Treaty it held that:

> [I]t cannot be argued that any unjustified enrichment on the part of the applicants exists.
>
> Indeed, equalization was designed to make up the difference in price between so-called imported scrap, which was more highly-priced and scrap recovered within the common market. According to the very principles underlying equalization, that extra cost was to be borne not by the applicants in proportion to the supplies of imported scrap which they received, but by the scrap consumers as a whole through the Fund. Thus the payment of equalization did not constitute an enrichment for the applicants by virtue of a payment which benefited them directly, but was the result of an operation bringing scrap delivered down to the price of the internal market. Moreover, an obligation to make restitution on the grounds of an unjustified enrichment also presupposes the absence of any justification whatever in the dealings between the parties. However, that legal justification exists independently of whether the equalization was paid directly to the scrap sellers, thus constituting the difference between the price on the internal market and the import price, or whether it was paid to the applicants to enable them to buy imported scrap instead of buying scrap coming from the internal Community market. Therefore in this instance the requirements of unjustified enrichment giving rise to restitution are not fulfilled.[15]

Considering each of these two requirements in turn, it is clear that both can be regarded as relating to the law of unjust enrichment. First, although it is immediately apparent that the requirement of an 'absence of justification' reflects the French approach of *enrichissement* sans *cause* or *répétition de l'indu* rather than the English *unjust* enrichment, this does not, of course, mean that the two systems would come to different conclusions, as was noted in chapters one and six.[16] What might in France be treated as either a fact rendering the sum due, or with cause, could in the English system be seen as providing a basis for the transfer, thus avoiding what is sometimes known as a failure of consideration outside contract. It is not clear from the ECJ's judgment what form this justification took, only that there was such a justification. However, AG Roemer explains in more detail that the certificates came from the Netherlands, where they were administrative measures and thus could only be rendered *voidable* by their shortcomings, not void. Since the Netherlands authority had not revoked the certificates, AG Roemer concluded that 'the scrap in respect of which the certificates were issued thereby kept the nature of scrap from third countries'.[17] In other words, the basis for the payment had therefore not failed, and (whether this is seen from the civilian or the English perspective), there was thus no reason for the payments to be returned.

[15] ibid 133.
[16] See above at pp 8–10 and p 192 onwards.
[17] *Mannesmann* (n 14) 150.

The second problem was, of course, that the SCU in question had not been enriched. Here, too, the ECJ's reasoning is the same as that found in the English and French systems. The applicant SCUs were never intended to pay more than the price for scrap recovered within the Community. The whole purpose of the equalisation scheme was to prevent them from ever having to pay the price for importing scrap. They therefore could not be said to be enriched by the payment of the difference by the Fund, as this was not a discharge of their debt. Had the lack of proper certification invalidated the Fund's payment, it is possible that the scrap *supplier*, Hansa, could have been said to be enriched, as the scheme was not set up for its benefit. Indeed, the ECJ stated that its judgment did not prejudice 'the High Authority's right to proceed against the perpetrators of the frauds [presumably for compensation as a response to wrongdoing] and against those who profited from them'.[18] That is, presumably, those who were unjustly enriched. The only action thus precluded was therefore an action based on unjust enrichment being brought against the applicant SCUs for return of the money.

Interestingly the applicants in *Mannesmann* had also tried to argue that the High Authority had acted beyond its competence by trying to use a public law power to create a claim for itself in private law. However, the ECJ decided that in operating the scrap equalisation scheme the High Authority was acting in a public manner, and since the right to repayment of the sums wrongly paid was directly connected to the obligation to pay the correct sums, the right to repayment came from a public law relationship and thus was within the competence of the High Authority. This is significant in that the ECJ thus clearly saw the relevance of both the public and private law issues in the case, a position which supports the argument made in part one and which therefore contrasts with the English approach. However, its significance is nevertheless limited by the fact that in the English cases discussed in previous chapters the public bodies were parties to private law actions in unjust enrichment. In contrast, the action in *Mannesmann* was for judicial review of the competence of the High Authority to demand repayment, albeit that the basis for that demand was the alleged unjust enrichment of the applicants.

Unjust Enrichment as a General Principle of EU Law

Although unjust enrichment-style reasoning could thus be found even in the very early days of the EC, it was in 1990 that the Court first recognised the prevention of unjust enrichment as a 'general principle' of EC law, holding that the Commission

[18] ibid 133. Cases of enrichment through discharge of debt are difficult in the English national system, see, eg: A Burrows, *The Law of Restitution*, 2nd edn (London, Butterworths, 2002) ch 8 and G Virgo, *The Principles of the Law of Restitution*, 2nd edn (Oxford, Clarendon Press, 2006) 222–40.

> cannot, without unjustly enriching the Community contrary to the general principles of Community law, refuse to take account of [certain relevant information] in calculating the correction to be made to the accounts of expenditure chargeable to the EAGGF [European Agricultural Guidance and Guarantee Fund] submitted by the Member State in question.[19]

This was reiterated in the subsequent cases of *Corus UK v Commission*,[20] discussed in further detail below, and *Vieira v Commission*.[21] However, in an echo of some of the French experience,[22] though not so much the English,[23] it has traditionally been much easier for the EC to obtain restitution, or for entities to obtain restitution in pursuance of EC goals, than it has been for private claimants to obtain restitution from the entities of the EC.

Staff Cases

For instance, obviously one group of individuals to which the EU regularly pays out money is its staff. Article 85 of the Staff Regulations provides two conditions in which a sum overpaid can be recovered; where the recipient was aware that there was no due reason for the payment, or where the fact of the overpayment was patently such that the recipient could not have been unaware of it. Thus in *Meganck v Commission*,[24] Meganck had informed the Commission, for which he worked, that his daughter had left school and been employed, so that he was no longer entitled to a 'head of the household allowance', but although his dependent child allowance and education allowance were stopped, his head of household allowance was not. When informed that the Personnel Department were seeking to recover the amount overpaid, Meganck argued that the Court should declare that he was not aware that there was no due reason for the payment; that the fact of the overpayment was not patently such that he could not have been unaware of it; and that there should therefore be no right on the part of the Personnel Department to recover the money. The Court held that since Meganck had not informed the Commission until three months after his change in status, he had no right to retain the overpayments received in this period.[25] For the period after notification the Court held that 'even a superficial examination of [some of the

[19] Case C-259/87 *Greece v Commission* [1990] ECR I-2845, [2] (summary publication).

[20] Case T-171/99 *Corus UK v Commission* [2001] ECR II-2967, [55].

[21] Case T-126/01 *Vieira v Commission* [2003] ECR II-1209, [86]: 'As the Commission points out, any other interpretation of the fisheries agreement would be contrary to the general principles of law common to the legal systems of the Member States, such as the principle which prohibits unjust enrichment'.

[22] See above, pp 181 and 197.

[23] It is true that *Auckland Harbour Board* (n 4) preceded *Woolwich* (n 4) by nearly 70 years, but decisions such as *Kleinwort Benson v Lincoln* (n 10) and *Deutsche Morgan Grenfell* (HL) (n 9) have been favourable to the private claimants and disadvantageous to the public body defendants. The statutory position is of course different, see eg pp 42–44 and 156.

[24] Case 36/72 *Meganck v Commission* [1973] ECR 527.

[25] ibid [17].

later] salary slips would have shown the applicant that he was continuing to receive an allowance in a capacity which was no longer his'.[26] However, the salary payments immediately after notification did not allow 'a person exercising normal diligence to recognise the undue payment of an allowance as head of household'.[27] Meganck was thus allowed to keep these, but only these, overpayments. Annemarie Kuhl[28] was also overpaid in her capacity as an official of the Council. This time the overpayment was of an education allowance for her children to go to school in Germany. After they had moved to the European school in Brussels, Kuhl informed the appropriate departments, but continued to receive the allowance for them to be educated abroad. Two years later, she was informed of the overpayment and the fact that 28 691 Belgian francs were being deducted from her salary. The Court held again that '[t]he applicant should have known that the change of school . . . involved a reduction of the education allowance'.[29] She was thus not entitled to retain the amount received before she notified the appropriate departments, and even after this,

> she continued to receive as before the same education allowance . . . the applicant should have been aware of the perpetuation of the error. In the circumstances the fact of overpayment was patently such that the applicant could not have been unaware of it.[30]

To an English lawyer, although the courts have referred only to 'the need to protect the Communities' resources' by asking for repayment, and to 'legitimate expectations' as a possible countervailing consideration,[31] this reasoning looks very like the argument that any change of position on the parts of Meganck and Kuhl could not have been bona fide.[32] Indeed, when Marcelle Exner did succeed in her claim against the Commission for annulment of the decision to reclaim her overpaid household allowance,[33] AG Reischl specifically held that she could not 'be said to have acted in bad faith, but must rather be regarded as having made an excusable error'.[34] Indeed, it could be argued that the references to legitimate

[26] ibid [19].

[27] ibid [20]. It is clear that the individual official concerned must be capable of noticing the discrepancy and carrying out any checks necessary to clarify the situation, see: Case 252/78 *Broe v Commission* [1979] ECR 2393; Case 310/87 *Stempels v Commission* [1989] ECR 43; and Case T-124/89 *Kormeier v Commission* [1991] ECR II-125.

[28] Case 71/72 *Kuhl v Council* [1973] ECR 705. See also: Case T-117/89 *Sens v Commission* [1990] ECR II-185.

[29] ibid [13].

[30] ibid [15]–[16].

[31] See, eg: Case T-111/89 *Schreiber v Council* [1990] ECR II-429, [28] and [41].

[32] As noted above, ch 5 pp 147–49, at present the 'bona fide' requirement in change of position in the law of England may be slightly narrower than this, involving something like 'sharp practice' rather than just knowledge: *Niru Battery Manufacturing Co v Milestone Trading Ltd* [2002] EWHC 1425 (QB); [2003] EWCA Civ 1446, [2004] QB 985, [135] and [164]. Nevertheless, in *Papamichael v National Westminster Bank* [2003] EWHC 164 (QB), [2003] 1 Lloyd's Rep 341, Judge Chambers QC held that he would be prepared to accept 'actual knowledge where good faith is concerned. This would include wilfully and recklessly failing to make such inquiries as an honest and reasonable man would make': [209].

[33] Case 142/78 *Marcelle Exner (née Berghmans) v Commission* [1979] ECR 3125.

[34] ibid 3147 (pt 2).

expectations simply support the argument made in chapter five that there is in fact a close link between that doctrine and the defence of change of position.[35]

These cases also illustrate the point made above, that apart from *Exner*, there is not much evidence of the operation of unjust enrichment *against* the EU, but plenty of evidence of the principle working to the benefit of the EU. Similarly, in *Danvin v Commission*,[36] Danvin had taken over the duties of the chief accounting officer while continuing to receive only his salary as an assistant accounting officer. When he claimed the difference on the basis of unjust enrichment, the ECJ refrained from deciding whether this principle could apply to such a contract of employment, but rejected Danvin's claim on the basis that 'a generally accepted principle in the national legal systems' was that the claimant must have suffered loss, and Danvin could not prove that he had. The references to damage are not helpful, but it is possible that the ECJ was simply denying the 'at the expense of the claimant' element of the cause of action. Another similar case was *Schina v Commission*,[37] where the Court, according to Magliveras,[38] 'ducked the question' and rejected the argument on the basis of a lack of evidence. Finally, AG Gand in *Danvin* attempted to discourage any future applicants from trying such a cause of action by holding that there was 'nothing to be gained from transposing concepts of private law into an area for which they have not been conceived'.[39] This seems to illustrate further recognition at European level of a distinction between public and private law,[40] and provides an interesting parallel with English law, where employment contracts have also given rise to debate over the proper spheres of public, as opposed to private, law.[41] However, it is clear from that context that, with respect, there is no reason at all why private law concepts of unjust enrichment should not be used in the public sphere, and conversely there is every reason why unjust enrichment actions should be available against the EU to the same degree as they are available in its favour.

Annulment Cases

Similarly, there has been a series of cases in which those who have paid fines to the EC have subsequently sought to have those fines annulled and recover the payments. Here again, although the situation has gradually improved, the ECJ has not always recognised the application of the principle of unjust enrichment against the European Institutions as it could have done.

[35] See above at pp 140–41, and see further below, pp 266–68.
[36] Case 26/67 *Danvin v Commission* [1968] ECR 315.
[37] Case 401/85 *Schina v Commission* [1986] ECR 3911.
[38] K Magliveras, 'Unjust Enrichment and Restitution in Community Law' (1997) 6 *Irish Journal of European Law* 190, 196.
[39] *Danvin* (n 36) 327.
[40] See further ch 8 p 241.
[41] See, eg: *Roy v Kensington Chelsea and Westminster Family Practitioner Committee* [1992] 1 AC 624 (HL) and P Craig, *Administrative Law*, 6th edn (London, Sweet and Maxwell, 2008) 26-016.

The Wood Pulp *Cases*

On 19 December 1984, the Commission adopted Decision 85/202 (the *Wood Pulp* decision), following a proceeding under what is now Article 101 of the Treaty on the Functioning of the EU (TFEU) (ex Art 81 EC), in which it stated that 400 wood pulp producers, together with three of their professional associations, had concerted on prices in breach of Article 101(1) of the Treaty. 36 of those addressees, including nine 'Swedish addressees', were fined amounts between €50,000 and €500,000. 28 of the addressees, not including the Swedish addressees, brought an action for annulment of this decision before the ECJ. The ECJ annulled part of the Commission's decision, holding that concertation was not the only plausible explanation for the parallelism of prices fixed by the addressees, and that the addressees had not had an opportunity to defend themselves effectively against an allegation of general concertation. The ECJ thus reduced the initial amounts of the fines by amounts between €125,000 and €2,000, taking them down to fines of €20,000 for each undertaking. Following delivery of this judgment on 31 March 1993,[42] the Swedish addressees asked the Commission, in a letter dated 24 November 1993, to re-examine their position in the light of the judgment and to refund the overpaid fines. This request was finally rejected by the Commission on 4 October 1995. The Swedish addressees then brought an action before the Court of First Instance (CFI) for annulment of this decision under Article 263 TFEU (ex 230 EC) and in *AssiDöman Kraft Products* the CFI held that:

> [T]he wood pulp decision, although drafted and published in the form of a single decision, must be treated as a bundle of individual decisions making a finding or findings of infringement against each of the undertakings to which it is addressed and, where appropriate, imposing a fine . . . Therefore, where an addressee did not bring an action under Article [263] for annulment of the wood pulp decision in so far as that decision relates to it, the decision continues to be valid and binding on it.[43]

The Swedish addressees were thus still bound by the wood pulp decision, as the time limit for bringing an action under Article 263 had expired. In order to review the Commission's subsequent decision not to reassess the position of the Swedish addressees following the annulment of the fines in other cases, the CFI had to find that this second decision was separate from the first, and not merely a reiteration of it which would not have been open to challenge.[44] This required it in turn to find that there was an obligation on the Commission under Article 266 TFEU (ex Art 233 EC)[45] to reassess the position of the Swedish addressees following the

[42] Cases C-89/85, C-104/85, C-114/85, C-116/85, C-117/85 and C-125 to C-129/85 *Ahlström Osakeyhtiö v Commission* [1993] ECR I-1307.

[43] Case T-227/95 *AssiDomän Kraft Products AB v Commission* [1997] ECR II-1185, [56] and [58].

[44] ie that Case C-188/92 *TWD Textilwerke Deggendorf GmbH v Germany* [1994] ECR I-833 did not apply.

[45] Art 266 provides that: 'The institution whose act has been declared void or whose failure to act has been declared contrary to the Treaties shall be required to take the necessary measures to comply with the judgment of the Court of Justice of the European Union'.

wood pulp decision, so that the second letter of 4 October 1995 could be considered as taken pursuant to that Article and therefore separate from the wood pulp decision. The CFI found that the Commission was indeed required:

> [I]n accordance with Article [266] of the Treaty and the principle of good administration—to review, in the light of the grounds of the Wood Pulp judgment, the legality of the wood pulp decision in so far as it relates to the Swedish addressees and to determine on the basis of such an examination whether it was appropriate to repay the fines.[46]

Having thus established the admissibility of the case, the CFI went on to consider the Commission's argument that it was neither required, nor entitled to repay the fines. The court held that:

> [T]he Community institutions are entitled, subject to the principles of the protection of legitimate expectations and of legal certainty, to withdraw, on the ground that it is unlawful, a decision granting a benefit to its addressee . . . That case-law applies a fortiori in situations where, as in this case, the decision in question merely imposes burdens or penalties on the individual. In such cases, the Commission is not precluded from withdrawing the decision by considerations relating to the protection of the legitimate expectations and vested rights of the person to whom the decision was addressed.[47]

Accordingly, the CFI continued that if the Commission were to conclude that the fines imposed on the Swedish addressees were unlawful:

> [I]f Article [266] were not to be deprived of all its practical effect, the Commission would also be required, in accordance with the principles of legality and of good administration, to repay those fines, as they would have no legal basis.[48]

However, the CFI rejected the Swedish addressees' claim for an order requiring the Commission to refund (with interest) part of the fines paid by them, since:

> Article [266] of the Treaty provides for a division of powers between the judicial and administrative authorities, under which it is for the institution whose act has been declared void to determine what measures are required in order to comply with a judgment annulling an act, such as the *Wood Pulp* judgment, and to exercise, subject to review by the Community judicature, the discretion which it enjoys in that regard while respecting the operative part and grounds of the judgment which it is required to comply with and the provisions of Community law.[49]

On appeal by the Commission, however, the ECJ set aside the CFI's judgment, holding that although Article 266 TFEU (ex 233 EC) required the institution concerned to ensure that any act intended to replace the annulled act was not affected by the same irregularities, this did not mean that the Commission must, at the request of interested parties, re-examine identical or similar decisions, allegedly affected by the same irregularity, addressed to addressees other than the

[46] *AssiDomän Kraft Products* (CFI) (n 43) [85].
[47] ibid [90]–[91].
[48] ibid [92].
[49] ibid [98].

applicant.[50] It was, the Court held, settled law that a decision which had not been challenged by the addressee within the time-limit laid down in Article 266 TFEU (ex Art 230 EC), became definitive as against him.[51] The principle of legal certainty thus precluded any necessity on the part of the institution which had adopted the decision to re-examine at the request of other addressees, in the light of the grounds of the annulling judgment, the legality of the unchallenged decisions.[52] In holding that Article 266 TFEU (ex Art 233 EC) placed the Commission under a duty to re-examine the position of the Swedish addressees in the light of the *Wood Pulp* judgment, the CFI had thus erred in law.[53]

AG Ruiz-Jarabo Colomer explained further that although the issue appeared to be 'deceptively simple', it in fact raised the 'difficult conflict' between substantive justice and legal certainty as soon as it was examined in detail.[54] He 'fully agreed' with the analysis of the *Wood Pulp* decision as a set of individual decisions, but in 'clarifying' the *erga omnes* effect of a judgment of annulment he explained that '[t]he legal basis of the obligation to re-examine final administrative measures adopted by Community institutions is . . . the need to give place, having regard to the general rule that such measures are not challengeable, to superior considerations of equity.[55] He thus disagreed with the CFI's view that such a duty arose from Article 266 TFEU (ex Art 233 EC) and the 'principle of legality'. Similarly, he agreed with the CFI's reasoning that the Commission was *entitled* to review the measure in respect of the Swedish addressees, but he disagreed with the CFI's conclusion that the Commission was thus *obliged* to repay the Swedish addressees' fines, pointing out that the principles of legality and good administration also require compliance with time limits and thus legal certainty and finality.[56] In proposing his alternative solution, he then returned to his theme of 'equitable considerations', holding that:

> [T]he proper solution to this dispute calls for the legal context chosen by the Court of First Instance to be abandoned. Any obligation which the Commission may be under to refund the fines to the Swedish undertakings should not be regarded as an emanation *ultra partes* of a judgment of annulment but rather as the recognition *by the legal order of an intolerable injustice.* That recognition is based therefore not on Article [266] but on *equitable considerations known to the laws of all the Member States, which are capable of overriding the general principle that administrative measures cannot be attacked outside the time-limit for instituting proceedings.* (emphasis added)[57]

He went on to list the equitable considerations which could have this effect as being divided into two kinds. On the one hand were categories which 'display the common feature of relying upon a new factor'. These are: pleas calling for

[50] Case C-310/97 P *Commission v AssiDomän Kraft Products AB* [1999] ECR I-5363, [56].
[51] ibid [57].
[52] ibid [63].
[53] ibid [71].
[54] ibid (point 2).
[55] ibid (point 45).
[56] ibid (points 45–46).
[57] ibid (point 48).

amendment (in favour of the interested party) of the factual or legal basis of the final measure being challenged; and pleas by which it is sought to rely on new evidence (or have existing evidence reappraised) prompting a decision more favourable to the person concerned. On the other hand, there were cases in which the defect prompting the challenge may have been inherent in the measure since the time of its adoption. These are: 'outright nullity'[58] and 'manifest infringement of the law',[59] the latter of which appears from his opinion to contain 'sets of measures producing discriminatory results'[60] and 'particularly severe penalties'.[61] Such cases must, he explained 'be exceptional and, in addition, must be strictly interpreted for fear of undermining the general rule that final measures are unchallengeable'.[62] He further stated that 'none of the circumstances making it advisable to restrict the degree of latitude ordinarily enjoyed by Community institutions'[63] were present in the case of the Swedish addressees. He thus concluded that:

> [S]ince there is no superior consideration of equity whatsoever, nor has there been claimed to be, the balancing of the various interests . . . can produce no result other than that pursued by the general rule, which is to preserve the finality of the contested penalty.[64]

It is this final sentence and the emphasised passages in the quote above which must be examined more carefully. It is clear from his reasoning that none of the 'considerations of equity' he listed applied to the present case, and that if these are the only 'intolerable injustices' to be considered then it was right to decide the case in favour of the Commission. However, it will be remembered from the discussion of the English law, and in particular the case of *British Steel plc v Customs and Excise Commissioners*[65] that one of the 'equitable considerations known to the laws of [at least England], which [is] capable of overriding the general principle that administrative measures cannot be attacked outside the time-limit for instituting proceedings'[66] is the presence of the event of unjust enrichment. It was seen in chapter three that since *British Steel* it has been possible for a claimant to bring a claim in unjust enrichment outside the public law time limits, but within the private law time limits, even when the claim is based on the public law unjust factor.[67] Clearly, then, in England at least, the unjust enrichment of the public body is seen

[58] This category has been received into the case law of the Court of Justice through the concept of *non-existent acts*: ibid (point 83).
[59] ibid (point 69).
[60] ibid (point 86).
[61] ibid (point 91).
[62] ibid (point 81).
[63] ibid (point 95).
[64] ibid (point 98).
[65] *British Steel plc v Customs and Excise Commissioners* [1997] 2 All ER 366 (CA). See above ch 3 pp 49–52 and ch 4 p 74 onwards.
[66] To paraphrase AG Ruiz-Jarabo Colomer cited with emphasis: (n 57).
[67] See pp 49–54, subject to the discussion of *Jones v Powys Local Health Board* [2008] EWHC 2562 (Admin). Even if the time limit should ideally be shorter than the full private law time limit, it should also be longer than the purely public law limitation period.

as a further example of an 'intolerable injustice' which can give access to the public law event even after the expiry of the administrative law time limit. Similarly, in France the courts ultimately allowed claims for the return of overpayments to social security pay-offices even when the claimant had not been a party to the case in which those payments had been held to be invalid.[68] It is possible that the *Wood Pulp* cases could be interpreted as being cases in which there was no ultra vires event as regards the Swedish addressees, on the basis that the decision could have become legal in their case by the lapse of time. However, the decision in *British Steel*, and AG Ruiz-Jarabo Colomer's receptiveness to certain other 'considerations of equity', suggest that this is not the case. Instead, the claimants should have argued, and the ECJ could have recognised, that the Swedish addressees had a claim in unjust enrichment, based on the common law viewpoint on the public law unjust factor, or from the civilian viewpoint on the absence of any justification which rendered the fines due.

Medici Grimm KG v Council[69]

To some extent, the effect of the *Wood Pulp* decision has been confined by a later decision of the CFI, and the way in which the Court reasoned in that case further bolsters the argument made here. In *Medici Grimm*, the Council had initiated a review to establish anti-dumping duties on handbags manufactured outside the EU. The applicant and its associate, Lucci Creation, did not participate in this process and a regulation was passed by the Council imposing anti-dumping duties. Six weeks after this, the Commission invited producers to submit evidence that this system should be reviewed and, this time, the applicants responded. These submissions were too late for inclusion in the initial procedure, but given the significant proportion of Chinese imports represented by the applicants, the Commission agreed to examine the information provided. As a result of this, the Council adopted a subsequent regulation reducing the anti-dumping duty to which the applicant companies were subject from 38 per cent to 0 per cent. However, the companies had argued that this regulation should be retroactive, which would entitle them to a refund of the anti-dumping duties already paid. The Council dismissed this application and the applicant companies consequently sought an Article 263 TFEU (ex 230 EC) review of the second, non-retroactive, regulation.

Having dealt with various admissibility and abuse of process issues, the CFI found that since the Institutions had themselves chosen the second investigation period and found that there should have been no anti-dumping duty during that period, the regulation should be retroactive. Further, it held that the Commission's power was not given for the purpose of penalising traders for their failure to participate in the initial anti-dumping investigation, so the retroactive application

[68] *URSSAF de Valenciennes c Sté Jeumont-Schneider* Cour de Cassation, Assemblée Plénière 2 April 1993; JCP 1993 II 22051, concl M Jéol, see further above pp 197–98.

[69] Case T-7/99 *Medici Grimm KG v Council* [2000] ECR II-2671.

of the contested regulation would not constitute an unjustified reward for the applicant companies:

> Furthermore, to accept the Council's position, even though the Court has held in this case that the Council was bound to abide by all the consequences flowing from the review findings, would result in the unjust enrichment of the Community at the applicant's expense.[70]

This last statement entirely supports the argument made above in relation to the *Wood Pulp* cases and it is therefore interesting to examine the ground on which the CFI distinguished that case. According to the CFI, whereas in that case, (*AssiDomän Kraft Products*) 'the applicant has already had an opportunity to submit for review by the Community judicature the act or conduct of the administration which is effectively the subject of the second claim', in this case 'the two actions arise as a result of different acts or conduct on the part of the administration, even if the financial outcome of the two actions is the same for the applicant'.[71] Thus here, because the applicant companies were asking for review of the *second* regulation on the basis that it was not retroactive, rather than a review of the *first* for imposing the 38 per cent charge, the two could be classed as 'different' and the *AssiDomän Kraft Products* ruling did not apply.

It has been argued here that there are already two different events even in the *Wood Pulp* cases, which could be classed as 'different' if the CFI so chose (the initial decision which was not challenged in time, and the consequent unjust enrichment of the Community). Thus alongside AG Ruiz-Jarabo Colomer's 'considerations of equity', *Medici Grimm* represents another exception from the basic *AssiDomän Kraft Products* principle, and when these existing exceptions are analysed (as they have been here), the *Wood Pulp* case *AssiDomän Kraft Products* should itself be included among them.

Corus UK (British Steel) v Commission[72]

Given the comparison drawn with *British Steel* above, it is perhaps appropriate that in another case involving British Steel (now Corus), the ECJ more openly recognised that unjust enrichment is indeed one of the general principles of European law[73] which does apply in the aftermath of an annulment decision. The Commission had imposed a fine of nearly €32 million for infringements of competition law in the steel beams market. In proceedings before the CFI, this amount was reduced to €20 million and the Commission repaid the €12 million difference. However, just as in *Woolwich*,[74] the Commission refused to pay interest on this sum. The CFI held first that payment of the interest was an 'essential component' of the Commission's obligation to restore the applicant to its original position following a judgment of annulment and complete reimbursement of a fine unduly paid could not leave out

[70] ibid [89].
[71] ibid [45].
[72] *Corus UK* (n 20).
[73] See above pp 211–12.
[74] *Woolwich* (n 4).

factors such as the effluxion of time. So far this is only evidence of the 'technical postscript' approach[75] which sees restitution simply as a response to the initial unlawfulness. But significantly the CFI continued by holding that:

> Second, a failure to reimburse interest could result, as is particularly the case in the present instance . . . in the unjust enrichment of the Community, which would be contrary to the general principles of Community law.[76] It follows that the Commission is required to reimburse not only the principal amount of the fine unduly paid, but also the amount of any enrichment or benefit it has obtained as a result of such payment.[77]

Finally, the right to receive such interest is not subject to proof of damage.[78]

Here the reasoning is no longer based on the annulment itself, but on the event of unjust enrichment. Further evidence of this comes from the fact that the CFI discussed the Member States' calculation of the amount of interest based on 'the lower of the two amounts corresponding to the enrichment and the loss'.[79] Not only is the case therefore significant in the specific context of repayments of interest on annulled competition law fines, but it also represents an important sign (in answer to the Commission's contrary assertion[80]) that unjust enrichment is one of the general principles of EU law, even, in some cases, where it is applied against the EU. It is therefore not impossible that, in the future, unjust enrichment may not only be a general principle, but also an 'equitable consideration' or a 'different issue' of relevance to all annulment situations.

Holcim (Deutschland) AG v Commission[81]

However, in the meantime, it has been made clear that the principle does not apply when, rather than paying the fine, the applicant chooses instead to provide a bank guarantee in favour of the Commission, albeit that the guarantee entails bank charges which are paid by the applicant. In *Holcim*, the applicant sought to reclaim these charges from the Commission and the CFI rejected its claim on the basis that:

> The Commission's failure to assume responsibility for the charges incurred in providing a bank guarantee does not entail any undue enrichment of the Community, since the bank guarantee charges are paid not to the Community but to a third party. Observance of the general principle prohibiting undue enrichment does not justify such reimbursement in

75 Discussed above, ch 2 at pp 31–35 .

76 On which it cited: *Greece v Commission* (n 19) [2] and *Corus UK* (n 20) [55].

77 *Corus UK* (n 20) [55]–[56].

78 *Corus UK (British Steel) v Commission* (n 20) [56], citing the Opinion of AG Trabucchi in Case 26/74 *Société Roquette Frères v Commission Société* [1976] ECR 677.

79 *Corus UK (British Steel) v Commission*, above (n 20) [60]. Though note now that in *Sempra Metals Ltd (formerly Metallgesellschaft Ltd) v IRC* [2007] UKHL 34, [2007] 3 WLR 354, the HL held that the measure of restitution was gain to the defendant rather than loss to the claimant. See further ch 4, note 32.

80 ibid [26]. As Jones notes, it also provides a further contrast with the decision in Cases C-279–281/96 *Ansaldo Energia SpA v Amministrazione delle Finanze dello Stato* [1998] ECR I-5025 in which it was held that national rules can continue to settle questions of payment of interest on sums charged by Member States, subject only to the usual requirements of equivalence and effectiveness: A Jones (n 12) 73–74.

81 Case T-28/03 *Holcim (Deutschland) AG v Commission* [2005] ECR II-1357.

> any circumstances. Quite to the contrary, if the Commission were to assume responsibility for the charges incurred in providing a bank guarantee, that would allow the undertaking concerned to be placed in the situation in which it was before the contested decision was adopted, but the Commission, on the other hand, would be penalised, since it would be required to reimburse to the undertaking sums of which it did not have the benefit.[82]

When Holcim appealed to the ECJ, AG Mengozzi took a slightly more lenient view, holding that the CFI had been wrong to exclude any possibility of undue enrichment of the Community on the ground that the expenses were paid not to the Community but to third parties.[83] In doing so, he continued, the CFI had 'lost sight of the fact that "enrichment" may occur not only when the person concerned enjoys an increase of assets but also where it benefits from a decrease of its liabilities (debts)'. From the English perspective, recognition that the saving of a future legal expense can constitute an enrichment would require at least a slight extension (or perhaps amalgamation) of the existing case law which currently only covers discharge of an *already existing* legal obligation[84] or saving of a *factually* necessary future expense.[85] Nevertheless, there are certainly policy arguments in favour of such a point of view. As AG Mengozzi points out, the actions of Holcim effectively mitigated its loss and certainly did reduce what the Commission would otherwise have been required to pay. As such, it may well be desirable to provide an incentive for parties to act in a similarly 'diligent'[86] and efficient way in future. From this point of view, it is disappointing that the ECJ did not discuss the issue of unjust enrichment at all, holding simply that the CFI had not erred in law when it found that, in imposing the fine in the first place, the Commission's breach of EC law had not been sufficiently serious to give rise to damages under the terms of *Bergaderm*.[87]

Although *Holcim* cannot therefore be regarded as an instance of the unjust enrichment principle in operation in EU law, there are two further points about the decision which are worth noting because they have also arisen in other cases.

Three-Party Cases

First, it is apparent from the decision in *Holcim* that the European courts, like their national counterparts, have much greater difficulty with cases of unjust or undue enrichment which involve three parties. In *Cantina Sociale di Dolianova Soc Coop*

[82] ibid [130].

[83] ibid [112].

[84] See, eg: *Exall v Partridge* (1799) 8 TR 308 (KB), 101 ER 1405 and *County of Carleton v City of Ottawa* [1965] SCR 663, (1965) 52 DLR (2d).

[85] eg: *Re Berkeley Applegate (Investment Consultants) Ltd (No 2)* (1988) 4 BCC 279 (Ch).

[86] ibid [115].

[87] Case C-352/98P *Bergaderm and Goupil v Commission* [2000] ECR I-5291. In this case the ECJ held that the same principles should be applicable to damages actions against the Community brought under Art 340 TFEU (ex 288 EC) EC as apply to damages actions against the Member States for breach of Community law in Cases C-46/93 and C-48/93 *Brasserie du Pêcheur SA v Federal Republic of Germany and R v Secretary of State for Transport, ex p Factortame* [1996] ECR I-1029.

Srl v Commission,[88] these problems did not prove insurmountable, though the claim as a whole was nevertheless unsuccessful. Under a Community scheme of 'preventive distillation', Regulation 337/79 EEC (as amended by Regulation 2499/82 EEC) provided that aid could be paid by national intervention agencies (NIAs) to distillers, who would then be obliged to pay the wine producers a minimum 'buy-in' price for the wine they received. The distillers could claim such aid in advance, but to do so they had to guarantee it by providing the NIAs with a security worth 110% of the amount of aid claimed. Producers wishing to have their wines distilled under this scheme had to conclude contracts with an approved distiller and then submit these contracts to the Commission and to a national intervention agency (NIA) for approval. The result was to create a three-party situation involving producers, distillers and the Commission in which the producers and distillers were in a contractual relationship, but the Commission was not. Instead, the Commission's actions were governed by Regulation 337/79 which provided only for payment to the distillers.

In *Cantina*, the applicants were wine producers who had provided a company of distillers (DAI), with a quantity of wine, which DAI distilled in accordance with the requirements of the regulations. In order to pay for the wine, DAI received 1 062 763 876 Italian lire (ITL) of aid from the Azienda di Stato per gli Interventi nel Mercato Agricolo (AIMA), the Italian NIA, in return for which it provided security in the form of a 1 169 040 262 ITL bond issued by an enterprise known as Assedile[89] for the benefit of AIMA. However, as a result of financial difficulties, DAI failed to pay the applicant producers for the wine they had received and DAI was later declared bankrupt. In the meantime, AIMA requested repayment of the aid from DAI, and when this was not received, AIMA applied to Assedile for payment of the security, which Assedile ultimately paid, following various instances of litigation in the Italian courts. As a result of this, the applicant producers lodged a complaint with the Commission requesting the Commission to call on AIMA and Italy to repay the amounts which they had not received in return for the wine delivered to the distillers. The Commission rejected that request and so the applicant producers brought an action under Article 263 TFEU (ex 230 EC) asking for that rejection to be annulled and for a declaration by the CFI that they should be entitled to receive the Community aid which had not been paid to them at the appropriate time by DAI and which had been redeemed by AIMA by way of the security and refunded to the EAGGF.[90] The CFI upheld the applicants' claim, holding that in the circumstances the Community had been unjustly enriched[91] and reaffirming that the prohibition on unjust enrichment was a general principle of EC law.[92] However, when the issue was brought before AG Sharpston and the ECJ,[93] the only

[88] Case T-166/98 *Cantina Sociale di Dolianova Soc Coop Srl v Commission* [2004] ECR II-3991.
[89] In full: Assicuratrice Edile SpA.
[90] European Agricultural Guidance and Guarantee Fund.
[91] *Cantina* (n 88) [159].
[92] ibid [160], citing *Greece v Commission* (n 19), *Corus UK* (n 20) and *Vieira* (n 21).
[93] Case C-51/05, decision of 17 July 2008 [2008] ECR I-5341.

question raised was the date from which time began to run against the applicants. Since AG Sharpston and the ECJ agreed that the CFI had taken too subjective an approach to this question,[94] and that the applicants were consequently out of time, they annulled the decision of the CFI without considering any of the issues relating specifically to the unjust enrichment of the Community. The decision thus cannot therefore be taken as authority in favour of recovery for unjust enrichment in a three-party context at the EU level.

Conversely, in *Masdar (UK) v Commission*[95] recovery in a three-party situation was not permitted. Under a Community programme of technical aid to the Commonwealth of Independent States, the Commission signed a contract with Helmico SA. Helmico then entered a sub-contract with Masdar whereby Masdar would provide some of the services for what were referred to as 'the Moldova Contract' and 'the Russian Contract'. This three-party situation therefore contained a two-contract chain from the Commission to Helmico and from Helmico to Masdar. However, although the Commission paid Helmico and Masdar performed the services as agreed, Helmico was late in paying Masdar. On one occasion, Helmico claimed that this was because it had been underpaid by the Commission, but when Masdar contacted the Commission, it discovered that Helmico had in fact received full payment. Perhaps unsurprisingly, in the light of this and similar discussions, the Commission eventually wrote to Helmico requiring repayment of over €2 000 000 because it had discovered Helmico to be guilty of fraud. Masdar then sued Helmico and brought an action for remuneration under Article 340 TFEU (ex 288 EC) against the Commission. At this stage, €200 000 had been paid by the Commission through Helmico's bank account and on to Masdar, but even more money had been paid by the Commission to Helmico (of which €453 000 was owing to Masdar but had not been paid) and further invoices sent by Helmico to the Commission were still outstanding. Masdar then tried to bring a case in the UK courts against Helmico for the €453 000 it was owed under the contract, but also brought an action in unjust enrichment against the Commission in the EU courts for the same amount, or, in the alternative, €249 314, which was the amount it was owed for the work it had completed after the discovery of Helmico's fraud. In the meantime, the Commission issued a recovery order against Helmico in respect of the Russian Contract and the Moldova Contract, totalling €2 091 168.07.

Unlike other previous references to the general principle of unjust or undue enrichment, the CFI's judgment in this case engaged much more directly with the specific requirements of *negotiorum gestio* and the action *de in rem verso*, apparently derived from a survey of the laws of Member States.[96] Its conclusion was that '[a]ny enrichment of the Commission or impoverishment of the applicant, as it arose from the contractual framework in place, cannot be described as being

[94] ibid [58] and [65].

[95] Case T-333/03 *Masdar (UK) v Commission* [2006] ECR II-4377, appealed as Case C-47/07, Opinion of AG Mazák (12 June 2008).

[96] See, eg: *Masdar* (CFI) ibid [91] and *Masdar* (AG Mazák) ibid [50]–[51].

without cause'.[97] Thus neither the action *de in rem verso* nor the action based on *negotiorum gestio* could succeed, and in addition the latter concept (with its connotations of benevolent intervention, inability of the principal to act on his own account and lack of knowledge by the principal of the manager's action) was thought particularly inapt to cover such an instance of contractual performance, albeit that the contract in question was between the applicant and a third party. On appeal to the ECJ, AG Mazák found no flaw in the legal reasoning of the CFI,[98] and the ECJ upheld its decision.[99] On the question of *negotiorum gestio*, the ECJ held that this claim could not succeed because Masdar continued to provide its services after discovering the irregularities committed by Helmico because Masdar believed that the Commission had undertaken to pay for those services, and its intervention could not therefore be described as 'benevolent'.[100] It also agreed with the CFI that the contracts between the Commission and Helmico on the one hand and between Helmico and Masdar on the other, had not ceased to exist. Enrichment, it held, could not be categorised as 'unjust' where it thus derives from contractual obligations.[101]

It is clear that these two specific concepts of the action *de in rem verso* and *negotiorum gestio* owe their terminology more to systems such as the French. From that perspective, it is easy to see why the latter doctrine is not particularly appropriate, but dismissal of the action *de in rem verso* is perhaps a little more difficult. To some extent, it is a question of policy whether such unjust enrichment actions should be allowed in triangular situations when parts of the triangle are covered by a contract, and it is clear that neither the French nor the English system currently do allow such actions.[102] Whether the issue is viewed from the civilian or the common law perspective, simply stating that services received under a contract were not 'unjust' 'undue' or 'without cause' just begs the question. The fact that those services had a cause or were justified in the relationship between Masdar and Helmico does not tell us anything about the extent to which they were caused or justified as against the Commission: this requires a further policy decision that a contract between A and B should be allowed to affect legal relations between B and C, and it is not completely and self-evidently apparent that it should[103] (although as already noted the weight of authority certainly leans in that direction). On the contrary, such a rule can lead to a potentially unfair discrepancy between cases such as *Cantina* (in which only one side of the triangle is covered by contract, and

[97] *Masdar* (CFI) ibid [99].

[98] ibid.

[99] Case C-47/07 *Masdar (UK) Ltd v Commission* (16 December 2008). [2008] ECR I-9761.

[100] ibid [67].

[101] ibid [54]–[57].

[102] See also: Burrows, *Law of Restitution* (n 18) 347–50 and ch 6. Nor does the Australian system, see the decision of the High Court of Australia: *Lumbers v W Cook Builders Pty Ltd (in liq)* [2008] HCA 27. This case was noted: A Goymour, 'Too Many Cooks: Three Parties, Contracts and Unjust Enrichment' (2008) 67 *Cambridge Law Journal* 469. I am very grateful to Graham Virgo for bringing this case to my attention.

[103] See in particular: K Barker, 'Restitution and Third Parties' [1994] *Lloyds Maritime and Commercial Law Quarterly* 305.

in which the CFI was keen to allow recovery in order to remedy what it saw as a 'lacuna' in the regulations which did not allow payment of aid to the wine producers in the event of the insolvency of the distiller)[104] and *Masdar*, in which two sides were contractual. In fact, without resorting to such potential discrepancies caused by blanket rules against recovery in three-party contractual contexts such as *Masdar*, there are more specific grounds on which recovery could have been denied in that case, as opposed to *Cantina*.

First, if the concern in three-party situations relates to the allocation of contractual risk then that issue can be examined specifically. In upholding the CFI's decision in *Masdar* the ECJ found that

> the Court of First Instance stated, rightly, that in all contractual relationships there is a certain risk that a party will not perform the contract satisfactorily or that it will become insolvent. That is a commercial risk inherent in the activities of economic operators.[105]

However true that is between two contracting parties, it says nothing about the existence of a potential unjust enrichment on the part of a third party. Instead, it is necessary to find a specific assumption of risk which does have implications for that third party unjust enrichment. In *Masdar*, for example, the applicants had been given the opportunity of contracting directly with the Commission and had chosen not to do so,[106] which might be thought to qualify Masdar as a speculative risk-taker.[107] Indeed in that case the CFI also pointed out that 'it is not without relevance that, according to case-law, it is the economic operators themselves who must bear the economic risks inherent in their operations'[108] and that:

> The applicant was not unaware that Helmico was not fulfilling its contractual obligations, but knowingly chose to continue to fulfil its own obligations rather than to take formal action. In so doing it ran a commercial risk which could be described as normal.

This point was reiterated by the ECJ.[109] Certainly, if Masdar did simply assume without any particular justification that the Commission would pay for its services, it is easy to see why the action should be rejected. But at the same time, neither court ruled out the possibility that Masdar had been 'induced' so to act,[110] which would run counter to this reasoning.[111] It is also unclear at which stage Masdar were offered the chance to contract directly with the Commission. If this occurred after the discovery of Helmico's fraud, then it is possible that the €249 314 worth of

[104] *Cantina* (n 88) [138].
[105] *Masdar* (ECJ) (n 99) [59].
[106] *Masdar* (CFI) (n 95) [88].
[107] cf Goymour (n 102) 471, citing P Watts, 'Does a Subcontractor Have Restitutionary Rights Against the Employer' [1995] *Lloyds Maritime and Commercial Law Quarterly* 398.
[108] *Masdar* (CFI) (n 95) [102], citing Case T-203/96 *Embassy Limousines and Services v Parliament* [1988] ECR II-4239, [75].
[109] *Masdar* (ECJ) (n 99) [58].
[110] *Masdar* (CFI) (n 95) [103] and *Masdar* (Mazák AG) (n 95) [101].
[111] Although it recognised this inducement he ECJ did not deal fully with this point, only raising it in relation to a specific argument based on legitimate expectations which it rejected on the basis that there had been no specific enough representation on the part of the Commission: *Masdar* (ECJ) (n 99) [80].

work that it completed afterwards might be unrecoverable, while the €203 686[112] completed before the fraud was discovered should not be ruled out.

A second, more specific reason for denying recovery is that of enrichment. Cases on non-monetary enrichment in general are notoriously difficult, though there are some circumstances in which a defendant can be estopped from denying that he, she or it has been enriched.[113] This might explain the decision of the CFI in *Cantina*, although (as noted above) that case was also motivated by a desire to remedy a perceived lacuna in the governing regulation.[114] However, other than this additional policy motivation, it cannot explain the difference between the decisions of the CFI in the two cases because, as noted above, both Courts also clearly refer to Masdar as having been 'induced' so to act by the Commission. Conversely, if a finding of enrichment estoppel requires an element of fault on the part of the defendant[115] rather than simple evidence that the defendant had requested and intended to pay for the completion of the project in question, then it would not be possible to make out an enrichment in either *Cantina* or *Masdar*. This issue is, as the Court pointed out, perhaps best dealt with as a question of legitimate expectations,[116] and it is particularly interesting here to note the close relationship between: (a) this doctrine in public law; (b) the concept of so-called 'sword' estoppel in private law[117] (which of course cannot be used in England); (c) the concept of 'free acceptance' (which apparently can);[118] and the issue of estoppel in establishing the defendant's enrichment. If instead, however, we are to remain with an attempt to find enrichment for the purposes of an unjust enrichment action, then in addition to the usual problems associated with enrichment by estoppel (given that we are dealing with three-party cases) it should be noted that a further question arises. This is whether, in making a request of B, A can be estopped from denying enrichment as against C.[119] Connected to this is a more

[112] ie €453 000 minus €249 314. It should be noted that this is the inverse of the claim made by Masdar against the Commission for €453 000 or at least the €249 314 for the work completed after discovery of the fraud.

[113] See, eg: *Brewer Street Investments Ltd v Barclays Woollen Co Ltd* [1954] 1 QB 428 (CA); *Sabemo Pty Ltd v North Sydney MC* [1977] 2 NSWLR 880 (SC); and perhaps also *Planche v Colburn* (1831) 8 Bing 14 (CA), 131 ER 305. See also: Virgo, *Principles* (n 18) 89–93; and, Burrows, *Law of Restitution* (n 18) 379–81.

[114] *Cantina* (n 88).

[115] Virgo, for example, suggests this as a possible distinction between *Brewer Street Investments* (n 113) and *Jennings and Chapman v Woodman Matthews and Co* [1952] 2 TLR 409 (CA): Virgo, *Principles* (n 18) 92.

[116] See further the decision of the ECJ in *Masdar* (ECJ) (n 99) [80]–[87], rejecting the claim based on legitimate expectations for want of a specific representation on which the expectation was based.

[117] As in *Walton's Stores (Interstate) Ltd v Maher* (1998) 164 CLR 387 (HC).

[118] See: *Rowe v Vale of White Horse DC* [2003] EWHC 388 (QB), [2003] 1 Lloyd's Report 418. As far as the question of enrichment is concerned, as in *Cantina* (n 88), it is arguable that by commissioning the work and ultimately intending to pay for it the Commission can be regarded as being enriched, and in this case the argument would be further strengthened if the work done by Masdar had subsequently been built upon in order to complete 'the Moldova project', though it is not clear from the report whether this was in fact the case.

[119] Although the considerations relating to contract and estoppel are obviously separate and different, if the law were to allow recovery in situations of three-party contracts there would be much to be said for not allowing the three-party bar to reappear at the level of enrichment.

significant point relating to the problem of enrichment, namely that in a typical three-party two-contract situation[120] the commissioning party cannot be enriched by completion of the commissioned work while that party remains liable to the middle, defaulting party, under the initial contract. In such a situation, the only party that can be regarded as enriched by completion of the work is the middle, defaulting party whose obligation to complete the work has been fulfilled by the third party in the triangle.[121] However, neither *Cantina* nor *Masdar* involved such a typical three-party two-contract situation. In *Cantina* the relationship between the Commission and the defaulting distillers, DAI, was governed by Regulation 337/79, under which the aid would only be paid to the distillers in the first place if it was guaranteed by a 110 per cent security and in the event this meant that the Commission was able to reclaim all its money and, a fortiori, it had no further liability to DAI. The facts of the situation are less clear in *Masdar*, because it is not apparent from the report exactly how much the Commission had paid to Helmico and how much of this represented work done by Masdar. Nor does the report reveal whether the Commission's claim to recover €2 091 168.07 from Helmico was successful or not. If it was successful and if this sum was equal to the amount it had paid Helmico in the first place, then the situation would be the same as in *Cantina*; apparently the Commission would no longer be under any liability to Helmico regarding the €453 000 claimed by Masdar, and if the Commission were then to have received the work done by Masdar without paying this amount in exchange it could thus be regarded as being enriched at Masdar's expense. Indeed, in its communications with Masdar the Commission specifically stated that it might consider 'further steps with regard to the use of the money' if it succeeded in reclaiming the money from Helmico.[122] Conversely, if Helmico were to have a counterclaim against the Commission for €453 000, it would be Helmico that had been enriched at Masdar's expense, not the Commission. If the Commission had initially paid Helmico *more* than the €2 091 168.07 and was only trying to recover from Helmico what it had paid *less* the €453 000 still owing by Helmico to Masdar, or if the Commission's claim for recovery from Helmico was unsuccessful altogether, then there would be even stronger grounds for rejecting the claim.

This would equally help to explain the difference between the CFI's decisions in the two cases. It was noted in chapter five that it is no longer necessary for a change of position to occur after receipt of the enrichment in order for it to found a defence; anticipatory change of position will also qualify as long as it is causally linked to the expected receipt of the enrichment.[123] It is clear that in *Cantina* there was no such change of position; as already mentioned, once AIMA (the Italian intervention agency) realised that the distillers, DAI, had applied for bankruptcy, AIMA requested reimbursement of the money paid to DAI and when this was not

[120] Such as: *Lumbers* (n 102).

[121] See further: A Goymour (n 102) 471, citing P Birks, *Unjust Enrichment*, 2nd edn (Oxford, Oxford University Press, 2005) 87–93.

[122] *Masdar* (CFI) (n 95) [35].

[123] pp 146–47.

forthcoming it applied to Assedile for the security, which Assedile paid.[124] In *Masdar*, by contrast, if the Commission had already paid to Helmico the €453 000 claimed by Masdar and this did not form part of the €2 091 168.07 which the Commission sought to recover from Helmico, or if the Commission's recovery from Helmico was altogether unsuccessful, then it could be regarded as having changed its position in such a way as to give it a defence.

The conclusion must therefore be that recovery in such three-party situations is unlikely to occur in the near future, and that this conclusion is in keeping with the laws of the Member States and indeed other countries.[125] However, there are also other, more specific grounds on which such claims can either be upheld or rejected, and it would therefore be open to the courts in a future case to use these more specific grounds in preference to such a blanket rule, should they wish to continue to distinguish clearly between cases such as *Cantina* and *Masdar*.

Unjust Enrichment: *Only* a 'General Principle' of EU Law

The second important feature common to *Holcim*, *Cantina* and *Masdar* is that, as the CFI pointed out in *Cantina*:

> The Treaty makes no provision among the remedies it puts in place for bringing an action for unjust enrichment. That does not however determine the validity of the plea alleging infringement of the rule prohibiting unjust enrichment, since the [claims brought] can be interpreted as meaning that the applicants are relying in particular on this rule in support of their claim for compensation.

As the ECJ explains in *Masdar*:

> Given that unjust enrichment . . . is a source of non contractual obligation common to the legal systems of the Member States, the Community cannot be dispensed from the application to itself of the same principles where a natural or legal person alleges that the Community has been unjustly enriched to the detriment of that person[126]

and:

> The possibility of bringing an action for unjust enrichment against the Community cannot be denied to a person solely on the ground that the EC Treaty does not make express provision for a means of pursuing that type of action. If Article [268 TFEU ex Art 235 EC] and the second paragraph of Article [340 TFEU (ex Art 288 EC)] were to be construed as excluding that possibility, the result would be contrary to the principle of effective judicial protection.[127]

[124] *Cantina* (n 88) [32].

[125] *Masdar* (CFI) (n 95), *Masdar* (AG Mazák) (n 95) and n 102 and surrounding text.

[126] *Masdar* (ECJ) (n 99) [47].

[127] ibid [50]. The right to effective judicial protection, it held, was contained, inter alia, in Art 47 of the Charter of Fundamental Rights of the European Union.

This claim, of course, must be brought via the Article 340 (ex 288) TFEU action for *damages* which, like the '*Francovich*'[128] action against Member States for breach of EU law, requires the applicant to prove a sufficiently serious breach of a superior rule of law or principle for the protection of the individual.

The precise practical interaction between Article 340 and the principle of unjust enrichment was explained by AG Mengozzi in *Holcim*:[129]

> The prohibition of undue enrichment, which is a general principle of Community law that applies to the Community as well, does not come into play in these proceedings as a separate basis for the appellant's claim that the Commission should be ordered to reimburse the bank guarantee charges. That claim . . . is a claim for damages based on the non-contractual liability of the Community under the second paragraph of Article [340] EC. The general principle of the prohibition of undue enrichment comes into play in this case, on the other hand, as a yardstick for interpreting the condition concerning a causal link which is relevant for the purposes of establishing such liability.

But the problem is that:

> Actions for unjust enrichment do not fall under the rules governing non-contractual liability in the strict sense, which, to be invoked, require a number of conditions to be satisfied, relating to the unlawfulness of the conduct imputed to the Community . . . They differ from actions brought under those rules in that they do not require proof of unlawful conduct—indeed, of any form of conduct at all on the part of the defendant, but merely proof of enrichment on the part of the defendant for which there is no valid legal basis and of impoverishment on the part of the applicant which is linked to that enrichment.[130]

Thus unjust enrichment claims must be brought through an essentially wrongs-based vehicle as a result of the specific wording of Article 340, notwithstanding (a) that they do not fit that cause of action terribly well; (b) that Article 340 refers more generally to the 'non-contractual' liability of the EU; and (c) that the 'general principle prohibiting unjust enrichment' could itself have been a direct ground of action against the EU if the Treaty had so provided. As it is, these last two factors cannot be put together to allow an individual a direct cause of action in unjust or undue enrichment against the EU. Instead, the prohibition of unjust enrichment is taken as a superior law for the protection of the individual, breach of which can sound in damages and a finding of undue enrichment on the facts is to be taken as proof that the EU has caused such 'damage' as required by the wording of Article 340.

[128] Cases C-6/90 and C-9/90 *Francovich and Bonifaci v Italy* [1991] ECR I-05357.
[129] *Masdar* (CFI) (n 95).
[130] *Masdar* (2008) (n 99) [49].

Conclusion

It is clear, then, that if the public body involved in an unjust enrichment claim is not a domestic entity but one of the institutions of the EU, the CFI and ECJ do recognise a 'general principle prohibiting unjust enrichment'. However, it is also clear, first, that that principle has tended to lead to success much more often in cases where the EU is the claimant than it has in cases where the EU is the defendant.[131] Second, just as in the domestic laws of the Member States, triangular situations present far more problems than those concerning only two parties. Most significantly of all, there is no way of bringing an action based on unjust enrichment against the European Communities directly: it can only ever be used as a general principle, breach of which may give rise to wrong-based *damages* under Article 340. As a result, although the European Courts have recognised the general concept of unjust enrichment, detailed discussion of its internal structure of the kind found in *Masdar*[132] is rare. Much more often 'unjust enrichment' is simply a general idea of a kind easily merged with other doctrines like legitimate expectation, as happened even in *Masdar* itself. When set against the distinctions drawn between so-called '*San Giorgio*'[133] and '*Francovich*'[134] actions in cases involving both the EU and the Member States,[135] the absence of such a distinction when such actions are brought against the EU institutions appears particularly stark. It is therefore to those cases involving both the EU institutions and the Member States that we should now turn.

[131] Contrast, for example: the staff cases of *Meganck* (n 24) and *Kuhl* (n 28), with those of *Danvin* (n 36) and *Schina* (n 37). Note also the failure of the claims in: *AssiDomän Kraft Products* (CFI) (n 43); *Masdar* (CFI) (n 95); and *Cantina* (n 88).

[132] *Masdar* (CFI) (n 95).

[133] *San Giorgio* (n 6).

[134] *Francovich* (n 128).

[135] See further ch 8. The key case to which this statement refers is *FII* (n 11), see pp 102–10 and 259–64.

8

Unjust Enrichment in National and European Law, and the 'Remedies' Jurisprudence of the ECJ

AT THE BEGINNING of the last chapter, three factors were identified which connect the EU to claims of unjust enrichment involving public bodies. The third, with which that chapter was concerned, was that the public body involved in the claim may itself be an institution of the EU. The first two, however, concerned the interrelation of EU law and national law in questions of unjust enrichment involving public bodies. In some of the cases considered in parts one and two,[1] the 'ultra vires'[2] nature of the public body's action arose from the application of European rather than national law. In other words, the source of the nullity was the EC, not the Member State. When this is the case, the 'remedies'[3] which must be provided by the Member State legal systems are governed in part by EU law as well as by national law. It is these two matters which will be the subject of this chapter.

However, closely related to these two issues are some of the fundamental themes of the EU legal order and its Member States. As a result these issues have 'revealed the larger problem of the articulation of Community and national law'.[4] In that sense, for an EU lawyer as much as for an unjust enrichment lawyer, the interplay between Member State and EU law in unjust enrichment claims can provide an

[1] Such as, most obviously, *Deutsche Morgan Grenfell v IRC* [2003] EWHC 1779 (Ch), [2003] 4 All ER 645 (first instance); [2005] EWCA Civ 78, (2006) Ch 243 (CA); and [2006] UKHL 49, [2007] 1 AC 558 (HL), which followed the decision of the ECJ in Cases C-397/98 and C-410/98 *Metallgesellschaft and Hoechst v IRC* [2001] ECR I-1727, and the French cases *Café Jacques Vabre* Trib d'inst du 1re arondissement de Paris, 8 January 1971, Cour d'Appel de Paris 7 July 1973: *D* 1974.159; Cour de Cassation 24 May 1975; *D* 1975.497; and *Fils Henri Ramel*, decision of the Cour d'appel de Lyon of the 30 November 1978 (1re Ch Civ) *D* 1979.371, note C-J Berr.

[2] Obviously this is a term of art used in England, rather than the French legal system. However, as was noted in ch 1, above p 12, it is used here as an 'umbrella' shorthand for any situation in which a public body is acting in excess of the legal limits of its powers.

[3] For discussion of this term see further below, p 242 onwards.

[4] See: A Barav, 'La Repetition de l'indu dans la Jurisprudence de la Cour de Justice des Communautés Européennes' (1981) 17 *Cahiers de Droit Européen* 507, 509, citing J Mertens de Wilmars (then president of the ECJ), 'Conclusions of work on the theme of the different national techniques of judicial protection against violations of Community law by national authorities, their details and efficacy' *Report of the 9th Congress of the International Congress for European Law* (Fédération Internationale pour le de Droit Européen) (London, 1980) vol 3, 8.1 and 8.5.

important insight into the ECJ's so-called 'remedies jurisprudence'. Comprehensive accounts of the essential principles of EU law can of course be found elsewhere,[5] but it is worth briefly listing those that are particularly important in this context.

Historical Development of the Relevant European Union Law

The first point to be made is that, of the 'three pillar' structure of the EU prior to the entry into force of the Lisbon Treaty in December 2009,[6] it was the first of the three, the so-called 'Community pillar' which was relevant to the current investigation. As is well-known, following the failure of early attempts at political union, the origins of the current Union are economic,[7] and only after the Treaty on European Union (TEU) was the term 'Economic' dropped from the title of the European Community which formed this first pillar (this is a matter of particular importance given that the law of unjust enrichment is specifically concerned with transfers of value).[8] Indeed, in the political sphere, the transfer of power to the Union from the Member States, either substantively or structurally, has not always been smooth and on many occasions the resulting division of competence or responsibility between the Member States and the Union has required arbitration, and in this the role of the European Court of Justice (ECJ) has been vital in further developing EU law.[9] For example, it was against the background of the so-called

[5] For a more detailed and general introduction to EU law see: P Craig and G de Búrca, *EU Law: Text, Cases and Materials*, 4th edn (Oxford, Oxford University Press, 2008) chs 1–2 and A Arnull and others, *Wyatt and Dashwood's European Union Law*, 5th edn (London, Sweet and Maxwell, 2006) chs 1–2.

[6] It was the Treaty signed in Maastricht (and therefore as frequently known by that title as by its official title, the Treaty on European Union (TEU)) which established what is known as the 'three pillar' structure of the Communities. The 'first pillar' comprised the three Communities (the EEC becoming known as simply the EC); the 'second pillar' (Title V TEU) comprises Common Foreign and Security Policy (CFSP); and the 'third pillar' (Title VI TEU) Justice and Home Affairs. As Wyatt and Dashwood note, '[t]he difference between the 'First Pillar' . . . and the 'Second and Third Pillars' . . . [lay] in the much lesser degree to which, in respect of the latter, the sovereign powers of the Member States have been curtailed': ibid 15. See also at 16 and 172–87. This three pillar structure has now largely been removed by the Treaty on the Functioning of the EU signed in Lisbon.

[7] Although the EEC Treaty avoided issues of political integration following the failure of the European Defence Community and European Political Community, there were calls throughout the 1960s for further political integration. However, from 1958–69, the French Presidency was held by Charles de Gaulle, whose view of the Community was at odds with that of other Member States and the Commission under the Presidency of Walter Hallstein. This was because de Gaulle favoured an intergovernmental, rather than supranational model of European cooperation. See: Craig and de Búrca (n 5) 8 and Wyatt and Dashwood ibid 4–7.

[8] An interesting example of the connection between the economic philosophy of a constitution and its implications for rules of unjust enrichment can be seen in the case of *Mafatlal Industries v Union of India* (1997) 5 SCC 536, [44] and [84].

[9] Craig and de Búrca state that 'Joseph Weiler . . . explains how the impediments to the attainment of Community objectives through the political process led to the growing importance of what he terms normative supranationalism. This is the relationship between Community policies and measures on the one hand, and competing policies and legal measures of the Member States on the other. The

'Luxembourg sclerosis' on the political front[10] that the ECJ developed the concept of direct effect and supremacy of what was then EC law, according to which EU Treaty provisions and other forms of legislation (regulations, directives and decisions) can be directly relied upon in national courts by individuals,[11] whether or not they have been implemented by national legislation, and whether or not there is conflicting national law, [12] regardless of whether that national law pre- or post-dates the EU law in question. Craig and de Búrca refer to the ECJ's 'bold theory'[13] in this context, and Arnull speaks of its 'central role' and 'creative' or 'surprising'

doctrines of direct effect, the supremacy of Community law, and pre-emption were central in this respect. They allowed the ECJ to develop EC law, notwithstanding the difficulties of securing the passage of the required regulations and directives through the legislative process': Craig and de Búrca (n 5) 127–28, citing J Weiler, 'The Community System: The Dual Character of Supranationalism' (1981) 1 *Year Book of European Law* 267 and J Weiler, 'The Transformation of Europe' (1991) 100 *Yale Law Journal* 2403, 2412–31.

[10] In 1965, the latent tension between France and the other Member States 'erupted into a crisis' when the time came under the transitional provisions of the Treaty for the move towards qualified majority voting in the Council of Ministers, in place of the unanimous voting procedure with its obvious veto power for Member States: Craig and de Búrca (n 5) 8. De Gaulle objected to the 'federalist' proposal that the Community raise its own resources, and when no compromise with the Council could be reached, France adopted what became known as the 'empty chair policy', refusing to attend any further meetings. This lasted from June 1965 until January 1966, when the 'Luxembourg Compromise' was reached. This provided that '[w]here in the case of decisions which may be taken by a majority vote on a proposal from the Commission, very important interests of one or more partners are at stake' and the Council has not been able within a reasonable time to reach a solution acceptable to all Members 'there is a divergence of views on what should be done'. '[T]he French delegation considers that . . . the discussion must be continued until unanimous agreement is reached' but 'the six delegations nevertheless consider that this divergence does not prevent the Community's work being resumed in accordance with the normal procedure': *Bull* EC 3-1966, 9. This resulted in the 'very important interests' provision being treated as a veto, so that there was a 'return to intergovernmentalism' rather than qualified majority voting.

[11] On direct effect generally, see: A Arnull, *The European Union and its Court of Justice*, 2nd edn (Oxford, Oxford University Press, 2006) ch 7; Wyatt and Dashwood (n 4) 72-109; Craig and de Búrca (n 5) ch 8; P Pescatore, 'The Doctrine of "Direct Effect": An Infant Disease of Community Law?' (1983) 8 *European Law Review* 155; P Craig, 'Once upon a Time in the West: Direct Effect and the Federalization of EEC Law' (1992) 12 *Oxford Journal of Legal Studies* 453; and M Lenz, D Sif Tynes and L Young, 'Horizontal What? Back to Basics' (2000) 25 *European Law Review* 509, 510. The only exception is of course, infamously, that directives do not have horizontal direct effect, meaning that they cannot be relied upon by an individual directly to found an action against another individual. See also: Cases 152/84 *Marshall v Southampton AHA* [1986] ECR 723 and Case 91/92 *Faccini Dori v Recreb* [1994] ECR I-3325. However, even this rule can in some cases be evaded or worked around, see also: Craig and de Búrca (n 5) 284–300.

[12] As with international law generally, the Member States of the EU are bound in their legislative, executive and judicial activities to follow EU law, and are unable to plead provisions of their domestic law or constitutions as a defence. This is obviously necessary in order to ensure the full effectiveness and uniform application of EU law, which in turn is necessary for the functioning of the internal market. As the ECJ held 'the law stemming from the Treaty, an independent source of law, could not, because of its special and original nature, be overridden by domestic legal provisions, however framed, without being deprived of its character as Community law and without the legal basis of the Community itself being called into question' Case 6/64 *Costa (Flaminio) v ENEL* [1964] ECR 585, 593–94.

[13] Craig and de Búrca state: 'In a series of judgments . . . The Court developed a bold theory of the nature of EC law, attributing to it the characteristics and force which the Court considered necessary to promote a set of dynamic and far-reaching common goals within a group of distinct and sovereign States. This became clear in its early case law in which the Court outlined what has become known as the 'direct effect' of Community law.' See Craig and de Búrca, *EU Law, Text, Cases and Materials*, 3rd edn (Oxford, Oxford University Press, 2003) 179. In the 4th edition they refer again to the ECJ's 'bold step' (n 5) 269.

use of its powers,[14] and it is these principles which provide the first way in which EU law has an impact on cases involving unjust enrichment and public bodies in the Member States. The principles of direct effect and supremacy mean that EU law imposes an additional set of limits on the powers of any public body in a Member State, so that a tax, contract, payment or other transfer of value can be invalidated, not just by domestic law, but also by EU law.

Most of this process has taken place through the dialogue between national courts and the ECJ provided for by Article 267 TFEU (ex Art 234 EC). However, as well as providing for preliminary rulings on interpretation of EU law, which can then have an impact at national level on the relevant domestic rules, Article 267 also provides for rulings on the validity of acts of the institutions of the Union (the Council, Commission and European Parliament) and of the European Central Bank. Challenges to validity can also arise under Article 263 TFEU (ex 230 EC) EC, although the relationship between the two is tightly controlled.[15] In particular, there is an interesting parallel between the presumption of exclusivity in favour of Article 263 over Article 267 on the one hand, and on the other, the earlier presumption of exclusivity in *O'Reilly v Mackman*[16] in favour of the public law procedure rather than the private law procedure in English law (where challenges were made to the validity of administrative actions). This is particularly so given the comparable protections available under Article 263 and Ord 53; short time limits and narrower standing requirements. Nevertheless, it should be noted, as is apparent from the case of *ex p Accrington Beef*,[17] that the two 'presumptions' operate separately. Thus *ex p Accrington Beef* was brought through the national public law procedure, but allowed to proceed at European level outside the procedural protections of Article 263. It would, conversely, be possible for a national issue to contain a private law cause of action (as in a European version of the *British Steel*[18] case), which would take it outside the public law procedure. However, in dealing with the incidental question of validity of a European administrative action, the applicant could be denied the Article 267 challenge to validity on the basis that he/she/it ought to have brought an Article 265 action.

[14] A Arnull, *The European Union and its Court of Justice* (Oxford, Oxford University Press, 1999) ix.

[15] Through a series of cases the ECJ has produced the following rules: 1. National courts can, without making an Art 267 reference to the ECJ, reject as unfounded challenges to the validity of EU acts, but they do not have the power to declare them invalid: Case 314/85 *Foto-Frost (Firma) v Hauptzollamt Lübeck-Ost* [1987] ECR 4199. While only the ECJ can hear 267 actions, 263 actions start before the Court of First Instance (CFI). 2. It appears that where it is clear that the matter could have been raised by a person who had standing under Art 263 within the time limit for a direct action (two months from publication/notification), that person will not be permitted to bring a challenge in the national courts using Art 267: Case C-188/92 *TWD Textilwerke Deggendorf GmbH v Germany* [1994] ECR I-833 and Case C-178/95 *Wiljo NV v Belgian State* [1997] ECR I-585. However, where it is not clear whether the applicant would have had standing for an action under Art 263, the ECJ is likely to be more willing to admit the indirect action through Art 267: Case C-241/95 *R v Intervention Board for Agricultural Produce, ex p Accrington Beef Co Ltd* [1996] ECR I-6699.

[16] *O'Reilly v Mackman* [1983] 2 AC 237 (HL).

[17] *ex p Accrington Beef* (n 15).

[18] *British Steel plc v Customs and Excise Commissioners* [1996] 1 All ER 1002 (QB); [1997] 2 All ER 366 (CA), see above at pp 49–52.

The Member State/EU Divide: Remedies in National Courts for Breach of European Law

The Principles of National Procedural Autonomy, Equivalence and Effectiveness, and the Three Phases of the ECJ's Case Law

Once the concepts of direct effect and supremacy had been established, a related question arose. There was no point in EC law, as it then was, being supreme unless it was also to be uniform and effective across the Member States.[19]

But how should the rights thus established be protected? How should jurisdiction be divided between the national courts and the ECJ? Three distinct phases can be identified in the Court's approach to answering these questions,[20] and it is notable that such issues have often arisen in cases where charges have been imposed by Member States in breach of the Treaty, so that it is here that European law has had its second big impact on unjust enrichment cases involving public bodies in the Member States.

The First Phase

The first phase of the ECJ's jurisprudence is typified by *Rewe-Zentralfinanz GmbH v Landwirtschaftskammer für das Saarland*[21] and *Comet BV v Produktschap voor Siergewassen*,[22] both of which contained such issues. In *Rewe-Zentralfinanz*, a claim had been brought before the German courts for the repayment (with interest) of charges which had, in an earlier case before the ECJ, been held to have an effect equivalent to customs duties within the meaning of Article 13(2) EEC.[23] *Comet* concerned levies imposed in breach of Community law, which the applicant could no longer claim back under national law, the national time limit for doing so having expired. The applicant thus wanted instead to set these amounts off against other amounts it owed to the defendant. The ECJ in *Rewe-Zentralfinanz* held that

> in the absence of Community rules on this subject, it is for the domestic legal system of each Member State to designate the courts having jurisdiction and to determine the

[19] Prechal states: 'It is a fact which is now too well-established to call for further explanation that national courts must protect the rights which individuals derive from Community law and, more objectively, that they must secure the full application of Community law provisions' See: S Prechal, 'EC Requirements for an Effective Remedy' in J Lonbay and A Biondi (eds), *Remedies for Breach of EC Law* (Chichester, Wiley, 1997) 3.

[20] The phases are identified by Arnull (n 11) ch 9 and by Craig and de Búrca (n 5) ch 9. Again, the dialogue between national courts and the ECJ took place through Art 267 references and preliminary rulings.

[21] Case 33/76 *Rewe-Zentralfinanz GmbH v Landwirtschaftskammer für das Saarland* [1976] ECR 1989.

[22] Case 45/76 *Comet BV v Produktschap voor Siergewassen* [1976] ECR 2043.

[23] Now repealed.

> procedural conditions governing actions at law intended to ensure the protection of the rights which citizens have from the direct effect of Community law.[24]

It ruled in almost identical terms in *Comet.*[25] This principle of national procedural autonomy was applied in several cases to permit the continued operation of various national laws. For example, in *Hans Just I/S v Danish Ministry for Fiscal Affairs*,[26] it permitted the application of a Danish rule relating to the passing on of the expense as a defence to a claim for the return of money unlawfully levied.[27] In *Société Roquette Frères v Commission*,[28] and *Express Dairy Foods v Intervention Board for Agricultural Produce*,[29] the question of interest was, on this basis, left to be determined by the national rules. In *Rewe-Handelsgesellschaft Nord GmbH v Hauptzollamt Kiel*, the ECJ affirmed that the Treaty 'was not intended to create new remedies in the national courts to ensure the observance of Community law other than those already laid down by national law'.[30] However, as Arnull notes, the significance of this remark should not be exaggerated since the court was not being asked to create a new remedy in that case.[31] Crucially, the ECJ in *Rewe-Zentralfinanz* had imposed two important limitations on the principle of national procedural autonomy:

- The principle of equivalence: the procedural conditions laid down by national law 'cannot be less favourable than those relating to similar actions of a domestic nature.[32]
- The principle of effectiveness: procedural conditions laid down by national law must not make it 'impossible in practice to exercise the rights which the national courts are obliged to protect.[33]

It was through these limitations that the law later began to develop.

[24] *Rewe-Zentralfinanz* (n 21) [5].

[25] *Comet* (n 22) [13]: 'In the absence of any relevant Community rules, it is for the national legal order of each member state to designate the competent courts and to lay down the procedural rules for proceedings designed to ensure the protection of the rights which individuals acquire through the direct effect of Community law'.

[26] Case 68/79 *Hans Just I/S v Danish Ministry for Fiscal Affairs* [1980] ECR 501.

[27] For further detail of the passing on defence, see ch 5 above at pp 152–57, and see also below, pp 254–56.

[28] Case 26/74 *Société Roquette Frères v Commission* [1976] ECR 677.

[29] Case 130/79 *Express Dairy Foods v Intervention Board for Agricultural Produce* [1980] ECR 1887. Again, these cases will be discussed in more detail below.

[30] Case 158/80 *Rewe-Handelsgesellschaft Nord GmbH v Hauptzollamt Kiel* [1981] ECR 1805, [44].

[31] Arnull (n 11) 273 states that instead it was being asked 'simply whether a remedy available under national law had to be provided to a claimant seeking to rely on Community law . . . [The Court held that it did have to be provided.] Moreover the judgment . . . [has] to be read in the light of the *Simmenthal* case [Case 106/77 [1978] ECR 629], decided less than four years previously. The effect of that case was that national courts could not be required to wait for a ruling from a higher court before they refused to apply a provision of national law which was incompatible with Community law. The result was that those who considered their rights under Community law to have been breached had a right of action in the ordinary courts which they would not have enjoyed had their claim been based exclusively on domestic law'.

[32] *Rewe-Zentralfinanz* (n 21) [5].

[33] ibid.

The Second Phase

The second phase of the ECJ's case law in this context was also heralded by another issue concerning the levy of illegal charges, this time health inspection charges, on the importation (by San Giorgio)[34] into Italy of dairy products from other Member States. Again, the question related to passing on, and in particular whether a particular charge could be *presumed* to have been passed on, in the absence of written evidence to the contrary, when the goods to which it related were transferred. The answer was no, the ECJ emphasising that 'any requirement of proof which has the effect of making it virtually impossible or excessively difficult to secure the repayment of charges levied contrary to Community law would be incompatible with Community law'.[35] The shift in the principle of effectiveness from 'not impossible in practice' to 'not *virtually impossible or excessively difficult*' (emphasis added) shows the increased judicial interventionism exercised by the ECJ in this second phase.

The approach taken by the Court in this phase also led to the development, in *Francovich and Bonifaci v Italy*[36] of the principle of state liability in damages for breach of EC law, the breach in question in that case being the failure to implement a directive. The relevant conditions, held the Court, were that the directive in question must have envisaged the grant of rights to individuals; that the provisions of the directive made it possible to identify the contents of those rights; and that there be a causal link between the state's failure and the loss suffered by the claimant.[37]

The Third Phase

However, subsequently the ECJ returned to a more conservative approach, promoting once more the principle of national procedural autonomy. Again, this phase contains a case on allegedly invalid taxes, *Fantask A/S v Industriministeriet*,[38] in which several companies sought to rely on an indirect taxes directive in order to reclaim certain taxes levied by the Danish authorities. One of the questions sent by the national court to the ECJ under Article 267 TFEU (ex 234 EC) was whether the time limit for reclaiming could begin to run before the Directive had been properly implemented. In reply, AG Jacobs distinguished the earlier complex case law on the matter,[39] holding that it could. This increased judicial restraint in the appreciation of national procedural rules was accompanied by a narrow approach to the further definition of the conditions in which state liability in damages arises.

[34] Case 199/82 *Amministrazione delle Finanze dello Stato v San Giorgio* [1983] ECR 3595.

[35] ibid [14].

[36] Cases C-6/90 and C-9/90 *Francovich and Bonifaci v Italy* [1991] ECR I-5357.

[37] ibid [38].

[38] Case C-188/95 *Fantask A/S v Industriministeriet* [1997] ECR I-6783. Two other important phase three cases also concern unjust enrichment issues: Cases C-397/98 and C-410/98 *Metallgesellschaft and Hoechst v IRC* [2001] ECR I-1727 and Case C-453/99 *Courage Ltd v Crehan* [2001] ECR I-6297. These will be considered in detail below.

[39] Case C-208/90 *Emmott v Minister for Social Welfare and AG* [1991] ECR I-4269.

Thus *Francovich* was succeeded by the well-known joined cases of *Brasserie du Pêcheur SA v Germany* and *R v Secretary of State for Transport, ex p Factortame Ltd* (*Factortame III*),[40] which established that liability would only exist for a 'sufficiently serious breach' which would arise when the Member State had 'manifestly and gravely disregarded' the limits on its discretion.[41]

However, it should be noted that phase three, which currently informs the decisions made by the ECJ, is not therefore a return to phase one, but rather a midpoint between phases one and two. In phase three, some of the developments towards increased effectiveness have been retained, but these requirements are now balanced more subtly against the justifications for the national procedural rules.[42] As before, cases on sums paid but not due have been central to these developments. For example, it is possible to introduce time limits which reduce the period within which repayment of sums collected illegally may be sought, as long as this period complies with various requirements. In *Marks and Spencer v Commissioners of Customs and Excise*,[43] M&S had overpaid VAT on gift vouchers since 1992 and when this was revealed to be the case by the decision in *Argos Distributors v Commissioners of Customs and Excise* on 24 October 1996,[44] M&S submitted a claim six days later. However, the Finance Act 1997 retrospectively 'capped' the recovery open to M&S, restricting repayment of VAT to three years before the making of the claim (that is from 1993 onwards only). The ECJ held that:

> Whilst national legislation reducing the period within which repayment of sums collected in breach of Community law may be sought is not incompatible with the principle of effectiveness, it is subject to the condition not only that the new limitation period is reasonable but also that the new legislation includes transitional arrangements allowing an adequate period after the enactment of the legislation for lodging the claims for repayment which persons were entitled to submit under the original legislation. Such transitional arrangements are necessary where the immediate application to those claims of a limitation period shorter than that which was previously in force would have the effect

[40] Cases C-46/93 and C-48/93 *Brasserie du Pêcheur SA v Germany and R v Secretary of State for Transport, ex p Factortame Ltd* [1996] ECR I-1029.

[41] The factors which would indicate that such a breach had taken place (listed ibid [56]–[57]) included: the clarity and precision of the rule breached; the measure of discretion left to the Member State; whether the infringement was intentional or involuntary; whether the error of law was excusable or inexcusable; whether or not the position adopted by a Community institution may have contributed to the breach; and whether there had been an adoption or a retention of national measures or practices contrary to EC law. On any view, a breach of EU law will be sufficiently serious if it has persisted despite a finding that the infringement is established, or it is clear from a preliminary ruling or settled case law. It is for the national courts to apply these criteria, see: *R v Secretary of State for Transport, ex p Factortame Ltd* [2000] 1 AC 524 (HL) (*Factortame V*).

[42] This third phase of the Court's jurisprudence has not been universally welcomed in its own terms, but this is beyond the scope of the current investigations. See eg: M Hoskins, 'Tilting the Balance: Supremacy and National Procedural Rules' (1996) 21 *European Law Review* 365.

[43] See: Case C-62/00 *Marks and Spencer v Commissioners of Customs and Excise* [2002] ECR I-6325 and M Chowdry, 'How long can section 80 last?' [2004] *British Tax Review* 106. For the final national chapter in the case, see: [2009] UKHL 8, [2009] 1 All ER 939.

[44] Case C-288/94 *Argos Distributors v Commissioners of Customs and Excise* [1996] ECR I-5311.

> of retroactively depriving some individuals of their right to repayment, or of allowing them too short a period for asserting that right.[45]

On the other hand, retroactivity is not absolutely fatal to the provisions as long as there are sufficient transitional periods.[46] In addition, the time limit must be reasonable and must not be specifically targeted at the effects of a particular decision of the ECJ.[47]

In coming to their conclusion in *Marks and Spencer*, the ECJ specifically recognised

> the argument of the United Kingdom Government to the effect that the enactment of the legislation at issue in the main proceedings was motivated by the legitimate purpose of striking a due balance between the individual and the collective interest and of enabling the State to plan income and expenditure without the disruption caused by major unforeseen liabilities.[48]

It then held that these arguments could justify reasonable limitation periods as long as they also ensured that rights conferred on individuals by Community law were safeguarded.

As was noted in chapter five, the Court will also examine the date from which the time begins to run in order to ensure that this too complies with the requirement of effectiveness. Accordingly, in *Preston v Wolverhampton Healthcare NHS Trust*,[49] the ECJ held that where the claimants were employed under temporary contracts, a time limit which ran for six months from the end of each contract rather than from the point at which that series of contracts (and thus the ongoing stable employment relationship) was interrupted, rendered the exercise of the Treaty right excessively difficult and was therefore precluded by EC law. Similarly, in *Manfredi v Lloyd Adriatico Assicurazioni SpA*,[50] the Court held that time could not begin to run from the date on which an anticompetitive agreement was concluded because that would mean the limitation period could expire before the infringement of competition law was brought to an end. This in turn could result in a situation whereby an individual could potentially suffer harm *after* the limitation period for challenging the source of that harm (namely the anticompetitive agreement) had already expired. However, in *Recheio-Cash and Carry SA v*

[45] *Marks and Spencer* (n 43) [38].

[46] In Case C-255/00 *Grundig Italiana SpA v Ministero delle Finanze* [2002] ECR I-8003, the ECJ held that retroactive time limits are possible as long as there is an adequate transitional period. For the UK application of these rules, see: *Fleming (trading as Bodycraft) and Condé Nast Publications Ltd v Revenue and Customs Commissioners* [2008] UKHL 2, [2008] 1 WLR 195.

[47] Case 309/85 *Barra v Belgium* [1988] ECR 355 and Case C-343/96 *Dilexport Srl v Amministrazione delle Finanze dello Statto* [1999] ECR I-579. See also *Marks and Spencer* (n 43) [36]: '[N]ational legislation curtailing the period within which recovery may be sought of sums charged in breach of Community law . . . must not be intended specifically to limit the consequences of a judgment of the Court to the effect that national legislation concerning a specific tax is incompatible with Community law'.

[48] *Marks and Spencer* (n 43) [41].

[49] Case C-78/98 *Preston v Wolverhampton Healthcare NHS Trust* [2000] ECR I-3201.

[50] Case C-295–298/04 *Manfredi v Lloyd Adriatico Assicurazioni SpA* [2006] ECR I-6619.

Fazenda Publica/Registo Nacional de Pessoas Colectivas,[51] the limitation period was permitted to run 'from the end of the period allowed for voluntary payment of the charges', and in *Edis v Ministero delle Finanze*,[52] the permissible period ran from the date of payment itself.

This balancing technique has also been applied to the requirement of equivalence which, having originally taken a back seat during the development of the principle of effectiveness, has now been developed more fully. In *Edis*,[53] another case concerning the reclaiming of money paid but not due, the ECJ held that as long as the same rule was applied to recovery of charges in breach of EC law as was applied to charges in breach of national law, the applicable national rule did not have to be the most generous rule available in any circumstance in national law. It was therefore perfectly acceptable for the Member States in both *Edis*,[54] and *Ministero delle Finanze v Spac*,[55] to lay down shorter limitation periods for cases involving public bodies than would be applicable to private claims, as long as those limits applied to all public claims and not just those involving EC law. This is not the only area in which EU law has recognised a distinction between public and private law at European level. For example, the Court has developed case law on the definition of the state both for the purposes of distinguishing horizontal from vertical direct effect (such as *Marshall v Southampton and South-West AHA*,[56] *Costanzo (Fratelli) SpA v Commune di Milano*[57] and *Foster (A) v British Gas plc*[58]) and for the purpose of establishing state liability in damages.[59]

All these principles, then, provide the basic constitutional structure for the development of EU law and its relationship with the legal systems of its constituent Member States. Indeed, it is these principles with which rules such as those contained in the Finance Act 2007 and Article L190 of the French book of fiscal procedures must be compatible.

[51] Case C-30/02 *Recheio-Cash and Carry SA v Fazenda Publica/Registo Nacional de Pessoas Colectivas* [2004] ECR I-6051.

[52] Case C-231/96 *Edis v Ministero delle Finanze* [1998] ECR I-4951. See also below at p 269.

[53] ibid.

[54] ibid.

[55] Case C-260/96 *Ministero delle Finanze v Spac* [1998] ECR I-4997.

[56] Case 152/84 *Marshall v Southampton and South-West AHA* [1986] ECR 723.

[57] Case 103/88 *Costanzo (Fratelli) SpA v Commune di Milano* [1989] ECR 1839.

[58] Case C-188/89 *Foster (A) v British Gas plc* [1990] ECR I-3313.

[59] *Francovich* (n 36).

Unjust Enrichment and Ultra Vires in National and EU Law; Two Different Models for Analysing the Division of Labour between the Member States and the EU

One of the problems with this process of dividing labour between the national and EU systems is that it is usually referred to as the ECJ's 'remedies jurisprudence', and yet the principle of leaving most of the responsibility for those 'remedies' to the Member States is often referred to as 'national *procedural* autonomy'. This lack of clarity in the terminology used is unhelpful,[60] and various academics or practitioners have studied the area in an attempt to analyse the division of labour in more precise terms.[61] One example of this is the work of van Gerven, who interestingly also chose to use a mapping process.[62] His aim was to try to resolve the tension between the ECJ and the national courts over the division of labour between them in enforcing European law.

The key to van Gerven's work, as his title indicates, is a distinction between 'rights', 'remedies' and 'procedures'. Rights to him are legal positions that a legal person may have, and which can be enforced by that person against some or all others before a court. This can be done by means of one or more remedies, which are classes of action intended to make good infringements of the rights concerned, in accordance with procedures which govern the exercise of such classes of action and are intended to make the remedy concerned operational. The concept of remedy then further subdivides into constituent and executive elements.[63] 'Rights' and 'constituent elements' of the remedies, he argues, are for decision by the ECJ. On the other hand, 'executive elements' of the remedy are for the Member States.[64]

van Gerven's own use of the word 'remedy' is interesting. In examining public law, it was seen that the division between public and private law has focused on the

[60] See also: C Kilpatrick, 'The Future of Remedies in Europe' in C Kilpatrick, T Novitz and P Skidmore (eds), *The Future of Remedies in Europe* (Oxford, Hart Publishing, 2000) 1 and 4.

[61] See, eg: C Kakouris, 'Do the Member States possess judicial procedural "*autonomy*"' (1997) 34 *Common Market Law Review* 1389 and S Prechal, 'Community law in national courts: The lessons from *Van Schijndel*' (1998) 35 *Common Market Law Review* 681.

[62] W van Gerven, 'Of Rights, Remedies and Procedures' (2000) 37 *Common Market Law Review* 501.

[63] Constituent elements, because of the principle of access to a court found in national constitutional rules or traditions and in Arts 6 and 13 ECHR are equal to the substantive underlying right: van Gerven, ibid 524–25. Executive elements include: the rules for determining who has standing against whom; the form and extent of the remedy, for example, available heads of damage; the standard of proof and permissible forms of evidence; and time limits.

[64] This is because the former must have a uniform content throughout the EU, thus so must the constituent elements of the remedy. On the constituent elements of the remedy, for van Gerven, the distinction between minimum effectiveness and adequacy is not only chronological (like the jurisprudence of the ECJ outlined in three phases above), but rather is a distinction between two different elements of the judicial process at any given time. That is, for procedural rules *stricto sensu* minimum effectiveness and equivalence is sufficient, but for the other executive conditions of the remedy adequacy must be guaranteed: ibid.

availability of public law 'remedies',[65] and in that context it was argued that at least some of the public law 'remedies' could be seen as 'responses' to ultra vires 'events' (for example, a quashing order for a biased decision). Here again, the word 'remedy' is at the heart of a legal division, but it is already clear that this time van Gerven does not just use the word 'remedy' as a synonym for 'response'.

Birks has argued that there are five different meanings of the word 'remedy'.[66] It is submitted that it is his first definition that best captures van Gerven's meaning: an 'actionable story' typified by the old English forms of action. It was Birks' argument that for many years the use of such forms of action obscured the true nature of unjust enrichment actions, and prevented the development of a clear event/response taxonomy. It is interesting, then, to see that the far newer and therefore less developed system of EU law should be, as van Gerven's work perhaps shows, at this same level of development, using the word remedy in sense one, as a general 'actionable story', rather than containing a more sophisticated division.

It is also apparent that van Gerven's and Birks' *concepts* of the word 'right' seem to align with each other,[67] but it is not so easy to establish the particular substantive rights to which van Gerven is referring in his article. It is arguable that there are in fact two separate categories of right at issue here, and as a result, two possible models for the precise division of labour between the national courts and the ECJ.

The EU[68] has gradually extended its jurisdiction over various matters, and has passed legislation of various sorts in addition to the treaties themselves, all with the purpose of changing the behaviour of the Member States and private entities and individuals in those states in various ways.[69] Also, as noted above, the supremacy of EU law means that where national law conflicts with the relevant EU law, the latter will prevail, and must be upheld by the national courts. As the ECJ held in *van Gend en Loos (NV Algemene Transporten Expeditie Onderneming) v Netherlands Inland Revenue Administration* 'the Community constitutes a new legal order of international law for the benefit of which the states have limited their sovereign rights, albeit within limited fields'.[70] The existence of those European limits thus renders unlawful any actions of the Member States which go beyond

[65] See ch 1 at p 11.

[66] P Birks, 'Rights, Wrongs and Remedies' (2000) 20 *Oxford Journal of Legal Studies* 1. Not only is his title strikingly similar to van Gerven's (n 62), the fact that they have independently undertaken work on such similar issues makes it possible to link their conclusions.

[67] Birks refers to rights as 'the conceptualisation of a legal response to events': ibid 5. van Gerven defines a right as 'a legal position which a person recognised as such by the law—thus a legal "subject" (hence the name "subjective" right)—may have and which in its normal state can be enforced by that person against (some or all) others before a court of law' (n 62) 502.

[68] This is true of the EU more generally, but it is what has previously been contained within the first EC pillar with which we are concerned here.

[69] As noted above, the fact that much of this legislation is passed to pursue economic goals, and to alter Member States', individuals' and undertakings' behaviour in an economic sense is particularly relevant to the context of unjust enrichment which deals specifically with wrongful shifts of wealth.

[70] Case 26/62 *van Gend en Loos (NV Algemene Transporten Expeditie Onderneming) v Netherlands Inland Revenue Administration* [1963] ECR 1, 12.

them, for example by creating an impediment to the four freedoms.[71] Conversely, in *Francovich* the ECJ held that

> the EEC Treaty has created its own legal system which is integrated into the legal systems of the Member States and which their courts are bound to apply. The subjects of that legal system are not only the Member States but also their nationals. Just as it imposes burdens on individuals, Community law is also intended to give rise to rights which become part of their legal patrimony.[72]

Thus the finding of EU law unlawfulness, as seen above, gives the individual concerned the 'right' to an effective/adequate 'remedy' which is equivalent to the national 'remedy' applicable in the same circumstances. If 'remedy' in this context does indeed mean 'an actionable story', then the EU law right of *adequacy/effectiveness* is the right to such an actionable story at national level, or as we would now understand it, the right to recognition that a particular event has occurred which in turn gives the claimant a right to certain responses.

It can thus be seen that there are two types of right being discussed here, the right to an actionable story of whatever kind, and the right within that actionable story which connects a particular legal event (to use the Birksian terminology) to a particular response. It is not clear to which of these two meanings van Gerven is referring when he says that definition of the 'right' requires a uniform content across the Member States, so that it should take place at the European level.

On the one hand, he could simply be referring to the EU 'rights' to the conceptualisation of an unlawfulness, leaving the whole of the remedy, in the sense of 'actionable story' to the jurisdiction of the Member States subject to the requirements of equivalence and effectiveness. Under this model, the fact that the 'substantive conditions underlying the right' and the 'constituent element of the remedy' are equal is simply a statement that the unlawfulness must be recognised by both the ECJ and the national court; a restatement of the supremacy of EU law. Under this model, the EU is only a general source of unlawfulness and as long as the Member State recognises that unlawfulness and gives some cause of action based on it, the Member State's EU obligations will be satisfied.

On the other hand, it is possible that the jurisprudence of the ECJ has developed beyond this, and that van Gerven could be referring to the second kind of right, namely the right to the law's conceptualisation of certain events entailing certain responses. On this basis, in terms of van Gerven's division of jurisdiction, definition of the *event* would require a uniform content across the Member States, so it should take place at the European level. If this were the case, then the second element of van Gerven's 'remedy', namely'executive conditions'[73]—would be the 'response', and it would be *this* which should, in van Gerven's words, be 'assessed

[71] Free movement of goods, workers, establishment/services and capital, see: Craig and de Búrca (n 5) 605.

[72] *Francovich* (n 36) [30]. It should be noted that the term appears in both the French and the English translations of the case.

[73] van Gerven (n 62) 525.

for consistency within the framework of adequacy', through a proportionality-style balancing test as in *van Schijndel and van Veen v Stichting Pensioenfonds voor Fysiotherapeuten*[74] and *Peterbroeck v Belgian State*,[75] while remaining within the jurisdiction of national courts. If this were the case, then the event/response division would fit with the EU/Member State substantive division of jurisdiction, with the EU providing a uniform definition of the event to which the Member States would be free to respond in their own way, subject to the requirements of equivalence and effectiveness.[76]

The distinction between these two models is not unlike the distinction between the two options identified in chapters two and six as justifications for recovery in a case such as *Woolwich Equitable Building Society v IRC*,[77] where it was pointed out that while English courts have regarded restitution following an ultra vires charge as being based on the private law principle of unjust enrichment, the courts of Canada have regarded it as a purely public law 'remedy' for the ultra vires nature of the charge itself, rather than a freestanding cause of action in itself.[78] The French courts have followed each of the two approaches, depending on the particular context.[79] The difference is, of course, that here the distinction is simply between the right to an actionable story in general (Model 1) and the right to a particular actionable story (Model 2, whether that specific story is in public or private law), whereas in chapters two and six the distinction was between an actionable story wholly in public law and an actionable story wholly in private law. Nevertheless, to the extent that the Canadian approach and the Model 1 approach described here do share a tendency to regard any restitutionary actions as part of a simple 'mopping up process', it is not impossible that conclusions drawn here about the stability of the Model 1 approach could potentially have implications for the Canadian approach.

Obviously, in the EU law context, it is important to determine which of these two models is operating in a particular area, because the more an area is governed by the reasoning of Model 2, the greater the influence of EU law on that area, even at the domestic level, and the greater the chance that the rules affecting the availability of the cause of action and its defences will derive, not from national law, but from EU law. Also, as is evident from the reasoning of Lord Goff in *Woolwich* noted

[74] Cases C-430–431/93 *van Schijndel and van Veen v Stichting Pensioenfonds voor Fysiotherapeuten* [1995] ECR I-4705.

[75] Case C-312/93 *Peterbroeck v Belgian State* [1995] ECR I-4599.

[76] This distinction between the first and second models should not be confused with the phases of development of EC law on remedies discussed above. In some ways, those phases can be seen as being divided by depth, or intensity of intervention by the Community. It may well be that model two does in practice entail more intense intervention by the EU, but this results from a more significant distinction based on subject matter. Indeed, it is the scope or content of the two models that is used to distinguish between them rather than their depth or intensity.

[77] *Woolwich Equitable Building Society v IRC* [1993] AC 70 (HL).

[78] See above pp 27–35.

[79] The French courts have, perhaps unsurprisingly, continued this relatively even split with some instances of recovery being based on 'nullity' while others are based on one of the unjust enrichment-related causes of action. See above pp 181–90.

at the beginning of chapter seven,[80] whatever the impact of EU law turns out to be, it is unlikely to be confined solely to cases raising an EU law element, but rather it has the potential to extend even into purely domestic situations, by analogy.

It is clear that in general there is evidence of both models operating at the European level. In the course of his investigation, van Gerven examines various different areas of EU law, and in the first of these, 'setting aside national measures', it is plain that only the first of the two alternative models is operating. EU law merely establishes an 'unlawfulness' that national law must supplement with its own 'actionable story' including both event and response. The claimant has a right to this actionable story, but the particular event contained in that story is to be defined by national, not EU law. Conversely, in cases involving 'compensation', the event is a wrong, and it seems reasonable to suggest that the elements decided by EU law[81] all relate to this wrong event, while the 'content and extent of the remedy', re-analysed as the 'response', of reparation is left to the national jurisdiction. This set of cases is thus the opposite of 'setting aside national measures' and they cannot be interpreted simply as 'illegalities' which trigger the national events. Of the two models, only Model 2 (EU event) can thus be operating in relation to claims for compensation. In a sense, this is not surprising, since it was noted at the end of chapter seven that in actions brought against the institutions of the EU there is a similar conception of an event of wrongdoing, and indeed the ECJ now deals with both sets of wrongs as sharing a single line of jurisprudence.[82]

Cases of unjust enrichment,[83] however, have generally tended to follow Model 1, and again, this may well be regarded as unsurprising given that in actions against the EU institutions, 'unjust enrichment' is a general principle only, not a freestanding cause of action like that relating to wrongs.[84] The Advocates General, on the other hand, tend more often to follow Model 2 reasoning, and more recently there has even been some evidence of this route being taken by the ECJ. Cases involving unjust enrichment generally divide into four types:

[80] pp 207–208

[81] Namely the nature of the breach (here 'sufficiently serious'); the type of rule breached (here one conferring rights on individuals); causality (direct causal link); and injury.

[82] See, eg: In *Brasserie du Pêcheur* (n 40), the ECJ derived its rules for state liability for breach of EC law from the rules it was already used to applying under Art 340 TFEU (ex Art 288 EC). Conversely in Case C-352/98P *Laboratoires Pharmaceutiques Bergaderm SA and Jean-Jacques Goupil v Commission* [2000] ECR I-5291, [41], the court completed the circle by referring to its rules for state liability in damages in dealing with an action under Art 340 TFEU.

[83] As was explained in ch 1 above, unjust enrichment claims are those in which there has been a transfer of value which is not a wrong. In the law of England, for a claimant to recover, he, she or it must demonstrate: that the defendant was enriched; that this was at the claimant's expense; that there are no defences to the claim; and that the enrichment was unjust (in the sense that there is some reason why restitution should be given, such as that the payment was made in error or under duress). In civilian systems, the approach is the opposite and the claimant must simply show that the payment was without a cause or basis, though this will, as discussed in ch 6, frequently lead to the same kind of arguments, because an intention to give would constitute a cause, but could in turn be vitiated if it was formed as the result of a mistake.

[84] See above pp 229–30.

1 Cases where a Member State levies money on behalf of the state but in contravention of EU law;
2 Cases where a national intervention agency (NIA) levies money on behalf of the EU, but this turns out to be contrary to EU law;
3 Cases where a Member State pays out money to private parties in breach of EU law (a) as an invalid state aid or (b) via an NIA; and
4 Cases where the EU pays out money to an individual in breach of EU law.

Though there are also cases which do not fall perfectly into this pattern, for example because EU money is granted on the basis of certain conditions and the grant is rendered invalid when those conditions are not fulfilled.[85] In practical terms (perhaps unsurprisingly)[86] as will be seen in what follows, the ECJ has demonstrated itself to be strictest in Cases 1 and 3(a). Indeed, cases in category 1 are the most frequent,[87] and have arisen since the days of the European Coal and Steel Community Treaty.[88] However, in conceptual terms there is a potential difference between Cases 1 and 2 on the one hand, and Cases 3 and 4 on the other, as a result of the way in which such cases tend to be reasoned.

Two important factors against Model 2

First, however, it is important to note that there are two key factors which operate against the introduction of Model 2 reasoning in this area. The first of these factors is that it is often the case that the right to recover, or the right even to an 'actionable story' at Member State level, comes not from jurisprudence at all, but from a directly effective piece of European legislation. Thus in the case of state aids, when these are found by the Commission to be invalid under the terms of Article 107 TFEU (ex Art 87 EC), Regulation 659/99 EC[89] lays down the conditions for their recovery. If the Member State fails to terminate or recover the aid, the Commission can bring Article 108(2) TFEU (ex Art 88(2) EC) infraction proceedings against it, and the Member States' only defence in such circumstances

[85] See, eg: Case C-336/00 *Republic of Austria v Hüber* [2002] ECR I-7699, discussed below at p 267. The opinion of AG Geelhoed in Case C-230/01 *Intervention Board for Agricultural Produce v Penycoed Farming Partnership* [2004] ECR I-937 also falls into this miscellany, but it will be argued below that this is not in fact an instance of unjust enrichment in the strict sense at all.

[86] In relation to the US, Holmes wrote: 'I do not think the United States would come to an end if we lost our power to declare an Act of Congress void. I do think the Union would be imperilled if we could not make that declaration as to the laws of the several States' O Holmes, *Collected Legal Papers* (London, Constable, 1920) 295–96. It is not impossible that similar reasoning drives the ECJ to be stricter with the Member States than with its own agencies, especially since we are not here discussing damages for breach of EU law in which differing levels of discretion on the part of the Member States, as opposed to the EU agencies, can offer an alternative explanation for differing levels of strictness between the two contexts.

[87] Barav states 'dans le cas le plus fréquent, il était question des actions en remboursement des sommes perçues par les autorités étatiques en vertu d'une mesure nationale incompatible avec le traité': Barav (n 4) 509.

[88] See, eg: Case 6/60 *Humblet v Belgium* [1960] ECR 559.

[89] 23 March 1999, OJ L 83/1. See further Commission Regulation (EC) No 794/2004 of 21 April 2004 OJ L 140, 30/04/2004 p 1.

is that the Commission's decision was unclear or unambiguous,[90] or that recovery is absolutely impossible.[91] It is therefore clear that at the European level, the recovery of the aid is *separate* from the decision finding the aid to be unlawful: it does not arise immediately upon such a finding. For example, in *Belgium v Commission (Tubemeuse)*, AG Tesauro noted that:

> It is true that the Commission normally notifies recovery of aid unlawfully granted in the same Decision which rules on compatibility. However, those two aspects of the question are independent of each other, to such an extent that, as the Court has observed, recovery *ab initio* of aid may be requested even if the aid is, at the same time, declared compatible, but only with effect from the future . . . The order to recover the aid is not an automatic consequence of unlawful implementation. It is the Commission which decides whether it should or should not adopt such an order on the basis of assessments in regard to which it has a wide discretion.[92]

The national court's obligation to recover the aid thus comes from the separate exercise by the Commission of its discretion under Article 108(2), and there is no unjust enrichment event at the European level, only a legislative requirement that the Member States provide their own 'actionable story' to recover the money. Similarly, in the case of levies by National Intervention Agencies, some levies on behalf of the EU but in contravention of EU law are covered by secondary legislation granting a right to reimbursement. Thus, for example, in the case of *FMC v Intervention Board for Agricultural Produce*,[93] Regulation No 1922/92 (amending Article 4 of Regulation No 1633/84) set out the applicable rules for calculating the amounts which operators who could rely on the invalidity could claim by way of reimbursement. Another example is Regulation No 450/2008 of the European Parliament and of the Council of 23 April 2008 which laid down the Community Customs Code (Modernised Customs Code).[94] Here again, while the Member States may translate the relevant requirements into unjust enrichment actions, the European rules are legislative and require no more than that some kind of 'actionable story' is provided at national level.

The second important reason why it is difficult to find examples of Model 2 reasoning in relation to unjust enrichment is that when given the direct choice, the ECJ has tended to opt specifically for Model 1. *Metallgesellschaft and Hoechst v IRC*[95] is of course well known to English lawyers as the starting point for the *Deutsche Morgan Grenfell* case discussed above in part one.[96] To reiterate the

[90] Case 70/72 *Commission v Germany (Kohlgesetz)* [1973] ECR 813.

[91] Case 52/84 *Commission v Belgium* [1986] ECR 89. This condition is extremely difficult to satisfy, see also: Case C-415/03 *Commission v Greece* [2005] ECR I-3875.

[92] Case C-142/87 *Belgium v Commission (Tubemeuse)* [1990] ECR I-959 [16].

[93] Case 212/94 *FMC v Intervention Board for Agricultural Produce* [1996] ECR 1-389.

[94] OJ 2008 L145/1.

[95] *Metallgesellschaft and Hoechst* (n 1).

[96] *Deutsche Morgan Grenfell* (first instance) (n 1). See above at p 75 onwards. See also: *Sempra Metals Ltd (formerly Metallgesellschaft Ltd) v IRC* [2004] EWHC 2387 (Ch), [2004] STC 1178. In that case, Park J held that compound interest would be available where the payment of interest was required by EC law: *Pirelli Cable Holding NV v IRC* [2003] EWCA Civ 1849, [2004] STC 130 and *Boake Allen NEC Semiconductors Ltd v IRC* [2003] EWHC 2813 (Ch), [2004] STC 489.

facts,[97] *Metallgesellschaft and Hoechst* concerned two separate cases involving companies resident in England whose parent companies had their seats in Germany. Companies whose parent is resident in England as well as companies whose parent is not, had to pay Advance Corporation Tax (ACT)[98] and Mainstream Corporation Tax (MCT).[99] The ACT was payable first, but could then be set off against the MCT paid later. Under the relevant legislation, two companies resident in the UK, one of which held at least 51% of the other, could make a group income election (GIE). The result of such an election was that the subsidiary could choose not to pay ACT on dividends which it paid to its parent company. Obviously, since the applicant companies in this case did not have parent companies resident in the UK, it was not possible for them to make a GIE, and thus ACT was payable on all the distributions made by them to their parent companies. This meant that, although this ACT was later offset against MCT, in the meantime they did not have use of the funds used to pay the ACT. Subsidiaries whose parent companies were also resident in the UK would have been able to retain the money in comparable circumstances by making a GIE. Metallgesellschaft and Hoechst (M&H) instituted proceedings before the High Court against the IRC, in which they sought a ruling that they had suffered loss by virtue of the fact that the distribution of dividends by the subsidiaries to their parent companies had been subject to ACT,[100] maintaining that they had suffered a 'cashflow disadvantage which subsidiaries of parent companies resident in the UK did not incur',[101] a disadvantage which they argued was indirect discrimination on the grounds of nationality contrary to the EC Treaty. The companies were not therefore claiming return of the principal sum: the ACT had already been offset against MCT by the time the proceedings were brought. The case instead concerned a claim for interest on the sum for the period between payment of the ACT and payment of the MCT. The High Court stayed the proceedings and sent various questions to the ECJ for a preliminary ruling under Article 267 TFEU (ex 234 EC), including the question whether the facts gave rise to a restitutionary right on the part of the claimant, or whether the interest was available, if at all, only through the Court's case law on damages for breach of EC law.[102] The High Court also asked whether the failure of the claimants to rely on EC law to challenge the unavailability of the GIE provided an answer to the claim.[103]

The ECJ ruled that it was indeed contrary to the right of establishment enshrined in Article 49 TFEU (ex Art 43 EC) of the Treaty for the tax legislation of a Member State to afford companies resident in that Member State favourable tax treatment when their parent company is also resident in that Member State, but

[97] See further discussion of the English domestic implications of the *Metallgesellschaft and Hoechst* case in ch 4.

[98] ACT was subsequently abolished by s 31 of the Finance Act 1988.

[99] Under the Income and Corporation Taxes Act 1988 (ICTA).

[100] *Metallgesellschaft and Hoechst* (n 1) [27].

[101] ibid [30].

[102] ibid [33] (question 2).

[103] ibid (question 5).

not when the parent company has its seat in another Member State.[104] This set the scene for the answer to the second question, whether the companies could claim the interest, either as a claim for restitution, or as a claim for compensation for damage resulting from breach of EC law. The UK Government argued that ACT should not be regarded as a tax levied contrary to EC law, since the subsidiaries were in any event bound to pay the tax. The companies' complaint, they argued, was the lack of availability of the GIE option, and this should be considered as giving rise to non-contractual liability.[105] This seemed to be motivated by the fact that the rules on interest and perhaps on mitigation would have been more favourable to the UK had the claim been classified as a wrong.[106] Second, the UK Government argued that if they were correct on the first point, and the claims were to be treated as claims for recovery of sums paid in breach of EC law, it was settled law that it is for the national system to determine whether interest is payable.[107]

In answer to the first aspect of the reasoning, on 'categorisation', the Court answered that:

> It must be stressed that it is not for the Court to assign a legal classification to the actions brought by the plaintiffs before the national court. In the circumstances, it is for Metallgesellschaft and Others and Hoechst to specify the nature and basis of their actions (whether they are actions for restitution or actions for compensation for damage), subject to the supervision of the national court.[108]

However, the ECJ then reiterated the well-known case law[109] on the right to refunds of charges 'levied in a Member State in breach of rules of Community law', indicating that an unjust enrichment analysis may be available. Turning to the question of national procedural autonomy on the question of interest, the Court continued by distinguishing this case from *Roquette Frères*[110] and *Express Dairy Foods*,[111] in which questions relating to interest were held to be for the national court. It pointed out that:

> In the main proceedings . . . the claim for payment of interest covering the cost of loss of use of the sums paid by way of ACT is not ancillary, but is the very objective sought by the plaintiff's actions in the main proceedings. In such circumstances, where the breach of Community law arises, not from the payment of the tax itself but from its being levied prematurely, the award of interest represents the reimbursement of that which was improperly paid and would appear to be essential in restoring the equal treatment guaranteed by . . . the Treaty.[112]

As a result, the case was not one of a claim for interest on a principal sum in the way such a claim is usually understood, but one in which the interest *was* the

[104] ibid [76].
[105] ibid [78]. It was supported in this by Finland: AG Fennelly (point 43).
[106] ibid, although the point is not made expressly.
[107] *Metallgesellschaft and Hoechst* (n 1) [79].
[108] ibid [81].
[109] ibid [84]. See further below at p 254.
[110] *Roquette Frères* (n 28).
[111] *Express Dairy Foods* (n 29).
[112] *Metallgesellschaft and Hoechst* (n 1) [87].

principal sum.[113] The Court concluded that Article 49 TFEU (ex Art 43 EC) entitled the companies to obtain interest accrued on the ACT paid before the MCT was payable 'and that sum may be claimed by way of restitution'.[114] On the other hand, it might not have to be so claimed, since if the case were to be considered as one of compensation for loss under the principle of state liability in damages, in order fully to repair the damage caused by the breach of Article 49 a sum representing the amount of interest would also be available. The UK Government's argument that the plaintiffs could not be awarded interest if they sought compensation in a claim for damages could not be accepted since it would render exercise of the right (practically) impossible. Thus while the ECJ refused to classify the relevant event in this case, it did make it clear that from its point of view both of the categories were open, and that the UK Government could not succeed in either case.

AG Fennelly, on the other hand, was not as reticent as the ECJ on the matter of the categorisation of the claim. He similarly concluded that the restriction on the availability of the tax advantage was incompatible with Article 49 of the Treaty,[115] and held that in terms of effectiveness, the mere fact that the loss was the result of only a temporary violation of EC law could not justify the refusal of a claim for around £800,000. He too, therefore, rejected the submission of the UK that the claim could not be regarded as restitutionary in nature.[116] So far AG Fennelly had gone no further than the ECJ, but he continued:

> I believe that it is more correct and more logical to treat the plaintiff's claim as restitutionary rather than as a compensatory claim for damages. ACT was . . . extracted from them in contravention of Community law and, therefore, unlawfully. In the period between payment of ACT and its being taken into account in respect of the [M]CT liability of the subsidiaries, it should have been repaid to the plaintiffs by the United Kingdom. If it had been possible to bring legal proceedings during this period, the plaintiffs would, in my view, have been entitled to interest. It is neither logical nor just to deprive them of this entitlement merely because, in the meantime, the liability of the United Kingdom to repay the principal sum has been discharged. In a practical sense, also, the claim for interest is closer to a restitutionary rather than a compensatory claim. The underlying sums are known and indisputable. All that is necessary is for the national court to establish an appropriate interest rate for the relevant period.[117]

In the alternative, AG Fennelly concluded that, should the Court disagree that a 'restitutionary claim' should be available, Article 49 did create rights for individuals;[118] that there was a causal link between the statutory exclusion of the companies and the loss suffered by the claimants; but that there was some question

[113] ibid [88].

[114] ibid [89].

[115] ibid (point 39).

[116] It was also stated that the ACT 'payments made by the claimants were made on the basis of national legislation which allowed them no choice. Since such legislation is not compatible . . . with Community law, they should, in principle, be entitled to seek restitution for those payments': ibid (point 51).

[117] ibid (point 52). It was suggested above pp 77–86 at that this is indeed the correct analysis of the claim.

[118] ibid (point 55).

whether the breach was 'sufficiently serious' as required by *Brasserie/Factortame III*, although this was a matter for the national court to decide.

In answer to the fifth question on mitigation, the Court held that, had the companies applied for a GIE, they would in any case have had their request refused, and had they appealed successfully after payment of the ACT they would still not, under English law, have had any right to reimbursement. Thus any reduction of the amount awarded on this basis would be contrary to EC law.[119] Similarly, AG Fennelly, who referred to this question as laches, concluded that the Member State may not plead that the taxpayer should have made use of statutory remedies and/or the primacy of EC law in order to reduce or exclude a claim, since 'a Member State must not be allowed to profit from its own wrong'.[120]

In terms of the analysis proposed here, AG Fennelly's opinion is relatively straightforward, being a clear example of Model 2 reasoning in which he clearly considers the two categories of causes of action and chooses the event of unjust enrichment (although in terminology he refers instead to a 'restitutionary claim')[121]. The reasoning of the ECJ is more difficult, and in fact appears to fall somewhere between the two models. Since the ECJ clearly distinguishes between claims for state liability in damages under *Francovich*[122] and claims for restitution, to this extent its reasoning falls into Model 2, but significantly, while acknowledging the difference between the types of claim, the ECJ refuses to classify the actions itself, stressing that this is for the national court. In terms of the specific rules relating to recovery in the case, the Court merely returns to its previous case law on equivalence, effectiveness and practical possibility. Furthermore it does not, even through these tools, define the event of unjust enrichment.[123] It is therefore clear that the ECJ's preference was for Model 1 reasoning, in which the whole 'actionable story' is to be provided at national level.

However, while this may be the case whenever the ECJ is able to exercise a conscious choice, there are circumstances in which it may not wholly be able to do so. It will be recalled from the discussion above that the ECJ's current approach to the imperatives of 'equivalence' and 'effectiveness' is to balance the reasons in favour of the relevant national rules against any detrimental impact they have on the

[119] ibid [107].

[120] ibid (points 58–59 and 60(3)).

[121] ibid (point 52).

[122] *Francovich* (n 36). See also: *Brasserie du Pêcheur* (n 40). The principle provides that where there has been a sufficiently serious breach of a superior rule of law which has caused damage to an individual the individual may recover damages against the state. In paragraph 55 of *Brasserie* the Court explains that 'the decisive test for finding that a breach of Community law is sufficiently serious is whether the Member State or the Community institution concerned manifestly and gravely disregarded the limits on its discretion'. The superior rule of law must be for the grant of rights to individuals and it must be possible to identify those rights from the legislative provision, but it does not matter whether the provision is directly effective or not. See: Craig and de Búrca (n 5) 328–41.

[123] As it was argued it did in *San Giorgio* (n 34). Nor does the Court (as it did in *Hans Just* (n 26)—cf Case C-377/89 *Cotter and McDermott v Minister for Social Welfare & AG* [1991] ECR 1-1155)—use the unjust enrichment basis of the case as a reason to treat it differently from cases which are not based on such an event, see below at 256–57.

application of EU law. This means that in some cases the ECJ will inevitably have to become involved in the reasoning behind the relevant national rules in order to determine whether that reasoning outweighs the EU concerns. In this context, the extent to which the ECJ must therefore move inevitably towards something more like Model 2 reasoning depends in part on the nature of the national rule in question. The result is that in some instances the nature of the question is such that while the Court still reiterates explicitly the principle established in *Metallgesellschaft and Hoechst*, implicitly, as a matter of substance, it has had to move away from that declaration. For this reason, there has been a slight difference between situations in which money has been levied in contravention of EC law by a Member State or NIA and those in which it has been wrongly paid out by those entities.

Cases in which a Member State or a National Intervention Agency Levies Money in Contravention of EU Law

In the very early cases in this context the reticence of the EC was such that in *Rewe-Zentralfinanz*[124]and *Comet*,[125] (where, as noted above, the principles of equivalence and effectiveness were first established) AG Warner held that he did

> not think that any such independent right of action was conferred on the plaintiffs by Community law: I think that it was for their national laws to lay down the remedies to which they were entitled in consequence of the invalidity of the fiscal legislation in question.[126]

This is a view which he reiterated two years later in *Pigs and Bacon Commission v McCarren and Co Ltd.*[127] Similarly, in *Roquette Frères*,[128] where the money had been levied by an NIA rather than the Member State, the Court held that:

> Disputes in connexion with the reimbursement of amounts collected for the Community are thus a matter for the national courts and must be settled by them under national law in so far as no provisions of Community law are relevant.[129]

[124] *Rewe-Zentralfinanz* (n 21). The charge in question was a phytosanitary inspection charge demanded and paid on the import of apples into Germany, which had been found in Case 39/73 *Rewe-Zentralfinanz GmbH v Direktor der Landwirtschaftskammer Westfalen-Lippe* [1973] ECR 1039 to be a charge equivalent to a customs duty, and thus contrary to Art 30 TFEU (ex Art 25 EC).

[125] *Comet* (n 22). This concerned a claim to set off charges levied, contrary to EC law, on the export of bulbs and corms of flowering plants from the Netherlands to West Germany.

[126] Opinion on *Comet* (n 22) and *Rewe-Zentralfinanz* (n 21) 2004.

[127] Case 177/78 *Pigs and Bacon Commission v McCarren and Co Ltd* [1979] ECR 2161. In the case it was stated 'in my opinion, if and in so far as Community law renders the levy unlawful, it invalidates not only the statutory provisions imposing it but also any agreement pursuant to which it was paid . . . where a charge has been levied in breach of Community law the amount of it should normally be refunded. The scope of the remedy is however a matter for national law' 2217–18.

[128] *Roquette Frères* (n 28).

[129] ibid [11].

However, in *Pigs and Bacon*, the ECJ held that since the pigmeat levy at issue was 'not due', 'any trader who is required to pay the levy has therefore the right to claim the reimbursement of that part of the levy which is thus devoted to purposes incompatible with Community law'.[130] This then paved the way for the establishment of the famous *San Giorgio* ruling that

> entitlement to the repayment of charges levied by a member state contrary to the rules of community law is a consequence of, and an adjunct to, the rights conferred on individuals by the community provisions prohibiting charges having an effect equivalent to customs duties or, as the case may be, the discriminatory application of internal taxes.[131]

Nevertheless, this still only meant that the Court was following Model 1 in requiring the national system to provide an actionable story for recovery of the money. The slightly more significant change came when the Court began to examine the impact of various national defences on the effectiveness of the remedies that those Member States were providing in this regard. Where the situation has involved a private party claiming from a public defendant, whether that public defendant was a Member State or an NIA, the defence often pleaded[132] is that of passing on, as the public entity seeks to argue that the claimant did not bear the charge personally, but passed it onto its clients or customers in its prices. In other words, as argued in chapter five, the essence of the defence is to argue that even if the defendant was enriched, this was not at the expense of this particular claimant as would be required for a successful unjust enrichment action. Originally this defence, confusingly known in the EU context as 'the defence of unjust enrichment' (on the basis that recovery would lead to the unjust enrichment of the claimant) was only recognised as a possibility by the Court in cases such as *Hans Just*,[133] *Amministrazione delle Finanze dello Stato v Denkavit Italiana*[134] and *Amministrazione delle Finanze dello Stato v Ariete*,[135] the ECJ holding that 'Community law does not prevent the fact that the burden of the charges which have been unlawfully levied may have been passed on to other traders or to consumers from being taken into consideration'.[136] However, in *San Giorgio*,[137] the Court held that the passing on defence was contrary to EC law in as much as it was 'subject to rules of evidence which render the exercise of that right virtually impossible, even where the repayment of other taxes, charges or duties levied in breach of national law is subject to the same

[130] *Pigs and Bacon* (n 127) [25].

[131] *San Giorgio* (n 34) [12].

[132] Although, as will be seen shortly, this defence was in use in Denmark and Italy, it should be remembered that of course in France the case of *Fils Henri Ramel* held that in France it would not be available because the requirement to show impoverishment of the claimant is not part of the claim in *répétition de l'indu* (*Fils Henri Ramel* (Decision of the Cour d'appel de Lyon of the 30 November 1978 (1re Ch Civ) *D* 1979.371, note C-J Berr) see above, ch 6 p 176). It was argued that this strengthens the connection between the defence of passing on and denial of the 'at the expense of' requirement of the common law claim in unjust enrichment.

[133] *Hans Just* (n 26).

[134] Case 61/79 *Amministrazione delle Finanze dello Stato v Denkavit Italiana* [1980] ECR 1205.

[135] Case 811/79 *Amministrazione delle Finanze dello Stato v Ariete* [1980] ECR 2545.

[136] *Hans Just* (n 26) [27].

[137] *San Giorgio* (n 34).

restrictive condition.[138] For this finding of incompatibility, as compared to the cases in which the Court had simply let the defence stand, AG Mancini had to consider the defence of passing on in more detail than, for example, AG Reischl in *Hans Just.* Thus AG Mancini held that in principle:

> The undue payment, it is true, remains the 'fact' which gives rise to entitlement to the refund. But if subsequently the person who made the payment passes on all or part of the burden to third parties, his right is extinguished to the extent, whether total or partial to which the charge is passed on.[139]

However, ultimately, he felt bound to reject this particular form of application of the defence for practical reasons, and an important reason of principle:

> There is an instance of unjust enrichment—the only one in this case which may be mentioned without fear of denial—which the [passing on] rule not only tolerates, but actually promotes: namely the unjust enrichment of the State which unlawfully levies a tax and does not reimburse the person who paid it.[140]

This was reiterated by AG Tesauro in *Comateb (Société) v Directeur Général des Douanes et Droit Indirects*,[141] and indeed a similar point was made in chapter five.[142] Although these opinions come from the Advocates General rather than the Court itself, it is nevertheless submitted that they form an important distinction between *Hans Just* on the one hand, and *San Giorgio* and *Comateb* on the other. As noted above,[143] by simply letting the passing on defence stand in the absence of any Community rules on the matter in *Hans Just*, the Court was simply recognising the existence of the national unjust enrichment event. However, even before the ECJ's third-phase 'balancing' approach to the issues of equivalence and effectiveness, in order to reject a defence the ECJ had, to some extent, to engage with the national reasoning behind that defence in order to work out why it was being pleaded at all. Since the defence of passing on relates specifically to unjust enrichment actions, even if the Court's reasoning was motivated principally or even exclusively by considerations of effectiveness, it nevertheless led the court, and even more so the Advocates General, to specify the boundaries of application of a defence specific to unjust enrichment and therefore inevitably to begin to define the boundaries of that event itself. In that sense, it represents an inevitable move towards Model 2, even if this is not what the Court would have chosen or intended, and although subsequent cases may refer to the basis for recovery in

[138] *Hans Just* (n 26) [18].

[139] *San Giorgio* (n 34) 3624.

[140] ibid 3627.

[141] Cases C-192/95 to C-218/95 *Comateb (Société) v Directeur Général des Douanes et Droit Indirects* [1997] ECR 1-165, 173, citing F Hubeau, 'La répétition de l'indu en droit communautaire' (1981) *Revue Trimestrielle de Droit Européenne* 442. Hubeau states «s'il y a enrichissement sans cause, c'est plutôt au bénéfice de l'autorité publique (*accipiens*) qui a perçu la taxe illicite, puisque la base légale sur laquelle la perception a été effectuée est mise postérieurement à néant, ce qui lui fait perdre toute cause» 451.

[142] p 156.

[143] p 254.

these cases as 'reimbursement' based on the '*San Giorgio*' principle,[144] to this extent they must in fact be regarded as being based on an EU level principle of unjust enrichment.

Similarly, in the context of claims from NIAs, in *Express Dairy Foods*[145] AG Capotorti had to deal with the defence of ministerial receipt,[146] argued by the NIA on the basis that they had only received the money by and on behalf of the Community. In concluding that the Member State should bear the burden in the first instance and then bring a claim against the EC, AG Capotorti made it clear that his reasoning was based on the concept of unjust enrichment and where, in the event, that unjust enrichment would be located.[147] In *ICC v Amministrazione delle Finanze dello Stato,*[148] the ECJ itself held that the passing on defence could deprive the claim for recovery of its legal foundation.[149] Here again, it is difficult to see why this should be the case unless that foundation was the event of unjust enrichment and the passing on defence deprived that claim of its legal foundation by denying that the enrichment, if any, was at the expense of that particular claimant. Thus once more, it is clear that the court did not want to become involved in the details of the 'actionable story', holding that 'national courts are entirely justified in determining the effect on the cases brought before them of a judgment declaring an act void given by the Court in an action between other parties'.[150] In this case even AG Reischl did not completely distinguish between issues of wrongdoing and issues of unjust enrichment.[151] Nevertheless, even in that phase of its jurisprudence the court could not reject the defence outright without becoming involved in the reasoning behind it to some extent, and therefore in doing so it inevitably had to move a little closer to Model 2. If this is true of the case law before the move to the phase three approach, in which the ECJ balances the reasoning behind the national rule against the detrimental impact it has on the enforcement of EU law, it is even truer since. Thus, for example, in *Fantask,*[152] one of the cases central to phase three, AG Jacobs clearly distinguished between unjust enrichment and wrongdoing, arguing that the duty to mitigate loss or damages established in *Brasserie du Pêcheur*[153] has 'no relevance to the restitutionary . . . element of the claim, ie the amount of the overpaid tax or benefit denied'.[154]

Further evidence for Model 2 comes from an argument made by A Jones, who contrasts *Hans Just*, in which the 'unjust enrichment' defence was accepted, with

[144] See, eg: Case C-446/04 *Test Claimants in the FII Group Litigation v Commissioners of Inland Revenue* [2006] ECR I-11753. 'FII' stands for 'Franked Investment Income'.

[145] *Express Dairy Foods* (n 29).

[146] See also: P Birks, *Unjust Enrichment*, 2nd edn (Oxford, Oxford University Press, 2005) 245–47.

[147] *Express Dairy Foods* (n 29) 1906.

[148] Case 66/80 *International Chemical Corporation v Amministrazione delle Finanze dello Stato* [1981] ECR 1191.

[149] ibid [25].

[150] ibid [15]. See also [21].

[151] ibid at [5], though conversely see also [6].

[152] *Fantask* (n 38).

[153] *Brasserie du Pêcheur* (n 40).

[154] ibid [81]–[83] (AG Jacobs).

Cotter and McDermott[155] in which it was rejected. In *Cotter and McDermott*, Irish social security legislation entitled married persons to an increase in social welfare, but in contrast to their husbands, wives had positively to prove that their husbands and children were dependent on them. The ECJ held this to be contrary to Directive 79/7 on equal treatment. The question thus arose whether the claimant wives could recover the amount they should have been paid, when in fact their husbands had been receiving it instead. The Irish Government argued that to pay the wives in such circumstances would be to enrich them unjustly, but the ECJ rejected this argument. Many commentators tried to reconcile *Cotter and McDermott* with *Hans Just* by focusing on the underlying legislation. Perhaps the equal treatment directive was more important than the breach of tax law at issue in *Hans Just*? Jones points out that the real difference between the two cases is not this at all, rather that only in *Hans Just* was there an event of unjust enrichment.[156] In *Cotter and McDermott*, the Irish Government was seeking to argue that there *would be* such an event if the money were to be paid, but since there does not appear to be a plausible reason for restitution available to them,[157] their argument had to fail.

There have, of course, also been important countervailing pressures. Thus even in the passing on context, the concern of the Advocates General to prevent the unjust enrichment of the Member States has led to a slight move away from Model 2, in effect if not in strict terms of reasoning. As noted in chapter five,[158] there are serious problems with applying the passing on defence in practice. Some relate to difficulties of proof, but even if in a particular instance it were possible to ascertain with 100% accuracy whether a particular price had changed solely as the result of an ultra vires tax, this would still not be the whole story. A further problem is that even if it has passed on the tax to its customers, by doing so the taxpayer may well have cost itself sales. In chapter five it was argued that while this cost ought also to be borne by the state, technically it cannot be considered to be part of the unjust enrichment investigation, because while the trader will have made a loss, there will have been no corresponding gain on the part of the taxing authorities. Such issues would therefore have correctly to be considered, if at all, via an action for state liability in damages under the doctrine established in *Francovich*.[159] However, given the already hugely complicated process of establishing the existence of passing on,[160] it hardly seems desirable to add in a further complication in the form of a second cause of action to deal with the loss of sales issue. It is not surprising, therefore, that the Advocates General have tended to deal with these issues together, while accepting their conceptual separation. Thus, for

155 *Cotter and McDermott* (n 123).

156 A Jones, *Restitution and European Community Law* (London, Mansfield Press, 2000) 88.

157 Or, from the civilian perspective, there seems to be nothing wrong with the cause of payment to the wives. See also: (n 83).

158 Above ch 5 p 157.

159 *Francovich* (n 36).

160 On which see also ch 5, p 157.

example, in pointing out the difficulty of justifying the passing on defence in *Commission v Italian Republic*,[161] AG Geelhoed points out that only in the event that price elasticity is zero will a trader be able to pass on the charge to the customer in full by means of a price increase which has no effect on sales.[162] In all other cases, as he puts it, 'partial passing on of amounts will be the rule rather than the exception'.[163] However, this partial passing on is, in AG Geelhoed's view, derived from three factors: there may be a drop in the volume of sales; as a result of that, if the tax is not a tax per unit but a general tax on the trader, the trader may end up having to pay the rest of that tax himself,[164] or it may be that he has to reduce his profit margin in order to absorb the tax.[165] Of these three scenarios, only the second[166] can really be regarded as relating to the unjust enrichment of the tax authorities at the expense of the taxpayer. Any loss of profit, either by a reduction in sales or a loss of profit margin, would not entail the corresponding enrichment of the taxing authorities. Nonetheless, it would obviously be undesirably complicated to try to establish precisely which of these scenarios had occurred in order for the claim to be classified correctly. It is therefore clear that although in a sense AG Geelhoed's reasoning follows Model 2 by referring to 'loss or damage' separately from passing on,[167] his ultimate conclusion that application of the passing on defence should be limited by all these considerations is much more indicative of Model 1 reasoning.

Slightly more evidence for Model 2 reasoning comes from the opinion of AG Jacobs in *Weber's Wine World v Abgabenberufungskommission Wien*[168] in which he distinguished between retroactive rules on passing on and retroactive time limits on the basis that:

> Since Community law does not require a right to reimbursement at all where unjust enrichment would ensue, the fact that, following a change to national law, a claim which might previously have succeeded can on that ground no longer succeed has no impact on the effectiveness of a right conferred by Community law.[169]

[161] Case C-129/00 *Commission v Italian Republic* [2003] ECR I-14637, see above ch 5 at p xx.
[162] ibid [75].
[163] ibid.
[164] eg: the trader sells units at £1 each, and is independently subject to a tax of 50p. He raises the unit price to £1.05 in order to try to pass on the tax, anticipating normal sales of 10 units, but since he only sells 5 units at the new increased price he has to bear the remaining 25p tax himself. Only 25p of the 50p tax can therefore be regarded as having been passed on.
[165] eg: the trader sells units at £1 each, but reckons he can put up the price by 10p without a reduction in sales because the market is so strong. However, as he increases the price a 10p per unit tax is imposed. He has therefore effectively lost his increased profit margin of 10p per unit. Such a situation would also be a perfect example of the difficulty in assessing whether the tax had been passed on in the first place and therefore of establishing who exactly had borne the tax.
[166] Assuming that the third scenario plays out as initially described in the note above, rather than being a price increase in order to pass on the charge.
[167] *Italian Republic* (n 161) [75]–[78]. This is borne out in both the French and English versions of the text.
[168] Case C-147/01 *Weber's Wine World v Abgabenberufungskommission Wien* [2003] ECR I-11365.
[169] ibid [69].

By again relating the defence of passing on specifically to the event of unjust enrichment and by reaffirming that the Community did not require restitution where the defence applies, AG Jacobs thus clearly conceives of an EU-defined event of unjust enrichment which will dictate the rules applicable at national level. However, the ECJ apparently did not accept this reasoning,[170] holding instead that:

> The adoption by a Member State of rules which retroactively restrict the right to repayment of a sum levied but not due, in order to forestall the possible effects of a judgment of the Court holding that Community law precludes the maintenance of a national duty, is contrary to Community law and, more particularly, to Article 10 [ex 5] EC [now repealed and replaced in substance by Art 4 TFEU].

By failing to make AG Jacobs' distinction between time limits which would restrict at national level a right recognised at European level, and the defence of passing on which can also apply to restrict those rights at the EU level itself, the Court thus clearly remains within the general reasoning of 'effectiveness' and 'cooperation' rather than engaging with the inherent logic of a conception of unjust enrichment adopted at EU level. Its reasoning is therefore firmly within the parameters of Model 1.

However, despite these countervailing pressures from the practical obstacles of the passing on defence, overall the move to phase three does mean that in principle there is more scope for engagement by the ECJ with the 'actionable story' itself. That this is so is illustrated by the limited extent to which, in subsequent cases, the ECJ has been able to follow in substance the clear boundaries that it set for itself in *Metallgesellschaft and Hoechst*.

The *Test Claimants in the FII Group Litigation v Commissioners of the Inland Revenue*[171] (*FII*) case was one of the many subsequent cases brought in the aftermath of the decision in *Metallgesellschaft and Hoechst*.[172] Again, to reiterate the facts,[173] as Henderson J, the English High Court judge dealing with the case at the domestic end put it, at the simplest level *FII* concerned 'factual situations which are the opposite of those which gave rise to the questions considered in *Hoecsht* and the ACT group litigation'.[174] Whereas *Metallgesellschaft and Hoechst* concerned UK resident subsidiaries of foreign parent companies which were prevented from making a GIE, the FII Group Litigation concerned foreign subsidiaries of UK parent companies and the tax treatment of dividends coming into the UK from abroad. As

[170] See also: A Jones, 'European Regional Digest' (2005) 13 *Restitution Law Review* 181, 186.

[171] *The Test Claimants in the FII Group Litigation v The Commissioners for Her Majesty's Revenue & Customs* [2008] EWHC 2893 (Ch), [2009] STC 254.

[172] See also Case C-201/05 *Test Claimants in the CFC and Dividend Group Litigation* (23 April 2008) and Case C-524/04 *Test Claimants in the Thin Cap Group Litigation* [2007] ECR I-2107.

[173] For discussion of the English domestic implications of the case see further ch 4, above pp 85–86 and 102 onwards.

[174] *FII* (UK) (n 171) [2].

[175] *FII* (ECJ) (n 144). The national rules in question were again the ACT regime at issue in *Metallgesellschaft and Hoechst*, which were held to be contrary to Arts 49 TFEU (ex 43 EC) and 63 TFEU (ex 56 EC) on freedom of establishment and free movement of capital.

with *Metallgesellschaft and Hoechst*, the ECJ had held the national rules to be in breach of EC law,[175] and so the question before Henderson J in the High Court in *FII* was how this finding should be applied to the facts of the case, and how the EC law findings should be translated into national law. However, this time, unlike *Metallgesellschaft and Hoechst*, the decision of the ECJ in *FII* gave more specific guidance on how this should be achieved.

The case concerned a series of different claims. Some of these were relatively straightforwardly for restitution of the tax payments[176] which had been found to be in breach of EC law, plus compound interest to represent the time value of those payments.[177] Others, however, were less straightforward. In particular, the application of the ACT regime to UK parent companies with foreign subsidiaries tended to lead to an 'ACT mountain'[178] building up within the company. ACT would become payable on the distribution of dividends, either within the company or to its outside shareholders to a greater extent than would have been the case with a wholly UK-based company, and then, whereas a wholly UK-based company would be able to offset these ACT payments against other liabilities, the scope for UK parent companies with foreign subsidiaries to do this was very limited.[179] As a result, companies in this position, such as the test claimants in *FII* tended to regard ACT not as *advance* corporation tax at all, but rather as an absolute and final form of liability with which they were stuck.[180] In order to minimise this, when ACT was abolished and 'shadow ACT' was introduced in its place, the claimants wanted to use up their surplus ACT as far as they could, lest they should lose the chance to do so altogether. They thus waived (or 'disclaimed') capital tax allowances for three years, thereby increasing their liability to MCT, against which they could then set off some of the surplus ACT. However, the ACT could only ever discharge a proportion of this MCT, so in *FII*, the claimants also sought to claim loss of use of the additional MCT thus paid. The claimants also set off their surplus ACT against 'Case V Corporation tax', which was itself one of the taxes which was unlawful as a matter of EC law. Finally, the claimants also sought to make use of their ACT mountain through what was known as the 'FID regime'.[181] UK-based companies

[176] ACT and Case V corporation tax.

[177] See: *FII* (UK) (n 171) [201]–[205] and [209]–[211] (Henderson J).

[178] ibid [33] (Henderson J).

[179] The main reasons for this were first that a UK resident company making a qualifying distribution to another UK-based company would be entitled to a tax credit. The total of the distribution and the tax credit was called Franked Investment Income (FII). The company would then only be liable to pay ACT to the extent that its dividends and the ACT referable to them exceeded the FII tax credit. However, a UK resident company receiving a distribution from a foreign company was not entitled to this credit. The amount of ACT payable in the first place would therefore be greater than that payable by a wholly UK-based company. In addition, companies were entitled to set this ACT off against MCT, but where a company received credit for foreign tax, this reduced the amount of MCT liability against which ACT could be set off. Thus UK based companies with foreign subsidiaries would both accrue more ACT and have less use to make of it than wholly UK-based companies. See further: ibid [19]–[23] (Henderson J).

[180] ibid [32], quoting from the witness statement of Mr K Hardman, Head of Tax at BAT industries, the group from which the test claimants were drawn.

[181] ibid [15], [164]–[191], [208] and [273]–[302].

distributing foreign profits to their shareholders could elect to treat them as 'Foreign Income Dividends' or 'FIDs'. The ACT paid on FIDs was in principle repayable and so the payment of dividends in the form of FIDs would substantially reduce the group's overall tax burden. Because there was virtually no other way in which surplus ACT could be used within the group, the claimants opted to make use of the 'FID regime'. However, FIDs had to be made on an all or nothing basis. A company could not elect to pay FIDs for recipients liable to UK income tax but not exempt shareholders; an election could only be made in respect of all the dividends on the same class of share. Also, shareholders could not receive tax credits for dividends paid under the FID system. Since 40 per cent of the claimants' shareholders were 'exempt shareholders', that is, those who would have received partial or full tax credits on normal dividends, it would not have been commercially viable for the claimants simply to start issuing dividends as FIDs without such credits. As a result, the claimants issued what became known as 'enhanced FIDs' made up of the original amount of the distribution, topped up to compensate the shareholders for the resulting loss of tax credit. In *FII*, the claimants claimed that had it not been for the unlawful ACT and FID system, they would not have paid 'enhanced FIDs', and that by compensating the recipient shareholders for the lack of repayable tax credits, they had enriched the Revenue by relieving it of its obligations in respect of those tax credits.

In the 'remedies' section of his judgment, AG Geelhoed reiterated the *Metallgesellschaft and Hoechst* principle that the classification of such claims under English law was a matter for the domestic courts rather than the ECJ.[182] However, in substance his decision clearly departs from this Model 1 reasoning in favour of a Model 2 approach, because he held explicitly that with one exception, the claims brought should be 'considered equivalent to claims for the recovery of sums unduly paid, that is to say, claims for recovery of charges unlawfully levied',[183] rather than as claims based on state liability for damages.[184] Indeed, not only was he happy, in apparent contradiction to the *Metallgesellschaft and Hoechst* principle, thus to classify the claims as a matter of EC law (which, as he pointed out, AG Fennelly in the *Metallgesellschaft and Hoechst* case had also done),[185] he also went on to point out that adoption at national level of this EC level classification might actually be required by the Community rules of effectiveness themselves. If the claim were to be regarded at national level as being based on the wrong of breach of EU law, then as noted above, under the decision in *Brasserie/Factortame III*[186] the state would only be liable in damages if that breach were to be regarded as 'sufficiently serious'. Where, in his view, as a matter of Community law a 'reimbursement claim could be brought, it was the duty of the national court to provide "an effective remedy" even where a claim for state liability in damages might not

182 *FII* (ECJ) (n 144) [129].
183 ibid [132].
184 For further discussion of this choice, see ch 4 pp 77–86.
185 *FII* (ECJ) (n 144) [131].
186 *Brasserie du Pêcheur* (n 40).

succeed'.[187] In other words, if the claims should be classified at the European level as being based on the principle of unjust enrichment (which, it was argued above, is how the '*San Giorgio* principle' of 'reimbursement' must be understood)[188] then classification of them at national level as being based instead on the wrong of breach of European law could itself be a breach of the EU principle of effectiveness. This is because the requirement of a 'sufficiently serious breach' could prevent recovery when a simple claim for reimbursement would have allowed it. Of all the cases discussed so far, then, this is probably the strongest indication of a move by an Advocate General towards Model 2 reasoning.

However, it is even more striking that this move to Model 2 reasoning was not, as in earlier cases, confined to the decision of the Advocate General, but extended also to the judgment of the ECJ. Like AG Geelhoed, the ECJ again reiterated the *Metallgesellschaft and Hoechst* principle that it was not for the ECJ itself to assign a legal classification to the actions brought before the national court.[189] 'However', it continued

> the fact remains that, according to established case-law, the right to a refund of charges levied in a Member State in breach of rules of Community law is the consequence and complement of the rights conferred on individuals by Community provisions as interpreted by the Court. The Member State is therefore required in principle to repay charges levied in breach of Community law.[190]

Thus, like AG Geelhoed, the Court regards the need for an effective remedy in the form of 'repayment' of the tax rather than state liability in damages (which may not be made out on the facts as a result of the 'sufficiently serious breach' requirement) as 'trumping', for practical purposes, the *Metallgesellschaft and Hoechst* principle that it is not for the ECJ to assign legal classifications to the cause of action.[191]

The conclusion must therefore be that however great the commitment to Model 1 reasoning as a matter of form, in substance there will inevitably be instances in which the nature of the question is such that the Court has, as a matter of substance to adopt Model 2 reasoning whether it wants to or not. The significance of this move should not be underestimated since, as was noted above, and as became evident in the subsequent High Court hearing in the *FII* case, a shift of this kind towards Model 2 reasoning decreases the role for national rules concerning a particular cause of action and increases the extent to which the definition and operation of the cause of action are determined instead at the European level.[192]

Thus, having regarded it as necessary to classify the claim in some instances, the ECJ and AG Geelhoed could not then avoid specifying the claims in the *FII* case which they did not regard as falling within the classification as unjust enrichment

[187] *FII* (ECJ) (n 144).
[188] See above pp 107 and 256.
[189] *FII* (ECJ) (n 144) [201].
[190] ibid [202].
[191] See also: ibid [203]–[206].
[192] *FII* (UK) (n 171) [271]. See also: ch 4.

or 'repayment' claims, thus continuing their classification of the claims at EC level. Given that we are now discussing the nascent EU concept of unjust enrichment which binds and perhaps even replaces the national rules on that cause of action, it is worth noting in more detail what these exceptions were. As far as AG Geelhoed was concerned, there was only one, concerning the claim for the FID enhancements, which he held were not necessarily 'a direct consequence of the UK's unlawful failure to grant an equivalent credit to the shareholders'.[193] The direct consequence was the extra tax levied on those shareholders, not the efforts made by the companies to alleviate this, although he did leave it to the national court to establish whether this was correct on the facts. As for the ECJ, it regarded *two* of the claims as falling outside the unjust enrichment *San Giorgio* principle. One, like AG Geelhoed, concerned the issue of enhanced FIDs and the other was the waiver of tax credits in order to increase the liability to MCT against which ACT could then be offset. According to the ECJ:

> Such waivers of relief or increases in the amount of dividends are the result of decisions taken by those companies and do not constitute, on their part, an inevitable consequence of the refusal by the United Kingdom to grant those shareholders the same treatment as that afforded to shareholders receiving a distribution which has its origin in nationally-sourced dividends.[194]

That being the case, it was for the national courts to decide whether these last two claims should instead succeed on the basis of state liability in damages for breach of Community law.[195] In the event Henderson J, the domestic High Court judge, followed AG Geelhoed and the ECJ on the FID enhancements and the ECJ on the waived/disclaimed tax credits, but also held that the set-off of ACT against the unlawful Case V corporation tax constituted a third exception. However, even in doing so it was clear that Henderson J regarded himself as applying 'the *San Giorgio* principle' reiterated by the ECJ and AG Geelhoed in *FII* and as applying their 'direct' or 'inevitable consequences' test.[196] In chapter four it was suggested that this approach was not necessarily to be welcomed.[197] First, it was argued that there may be relatively few situations in which a given consequence is truly an *inevitable* result of a particular charge. Accordingly, the approach of AG Geelhoed and the ECJ might therefore be better understood as allowing the claimants to bring actions for repayment on the basis of unjust enrichment under *San Giorgio* only where the loss has been allowed to lie where it fell, and not where the claimant has done something to mitigate that loss. Second, it was argued there that this state of affairs is not desirable in terms of either principle or policy. From the point of view of principle, while it is true that claimants *are not required* to mitigate their loss before bringing a claim in unjust enrichment,[198] this should not be allowed to

[193] ibid [133].
[194] ibid [207].
[195] ibid.
[196] ibid [271].
[197] See further above, pp 113–16.
[198] *Fantask* (n 38) and accompanying text at (n 152).

slide into a rule that claimants *are required not* to mitigate their loss, not least because, as a matter of policy, such a rule could have potentially inefficient results. If claimants genuinely can mitigate their loss this should be encouraged by ensuring that where they have in fact not managed to do so they are not penalised for having tried. Given that national courts are now to be bound by these principles, as was Henderson J in *FII*, and given that the ECJ has thus assumed responsibility for the cause of action in this regard, further and more careful consideration of this point in future cases would be desirable.

In sum, then, where the claims are brought by private entities against public authorities, the defences with which the ECJ and its Advocates General have had to grapple have tended to concern defences specific to the issue of unjust enrichment. Where this is the case, particularly in the third 'balancing' phase of the ECJ's case law on effectiveness and equivalence, but even before that point, it has been difficult for the Advocates General, and even in some cases the Court, to reject a national defence without engaging in at least a general understanding of the reasoning behind it. In doing so, and in establishing the acceptable boundaries of such defences, the Court has therefore ended up becoming involved to some extent in the 'actionable story' itself, rather than acting as a pure source of nullity which is then translated into this 'actionable story' wholly at national level. This runs against the Court's own choice, most clearly expressed in *Metallgesellschaft and Hoechst*,[199] and there are important competing practical pressures towards Model 1 given the difficulties of proof involved in the passing on defence. Nevertheless, the degree of tension between the Court's stated aims and the inevitable result of its reasoning has meant that it has had to move a little closer towards Model 2. The most striking development in this vein took place in the *FII* case, in which both AG Geelhoed and the ECJ did classify the claims at issue even as they reiterated the *Metallgesellschaft and Hoechst* principle that this classification was in principle for the national courts. In some cases, such a move towards Model 2 is vital if the reasoning of the ECJ is to become comprehensible in a way that general references to 'national procedural autonomy' and 'remedies jurisprudence' are not. Without reference to the presence or absence of unjust enrichment, for example, it would not have been possible to understand the distinction between *Hans Just*[200] and *Cotter and McDermott*.[201] However, the move also carries responsibilities as can be seen from the fact that more attention could perhaps have been given to the mitigation issue in *FII*. If the ECJ and its Advocates General are to classify causes of action and their detailed requirements in a manner which may replace, or at least have important repercussions for, national law, they must ensure that the reasoning behind their decisions is fully thought out in terms of both principle and policy.

199 *Metallgesellschaft and Hoechst* (n 1).
200 *Hans Just* (n 26).
201 *Cotter and McDermott* (n 123).

Cases in Which an NIA or the EU Pays Out Money in Breach of EU Law which it then Seeks to Recover

Conversely, where the roles are reversed and the private entity is the defendant, there has generally been less evidence of Model 2 reasoning. The reason is that the defences most commonly used in this context are less specific to the issue of unjust enrichment and thus in considering them the ECJ and its Advocates General are less inevitably drawn into defining the boundaries of that event and they are better able to remain at the level of general principle. The defence in question is that of change of position which, as noted above in chapter five,[202] may well be closely connected to other arguments based on legal certainty and the rule of law, such as legitimate expectations. Thus in *Deutsche Milch-Kontor GmbH v Germany*,[203] a case involving an NIA, the ECJ was asked to rule on the compatibility of paragraph 48 of the Verwaltungsverfahrengesetz (VwVfG) with Community law and the obligation to recover charges. The paragraph provided that

> an unlawful administrative decision granting a pecuniary benefit may not be revoked in so far as the beneficiary has relied upon the decision and his expectation, weighed against the public interest in revoking the decision, merits protection; the recipient of such a benefit may plead loss of enrichment in accordance with the relevant rules of civil law unless he knew, or was unaware of owing to gross negligence on his part, the circumstances which made the grant of the benefit unlawful . . . the amount unduly paid cannot be recovered where the authority knew, or was unaware owing to gross negligence on its part, that it was granting the benefit unlawfully.[204]

The ECJ replied that

> the principles of the protection of legitimate expectation and assurance of legal certainty are part of the legal order of the Community. The fact that national legislation provides for the same principles to be observed in a matter such as the recovery of unduly-paid Community aids cannot, therefore, be considered contrary to that same legal order.[205]

Thus:

> Community law does not prevent national law from having regard, in excluding the recovery of unduly-paid aids, to such considerations as the protection of legitimate expectation, the loss of unjustified enrichment, the passing of a time-limit or the fact that the administration knew, or was unaware owing to gross negligence on its part, that it was wrong in granting the aids in question, provided however that the conditions laid down are the same as for the recovery of purely national financial benefits and the interests of the Community are taken fully into account.[206]

[202] pp 140–41.
[203] Cases 205–215/82 *Deutsche Milch-Kontor GmbH v Germany* [1983] ECR 2633.
[204] ibid [28].
[205] ibid [29].
[206] ibid [33].

It was argued in chapter five that the defence of change of position (which is the English version of the German defence described above in paragraph 48(2) of the VwVfG) is very closely connected to the public law protection of legitimate expectations. This argument is, it is submitted, well supported by the excerpt from the German law quoted above, which very closely links the defence of change of position (or 'loss of enrichment')[207] in paragraph 48(2) to the protection of legitimate expectations in paragraphs 48(1) and 48(3). This point is also made by Jewell, in a comparative study of the German and English law on change of position.[208] However, since references to 'loss of enrichment'[209] were therefore combined with a variety of other considerations such as legitimate expectations, this meant that the Court did not have to become involved in defining the boundaries of unjust enrichment specifically.

The *Deutsche Milch-Kontor* principles were reiterated in *Oelmühle Hamburg AG v Bundesanstalt für Landwirtschaft und Ernährung*,[210] where the Court came a little closer to model two by stating that *the plea of loss of enrichment* itself was part of the general principles of EC law,[211] rather than just the general idea of reliance, expectations and certainty, but no references were given for this assertion. Indeed, the Court again referred to a range of different justifications for the defence so that while legitimate expectations were certainly relevant, they could not be said to be the sole basis for the defence. Rather it was referred to variously as 'lost enrichment',[212] 'legitimate expectation'[213] (which, together with references to the foreseeability of the risk[214] and the need for good faith[215] refer instead to the defendant's reliance on the sum and ideas of non-retroactivity) and 'passing on of benefit'[216] (which is not only a third option, but is not really a defence at all since it is the mirror-image of one of the interpretations of passing on and suggests that

[207] The exact application of the defence is still a matter of debate in the English system and 'loss of enrichment' is one suggested definition.

[208] Jewell writes that: 'The public law approach is based on the concept of *Vertrauensschutz*. This translates as 'protection of legitimate expectations' or 'protection of reliance'. Like BGB §818(III) [the change of position defence in German private law], it protects a defendant who has changed his position in reliance on the wealth which has flowed to him at the plaintiff's expense. However, there are two major differences. The first is that *Vertrauensschutz* explicitly involves weighing up all the factors so as to decide whether it would be fair to order restitution. It is an immediate enquiry as to what would be a fair result, with the continued enrichment of the defendant being only one of the considerations. The second is that the role of fault in excluding the defence is different.' M Jewell, 'The Boundaries of Change of Position—a Comparative Study' (2000) 8 *Restitution Law Review* 1, 6. The different role of fault will be dealt with below, at p 267.

[209] For discussion of the precise relationship between loss of enrichment and change of position, see also: A Burrows, *The Law of Restitution*, 2nd edn (London, Butterworths, 2002) 512–17.

[210] Case C-298/96 *Oelmühle Hamburg AG v Bundesanstalt für Landwirtschaft und Ernährung* [1998] I ECR 4767.

[211] ibid [31].

[212] ibid [17]. See: Burrows, *Law of Restitution* (n 209).

[213] ibid [24].

[214] ibid [18].

[215] ibid [29].

[216] ibid [18] and [38].

the claimant has simply chosen the wrong defendant). Certainly the Court held that it would be necessary for the defendants to show that they could not recover the benefit from those on whom it had been conferred[217] and it was also made clear that the defence only applies in this category of cases, and not in relation to state aids.[218]

These principles were reiterated in the subsequent case of *Republic of Austria v Hüber*,[219] in which Austria had made a grant to Hüber without informing him that its validity was dependent on his fulfilment of various conditions. When these conditions were not fulfilled and the money was reclaimed, the ECJ simply confirmed that EC law did not preclude the application of the principles of the protection of legitimate expectations and legal certainty in order to prevent the recovery of aid which has been wrongly paid, provided that the interest of the Community was also taken into consideration and assuming the good faith of the beneficiary of the aid in question was also established.[220] AG Alber, on the other hand, more specifically indicated that:

> When weighing up the Community interest in the recovery of the unduly received aid and the protection of the recipient's legitimate expectations, criteria such as the recipient's good faith, negligent conduct on the part of the national authorities and the fact that the enrichment has since disappeared may be taken into account, provided that the same conditions apply as for the recovery of purely national aid and that the interests of the Community are taken fully into consideration.[221]

Interestingly, he also pointed out that in *Hauptzollamt Hamburg-Jonas v Firma P Krücken*,[222] the Court had established that 'the principle of legitimate expectations cannot be relied upon against a precise provision of Community law'.[223] *Krücken* did not concern the use of legitimate expectations as a defence, but rather its 'sword' form, with the applicant arguing that it should receive a pre-agreed higher rate of export refund than that which had been granted to it by the Hauptzollamt Hamburg-Jonas when it applied the rate in force at the time of exportation. Thus by referring to this case in the context of *Hüber*, AG Alber again strengthened the link between legitimate expectations more generally and the defence of change of position,[224] while at the same time decreasing the unjust-enrichment specificity of the defence in this context. The same can be said of cases where it is the EU that has paid out the

[217] ibid [34].

[218] ibid [37]. The ECJ in Case C-24/95 *Land Rheinland-Pfalz v Alcan Deutschland GmbH* [1997] ECR I-1591 held that the provisions set out in Para 48(4) of the VwVfG could not in general apply as a defence in state aids cases. See: Jones (n 156) 139.

[219] *Hüber* (n 85).

[220] ibid [59].

[221] *Hüber* (n 85) point 138.

[222] Case 316/86 *Hauptzollamt Hamburg-Jonas v Firma P Krücken* [1988] ECR 2213.

[223] ibid point 129.

[224] Particularly in the context of the extent to which the defence should be allowed to qualify the 'ultra vires principle', see above ch 5 p 141.

money it now seeks to recover, such as *Netherlands v Commission (EAGGF)*[225] and *Stichting ROM-projecten v Staatsecretaris van Economische Zaken.*[226]

The final case to consider in this context does not in fact fit very well, either into this category or into the context of unjust enrichment more generally. In *Intervention Board for Agricultural Produce v Penycoed Farming Partnership*,[227] the defendant had produced milk without a quota to do so but had failed to pay the relevant levy required by the Community regulations governing the scheme. In return for the milk that it delivered, Penycoed received a price guaranteed by the Community which was in part subsidy. The Intervention Board which ran the Community Scheme within the UK sought to recover the levy owed by Penycoed, but in fact the regulation only provided for the levy to be recovered from the *purchaser* of the milk, not from producers such as Penycoed. The national court thus made a reference to the ECJ under Article 267 TFEU (ex Art 234 EC) asking whether the money could instead be recovered directly from Penycoed. The ECJ held that it could, holding that although no such right could be found in the regulation itself, that was not an exhaustive source of such powers, and the duty of cooperation under Article 4 TFEU (replacing Art 10 EC, now repealed) could instead provide the authorisation for such a direct action. Unsurprisingly, given its decision in *Metallgesellschaft and Hoechst*,[228] the ECJ did not specify the basis for this action in national law, only in EC law. However, AG Geelhoed went much further, arguing that the power to demand the levy from Penycoed could be derived from *two* legal principles; the principle of effectiveness (which ties in with the duty of cooperation under Art 4) *and* the principle prohibiting unjust enrichment. According to AG Geelhoed there had been an unjust enrichment at the expense of Community resources which must be recovered because Penycoed had

> obtained an economic advantage by receiving money to which it was not entitled. Furthermore, that was money the amount of which is guaranteed by the Community. There is also a debt to the European Community, as a consequence of which the latter sustains a loss, since it is incurred at the cost of the resources available for expenditure in the milk sector.[229]

With respect, A Jones is right to point out that it is very difficult to regard this as a case of unjust enrichment in the usual sense. As she notes, even if the higher price Penycoed had received for the milk, partly subsidised by the Community, were to be regarded as an economic advantage, it was not this amount that the Intervention Board was trying to recover. Instead, it was trying to recover an independent levy which ought to have been paid by the milk purchasers.[230] In a sense,

[225] Case 11/76 *Netherlands v Commission (EAGGF)* [1979] ECR 245, [8].

[226] Case C-158/06 *Stichting ROM-projecten v Staatsecretaris van Economische Zaken* [2007] ECR I-5103. In this case, the Court also pointed out that where the breach is attributable to a Member State it can in any event be recovered from that State and does not therefore have to be recovered from the private entity.

[227] *Penycoed Farming Partnership* (n 85).

[228] *Metallgesellschaft and Hoechst* (n 1).

[229] *Penycoed Farming Partnership* (n 85) point 76.

[230] A Jones, 'European Regional Digest' (2003) 11 *Restitution Law Review* 194, 200.

by using the unjust enrichment terminology as a joint basis for recovery, AG Geelhoed's reasoning ought perhaps to be classified as belonging in Model 2, in contrast to the ECJ's standard Model 1 tendency to specify the required result while leaving the choice of basis to the Member State. Yet in fact, by using the concept of unjust enrichment as such a broad and general principle, rather than as a clearly defined and structured cause of action, AG Geelhoed arguably moved further away from the development of an EU law of unjust enrichment capable of supplementing or interacting with those found at national level.

In summary, then, where the private entity is the defendant from whom an NIA or the EU seeks to recover, the Court and its Advocates General have wholly avoided any move towards Model 2 reasoning by referring to any defence such as change of position alongside other related arguments such as legitimate expectations. These cases therefore provide strong support for the argument made in chapter five that there is a close relationship between these different concepts and that use of the change of position defence against hybrid claims is not to prioritise private law to the exclusion of public law concerns.[231] They do not, however, provide any indication of the ECJ becoming involved in the definition of the 'actionable story' itself, far less so than in cases where the money was levied or charged in contravention of EC law by a public authority.

What, then, of the other, public law event at the heart of such claims?

Is there an EU Law 'Event' of Ultra Vires in Cases involving both EU and National Law?

As noted above,[232] just as the balance between the efficacy principle and the defence of passing on led the ECJ inevitably to have to engage with principles of unjust enrichment, so the principle of equivalence to some extent led the ECJ to acknowledge the distinction between public and private entities, specifically in relation to the shorter time limits available to the former.[233] It was noted in chapter seven that in cases concerning only EU law, the ECJ also recognises a public/private divide.[234] However, as with its recognition of unjust enrichment, the ECJ has never consciously chosen a Model 2 approach, and thus it does not recognise a distinction in this sense between illegality as a matter of private, as opposed to public, law. When it acts as a Model 1 'source of unlawfulness' only, it does not choose to distinguish between these very different kinds of unlawfulness.

Whereas cases involving public law illegality usually concern taxes or charges of some kind, cases involving private law illegality often come from the competition

[231] See above pp 140–41.
[232] p 256.
[233] *Edis* (n 52).
[234] Above p 211.

sphere,[235] specifically Articles 101 and 102 TFEU (ex Arts 81 and 82 EC).[236] Both articles may affect the validity of contracts, Article 101(2) more so than Article 102. Article 101(2) renders the contract void unless the agreement is subject to an individual or block exemption.[237] Article 102 does not contain an equivalent to Article 101(2), but Jones argues that its effect on agreements could be considered to be the same, given that it implicitly prohibits many contracts and contractual terms.[238]

Articles 101(1), 101(2) and 102 are directly effective, so that the national courts have a duty to safeguard the rights of individuals to which they give rise,[239] and as Jones notes, the relationship between unjust enrichment and the enforcement of competition rules is becoming extremely important.[240]

In England, this issue has been raised in the context of the 'Beer Tie' cases, in which the tenancy agreements of the publicans have obliged them to buy their drinks only from certain suppliers. In *Gibbs Mew plc v Gemell*,[241] the English courts held that an action for restitution did not lie where the agreement infringes Article 101(1). This was for various reasons. First the Court of Appeal held that in contrast to Article 102, Article 101 was designed to protect third-party competitors, not the parties to the prohibited agreement. Second, English law did not allow a party to an illegal agreement to claim damages from the other party for loss caused by being party to an illegal agreement. There was also a concern that it would not be possible for the claimant to make counter-restitution. This decision was followed in *Trent Taverns Ltd v Sykes*[242] However, Jones notes that the same result was not reached in Germany, Italy, Denmark, Ireland, the Netherlands or Portugal, where benefits conferred under an agreement which is void for infringing Article 101(1) were recoverable.[243] In Spain, the action also lies, except where the claimant was responsible for the nullity.

[235] See generally: Jones (n 156) ch 6.

[236] Art 101(1) provides that: 'The following shall be prohibited as incompatible with the internal market: all agreements between undertakings, decisions by associations of undertakings and concerted practices which may affect trade between Member States and which have as their object or effect the prevention, restriction or distortion of competition within the internal market . . .' A number of agreements are then specifically prohibited, and Art 101(2) provides that '[a]ny agreements or decisions prohibited pursuant to this Article shall be automatically void'. Art 102 provides that: 'Any abuse by one or more undertakings of a dominant position within the internal market or in a substantial part of it shall be prohibited as incompatible with the common market in so far as it may affect trade between Member States.' Again, specific examples of such abuse are given.

[237] See also: Craig and de Búrca (n 5) ch 25.

[238] Jones (n 156) 151.

[239] Case 127/73 *Belgische Radio en Televisie v SABAM SV* [1974] ECR 51, [16] and *van Gend en Loos* (n 70). This was accepted by Peter Gibson J in *Holleran v Daniel Thwaites plc* [1989] 2 CMLR 917 (Ch) 921.

[240] Jones (n 156) 152.

[241] *Gibbs Mew plc v Gemmell* [1999] 1 ECC 97 (CA).

[242] *Trent Taverns Ltd v Sykes* [1999] Eu LR 492 (CA).

[243] Jones (n 156) 153 quoting the results of a survey published by the European Commission on the 'Application of Articles [101] and [102] of the EC Treaty by National Courts in the Member States'.

In *Courage Ltd v Crehan*,[244] the ECJ finally had the chance to rule on the compatibility of such English rules with EC law. Again this was a Beer Tie case, Mr Crehan being one of Courage and Grand Metropolitan's tenants. Courage sued Crehan for £15,000 for unpaid deliveries of beer and Crehan counterclaimed on the basis that the beer tie under which they had been delivered was contrary to Article 101. Relying on the direct effect of Article 101,[245] AG Mischo held that national rules were precluded by EC law if they prevented parties to the agreement from recovering damages. It was true that as a matter of EC law parties could not assert claims by relying on their own wrongs,[246] but this would only apply where the party 'genuinely bears' responsibility for the distortion of competition, not where the party was 'too small to resist the economic pressure imposed on it by the more powerful undertaking'.[247] The ECJ agreed, though its choice of words was slightly different, excluding only those who bear 'significant' responsibility for the agreement.[248]

Clearly, then, the ECJ was as happy to apply its general 'remedies jurisprudence' and its requirements of equivalence and effectiveness to cases between private parties as it was to cases involving public bodies,[249] and thus any recognition of the difference between these two forms of unlawfulness is for the national legal systems alone. From this point of view, Jones is right to argue that in cases such as *GT-Link A/S v De Danske Statsbaner (DSB)*[250] (levy by a port authority in contravention of Art 102 of the EC Treaty) and *Barra*[251] (wrongful charge of a 'minerval') the obligation would have applied equally had the recipients of the wrongful charges been private entities instead of public ones.[252]

Conclusion—The Impact of EU Law on National Unjust Enrichment Claims involving Public Bodies

As was noted at the outset, it is clear that in practical terms EC law has had an important impact on claims in unjust enrichment involving public bodies in national systems. The limit on a public body's 'vires' to charge a particular tax or levy can come from its EU obligations as well as from national law. In EU law, if it exceeds those obligations it has a duty to repay, regardless of whether such a duty

[244] Case C-453/99 *Courage Ltd v Crehan* [2001] ECR I-6297. See: R Williams, 'European Competition Law-Beer Tie Cases-Restitution—In Pari Delicto Rule' (2001) 23 *Dublin University Law Journal* 194.

[245] Established in: *Belgische Radio en Televisie* (n 239) and Case C-234/89 *Delimitis v Henninger Bräu AG* [1991] ECR I-935.

[246] *Nemo auditur propriam turpitudinem allegans*: *Courage v Crehan* (n 244) (point 68).

[247] ibid (points 42–44).

[248] ibid [31].

[249] ibid [29].

[250] Case C-242/95 *GT-Link A/S v De Danske Statsbaner (DSB)* [1997] ECR 1-4449.

[251] *Barra v Belgium* (n 47).

[252] Jones (n 156) 61–62.

exists at national level.[253] No wonder, therefore, Lord Goff in *Woolwich* felt an added impetus to create such a cause of action even in purely domestic situations.[254] In addition, the EU has an important impact not only on the duty to repay, but also on any time limits,[255] rules of interest[256] or defences[257] applicable to it.

Thus, first, although the ECJ did not provide the conceptual reasoning for the important cases of *Woolwich* and *Deutsche Morgan Grenfell*, the interplay between the EU and the national system in England has, even before the *FII* case, been fertile ground for development of the domestic law, without which the latter may not have reached its current stage of development. Second, when the ECJ has become involved in discussing particular aspects of a cause of action, such as the defence of passing on, it has provided a channel through which principles familiar to some Member States are then given their own European components, and are then in turn discussed by the legal systems of other Member States.[258] Thus even if the EU has not always directly controlled the conceptual development of these causes of action and associated defences, it can nevertheless have an indirect impact on their development. Third, the principle of national 'procedural' autonomy and the maintenance of 'Model 1' reasoning is not without cost. Nor is it necessarily sustainable. Returning to the case of *Courage v Crehan*[259] it will be remembered that the basis for the claim was that the contract between the parties was void for infringement of EC competition law. However, it should be noted that the parties' claim in *Courage* was not formulated in terms of unjust enrichment, but rather in terms of 'damages'.[260] Unsurprisingly, given its decision in *Metallgesellschaft and Hoechst*,[261] the ECJ did not reclassify this claim or express any opinion on the relevant national law event. As in *Metallgesellschaft and Hoechst*, it is true that AG Fennelly was prepared to go further than the ECJ, pointing out that 'if a party who bears no significant responsibility for the distortion of competition is debarred from seeking damages, the other party would gain an unjustified advantage from its unlawful conduct at the expense of its co-contractor'.[262]

However, the ECJ was even *less* prepared to enter this discussion than it had been in *Metallgesellschaft and Hoechst*. In previous cases when the ECJ has referred to 'unjust enrichment', it has done so in the specific context of what an English lawyer would call the passing on defence and it was argued above that in some cases this has provided evidence of 'Model 2' behaviour by the ECJ, in which both

[253] *San Giorgio* (n 34).
[254] See above pp 207–208.
[255] *Marks and Spencer* (n 43).
[256] *Sempra Metals* (n 96).
[257] Such as passing on and change of position, see above pp 136–49 and 152–57.
[258] See, eg: the discussion of the EC jurisprudence on passing on in *Commissioners for Customs and Excise v National Westminster Bank plc* [2003] EWHC 1822 (Ch), [2003] STC 1072.
[259] *Courage v Crehan* (n 244).
[260] Which Jones has correctly criticised as 'unfortunate': Jones (n 156) 154 and 185–89.
[261] *Metallgesellschaft and Hoechst* (n 1).
[262] *Courage v Crehan* (n 244) (pt 54).

the unlawfulness and unjust enrichment are provided at EU level.[263] But in *Courage v Crehan*, there was no such 'passing on' issue and yet the ECJ still referred to 'unjust enrichment', using the term simply as a parallel for the rule that a party cannot make undue profit from a breach of EU law. As with AG Geelhoed's opinion in *Penycoed*,[264] in one sense this specification of a potential legal basis could be seen as Model 2 reasoning but, as in that case, it can also be seen as a generalised reference to the term which represents a move away from an attempt to create a clearly defined cause of action based on unjust enrichment of the kind found in national systems.

In the case of *Courage v Crehan*, however, reluctance on the part of the ECJ to discuss the basis for the claim actually had the potential to reduce the usefulness and applicability of its decision. After the decision in that case it was suggested[265] that the ECJ may in that case have been extending the action for *compensation* under *Francovich* and *Brasserie/Factortame III* to cover damage caused through a breach of EC law by *private* rather than state parties. It does indeed appear from the subsequent *Manfredi* judgment that this was the case.[266] However, if *Courage v Crehan* was not a case of 'damage' and of 'wrongs' at all but rather a case about 'unjust enrichment',[267] then *Courage v Crehan* itself cannot be taken as authority for this proposition.

Clarifying the basis for the claim in *Manfredi* in this way does have an impact on the autonomy of the national legal systems to a greater extent, but by doing so, the import of the decision becomes clearer and its impact on other cases more readily understood than was *Courage v Crehan*. Given the primacy of EU law, it was hardly a benefit to the Member States that in the period between *Courage v Crehan* and *Manfredi* they should be bound by a decision whose basis was not wholly clear, even if that lack of clarity left the potential for the decision to be interpreted more narrowly than the decision in *Manfredi* now provides. It will be remembered that the same argument of course applied to the distinction between *Hans Just* and *Cotter and McDermott* noted above.[268] Without Jones' analysis of the cause of action being used by the ECJ, on the surface it was very difficult to explain the differences in outcome between these two cases, which led to confusion and a lack of certainty over which would be followed subsequently.

Finally, as noted above in relation to the *FII* case, there may simply be some cases in which the principle of effectiveness itself undercuts the *Metallgesellschaft and Hoechst* principle that classification and definition of particular causes of action should be left to the Member States, and it becomes inevitable that the ECJ will have to move towards Model 2. This is not to suggest that in normative terms dictation by the ECJ is to be preferred to national 'procedural' or indeed substantive

[263] See above at p 255.
[264] In a manner not unlike that of AG Geelhoed in *Penycoed Farming Partnership* (n 85).
[265] See, eg: Craig and de Búrca (n 5) 334.
[266] *Manfredi* (n 50).
[267] As has been suggested by Jones (n 156) ch 6.
[268] pp 256–57.

autonomy. Rather, it is simply to point out that the decided cases cast serious doubt on the ECJ's ability to maintain its earlier stance of protecting its imperatives of equivalence and effectiveness, balancing them against the reasoning adopted by the Member States, without at some stage becoming involved in the definition and operation of the 'actionable story' of unjust enrichment, as, of course, it has already done in the case of wrongdoing and the cause of action in state liability in damages. If this conclusion is correct, and the adoption of Model 2 is inevitable, this conclusion carries with it important responsibilities on the part of the Advocates General and the ECJ to develop clear and coherent rules for the cause of action which make good use of the work already done at national level and which strike a desirable balance in terms of both principle and policy. Much of this book has been devoted to establishing the care and particular treatment needed in dealing with instances of unjust enrichment where the reason for restitution is provided by public law. As the *FII* case demonstrates, these requirements do not vanish if the operation of the 'actionable story' of unjust enrichment is defined by EU rather than by national law. For claims in unjust enrichment involving public bodies to work successfully in future, it is therefore imperative that whichever system is responsible for the ultimate parameters of the claim, this does not result in a failure to provide that care and particular treatment.

Conclusion

FROM THE OUTSET it was clear that this book would be about the intersection of the reasons for restitution in unjust enrichment actions and the division between public and private law. All of the key cases considered in part one thus began with an application for judicial review (*Woolwich*,[1] the swaps cases, and in a sense even *Deutsche Morgan Grenfell*),[2] followed later by an action based on unjust enrichment in private law. This dual aspect of the cases is crucial and is not changed by either the fact that the two actions took place separately nor by the fact that following *British Steel*[3] it is now possible to bring both claims through the same procedure.[4]

It is therefore not surprising that when faced with the task of accommodating both public and private law in the reason for restitution, the House of Lords in *Woolwich* struggled to fit the case into any of the existing private law 'unjust factors' of inequality, incapacity, illegality, or absence/failure of basis. None of these were sufficient on their own precisely because all of them are relevant: when a private entity pays an ultra vires tax, makes a payment under an ultra vires contract or receives an ultra vires grant, the situation involves a relationship between public power and private entities in which the public powers are inherently limited; exceeding those powers constitutes an unlawful action from the point of view of public law, and this in turn renders the transaction void *ab initio*.[5]

Conversely, it is no more possible to absorb the private law unjust enrichment aspects of the claim into a purely public law 'remedy' as took place in the Canadian case of *Kingstreet Investments*.[6] Such an approach can explain why some kind of

[1] [1993] AC 70.

[2] *Deutsche Morgan Grenfell v Commissioners of Inland Revenue*: First Instance: [2003] EWHC 1779; [2003] 4 All ER 645; Court of Appeal: [2005] EWCA Civ 78; [2006] Ch 243; House of Lords: [2006] UKHL 49, [2007] 1 AC 558. In Cases C-397/98 and C-410/98 *Metallgesellschaft & Hoechst v IRC* [2001] ECR I-1727, the ECJ ruled on the requirements of EC law which, via the 1972 European Communities Act impose limits on the powers of public bodies. Thus although the ECJ cannot itself strike down national actions or legislation (see further ch 4 at p 81), by defining the EC requirements in this way it became apparent that the national courts would have to hold the Revenue to be in breach of Community law and thus acting beyond its powers. In this sense the decision of the ECJ is not so far removed from a judicial review action such as those which occurred in *Hazell v Hammersmith* [1992] 2 AC 1and *R v IRC, ex p Woolwich Equitable Building Society* [1990] 1 WLR 1400.

[3] *British Steel plc v Customs and Excise Commissioners* [1997] 2 All ER 366.

[4] See above pp 49–52.

[5] See further p 36.

[6] *Kingstreet Investments Ltd v New Brunswick (Finance)* 2007 SCC 1, [2007] 1 SCR 3.

response is necessary, but not, for example, why that response should take the form of requiring the public body to repay the money to the private claimant.

The point is that it is both the public and private aspects of the claim which are relevant. It is therefore wholly undesirable for courts to choose between these two equally important aspects of the claim, though it is perhaps inevitable that when they do feel constrained so to choose the result should be an almost even split, with the House of Lords opting for the wholly private viewpoint in *Deutsche Morgan Grenfell*, the Supreme Court of Canada opting for the wholly public viewpoint in *Kingstreet Investments* and the courts in France opting sometimes for the one and sometimes for the other.[7]

The correct approach is instead that the law must recognise the inherently hybrid nature of such claims and address the concerns of both areas of law. While the enrichment, expense and some of the defence aspects of the claims can be derived from the private law of unjust enrichment, the reason for restitution is simply 'public law'. Once this is properly understood it then becomes possible to answer many of the questions left open by *Woolwich* about the proper scope and functioning of the reason for restitution that case created. We know, for example, that there need be no demand on the part of the public entity, no protest on the part of the private party; we know the kinds of bodies and payments to which this reason for restitution applies. The answer to such questions is simply that the scope and function of the reason for restitution is the scope and function of public law itself.[8]

Not only does this allow us fully to understand the *Woolwich* decision, it also allows us to draw some other important conclusions. First, it becomes apparent that there is no further need to separate cases in which the public body is the defendant from those in which it is or could be the claimant. Thus cases such as *Auckland Harbour Board v the King*[9] can be placed in the same category as *Woolwich.* Nor need we separate cases in which the ultra vires action was the conclusion of a contract, as in the swaps cases, from those in which it was, for example, an unlawful levy or tax as in *Woolwich* or *Deutsche Morgan Grenfell.*

Second, not only *can* the public law reason for restitution provide a more straightforward route to restitution in such cases than any private law 'unjust factor', and not only *can* it group together all public body cases, normatively it *should* do so. Only this way can the law achieve sufficient access to both the relevant events, public and private, which give rise to such a claim. Public law concerns do not vanish simply because the action is brought through private law, nor because those public law concerns were discovered separately in a judicial review action before the private law proceedings commenced. It still remains necessary to balance protection for public bodies against the need to protect the citizen, often within the additional requirement of compliance with EU law and in particular the

[7] See further pp 31–38 and 181–90.
[8] See further pp 38–40 and ch 3.
[9] [1924] AC 318.

need to provide an adequate and effective remedy for breach of that law.[10] Striking this kind of balance is not a novel experience; it is in many ways the essence of public law. By failing to give public law pre-eminence as the reason for restitution in such cases the courts deprive themselves of the set of tools already developed for precisely this purpose. Instead, private lawyers are left trying to re-invent the public law wheel. This is not only inefficient, it also runs the risk that the law itself will be distorted in the process as public law concepts are forced through private law concepts into which they do not fit. An ultra vires event is not necessarily comparable to a tort.[11] The rules relating to the setting aside of contracts may well be different from those relating to invalidity in public law.[12] A finding that an action was void *ab initio* because ultra vires does not require the law of unjust enrichment to concern itself with an 'absence of basis' approach,[13] and a situation in which the House of Lords splits 4:1 over whether a mistake can be made at all in such circumstances, 3:2 over whether in fact the claimant was labouring under a mistake when it made the relevant payments, and suffers a further 2:1 split among that majority concerning the content of the mistake, to say nothing of differences between the three levels of court, or between different courts in different branches of the subsequent litigation,[14] can hardly be regarded as a successful and clear method of dealing with a case.[15] It is true that the facts of *Deutsche Morgan Grenfell* were in any event complex, but the extra complexity added by the mistake issue would be rendered entirely unnecessary if the true nature of the case was fully understood.

On this basis the series of appeals in *Deutsche Morgan Grenfell* represent a wasted opportunity. The judgments of the Court of Appeal came closest to the position advocated here, but even these were based too little on principled analysis and too closely on the previous judgments of Lord Goff for their full implications and potential to be properly realised. Then in turn the House of Lords' reluctance to maintain the hierarchy established by the Court of Appeal stemmed mainly from a failure to understand how and why this hierarchy should operate. Had their Lordships had the benefit of a pair of public law spectacles as well as their private law ones[16] they would have understood that they were not being asked to carve out a random exception to the mistake of law unjust factor, nor to

[10] On which see further p 237.

[11] See the argument above at p 12–13 and 147–49 that Henderson J was wrong in *Test Claimants in the FII Group Litigation v The Commissioners for Her Majesty's Revenue and Customs* [2008] EWHC 2893 (Ch) at [339] to analogise a finding of ultra vires with the tort of conversion.

[12] See the discussion of the judgment of Lord Scott in *Deutsche Morgan Grenfell*, above pp 77–86.

[13] See above p 36.

[14] See, eg: Mummery LJ in *Boake Allen Limited v Revenue and Customs Commissioners*, [2006] EWCA Civ 25, [2006] STC 606. The case was also known and subsequently heard in the HL as *Boake Allen* (HL) at [161], quoted above, p 109, and the odd use of relatively unspecific mistake by Henderson J in the *FII* decision, above n 11.

[15] For further, detailed, analysis of the complexity of different treatments of mistake in *Deutsche Morgan Grenfell* see further C Mitchell, 'Mistaken Tax Payments' (2007) RLR 124.

[16] The phrase is Burrows'. See: A Burrows, 'Public Authorities, Ultra Vires and Restitution' in A Burrows (ed) *Essays on the Law of Restitution* (Oxford, Clarendon Press 1991).

overturn *Henderson v Merrett*.[17] Instead they would have realised they were simply being asked to follow the principle already established in cases such as *O'Reilly v Mackman*[18] and *Clark v University of Lincolnshire and Humberside*,[19] in preserving public law's access to the ultra vires aspects of the claim and preventing the concerns applicable to this ultra vires event from being circumvented, mistranslated or distorted by private law.

Instead, public law should be regarded as the only ground for recovery in such claims, whether the public body is the claimant or defendant. This approach, unlike that adopted following the House of Lords decision in *Deutsche Morgan Grenfell*, is perfectly compatible with the EU principles of equivalence and effectiveness and it brings the domestic reason for recovery completely in line with that used by the ECJ in *San Giorgio*.[20] When questions arise in subsequent cases, such as those raised in the *FII* litigation,[21] once the reason for recovery is properly understood it can potentially play an important and helpful role in answering those questions.

One important example of this concerns the tailoring of both public law and private law defences. Understanding the reason for restitution in this way and allowing the law access to both the public and the private aspects of the claim by prioritising the public law reason for restitution will also allow that balance to be carried through into the defences available to such claims. The practical result of this is that very few of the proposed defences from private or from public law will be able to apply fully, either because of practical difficulties, because of the threat to the EU principle of effectiveness, or a combination of the two. It therefore becomes clear that it is crucial to set an appropriate time limit which balances the concerns of both public and private law, and which is applied prospectively, with an adequate transitional period for its implementation. Then all cases in which there has been an enrichment as the result of a public law ultra vires event, whether the public body is the claimant or the defendant, should be brought on the basis of the public law unjust factor subject to this time limit, set specifically for such claims.[22]

It is therefore perfectly possible to accommodate the requirements of both public and private law within the current approach of finding specific 'reasons for restitution' or 'unjust factors'. We need not conclude, as Birks did,[23] that such cases can only be dealt with properly by a move to the 'absence of basis' approach. When the French experience is examined it becomes apparent that not only would such a move be unnecessary, it would also be insufficient on its own. Indeed the French system has five important lessons it can teach us in this regard. First, France

[17] *Henderson v Merrett Syndicates Ltd* [1995] 2 AC 145.

[18] [1983] 2 AC 237.

[19] [2000] 1 WLR 1988.

[20] Case 199/82 *Amministrazione delle Finanze dello Stato v San Giorgio* [1983] ECR 3595. See further above, ch 8.

[21] Above n 11.

[22] See further ch 5.

[23] P Birks, *Unjust Enrichment* 2nd edn (Oxford, Oxford University Press, 2005) at 113–4.

automatically adjusts its 'quasi-contracts' in their application to cases involving public bodies. Second, as noted above, the French experience provides further evidence that when forced to choose between two events, nullity and unjust enrichment, both of which are relevant to a particular claim, some courts will choose one and others the other. Third, in addition to adjusting its quasi-contracts for public body cases, French law also distinguishes between public law rules and public law procedure so that, as suggested in England and Wales, even within the private procedure it becomes possible to make adjustments to take account of the public nature of the claim. However, for an exact parallel with the situation in England and Wales the key French cases are those in which the claim is brought within private law and before the private law courts, but those courts need to take account of the public law nature of the claim in relation to the substance of the claim itself, rather than just the procedure and time limits applicable to it. Here we learn two particularly interesting things from the French experience. First, as noted above, the absence of cause approach does not necessarily prove to be better adapted to dealing with claims involving public law. Instead, and second, in France as in England, the need to accommodate public bodies in private claims has a tendency to change the rules of private law. Thus, just as the English courts' struggle to accommodate both the public and private law events led them to examine 'transactional inequality' and then to resort to the civilian language of absence of basis, the availability of such an 'absence of basis' approach elsewhere in French law did not prevent the Cour de cassation in cases of *répétition de l'indu* from flirting with a move towards the common law system. When the French courts did finally move towards the 'absence of cause' approach, at least for *répétition de l'indu objectif*, this did not seem to differ much from the common law approach in anything other than burden of proof; investigations will still tend to focus on positive factors, whether these are reasons for repaying the money or reasons for denying repayment, and indeed both sets of factors seem likely to require an investigation into the intentions of the payer-claimant. Furthermore, even if they reverse the burden of proof, the civilian rules do not seem to remove the purely private perspective rejected in part one. So, whether one starts from the specific unjust factors approach or from the civilian absence of cause approach the problem is the same; attempting to deal with hybrid public and private claims solely through the rules of private law has a tendency to put more strain on that system than it can bear and in turn this can lead to a distortion of the structure of that law itself.[24]

Thus in that sense, not only are the civilian rules likely to be little different from those in the common law, they also, perhaps unsurprisingly, appear to be *less* well adapted to the public body context than a reason for restitution which takes account not only of the absence of full and free consent (in identifying the public power of one of the parties) and the voidness of the transaction or payment, but also the public law event which gave rise to these considerations. In other words,

[24] See further ch 6.

the importance of the French system's approach to public body cases lies not so much in the fact that it focuses on the *absence* of cause for the payment, but rather in the further adjustments that it makes to accommodate those bodies. It can therefore be concluded that not only is the 'absence of cause' approach unnecessary, as argued in part one, it is also arguably less desirable than an approach which is able to take account of both the private and public aspects of the claim at the stage of establishing the reason for return of the money.

In neither system, finally, would our investigation be complete without an examination of the influence of the EU on such claims. This is for three important reasons. First, it may well be the case that the public body involved in the claim is not a domestic body at all but one of the institutions of the EU itself. Relatively early on it became apparent that it would not be possible for the ECJ to avoid questions relating to unjust enrichment and in *Greece v Commission*,[25] *Vieira and others v Commission*[26] and *Corus UK v Commission*[27] the ECJ established that the prohibition of unjust enrichment was a general principle of the EC. However, consideration of the staff and annulment cases reveals that, in a reflection of the French experience, though less so the English,[28] it is far easier for the EU institutions to obtain restitution for unjust enrichment than it is for a claimant to obtain restitution from them. As in both national systems, recovery is particularly unlikely in three-party cases. Most importantly of all, however, while the prohibition of unjust enrichment is a general principle of the EU, it is also *only* a general principle, not a freestanding cause of action in itself as is the wrong of breach of European law under Article 340 TFEU (ex Art 288 EC). Therefore unjust enrichment claims against the Union must be brought through essentially a wrongs-based vehicle, notwithstanding that unjust enrichment claims unsurprisingly do not fit terribly well into this channel, that Article 340 does refer more generally to the 'non-contractual' liability of the Union and that the general principle could itself have been a direct ground of action had the Treaties so provided.[29]

Second, as far as the Member State–EU relationship is concerned, the EU's free movement and anti-discrimination rules have provided an important source of nullity in the sense that the power of Member State public bodies is limited not just by domestic law but also by the requirement that they comply with their EU obligations. This was seen clearly in French law in cases such as *Café Jacques Vabre*[30] and

[25] Case C-259/87 *Greece v Commission* [1990] ECR I-2845, summary publication, para 2.

[26] Case T-126/01 [2003] ECR II-1209, [86]: 'As the Commission points out, any other interpretation of the fisheries agreement would be contrary to the general principles of law common to the legal systems of the Member States, such as the principle which prohibits unjust enrichment'.

[27] Case T-171/99 [2001] ECR II-2967, [55].

[28] For the French law see above pp 181 and 197. As far as English law is concerned, it is true that *Auckland Harbour Board v the King* [1924] AC 318 preceded *Woolwich* (above n 33) by nearly 70 years, but decisions such as *Kleinwort Benson v Lincoln CC* [1999] 2 AC 349 (HL) and *Deutsche Morgan Grenfell* [2006] UKHL 49, [2007] 1 AC 558 have been favourable to the private claimants and disadvantageous to the public body defendants.

[29] See further ch 7.

[30] Trib d'inst du 1er arondissement de Paris, 8 January 1971, Cour d'appel de Paris 7 July 1973; *D* 1974.159; Cour de cassation 24 May 1975; *D* 1975.497.

Fils Henri Ramel.[31] Similarly, in England, one of Lord Goff's reasons[32] for allowing recovery in *Woolwich,*[33] was that 'it would be strange if the right of the citizen to recover overpaid charges were to be more restricted under domestic law than it is under European law',[34] and of course all the ACT litigation in cases such as *Deutsche Morgan Grenfell* and *FII* can ultimately be traced back to decisions of the ECJ. Third, should they breach EU law in this respect, the 'remedy' provided by the Member State for that breach must comply with the EU requirements of equivalence and effectiveness. Thus time limits, interest and defences in national law are all affected by the necessity of complying with EU law.[35]

On this question of the interrelationship of EU and national law, the ECJ's 'remedies jurisprudence' is unclear, referring sometimes to 'remedies' but at other times to national 'procedural' autonomy. However, on further analysis there appear to be two models that this jurisprudence could follow. Under the first model the EU is simply a 'source of unlawfulness' from which a claimant derives a right to an 'actionable story' of some kind at national level, but the precise definition and operation of that story remain the responsibility of the national courts alone. Under the second model, however, which, for instance applies to the action for state liability in damages under *Francovich*[36] and *Brasserie/Factortame III,*[37] the EU generates not only the initial unlawfulness but also provides the right to a *particular* cause of action at national level, and the ECJ takes responsibility for the definition of this cause of action.

It is clear that as far as unjust enrichment claims are concerned, some claims are covered not by case law at all but by statute, and in any event the ECJ's conscious choice in *Metallgesellschaft and Hoechst*[38] was for Model 1. Nevertheless, it may not always be able to maintain this approach in practice. Where money is paid out by a public body and the private party is the defendant it is easier for the ECJ to maintain Model 1 reasoning, because the defences on which it is asked to rule in terms of equivalence and effectiveness tend to focus on matters of change of

[31] Decision of the Cour d'appel de Lyon of 30 November 1978 (1re Ch Civ) *D* 1979.371, note C-J Berr.

[32] In addition to general motivations based on constitutional principles and justice, Lord Goff cited six further reasons for granting recovery in *Woolwich.* Four of these were relatively pragmatic dealing with the limited practical effect of the judgment in this particular case, the fact that the opportunity to make a similar decision would not arise again, the fact that the issue was at the time under active consultation by the Law Commission and the fact that if any action were to be taken it would have to be taken by the courts, because it would obviously not be in the Treasury's interest for the government to initiate legislation along the same lines (*Woolwich Equitable Building Society v Inland Revenue Commissioners* [1993] AC 70 176-177). Two, however, were more conceptual, and related to ideas of parity with other contexts. As seen above (p 56) one of these was the ability of the Crown to obtain restitution in cases like *Auckland Harbour Board v The King* [1924] AC 318, but the other was the comparison with the situation in cases involving EC law noted here.

[33] ibid.

[34] ibid.

[35] See further pp 236–41.

[36] Cases C-6/90 and C-9/90 *Francovich & Bonifaci v Italy* [1991] ECR I-5357.

[37] Cases C-46/93 and C-48/93 *Brasserie du Pêcheur SA v Germany* and *R v Secretary of State for Transport, ex p Factortame Ltd and others* [1996] ECR I-1029.

[38] Cases C-397/98 and C-410/98 *Metallgesellschaft and Hoechst v IRC* [2001] ECR I-1727.

position and, as argued in chapter five, defences of this kind based on security of receipt tend to merge with more general defences such as legitimate expectations. It is therefore possible for the ECJ to rule on them in general terms of 'effectiveness' without being drawn into the definition of a particular cause of action or the defences specific to it. However, where the public body is the defendant and the private party the claimant, the defence most often argued is that of passing on. This defence *is* inherently bound up with the nature of unjust enrichment, since it arguably denies the 'at the expense of' element of the claim.[39] In such cases the ECJ's current case law requires it to balance the reasoning in favour of the Member State rules against the requirements of equivalence and effectiveness, but the process of doing so makes it very difficult for the ECJ to avoid becoming drawn into the definition of the boundaries and operation of the unjust enrichment action itself. What is there to be said for the Member State defence of passing on if not for the fact that it denies an important element of the claim? And how can the court reach this conclusion without itself having a concept of that claim?

However, by far the most striking case is that of *FII* in which not only the Advocate General but also the ECJ held that in some instances, where the sufficiently serious breach necessary for an action for state liability in damages would not be made out, the principle of effectiveness might itself require a '*San Giorgio* claim' for reimbursement of the sum to be granted instead. Thus while the Court and the Advocate General both formally reiterated the *Metallgesellschaft and Hoechst* principle that the choice and form of action were for the Member State only, this commitment to Model 1 was immediately undercut in substance by their use of the principle of effectiveness to require one cause of action to be given when the requirements of another would not be fulfilled.

In many ways this shift to Model 2 should not be surprising. As becomes evident from consideration of cases such as *Courage Ltd v Crehan*[40] and *Cotter and McDermott*,[41] the 'remedies' jurisprudence per se may well be too amorphous and lacking in analysis to provide real guidance for the national courts. Only with the addition of unjust enrichment reasoning can either decision be fully understood and interpreted. However, the result of this shift is, as seen in *FII*, that the EU now has potentially far greater responsibility for defining the parameters and operation of the unjust enrichment event in such cases even at the domestic level. Also, as is evident from *Woolwich* itself, any decisions it makes in this regard may not remain confined wholly to EU only cases but have the potential to 'leak' into wholly domestic contexts.

The conclusion must therefore be that it is imperative that both the domestic system and the EU system take much greater care than they have so far to analyse carefully the requirements of cases involving public law and to ensure that such

[39] See further p 255.

[40] Case C-453/99 [2001] ECR I-6297. See RA Williams, casenote [2001] 23 *Dublin University Law Journal* 194.

[41] Case C-377/89 *Cotter and McDermott v Minister for Social Welfare & Attorney General* [1991] ECR I-1155.

cases are treated appropriately. At the EU level, if the ECJ is to take responsibility for the claims in this way then it must match this with the responsibility of developing a proper framework for analysis. It should move beyond the concept of unjust enrichment as a general principle, develop a more precise analysis of unjust enrichment or enrichment without cause[42] as a cause of action, avoid reference to the general principle when the requirements of this more specific cause of action are not made out,[43] and consider carefully the practical and policy implications of its decisions on specific issues such as causation.[44] In the domestic system, precedence should be given to the public law reason for restitution; all cases in which the reason for restitution is public law should be grouped together, whether the public body is the claimant or the defendant and whatever the nature of the ultra vires action; the parameters and operation of such claims should in future be informed by reference to public law as much as to private law, and defences should be tailored to take account of the hybrid nature of such claims, with the creation of a specific time limit in particular.

It is nearly 60 years since administrative law first began to develop to its current state, and it is time that private law recognised this. We need a public law of unjust enrichment.

[42] Even if, following the *FII* decision the ECJ will specify that an unjust enrichment-type action must be used it seems unlikely that at this stage EU law will go so far as to specify the specific ground for restitution whether it is absence of cause or a specific reason for restitution. Thus at present the arguments made here concerning the approach to this question are directed primarily at the domestic system of England and Wales. Nevertheless, should this situation alter at any stage those arguments would remain and would simply be directed at the EU instead.

[43] As it should have done in Case C-230/01 *Intervention Board for Agricultural Produce v Penycoed Farming Partnership* [2004] ECR I-937.

[44] As in the FII case.

INDEX